ROYAL ARTILLERY
IN THE SECOND WORLD WAR

ROYAL ARTILLERY
IN THE SECOND WORLD WAR

RICHARD
DOHERTY

First published 2008 as *Ubique: The Royal Artillery in the Second World War*
This paperback edition published 2023

The History Press
97 St George's Place, Cheltenham,
Gloucestershire, GL50 3QB
www.thehistorypress.co.uk

British Library Cataloguing in Publication Data.
A catalogue record for this book is available from the British Library.

ISBN 978 1 80399 556 4

Typesetting and origination by The History Press
Printed and bound in Great Britain by TJ Books Limited, Padstow, Cornwall.

Trees for Life

Contents

Dedication

To all those men and women who served the guns from 1939 to 1945, especially those who gave their lives so that our world might have peace.
Ubique Quo Fas et Gloria Ducunt

For the whole earth is the tomb of famous men; not only are they commemorated by columns and inscriptions in their own country, but in foreign lands there dwells also an unwritten memorial of them, graven not on stone but in the hearts of men. Make them your examples . . .
(From Pericles' funeral oration for the Athenians)

By the same author

Wall of Steel: The History of 9th (Londonderry) HAA Regiment, RA (SR); North-West Books, Limavady, 1988

The Sons of Ulster: Ulstermen at war from the Somme to Korea; Appletree Press, Belfast, 1992

Clear the Way! A History of the 38th (Irish) Brigade, 1941–47; Irish Academic Press, Dublin, 1993

Irish Generals: Irish Generals in the British Army in the Second World War; Appletree Press, Belfast, 1993

Key to Victory: The Maiden City in the Second World War; Greystone Books, Antrim, 1995

The Williamite War in Ireland, 1688–1691; Four Courts Press, Dublin, 1998

Irish Men and Women in the Second World War; Four Courts Press, Dublin, 1999

Irish Winners of the Victoria Cross (with David Truesdale); Four Courts Press, Dublin, 2000

Irish Volunteers in the Second World War; Four Courts Press, Dublin, 2001

The Sound of History: El Alamein 1942; The History Press, Stroud, 2002

The North Irish Horse: A Hundred Years of Service; The History Press, Stroud, 2002

Normandy 1944: The Road to Victory; The History Press, Stroud, 2004

Ireland's Generals in the Second World War; Four Courts Press, Dublin, 2004

The Thin Green Line: A History of The Royal Ulster Constabulary GC, 1922–2001; Pen & Sword Books, Barnsley, 2004

None Bolder: A History of 51st (Highland) Division 1939–1945; The History Press, Stroud, 2006

The British Reconnaissance Corps in World War II; Osprey Publishing, Oxford, 2007

Eighth Army in Italy: The Long Hard Slog; Pen & Sword, Barnsley, 2007

The Siege of Derry 1689: The Military History; The History Press, Stroud, 2008

Only the Enemy in Front: The Recce Corps at War, 1940–46; The History Press, Stroud, 2008

A Noble Crusade: The History of Eighth Army 1941–45; The History Press, Stroud, 2008

Acknowledgements

This book came about as the result of a suggestion by my publisher, Jamie Wilson, who asked if I would be interested in doing something about the Gunners. The idea appealed to me but we both hesitated as we were certain that there had been many books about the Royal Regiment of Artillery in the Second World War. However, a little research showed that the last book to cover the Regiment in all its roles during that conflict came from the pen of the late Brigadier Peter Mead as far back as 1982. Since then there have been many histories of individual regiments or batteries – for one of which I was responsible – as well as the volumes of the *History of the Royal Regiment of Artillery* being produced by the Royal Artillery Institution. It seemed, therefore, that there was room for a new book on the Regiment's work between 1939 and 1945. My first thanks go to Jamie for his inspiration and support of this project. I should mention at this stage that both of us have a vested interest in the Gunners: my late father served in a Gunner regiment during the war, although he had been a pre-war infantryman, and Jamie served in the Honourable Artillery Company, part of the Artillery family and the oldest unit in the Army.

I am very grateful to Lieutenant Colonel W A H Townend MA, Secretary of the Royal Artillery Historical Society, for his invaluable advice and support and his prompt and full answers to my queries. In particular he ensured the accuracy of my account of the run-in shoot on the Normandy beaches on 6 June 1944 as several otherwise reliable sources conflicted. Firepower, the Museum of the Royal Regiment of Artillery at Woolwich was another invaluable source and well worth a visit to see many of the weapons included in this book. At Kew, the National Archives house many of the wartime records of the Gunners, as well as many pre-war documents that were invaluable in describing the Regiment in the years before the war. For more than two decades I have found the staff of the reading and search rooms at Kew to be extremely helpful and their enthusiasm makes researching in the Archives a pleasure. I also used the Department of Printed Books at the Imperial War Museum, Lambeth Road, London where, once again, a team of enthusiastic and expert staff ease the way of any researcher. An invaluable source for anyone studying the history of the Royal Artillery in the Second World

War is the *Royal Artillery Commemoration Book*, edited by Brigadier W E Duncan. A copy of this work is in the Linenhall Library, Belfast where I was able to study it. My thanks are due to the Library for their cooperation and assistance.

Major Mike Shaw, editor of *The Gunner*, the magazine of the Royal Artillery, very kindly carried appeals for information from veterans for which I thank him. However, the passage of over sixty years since the end of the war means that the number of veterans is now quite small but to those who got in touch I extend my gratitude. Major Douglas Goddard MBE FCIS RA (Retd) provided me with much valuable material on 112th (Wessex) Field Regiment in which he served; Mr V J Emery, who was a signaller with 112th (Durham Light Infantry) LAA Regiment also provided information and a photograph while Alfred Tubb contacted me with information on the Maritime Royal Artillery in which he served. Billy Smyth, a sergeant in 25 HAA Battery, outlined an experience as an OP sergeant when his battery – in which my father also served – was firing in a field role near Pisa in Italy. Sadly, Billy died just over three weeks later. Others who helped me included Major Bill Lemon, Major Arthur Hogg, Robert Hamilton and William Sherrard, the late Colonel Harry Porter, Colonel Sir Robin Kinahan, Major Cunningham Fowler, Major Ernest McClure, Captain Eric Woodburn, Tom Reynolds, Bertie Cuthbert, John Ormsby, Tom Patton and Eric Wilson.

The photographs that appear in this book were supplied by a number of institutions and individuals to all of whom I am grateful: the Photographic Archive of the Imperial War Museum; the National Archives of Canada; the United States Navy Photo Archives; 9th (Londonderry) HAA Regiment Archive; 6 LAA Battery OCA; Royal Ulter Rifles Museum, Belfast; *ARHAM (Association de Recherches Historiques et Archeologiques Militaires)*; the Wimbledon News/Newsquest; Evening Courier, Halifax, especially Colin Drury; Arthur Hogg, Londonderry; Ronnie Gamble, Coleraine, Co. Londonderry; Dominique Faivre, France; Ray Goodacre, Bookham, Surrey; Joe McCready, London; Major Douglas Goddard MBE; and to others who provided photos. Thanks are also due to David Rowlands for his kind permission to reproduce two of his paintings and to the Royal Artillery Historical Trust for permission to use two photographs taken in Firepower, the Royal Artillery Museum.

Thanks are also due to my friend Bob O'Hara who carried out research for me at the National Archives when I was unable to visit myself and to Ronnie Gamble, for his support and for providing additional material on 6 LAA Battery.

Jamie Wilson and Shaun Barrington at The History Press provided enthusiastic support for this book and have ensured its completion as a polished production. To them and all the team, I offer my thanks.

Finally, but not least, thanks are also due to my family for their constant support: my wife Carol, my children Joanne, James and Catríona and to my grandson Ciarán.

Richard Doherty
Co. Londonderry

Prologue

On 27 June 1945, in a message to the men of the Royal Artillery of 21 Army Group, Field Marshal Sir Bernard Montgomery wrote:

> I would like to pay a compliment to the gunners, and I would like this to be passed on to every gunner.
>
> The gunners have risen to great heights in this war; they have been well commanded and well handled. In my experience the artillery has never been so efficient as it is today; it is at the top of its form. For all this I offer you my warmest congratulations.
>
> The contribution of the artillery to final victory in the German war has been immense. This will always be so; the harder the fighting and the longer the war, the more the infantry, and in fact all the arms, lean on the gunners. The proper use of the artillery is a great battle-winning factor.
>
> I think all the other arms have done very well too. But the artillery has been terrific and I want to give due weight to its contribution to the victory in this campaign.

Montgomery's praise may have been directed specifically to the Gunners of his own command – 21 Army Group, which comprised Second (British) and First (Canadian) Armies – but it applied in equal measure to the Gunners in other theatres. Since 1833, the single battle honour of the Royal Regiment of Artillery has been *Ubique* – Everywhere – and that word rang as true as ever in the Second World War. Gunners had served in all the campaigns fought by the British armies in Europe, Africa and Asia as well as serving under Admiralty command on board ships plying the convoy routes that sustained Britain, and under RAF command in defence of Britain itself in the dangerous days of the blitz and in the V1 offensive of 1944–5. In every campaign, and in every role, they had indeed been terrific.

It would be impossible to tell the full story of the Royal Artillery's wartime roles and achievements in one book and it is not the author's intention to attempt so to do. Instead this book will seek to demonstrate the ubiquity of the Gunners, their efficiency and effectiveness, and their contribution to both local success and overall final victory by telling the stories of elements of the Royal Artillery's experience in various theatres and using those stories to illustrate the critical importance of the Gunners.

Since the Royal Artillery was also the largest single element of the Army during the Second World War, comprising more than a quarter of its manpower when it peaked at about 700,000 in some 700 regiments and with almost as many personnel as the Royal Navy, this also compels the author to point the way to the bigger picture through the selective use of stories from various theatres and elements of the Royal Regiment. It may also be noted that the term 'manpower' is misleading: the Royal Artillery included women in many of its units. While these female soldiers were, strictly, not Gunners but members of the Auxiliary Territorial Service (ATS), those who served in the mixed regiments of Anti-Aircraft Command have been regarded as honorary gunners and have their own branch of the Royal Artillery Association.

The growth that led to the Royal Artillery becoming the Army's largest element began before the war and reached a significant milestone with the doubling of the Territorial Army in early 1939. This occurred in the wake of the Munich crisis and following the German occupation of Memel when units of the TA were asked to form duplicates. On 30 March 1939, six days after the German takeover, the War Office announced its plan to double the size of the TA. However, there were no clear plans for equipping and training the new units.

However, that was not the only aspect of the burgeoning of the Royal Artillery in the 1930s. After several years of neglect, the anti-aircraft artillery arm of the regiment began to receive attention, and by the time war broke out in September 1939 Anti-Aircraft Command had been formed to provide the gun aspect of the air defence of Great Britain. The bulk of that work was to be performed by units of the Territorial Army. Included in AA Command were searchlight units which had previously been the responsibility of the Royal Engineers but which the Gunners began to take over in 1938. It was in the same year that dedicated anti-tank units began to appear in the order of battle which seems to have been a very belated acceptance of the role of tanks on the battlefield but may have been as much to do with government parsimony.

These changes not only swelled the ranks of the Royal Artillery but also made it a very diverse family, not only in terms of the many roles that the regiment would play in the Second World War but also in terms of the origins of many of its soldiers. We have already noted the presence of women soldiers from the ATS and former Sappers from the Royal Engineers but the inter-war period also saw a number of TA units from other arms re-roled as gunners. Thus Yeomanry units such as those of Leicestershire, Shropshire and South Nottinghamshire became Gunner regiments as did TA infantry units such as the City of London Rifles, the Finsbury Rifles and 1st Monmouthshire Regiment.[1] In this new role they were joined by some war-formed infantry battalions, including 12th King's, 7th Loyals and 8th Royal Ulster Rifles, which became, respectively, 101st, 92nd and 117th Light AA Regiments. Those units transferring from other arms were often given permission to retain the distinctions of their original regiments giving rise to the sight of Gunners wearing infantry cap badges and distinctions such as the black buttons of the Ulster Rifles.

The ability of the Royal Artillery to absorb such units and yet retain pride in their origins with different badges, buttons and flashes enriches the story of the Royal Regiment during the Second World War and makes its story all the more fascinating. It is the aim of this volume to tell something of that story with all its richness and variety, its tragedies and triumphs, its endeavours and achievements and in so doing show how valuable was the contribution of the Regiment to final victory.

Notes

1 As 154th (Leicestershire Yeomanry) Field Regiment, 76th (Shropshire Yeomanry) Medium Regiment, 107th (South Nottinghamshire Hussars Yeomanry) Regiment Royal Horse Artillery, 31st (City of London) Searchlight Regiment (formerly 31st Anti-Aircraft Bn, RE), 61st (Finsbury Rifles) AA Regiment and 1st (Rifle) Bn The Monmouthshire Regiment (68th SL Regiment).

Chapter One

Rumours of War

When the Great War ended the Royal Regiment of Artillery could reflect on having made a major contribution to Allied victory. Many lessons had been absorbed and gunnery had evolved greatly from the early days of war with the Gunners developing principles which survive to this day and which were put into effect during the Second World War. Not least of these was the principle of concentration of fire and speed in so doing, but there were others: there should be only one artillery commander at each level who must command all types of artillery allotted; gunner command and control must be linked directly to the tactical plan; operations without a fireplan are doomed to failure; artillery command must be well forward, and mobile. These were summarised by the late Sir Martin Farndale:

> No other part of the Army can meet the severe demands of the principles of war as successfully as can the Gunners. Whether it be the persistent *maintenance of the aim*, day or night, in any weather or on any ground; the *maintenance of morale* by *offensive action*, which is the hallmark of all artillery operations; *surprise* – no Arm can produce surprise as can the Gunners; nothing is more surprising than the sudden, unexpected arrival of tons of high explosive on an unsuspecting target; no Arm can *concentrate force* as rapidly at one point on the battlefield, without the movement of its units, as can a divisional artillery correctly handled; a fundamental facet of the *security* of any position is an effective defensive fireplan; *economy of effort* cannot be better demonstrated, when needed, provided all guns are in range of the target; *flexibility* must be one of the most powerful characteristics of artillery, whether in method of attack, timing of attack or place of attack; no Arm relies so much on *cooperation* to achieve its aim. Alone it is effective but limited – with its comrades in the cavalry and infantry in full concert it is unbeatable; however, finally, without effective *administration* and, in particular, the provision of the weapon itself – the shell – it is useless.
>
> But this is not all. Artillery command, control and communications must be second to none or all is lost. Battery commanders and forward observers without

> communications are useless. Guns out of contact with the battle are little more than mobile road blocks. In any operational plan the fireplan is paramount, for what is war but a gigantic fireplan? Artillery is flexible but is never unlinked to the main manoeuvre battle. It has never made, and must never make, the mistake of air-power which is totally flexible and, in the pursuit of flexibility, has disconnected itself from the operations of ground troops. Artillery must be kept clear of the manoeuvre battle but must remain an integral part of it.[1]

By 1919 the Royal Regiment was the world's most professional artillery arm and faced the future with confidence. However, the 1920s became a decade of retrenchment as the Regiment reduced in size with the anti-aircraft element – built up so painstakingly in the late war – dismantled to leave but a single gun brigade[2] and a searchlight battalion in the regular army; there were no AA units in the Territorial Army, re-formed in 1922, although the Territorial Force had provided a major element of the wartime strength of the artillery arm. Worse still, such had been the speed with which the War Office had run down the post-war Army that no evaluation of AA artillery, its tactics and the technical and logistic aspects of this field of gunnery had been made and thus no AA gunnery doctrine had been formulated while those with recent experience were still in service. Indeed, for six years there was no development at all in the field or, as Brigadier N W Routledge describes it, 'there followed stagnation in the state of the art'.[3]

Unfortunately, this set the pattern for the inter-war years. The Army had to make do with what it had as the Treasury imposed the 'ten-year rule' which decreed that there would be no war in Europe for at least ten years. While this might have been fine had the rule been applied as a 'one-off' in 1919, it became a Treasury principle with a rolling 'ten-year rule' ensuring that the services remained short of funds until almost too late. Not until 1932 did the Cabinet abandon this rule. In the light of the history of the United Kingdom in the Second World War, it is worth noting that one of those who first promulgated the rule 'that the British Empire will not be engaged in any great war during the next ten years, and that no expeditionary force is required for this purpose', held the portfolios of War and Air. He was Winston S Churchill who, as Chancellor of the Exchequer in 1925 continued upholding the rule and used it to oppose plans to upgrade the Singapore naval base. In 1928 Churchill recommended that the rule 'should now be laid down as a standing assumption that at any given date there will be no major war for ten years from that date'.[4]

Fortunately common sense prevailed in 1932. The rule was abandoned and investment began trickling into the services but there were many demands from all three services which could not be met immediately. Some investment in the Royal Regiment ensured that the bulk of the field artillery would be mechanised by 1939. New equipment was also funded, including that classic of field pieces, the 25-pounder, and the finest AA gun of the war, the 3.7. Since the size, diversity and range of roles of the Regiment meant that it sought a very large slice of the money available to the Army, it is appropriate to review the contemporary organisation of the Royal Artillery.

The division into Royal Field Artillery and Royal Garrison Artillery had been abandoned in 1924. (As if to add confusion, the Royal Horse Artillery was the *corps d'elite* of the Royal Field Artillery while the Honourable Artillery Company, a TA unit, also belongs to the regimental family.) However, it was decided that, once again, the Regiment should be split into two branches: Field Army and Coast Defence and Anti-Aircraft. The former included units designated as field brigades – later regiments – as well as medium, mountain and anti-tank units plus 1st Heavy Brigade, a survey company and section, and both mountain and medium units of the Hong Kong and Singapore Royal Artillery (HKSRA) while the latter took responsibility for coast defence and AA artillery, all heavy brigades and batteries other than 1st Heavy Brigade, home fixed defences and fire commands, and the AA and coast defence elements of the HKSRA. The paired functions of coast defence and AA were further divided into twin elements. Coast artillery included close defence guns and counter-bombardment guns with the former using automatic sights that measured and set target ranges while the latter carried out longer range tasks. In the AA role there were heavy and light guns, the former deploying against high-flying targets and the latter against low-flying aircraft. (Searchlights, a Royal Engineer responsibility before the war, would be transferred to the Royal Artillery.) To complicate matters further, light AA units would also be assigned to the Field Army, initially at corps and later at divisional level. This re-organisation took effect in 1938, the creation of the Coast Defence and Anti-Aircraft branch having received Royal approval on 30 March.[5]

Also in 1938 a re-organisation of artillery units saw the lieutenant colonel's command redesignated from brigade to regiment.[6] The most important fire unit continued to be the battery to which, of course, Gunners owe their first loyalty. However, the new organisation established a field regiment of two twelve-gun batteries whereas field brigades had had four six-gun batteries. In regular regiments this led to a pairing of batteries so as to maintain the traditions of every battery: thus, for example, 19th Field Brigade's 29, 39, 96 and 97 Batteries became 19th Field Regiment's 29/39 and 96/97 Batteries.[7] Royal Horse Artillery units were also re-organised; the three RHA brigades became 1st, 2nd and 3rd Regiments RHA but since the original brigades had included three six-gun batteries, the new organisation was achieved by withdrawing E Battery from India – linked with A Battery it joined 1st Regiment – and redesignating two onetime RHA batteries, H (Ramsay's Troop) and P (The Dragon Troop), which had been in 8th Field Regiment and 21st Anti-Tank Regiment respectively. In the RHA, batteries were divided into two six-gun troops, thus allowing the troop to maintain the identity of the battery it had formerly been. A proposal that the twelve-gun unit should be styled a 'battalion' with the term 'battery' retained for the six-gun unit came to nothing.[8]

For the Territorial Army the effect was not so traumatic as re-organisation coincided with the decision to double the TA. Thus each TA field regiment could throw off two batteries to form a duplicate unit; 60th (North Midland) Field Regiment's second and fourth batteries – 238 and 240 – became 115th Field Regiment RA (North Midland) (TA), a pattern repeated across the TA throughout Great Britain.[9] Medium, heavy, coast and anti-aircraft regiments did not suffer to the same extent as field units, apart from some pairing of regular medium batteries.

Field batteries were now divided into three troops, each of four guns, with command posts at both battery and troop. A battery command post was manned by the command post officer (CPO) with the necessary assistants, telephonists and radio-operators, a format mirrored at troop level with the officer in charge being the gun position officer (GPO). On active service the battery commander (BC), a major, would have his own HQ with that of the infantry unit he was supporting; if he was not present himself then he would have an officer representing him but this would have been the exception rather than the rule. He would also have established observation posts (OPs) at locations from which possible targets could be seen clearly. In addition, forward-observation officers (FOOs) would deploy with advanced infantry units or elements of such units. These FOOs, whose role proved critical on many occasions during the war, could initiate engagement of any enemy target by sending fire orders to the GPOs over landline telephone or wireless; alternatively, signal lamps, flags, semaphore or heliograph might be used. During the 1930s the first steps were also taken in using air observation with RAF pilots trained to pass observations by coded radio messages to CPOs or GPOs. This would develop into the aerial observation post (AOP) system that proved invaluable in the war years.

Of course, information or fire orders passed back from FOOs, OPs or AOPs had to be checked by the GPO and allowances made for variables such as wind speed and temperature or uneven spacing of the guns of the battery or troop. To this end, the GPO's assistant (the GPO Ack) used the artillery board, a portable table with a squared chart on which were marked the gun position as well as the target positions. It will be recognised that Gunner officers needed scientific training and a solid grasp of mathematics. Alongside officers of the Royal Engineers, Royal Signals and Royal Tank Corps, they were trained at 'the Shop', the Royal Military Academy at Woolwich, the home of the Royal Artillery, rather than at the Royal Military College, Sandhurst where infantry and cavalry officers underwent training.

Throughout most of the interwar period, the Royal Artillery's guns were those with which it had fought the Great War. Some weapons, already obsolescent by armistice, were no longer suitable for a modern artillery arm by the early 1930s. But modernisation came painfully slowly as the Gunners jostled in the queue for the funds that began to come from the Treasury in that decade. As late as 1936 a senior officer could comment that current heavy artillery equipments 'are out of date in their ballistics' and 'cumbersome in their method of progression'. Perhaps the classic case of a completely outdated weapon was the 9.2-in howitzer which, weighing in at 21 tons, could be moved only in three loads and took about five hours to bring into action. This was hardly a weapon with which to fight a modern war. A new split-trail 7.85-inch howitzer had been proposed; this would weigh 14–15 tons, was more mobile and could come into action in under thirty minutes.[10]

The quest for new heavy weapons led to information being sought on equivalents in the armies of Germany, France, Italy, the USSR and the USA while the Chief of the Imperial General Staff (CIGS), the Army's professional head, showed interest in the 7.85-inch howitzer proposal, as well as a 10-inch howitzer and a 6.85-inch gun. The Director of Artillery added a 6-inch gun capable of firing a 112lb shell over a range of 30,000 yards. By May 1939, Vickers Armstrong had received specifications for two new heavy projects: a 9.2-inch howitzer, really a re-working of the older equipment, and a 6-inch gun, designated Mk XXIII.[11] The 9.2-inch howitzer proposal came to naught and when it became clear that this was a 'sterile exercise' it was decided to modify yet another Great War veteran equipment: the 8-inch howitzer was to be re-lined to increase its range from 12,400 to 15,500 yards. This became the 7.2-inch howitzer, mounted on a modified 8-inch carriage – later it was fitted to a modern American carriage – which could fire a 200lb shell to 16,900 yards and which saw widespread service beginning in the North African campaign.[12]

This almost leisurely pace had already caused concern with the Director of Artillery writing to the Director of Staff Duties at the War Office on 3 March 1937 to state that he was 'disturbed about lack of progress with our New Heavy Artillery piece. Time slips away and then we are rushed.' He then quoted 'from my own experience' three examples of the time it took to bring new projects to fruition: the 25-pounder had taken five years of discussion, as had the 3.7-inch anti-aircraft gun, while the 2-pounder anti-aircraft gun had taken two years.[13]

That Gunners had been considering the deployment of their heavy equipments on the mainland yet again was illustrated by requests to the military attachés in the embassies in Paris and Brussels, in October 1936, for information on whether bridges in northern France and Belgium could support heavy artillery. In both cases the responses were positive: for France maps were provided showing suitable routes while for Belgium it was believed that all bridges on first-class roads could carry heavy artillery.[14] While this investigation showed commendable foresight, it might also be interpreted as suggesting that a future war would develop on lines similar to the previous conflict.

The typical heavy artillery unit that was expected to use those bridges should war erupt again in Europe was still designated a heavy brigade and would remain so until 1 November 1938 when it would become a heavy regiment. However, the change in designation did not affect the order of battle: a heavy brigade/regiment included four batteries each deploying six weapons; these were a battery of 8-inch howitzers, firing a 200lb shell over a range of 12,400 yards, two batteries of 9.2-inch howitzers, firing a 290lb shell over 13,000 yards, and a battery of 6-inch Mk XIX guns, with a range of 18,750 yards at 38 degrees elevation, firing a 100lb shell.[15]

Although it only began re-equipping with some of its new guns by the end of 1938, the Royal Regiment had passed one major milestone: the mechanisation of the bulk of its field artillery. The iconic vehicle of the new era was the Morris-Commercial Quad, subsequently the principal towing vehicle for the new 25-pounder field gun. However, the Quad, a four-wheel-drive vehicle, was designed originally by Guy Motors who produced such a unique shape that, with its metal covering, many believed that the vehicle was bullet-proof. In fact, it was not even splinter-proof; the shape had been designed for ease of washing down after exposure to poison gas;[16] since gas had been used in the Great War, it was expected that it would be deployed again. Later in the war the Quad was also used to tow the 17-pounder anti-tank gun.[17]

Between the wars there had been much experimentation with gun tractors, including tracked vehicles, one of which, the Light Dragon, led to the various carriers that saw widespread service with the Army during the Second World War.[18] Some Dragons remained in Gunner service in 1939 and went to France with the British Expeditionary Force; these were Mk IIs, used mainly to tow guns of the newly-formed anti-tank units. When Royal Horse Artillery brigades were mechanised in 1936 the vehicle adopted was the Dragon.[19] Other gun-towing vehicles included four- and six-wheel lorries from companies such as AEC, Bedford, Guy and Scammell. When war was declared on 3 September 1939 Britain's army was the most mechanised in the world. But what of the guns towed by Royal Artillery vehicles?

During the Great War the standard field gun had been the 18-pounder alongside which had been operated the 4.5-inch howitzer. Both were replaced by the 25-pounder which was designed as a gun/howitzer. In other words, it could fire in both the 'lower' and 'upper' registers: the barrel could be elevated above 45 degrees. However, the first of the 25-pounder family were 18-pounders fitted with re-bored barrels of 87.5mm calibre and with carriages adapted for pneumatic tyres to allow the equipments to be towed at higher speeds by petrol- or diesel-engined vehicles. These re-bored guns were designated Ordnance QF 25-pounder Mk I; about 1,000 were produced. However, this 18/25-pounder was an interim equipment and the true 25-pounder, the Ordnance QF 25-pounder Mk II, was being developed simultaneously. Commenting that few Second World War weapons resulted from clearly defined requirements from the General Staff, Shelford Bidwell pointed out that they were either civil inventions, such as radar, 'or largely unprompted "doodles" by the technical staff, like the 25-pounder, the child of an unblessed liaison between the technical staff and the School of Artillery'.[20]

Initially this new design incorporated a split trail, and the first order was for guns to this design, but the Inspector Royal Artillery approached the Director of Artillery 'to say there was a strong feeling in the Regiment' that the weapon should have a 'box-trail-cum-platform'.[21] This would allow the higher elevations of a howitzer, and could traverse through 360 degrees, thanks to a circular platform specified by the Royal Artillery Committee. This platform resembled an old-fashioned cartwheel fitted with toeplates which dug into the ground; the gun could be towed onto the platform in seconds and fixed by tie-rods. The recommendation for the box trail was accepted and was a principal factor in the gun's success. Such was that success that the 25-pounder served the Royal Artillery not only throughout the Second World War but for many years thereafter, finally going out of service in 1967. (However, it continued to be used for ceremonial duties and was last used in action by British troops at Mirbat in Oman in 1972 when SAS troops used an Omani army 25-pounder.) It also served in a variety of roles and was adapted as a self-propelled weapon as well as being the standard field gun in Commonwealth and Imperial forces. When the BEF went to France in late 1939 many field regiments were still equipped with 18-pounders and 4.5-inch howitzers although some included both 18-pounders and 18/25-pounders.[22] Not until April 1940 was the first 25-pounder Mk II issued; these went to Royal Canadian Artillery units in Britain. Later that month, and in early May, Mk IIs of 203 Battery 51st Field Regiment went into action in Norway in the 25-pounder's baptism of fire.[23]

Medium regiments continued with the 6-inch howitzer and 60-pounder gun. The former dated from 1915 while the latter was even older with an ancestry going back to 1904, although it had been updated by Vickers Armstrong in 1918 with a new carriage, improved breech mechanism and a piece that was five calibres longer. Replacements for both equipments were on their way but the 6-inch howitzer and 60-pounder had to soldier on until the new weapons arrived.[24] In the case of the 60-pounder, it could be said that the old gun replaced itself as the barrel was relined to 4.5 inches and its carriage fitted with pneumatic tyres. Attempts to modify the 6-inch gun in like fashion were unsuccessful and a new weapon was developed to fire an 80lb shell to 18,500 yards; this became the 5.5-inch medium gun which would enter service in North Africa and see its last action in Borneo in 1964.[25]

In the heavy regiments there was yet another ancient weapon. The 6-inch gun – adapted in 1915 from a design dating back to the Boer War – had been built in small numbers, with little more than a hundred produced for British service.[26] Three heavy regiments went to France with the BEF and left behind all their 6-inch guns. Their other equipments were 8- and 9.2-inch howitzers, most of which were also left behind.[27] Although these weapons were of little value in modern warfare, some limited use was made of the 6-inch gun in the Middle East while the 8-inch howitzer provided the stepping stone to the 7.2-inch howitzer; the 9.2 was last used as an anti-invasion weapon on England's south-east coast. Also in the BEF order of battle were three super-heavy batteries, equipped with 9.2- and 12-inch howitzers, the latter an enlarged version of the former. The 12-inch howitzer also ended its career as an anti-invasion weapon.[28]

Anti-tank regiments were receiving a weapon that, when approved on 1 January 1936, was probably the best anti-tank gun in any army; its 2lb armour-piercing (AP) shot could penetrate 42mm of armour, sloped at 30 degrees, at a range of 1,000 yards. Sadly, by 1940 the gun was no longer the best, but it had to soldier on for some time yet. Not surprisingly, there were insufficient 2-pounders to equip the BEF's anti-tank regiments and 37mm anti-tank guns had to be bought from the Swedish firm of Bofors. The 2-pounder was a light gun – its weight in action was 1,757 lbs – on a three-legged mounting that allowed an all-round traverse. Its semi-automatic breech mechanism gave a high rate of fire and it was fitted with an excellent telescope sight. Although capable of dealing with early German and Italian tanks, it was soon outclassed and its high profile made it hard to conceal, allowing enemy tanks to stay out of range while shelling the gun and killing its detachment.[29]

Although anti-tank regiments received a gun on the verge of obsolescence, this was not the case with their comrades in anti-aircraft units where two remarkable equipments were reaching front-line units as the final months of peace faded. These were the Vickers Armstrong-designed 3.7-inch heavy anti-aircraft gun, 'an extremely advanced weapon for its time'[30] and the Swedish Bofors 40mm light anti-aircraft gun. Although there were other AA weapons, such as the 4.5-inch heavy AA gun, the 3.7 and the Bofors were to be the principal British AA equipments of the war and the former can be regarded, with no trace of chauvinism, as the best gun in its class in the world – and that includes the German 88mm.

Coast artillery units operated some of the Army's oldest equipments. The 12-pounder dated back to 1894, when it began life as a naval gun for close defence against light, fast craft while the 4.7-inch gun had entered naval service in 1887 and joined the Army in the 1890s, but both were beaten in terms of age by the 6-inch coast gun which began life as the 80-pounder as far back as 1882.[31] There was also the twin 6-pounder coast gun which mounted two 6-pounders – a weapon also dating to the 1880s but superseded as a solo weapon by the 12-pounder by the 1920s when it was relegated to training and practice – with semi-automatic breeches and a rate of fire per barrel of 40 rounds each minute. These were intended for harbour defence, a role in which they proved themselves beyond doubt when the Italian navy, the *Regia Marina*, attacked Malta's Valetta harbour in July 1941, an incident outlined later in this book.[32]

It was therefore with a mixed bag of weaponry that the Royal Artillery entered the Second World War. Some of its guns were new and excellent, some were old and in need of replacement and, in the case of the 2-pounder anti-tank gun, at least one was new and already almost outdated. Irrespective of the quantity or quality of the guns available in September 1939, the Regiment had one great advantage over the rest of the Army – it was the best trained of all the arms. One Gunner historian has argued that its standard of training was unsurpassed in any army.[33]

This training regime was a result of the many lessons absorbed from the Great War, which also led to the abolition of the distinction between field and garrison artillery in 1924. Four years earlier, the School of Artillery had been established at Larkhill, quickly becoming the nerve centre of the Regiment although its soul remained at Woolwich. The School's role was to teach instructors by selecting officers and NCOs from throughout the Regiment to attend the long Gunnery Staff Course and qualify to become Instructors in Gunnery, or IGs. Thus was created the 'Gunnery Staff', a body unique to the Royal Artillery, with the role of ensuring that high standards were achieved consistently across the Regiment. It was the IGs' duty 'to go wherever the units of the Royal Artillery were stationed like missionaries and propagate the gospel according to Larkhill. In India there was a subsidiary School, at first at Kakul near Abbotabad, and later at Deolali.'[34]

New regimes are rarely popular initially, and so it was with the IGs but their value soon became apparent as these zealots from Larkhill descended on units that were carrying out their regular training to observe in detail all that happened. Departures from official drills were commented upon, as were any miscalculations. In time, this led to a uniform doctrine throughout the Regiment which proved of great benefit in the war years. Larkhill not only produced IGs; it also played a major part in training newly-commissioned Gunner officers. From 1926 all subalterns were sent to Larkhill from Woolwich to undertake the Young Officers' Course. No longer was the training of new Gunner officers left to the vagaries of their seniors when they joined their batteries.[35] Larkhill and the YOs' Course ensured uniform training in the service of the gun.

In his seminal work *Gunners at War*, Shelford Bidwell noted that the School of Artillery:

> was apt to disapprove of or pour cold water on innovations [and] ... remained insulated from and indifferent to the dynamic thinking going on in the new Royal Tank Corps: no one attending the School in the early thirties would have guessed that a violent military storm was raging outside its walls, or that tanks existed. There was a tragic failure to build a bridge between the old arm and the new. Nevertheless, the School made an immense contribution to the Regiment and thereby to the Army as a whole.[36]

Who knows what innovations might have stemmed from a close link between Gunners and the Royal Tank Corps? Perhaps self-propelled artillery, both field and anti-tank, might have made an earlier appearance, although it has to be noted that the Regiment experimented with a self-propelled field gun, the Birch gun (an 18-pounder mounted on a tracked body), and 9th Field Brigade's 20 Battery formed part of the Experimental Mechanised Force with such SPGs. The Birch gun, named for General Birch, then Master General of the Ordnance, began life as a turret-fitted 18-pounder mounted on a tracked body developed from the Medium Mk I tank which proved deficient in a number of ways including low power-to-weight ratio and restricted gun traverse and elevation. Thus the concept was modified to a pedestal-mounted 18-pounder fitted to the turret ring and protected by a shield.[37] The Experimental Mechanised Force was created in May 1927 and disbanded, prematurely, a year later. No development of SPGs followed. For the Gunners the experiment was not entirely propitious as the 18-pounder was insufficiently flexible to provide an effective close support weapon for a mechanised force. In fact, the end result of the experiments, the 1929 training manual entitled *Mechanised and Armoured Formations* and its 1931 revised edition, *Modern Formations*, made no mention of artillery in the close support role which was allotted to a 'close support tank battery'. Although no close support tank existed at the time, it was implied that, when it did come into service, it would be manned by the Royal Tank Corps rather than the Royal Artillery.[38] Nothing makes clearer that 'tragic failure' to bring together in harmony the Gunners and the Tankers.

Not until the North African campaign were further efforts made to provide a self-propelled gun with the resulting compromise a 25-pounder mounted on a Cruiser tank. As with all compromises, it lost something from both aspects: the 25-pounder's performance was restricted and the low silhouette of the mated tank – the Valentine – disappeared to produce Bishop. Ironically, the experiments with a mobile or armoured division had presaged quite closely the mid-war composition of an armoured division, but the latter was arrived at, eventually, by dint of painful experience in action. In the post-war era, one Gunner historian was prompted to comment on

> the curious blind spot in the minds of military technicians, who followed with painstaking alacrity the gun-*versus*-armour conflict but pondered two years of warfare's bitterest lessons before they managed to provide artillerymen with the protection of self-propelled guns.[39]

By 1939 the Gunners were much more mobile than ever and determined to prove their worth. While the doubling of the TA so close to the outbreak of war created many problems for trainers and logisticians, as well as weapon manufacturers, there was a quiet confidence in the Royal Regiment that, once again, there would be a job well done.

Notes

1. Farndale, *History of The Royal Regiment of Artillery: Western Front, 1914–18*, pp. 335–6
2. At this time, and until 1938, a lieutenant colonel's command of two batteries. From 1938 a lieutenant colonel's command was redesignated a regiment.
3. Routledge, *History of The Royal Regiment of Artillery: Anti-Aircraft Artillery, 1914–55*, p. 40

4 Corrigan, *Blood, Sweat and Arrogance*, p. 58 (for the initial formulation of the rule) and pp. 86–7 (for Churchill's role as Chancellor).
5 NA Kew, WO32/4619 'Formation of a separate Coast Defence & Anti-Aircraft Branch RA'
6 Army Order (AO) 204, September 1938
7 Frederick, *Lineage Book of British Land Forces, 1660–1978*, p. 504
8 Maj W G Clarke, 'Options for Change' – c 1938, Gunner, Feb 1992
9 Frederick, op cit, p. 517 & 529
10 NA Kew, WO32/4617, 'Heavy Artillery – Reorganization & Re-equipment, 1936–40'
11 Ibid
12 Ibid; Bidwell, *Gunners At War*, pp. 106–7; Hogg, *Allied Artillery of World War Two*, pp. 70–1
13 NA Kew, WO32/4617, op cit
14 Ibid
15 Ibid
16 Ventham and Fletcher, *Moving the Guns*, p. 81
17 Hogg & Weeks, *The Illustrated Encyclopedia of Military Vehicles*, p. 257
18 Ibid, p. 256; Ventham & Fletcher, op cit, pp. 26–73
19 Ventham & Fletcher, op cit, pp. 71–2
20 Bidwell, op cit, p. 100
21 Duncan, *Royal Artillery Commemoration Book*, p. 35
22 Hogg, *British & American Artillery of World War 2*, pp. 26–8
23 Henry, *The 25-pounder Field Gun 1939–72*, pp. 23–4
24 Hogg, op cit, pp. 50–1 (6-inch howitzer); p. 44 (60-pdr)
25 Bidwell, op cit, pp. 105–6
26 Hogg, op cit, p. 137
27 Farndale, *History of The Royal Regiment of Artillery: The Years of Defeat*, p. 264
28 Information on these weapons also from Hogg.
29 Hogg, op cit, pp. 73–5
30 Ibid, pp. 107–9
31 Ibid, pp. 188–193
32 Ibid, p. 186
33 Bidwell, op cit, p. 58
34 Ibid, p. 57
35 Ibid, pp. 58–9
36 Ibid, p. 58
37 Bidwell, op cit, pp. 72–3
38 Ventham & Fletcher, op cit, pp. 56–61
39 Johnston, *Regimental Fire*, p. 17

Chapter Two

First Blood

At 11.15am on Sunday 3 September 1939, Prime Minister Neville Chamberlain broadcast to the nation. In tired tones, he told listeners that Germany had ignored a Franco-British ultimatum to withdraw from Poland, which it had invaded on the 1st, and, therefore, the United Kingdom was at war with Germany.

Gunners were already prepared for action throughout the United Kingdom and there is a claim that the first British shot of the war was from 188 (Antrim) Heavy Battery when it 'fired across the bows of an incoming vessel on the morning of 3rd September 1939, some three hours before war was declared'.[1] However, this is contradicted in the authoritative account of Ulster's coast defences which describes how at '08.15 hours on *5* September the small coasting steamer SS *E Hayward* entered the [Belfast] lough quite unaware that war had been declared with Germany' and that one plugged (no explosive filling) round was fired. This statement is based on the war diary for the 5th which states that at 0815 'Steamer *E Hayward* brought to by firing plugged shell across her bows'.[2] This was the sole occasion on which Grey Point's guns fired in anything resembling anger. The quiet war of 188 Battery which, with the newly-created 200 Battery, formed the Antrim Heavy Regiment RA from 1 March 1940, was not to be the experience of many of their Royal Artillery comrades.

Arguably the first true shots in anger were fired by 71st (Forth) Anti-Aircraft Regiment on 16 October. The regiment had deployed to protect the Forth bridge and detachments were undergoing gun drill when German aircraft were spotted. In the ensuing action the guns and RAF fighters shot down two aircraft, the first two enemy planes shot down by British forces during the war. The guns of 71st (Forth) AA Regiment could, therefore, claim to have been the first British guns to fire on the enemy.[3]

Most regiments had begun mobilising on 1 September although some, especially AA units, were already at war stations. Lord Gort of Limerick VC was told that he was to command the British Expeditionary Force (BEF) which would cross to France to support the French armies against German aggression.

The creation of the BEF in March 1939 had marked a reversal of British policy for the Army, which hitherto had been seen as defending the UK, imperial policing, protecting overseas' possessions and ports, and dealing with a second-class Middle Eastern power. Although it was intended that the BEF would include nineteen divisions, to the chagrin of the French this would take more than a year to accomplish; only 1st and 2nd Divisions were ready to cross the Channel at the beginning of September. Making up I Corps, under Lieutenant General Sir John Dill, these began moving to France within days.[4] However, it was not until 22 September that the main bodies of both began to move.[5] I Corps' Gunner complement included six field regiments, under the Corps Commander Royal Artillery (CCRA), Brigadier F H N Davidson. In 1st Division, whose Commander Royal Artillery (CRA) was Brigadier C W P Perceval, were 2nd, 19th and 67th Field Regiments while 2nd Division deployed 10th, 16th and 99th (Royal Buckinghamshire Yeomanry) Field Regiments with Brigadier C B Findlay as CRA. Of these six regiments, 67th Field, a South Midland TA unit, had not completed training and did not cross to France until January 1940.[6]

II Corps, under Lieutenant General Sir Alan Brooke, a distinguished Gunner, followed I Corps and began moving into the line on 12 October. Composed of 3rd and 4th Divisions, it also deployed six field regiments: 7th, transferred from 5th Division, 33rd and the TA 76th (Highland) were in 3rd Division with Brigadier R H Towell as CRA while 4th Division included 22nd, 30th and 77th (Highland) under Brigadier G E W Franklyn; Brigadier E C A Schreiber was CCRA. Once again the field artillery was not complete in France until January 1940.[7] In all, the planned Gunner complement of the initial BEF included twenty field regiments, seven medium, four light AA, three AA (the designation HAA had yet to be introduced), one heavy regiment and two light AA batteries.[8] Field regiments were equipped with 18-pounders and 4.5-inch howitzers in the case of the TA units or 18/25-pounders in the Regulars while most other regiments had vintage equipment, save for the Bofors 40mm guns equipping some light AA units.

While the allocation of three field regiments to a division gave each brigade a supporting field regiment, the two-battery composition did not permit a battery to be assigned to each battalion. This situation was exacerbated by the fact that, at battery level, there were only two groups of Gunner commanders for an infantry brigade, leaving one battalion bereft of artillery command and control, 'a most serious omission'. How had this come about? Quite simply, the two-battery structure had been selected because it had been considered that the survey process to make three eight-gun batteries ready to fire together in a fast-moving situation would have taken too long. Thus it was decided to survey one battery and pass the resulting data to the other. Although faster, this created the undesirable operational situation that we have noted. Eventually, this problem would be eliminated through adopting a three-battery organisation but in the meantime it was alleviated, to some extent, by the availability of army field regiments, several of which were held at corps level and which the CCRA could deploy to reinforce divisions as necessary.[9]

Throughout the autumn and winter the BEF increased its strength and built defensive positions in its assigned sector. That sector, which was to be held by two field armies – First and Second – by summer 1940,[10] was along the Belgian frontier where the Maginot Line, the French defensive system, did not extend. British troops did much digging and building to create what was dubbed the Gort Line. Weather conditions were atrocious that winter, one of the region's worst, making construction tasks even more difficult. It also created problems for the BEF's training programme, especially since training standards following such a speedy mobilisation were not as high as was necessary. Thus war diaries tell of treacherous road conditions, of sharp frosts and frozen ground, and of the quagmire following the thaw. The latter led the French authorities to impose 'thaw precautions' to preserve their roads; 75th (Highland) Field Regiment noted that it was unable to move for 'at least two days' as a result.[11] At one stage, nocturnal temperatures were so low that vehicles had to be kept 'running all night to prevent them from freezing up'.[12] While training was carried out by the artillery, realism could not be achieved due to a French ban on using radios, even for training. This resulted, as might be expected, in 'an almost total communication failure' whereas allowing signallers to train might have ensured much better command, control and communications in the fluid days of May 1940.[13]

As the BEF grew so additional Gunner units arrived, including field, medium and heavy regiments. Air defences were not neglected and would grow to include six AA brigades: 1, 2, 3 (Ulster), 4, 5 and 12 AA Brigades.[14] These deployed eleven heavy AA regiments – still defined as AA regiments as the HAA definition was not adopted until May 1940 – as well as four light AA regiments, four searchlight regiments, four non-regimented heavy AA batteries and two non-regimented light AA batteries. In addition, three light AA regiments were serving as corps troops and a combined light AA/anti-tank regiment arrived with 1st Armoured Division. Anti-tank units were arriving with their parent divisions although most TA units, and some Regulars, had the French Hotchkiss 25mm guns, carried on 15cwt trucks; Regular units using the Hotchkiss included the four batteries (36, 61, 68 and 88) of 14th Anti-Tank Regiment in 4th Division.[15]

Although Germany and the USSR overran Poland quickly, the Germans did not turn their attention immediately to the west. A lengthy period in which Wehrmacht forces were transferred from the eastern front in preparation for the assault on France became known as the 'Phoney War' or '*Sitzkrieg*'. This was not a period of inactivity for the BEF in which, as we have noted, training and preparation continued apace. Gunners trained with their equipments, to get to know the area of front on which they would be fighting and to refine operational procedures, often under the watchful eyes of IGs.

Among Gunner roles was the protection of the bases of the Advanced Air Striking Force (AASF);[16] this was undertaken by 12 AA Brigade. One Royal Air Force responsibility was army co-operation but, in 1939–40, this was an area in which the air element was weak. The principal army co-operation aircraft, the Westland Lysander, was a slow, single-engined, high-winged monoplane, five squadrons of which were included in the BEF's Air Component. The Lysander proved of little value in battle, although it later created a unique niche in special duties. Thus the Army had no eyes of its own and no airborne striking power in contrast to the German forces where the Luftwaffe co-operated closely with ground forces and provided airborne artillery. However, the CIGS, General Ironside, a Gunner, had produced a paper on Army/Air co-operation which went to the Cabinet on 25 September 1939. In response the Cabinet 'stressed the need for the Army to have control over its own aircraft requirements'. This was followed by a War Office affirmation of the need for 'a new type of light aeroplane to improve the application of artillery fire to be piloted by Army officers especially trained for this work.'[17]

From this was born the Royal Artillery Air Observation Posts which proved so valuable later in the war. Several Gunner officers had already devoted much time and effort to developing air observation in the pre-war years. Prominent among them was Jack Parham who, writing in the Royal United Services Institute (RUSI) *Journal* in August 1933, had noted how a battery commander had to call on a distant RAF unit to help him should he wish to see a target out of sight behind a hill whereas 'five minutes in the air above his own battery position – even a thousand feet up – would meet all his requirements'. Parham was thinking of an autogiro which could be based with the Gunner unit and flown by one of its officers; he himself was qualified to fly such a machine. Not until 1935 were trials authorised with RAF Lysanders but with Gunner officers as passengers, thus making it more difficult to spot and correct the fall of shot.[18]

Meanwhile, a small group of officers formed the Royal Artillery Flying Club in November 1934. Its president was the BRA Southern Command, Brigadier H R S Massy, later Director of Military Training from September 1938 until October 1939, with Captain Charles Bazeley as the secretary. The pair did much to work out the AOP concept with Gunners flying *and* observing. Bazeley transferred on secondment to the RAF in 1935, serving as an Army Co-operation pilot until 1940, during which time he presented the idea of what he described as Flying Observation Posts, 'light aircraft manned by Gunners in direct contact with the guns at all times' that would operate in conjunction with their ground-based colleagues; the aerial OPs would usually fly above the guns.[19]

Following trials supervised by the Schools of Artillery and Army Co-operation, it was agreed to develop flying OPs and, in summer 1939, discussions between the Deputy CIGS and Deputy Chief of the Air Staff accepted that a Gunner officer in an 'Air OP' was the ideal solution to the problem of artillery observation from the air. A simple, slow aeroplane, to remain RAF property, was necessary. Agreement was also reached on a scale of machines – twelve per corps – and trials began before the summer was out. Aeroplanes under trial included the American Taylorcraft, which was eventually manufactured by a British company, the British Mosscraft and another American product, the Stinson.[20] However, this was not the end of the story: further trials were to be undertaken at Old Sarum in Wiltshire in early 1940 by D Flight RAF, a joint Royal Artillery/Royal Air Force unit commanded by the now-Major Bazeley. Four machines were assessed, a Taylorcraft and a Stinson from the USA, and a General Aircraft Cagnet and a Comper Fly from Britain. Trials included co-operation with French artillery at their ranges at Mailly, by which time D Flight was operating only a Stinson 105 and three Taylorcraft Ds. The American designs were the most promising and with a British company in Leicester licensed to build the Taylorcraft, this was the final choice.[21] No operational trials were conducted in France. Although scheduled to begin on 9 May 1940, the German attack through the Low Countries on the 10th meant that the plan went into abeyance.

By the time the Germans launched their attack, Jack Parham was commanding 10th Field Regiment with 2nd Division in II Corps. The offensive meant that Gunners were fighting on two fronts on the continent: Norway and France. Already a month old, the Norwegian campaign saw several Gunner units involved under command of 6 AA Brigade, including 51st (London) and 82nd (Essex) AA Regiments, 55th (Devon) Light AA Regiment and HQ and 167 Battery 56th (East Lancashire) Light AA Regiment, 3 LAA Battery, 203 Field Battery (from 51st (Westmorland and Cumberland) Field Regiment) and 10 Army Observation Unit. In this short but vicious campaign those Gunner units played a significant role.[22]

The Norwegian campaign arose from a German naval desire for bases 'for a fundamental improvement in our strategic and operational situation' with the ice-free ports of Narvik and Trondheim the most desirable.[23] A visit to Berlin by a former Norwegian defence minister, Vidkun Quisling, founder of a Nazi-style party, *Nasjonal Samling*, revived Hitler's interest and led to *Studie Nord*, a study for the occupation of Norway by peaceful or other means.[24] When HMS *Cossack* liberated *Graf Spee*'s prisoners from the supply ship *Altmark* in a Norwegian fjord on 16 February 1940, the incident probably focused Hitler's mind on Norway and, on 1 March, he issued a formal order to occupy both Denmark and Norway. This did not happen immediately, although plans were drawn up with the Luftwaffe in a leading role; the initial attack would involve troops transported by air.

Britain was also concerned about Norway and especially about maintaining its neutrality. However, since intelligence suggested that the Germans intended to invade, it was decided to send an expeditionary force to assist the Norwegians as soon as the first Germans entered the country, or as soon as it became clear that invasion was imminent. In this Britain was supported by France and French troops were also assigned to the expeditionary force. On 2 April Hitler issued orders for Operation WESERÜBUNG, the invasion of Denmark and Norway, and five days later the Allied expeditionary force sailed for Norway. Then, on 9 April, German forces invaded both Denmark and Norway. With the former overrun in hours, the Germans could concentrate on Norway. Opposing forces were engaged at sea and the Kriegsmarine suffered heavily in the battle of Narvik. However, the small Norwegian forces were hard-pressed and the Luftwaffe controlled the skies. Within eight days German troops dominated southern Norway and when British troops of 148 Brigade arrived to join the defending Norwegians they were soon beaten by their foes who were better trained, better led and better equipped. Elements of two British brigades, 15 and 146, which landed near Namsos in mid-April had been evacuated by the beginning of May, leaving almost all central and southern Norway to the Germans.

The struggle continued in the north where the German commander, General Dietl, lost Narvik to a force of British, French and Polish troops. Dietl's mountain troops had been deprived of their naval transport and logistic support by the Royal Navy and Narvik was in Allied hands by 28 May. By then, however, it had been decided to evacuate Norway and orders to that effect had been issued.

How had the Gunners fared during this brief campaign? As already noted, the Gunner contribution to the expeditionary force was 6 AA Brigade who went to Harstad but did not begin landing until 6 May. They were soon engaged heavily against Luftwaffe aircraft attacking ships in the fjord. Many barrages were put up and 152 AA Battery reported firing for four hours on one occasion. One unit had arrived earlier: 3 LAA Battery began disembarking at Harstad on 15 April and, next day, some of its guns were in action while still aboard the ships; BQMS Morgan claimed one enemy aircraft downed with a machine gun. Within a week the guns were deployed around the harbour and in action daily against Luftwaffe raids. Then came orders to detach guns for other tasks: 1st Troop was sent to Skaanland on the 27th and on 4 May two guns were ordered to Bardufoss airfield. Such were the road conditions that it took Lieutenant T S Wilkinson and his two guns some fourteen hours of digging and winching to reach their destination. Four days later, 2nd Troop left for Gratangen to provide AA defence for the French. By this time, 55th LAA Regiment had arrived at Harstad to defend the airfield and was ordered to detach a troop of 164 Battery to Skaanland. Those guns were in action next day, the 10th, the day on which the Germans invaded the Low Countries, and claimed a German aircraft shot down and its pilot captured. On 18 May, BHQ 164 Battery and eight of its guns were at Bardufoss defending the airfield when a squadron of sixteen Gloster Gladiator biplane fighters arrived. The Gladiators were followed by a squadron of fourteen Hawker Hurricanes on the 27th but the campaign was all but over. Orders to destroy the guns and embark for home were received on 5 June. The battery was home eight days later.[25]

Elsewhere the Gunners had also played their parts in the doomed campaign. When Sickleforce – 148 Brigade with only two battalions – landed near Åndalsnes the Germans deployed a force from Oslo to relieve Trondheim, which 148 Brigade turned south to meet. Following tough fighting in deep snow, 148 Brigade had to retreat. To their assistance came 15 Brigade with 260 AA and 168 LAA Batteries, which linked up with 148 Brigade by 21 April. At Otta, Sickleforce came under sustained aerial attack on the 25th; three of 168 LAA Battery's Bofors shot down three enemy aircraft. However, a direct hit on one Bofors killed or wounded the detachment members and knocked out the gun. Before long the other guns had also been knocked out but the trio had put up 'a splendid effort against superior odds'.[26]

When Sickleforce was evacuated from Namsos on the nights of 2 and 3 May, some 9,000 men and most of 15 Brigade were saved. By then Allied efforts were concentrated on the one area where some success had been achieved: Narvik. French troops made contact with the Germans at Lake Storvatn, having reached the high ground overlooking the town across the Beisfjord. The *Chasseurs Alpins*' morale was boosted considerably when a section of 203 Field Battery joined with their two 25-pounder Mk IIs. The Battery's guns, and a troop of 3 LAA Battery, played a key role in the capture of Narvik by destroying a determined German counter-attack. These were, as noted in Chapter One, the first 25-pounders to see action.[27]

The principal Allied attack on Narvik was launched on 17 May by a force including Norwegian, British, French and Polish troops. The Poles relieved the *Chasseurs Alpins* to attack Beisfjord while 1st and 2nd Battalions of 13 Demi-Brigade *Légion étrangère* landed north of the town. A German counter-attack met withering fire from 203 Field Battery's 25-pounders and the guns of 2nd Troop 3 LAA Battery, operating under French control. The Gunner efforts did much to persuade the Germans to abandon their attack. The Luftwaffe also attacked French positions at Bjervik during which 2nd Troop 3 LAA Battery shot down one attacker. The 25-pounders of 203 Battery moved to support the Poles as their brigade attacked Ankenes on the night of the 27th, an attack also supported by Royal Navy ships. The operation was successful and on the 28th Narvik was in Allied hands.

There had been a German move to support their troops at Narvik which involved some of those troops now released from the south following the Allied evacuation moving towards Narvik. To counter this, a British blocking force was despatched to Mö. Consisting of 1st Scots Guards with a troop of 203 Battery, a Bofors troop of three guns from 55th LAA Regiment and a detachment of 230 Field Company Royal Engineers, this little force advanced to Stein to await the approaching Germans. At 6.30pm on the 17th the Germans attacked. Although outnumbered, the Gunners and Guards held their line. Command of the force, now dubbed Scissorsforce, was assumed by Brigadier C McV Gubbins who eventually ordered a withdrawal to Viskiskoia. Here, again, Scissorsforce engaged the enemy and, again, was forced to retire. Reforming at Pothus in bitterly cold conditions, Gunners and infantry once more stood in the path of the enemy advance. Reinforced by additional infantry and renamed Stockforce, but still commanded by Brigadier Gubbins, the intention was to hold the enemy in the Saltdalen valley.

The 25-pounders of 203 Battery proved their worth time and time again by wreaking execution on the attackers. But the Germans had weight of numbers and air superiority on their side, as well as artillery and tanks. Their mortars and machine guns were dug in on high ground and their final assault was supported by five Heinkel He111 bombers that strafed the infantry positions. At the same time the infantry assault went in and the 'British 25-pounders and Norwegian mortars caused many casualties as the enemy rushed over the bridge, hurling grenades'.[28] Such was the pressure of the German attack, with its armour, artillery and air support, that another withdrawal was necessary, this time to Bodö for evacuation. On 31 May, the 25-pounder detachments had the sad duty of destroying their equipments before embarking for Harstad. By 7 June the expeditionary force had quit Norway. The campaign was over but the Gunners had acquitted themselves well and taken a deadly toll of their enemy.

The failure of the Allied campaign in central Norway was a factor in what became known as the 'Norway debate' in the House of Commons which led to the resignation of Neville Chamberlain and Winston Churchill's appointment as Prime Minister. Churchill assumed office on 10 May, the very day on which the Wehrmacht attacked the Low Countries.

The BEF's artillery was emplaced along the Franco-Belgian frontier when the German attack came. Those positions, part of the Gort Line, prepared carefully and with much sweat, were abandoned as the BEF moved into Belgium to meet the Germans. Once again it proved an unequal struggle and, with French armies crumbling, the BEF retreated to the Channel coast, eventually to be evacuated through several ports, most famously Dunkirk. The battle that followed the German attack lasted for twenty-eight days and fell into four phases, although these cannot be defined sharply, merging as they did into each other. In phase one, the BEF advanced to the Dyle river in Belgium, deploying between Louvain and Wavre. Then came the battles to defend that line, followed by withdrawal, via intermediate positions on the Senne and Dendre rivers, to the Escaut river; this was the second phase. The vital role played by the Royal Artillery is demonstrated by the comment of 3rd Division's GOC, Major General Bernard Montgomery, that 'it was entirely due to the Gunners that the 3rd Division was able to get away from Louvain successfully in May'.[29] Phase three came with the Germans isolating the northern group of Allied armies, including the BEF, in the Dunkirk perimeter. The final phase was the evacuation itself. With hindsight one can make such an analysis; it is doubtful if anyone on the ground saw things quite so clearly in May 1940.

For those who served through the campaign it seemed to be a series of battles and skirmishes fought by divisions, brigades and even battalions reacting to enemy action as best they could while trying to conform to corps and army commanders' orders. There is no more difficult manoeuvre than to retreat in the face of a superior enemy force. It calls for much courage and resolution, not least from the artillery who were often called on to cover their comrades in rearguard actions, engaging German troops over open sights. That they did their duty well is one of the reasons the BEF was extricated successfully from France; but the cost was heavy.

The Gunners' part in the campaign was great,

> for they remained constantly in action, changing their allegiances frequently as they covered first one and then another formation in the confusion of the retreat which it rapidly became. The Gunners did, however, enable General Gort and his corps, divisional and brigade commanders to retain a battle framework around which they could act. Without this even greater confusion would have resulted. They provided the long-range firepower. Thus they had the job of holding the advancing enemy at bay while the rest of the Army withdrew. This job fell mainly to the field and anti-tank Gunners but the mediums and the heavies played their part while all the time the anti-aircraft batteries did their best to keep the Junkers, Heinkels, Messerschmitts and Dorniers from causing too much damage. It was a campaign of great speed, emergency following emergency, where orders were out of date as soon as given and where there was constant confusion. The Germans were better and more professional in almost every sphere and ruthlessly followed the principles of war.[30]

For all their skill and professionalism, the Germans never once managed to break the BEF's front.[31] Had they done so, the story of the campaign might have been very different. That they did not do so owes much to the Gunners. The story of Dunkirk may be one of defeat but the story of the Gunners in that campaign is one of success: in Farndale's words 'a story of victory in defeat' and 'one of which the Regiment may be justifiably proud'.[32] We may see that story of victory in defeat through the actions of a number of Gunner units as they served their guns in the BEF's retreat.

When the German attack was launched on 10 May, Lieutenant Colonel Jack Parham's 10th Field Regiment was training well behind the Gort Line but its batteries – 30/46 and 51/54 – were in front-line positions by the 13th. Within thirty-six hours their guns were harassing enemy troops and, next day, were engaging attacking infantry. During the evening of 15 May Parham's regiment put paid to a significant number of enemy tanks that must have considered themselves safely concealed in a wood. In his own account of this incident, Jack Parham recalled that

> I was rung up from the right OP, overlooking Wavre, by M who said his lookout man (actually his signaller) had spotted Boche tanks camouflaging themselves on *our* side of a wood. The inference was that if some were *there*, there were probably

> lots more inside so I ordered a regimental concentration, all exactly as per miniature range, and at zero hour, some ten minutes later, we put 500 rounds at rate intense into the wood without any preliminary ranging. It was a grand crash and excited chuckles down the OP wire confirmed that we had struck a winner. That wood blazed for several hours with big black columns of smoke indicating petrol fires. A good effort on the part of an alert OP.[33]

The regimental concentration – all twenty-four guns firing simultaneously – caught a German tank battalion refuelling and inflicted heavy loss in vehicles and personnel. According to Bidwell, this

> was the first fully predicted, radio-controlled concentration on an opportunity target ever fired by the Royal Artillery in war. This lesson Parham, who was to become a brigadier, and the CRA of 38th Division the following year, took back to England with him.[34]

Not every regiment could deploy all its guns at once and there were many instances of actions by batteries, troops and sections. Even single-gun actions were fought to delay the enemy's inexorable advance. These smaller actions led to some spectacular battles and perhaps none more so than that at the Belgian village of Hondeghem on 27 May involving F Troop K Battery Royal Horse Artillery.

Hondeghem, midway between Cassel and Hazebrouck, lay on a main line of advance for the Germans and it was vital that they be delayed there as long as possible. The sole forces available were K Battery, with Mk II 18-pounders, modernised with pneumatic-tyred road wheels, and a detachment of an officer and eighty men of 2nd Searchlight Regiment. F Troop 'was pulled out of the huge convoy travelling along the main road … by Brigadier Somerset'. The Troop Sergeant Major, TSM Ralph Opie, was 'given the task of commencing the deployment of the Troop in an anti-tank role in and around the village'.[35] Major Rawdon Hoare, commanding K Battery, charged F Troop, under Captain Brian Teacher, with four 18-pounders, some Bren and Lewis machine guns and Boys anti-tank rifles, with defending the village; there was also a small Battery HQ under BSM Millard. Roads into Hondeghem were blocked and two guns, I and J Sub-Sections, were deployed on the outskirts while the other two were in the village square. The guns were in position on the afternoon of the 26th and the evening passed without incident.[36]

Next morning, at 7.30, the Germans appeared and were engaged by the guns on the edge of the village. It was an uneven struggle and although the guns knocked out several enemy vehicles and two or three tanks they were overrun. I Sub-Section was hit and knocked out by a panzer at ninety yards' range at which stage enemy infantry supported by tanks moved out to the left. TSM Opie, with J Sub-Section, ordered his Bren gunners to engage these troops. Their fire caused many casualties amongst the attackers before a panzer closed on J Sub-Section, engaging its target with its machine gun and killing the gun's Number 2 and hitting the 18-pounder with its main armament. Another member of the detachment was killed while Opie and Gunner Reginald Manning were wounded, the latter 'very badly … around the head and chest'.[37] Manning suffered further wounds to both legs from small-arms fire but remained at his post. Opie tried to get the gun back into action by dragging the dead Number 2 from his seat only to find that the sights had been smashed. With Manning close to death but refusing to move, Opie 'was forced to push him down between the shield and his seat to get him out', although 'he still insisted he was all right and wanted to go back to his position'.[38] I Sub-Section engaged the tank just before being knocked out. Finally, German infantry dashed forward to capture the surviving members of J Sub. By remaining at their posts, Opie and Manning had demonstrated courage in the highest traditions of the Royal Artillery.[39] Manning died in captivity.[40]

The destruction of I and J Subs allowed the Germans to advance into Hondeghem where the other two guns opened fire at close range, hitting and destroying vehicle after vehicle. Thus began a battle that lasted eight hours. The Germans tried to establish machine-gun posts in the upper floors of nearby buildings but were countered by Gunners blasting them out. At one stage a German machine gun was brought into action in the building on the edge of the main square which was being used as the battery cookhouse. L Sub-Section manhandled their gun into a new position and fired through a window into the cookhouse. One round was sufficient to silence the machine gun, the remains of which became a valued trophy for the Battery. The building was also set on fire. There was one note of regret: breakfast had been destroyed.[41]

Throughout the day the actions at Hondeghem continued in like vein. When another enemy machine-gun team set up shop in a farm building that was garaging some Battery vehicles, that building too became a target. Although no one was certain that all the drivers had left the building, the silencing of the machine gun was vital. A round from K Sub did just that by demolishing the building. The one driver who was still inside escaped to rejoin the Battery. All through that morning battle continued, the two 18-pounders more than holding their own against the attackers. Both guns were firing at ranges of no more than 100 yards and there were plenty of targets, with the guns constantly being moved to engage the latest building in which the enemy had installed a machine gun. Each new location was soon put out of action. For the Germans it was essential that they wipe out the gun detachments and the best way of doing that was with machine-gun fire, but the speed and efficiency of the Gunners continued to deny the village centre to their foe.[42] Here the old 18-pounders proved advantageous: much lighter than the 18/25-pounder, they were more easily manhandled from position to position as the tactical situation demanded.

At one stage a smoke round was fired in error by one gun. This might have given the Germans some cover but both detachments used rapid fire with high-explosive rounds to disperse the smoke. Some assistance was provided by the other four guns of K Battery early in the afternoon when they fired several defensive concentrations around the two guns in Hondeghem. These other weapons were D Troop's guns, sited three miles north of the village but with an OP in Hondeghem's church tower. Such was D Troop's accuracy that fire was brought down to within fifty yards of K and L Subs. D Troop's support was short-lived as three of its guns were knocked out by enemy fire soon afterwards.[43]

Ammunition was running low by mid-afternoon and, from 3.30pm, all soldiers with rifles were called on to harass any Germans who appeared in nearby buildings. Not long afterwards, at 4.15pm, K Battery was ordered to withdraw to St Silvestre, two miles away on Cassel road. K Battery had delayed the German advance for six hours but its travails were not over as St Silvestre had been occupied by the enemy with both infantry and tanks in the village. Once again the surviving guns came into action close to the village church where they were joined by about twenty men of the Royal Army Service Corps, armed with rifles and machine guns. The Troop Commander decided on an audacious course of action. Although his men were half surrounded by the enemy he ordered a charge. With every man yelling as loud as his lungs would allow, the small group raced towards the Germans who, unnerved completely, ran off. Having fired its remaining ammunition after the fleeing Germans, the column moved off, although one quad and gun were destroyed by a direct hit; the detachment's survivors climbed into other vehicles as the column made off down the road, still under fire.[44]

> There were more casualties to vehicles on the way, but the Battery finally extricated itself after a battle in which every single man had played his part in refusing to be beaten by an enormously superior force, and in which the task given to the Battery had been carried out triumphantly.[45]

Not only were Battery members awarded a DSO, an MC, a DCM, an MM and three Mentions in Despatches, but K Battery was subsequently awarded an honour title to become K (Hondeghem) Battery.[46]

The war diary of the attacking German unit, I/4th Rifle Regiment noted that

> the company approached the town only with great difficulty and heavy casualties. An exceedingly courageous detachment of English soldiers had dug in there. Guns had been skilfully emplaced for direct fire.[47]

K Battery's stand at Hondeghem was probably the most outstanding example of that devotion to duty that typifies Gunners *in extremis*. However, there were many other instances in which detachments fought to the bitter end. Just days earlier, on the 23rd, 392 Battery 98th Field (Surrey and Sussex Yeomanry), with seven 18-pounders, defended seven crossings of the Aire canal. Each gun fought alone and imposed considerable delay on the enemy. Such were this battery's exploits – its Gunners had been part-time soldiers only months before – that it received special mention in the Official History.[48] Major L F Ellis, author of *The War in France and Flanders*, related in some detail the actions of the seven individual detachments, noting that

> On the 22nd two troops ... were hastily sent up to form part of the defence between St Momelin and Wittes. They had only seven guns for one was being repaired in workshops. One gun with its detachment was therefore sent to cover each of the bridges at St Momelin, St Omer, Arques, Renescure, Wardrecques, Blaringhem and Wittes.[49]

The gun that was to deploy to St Omer was diverted to Hazebrouck since St Omer was already in enemy hands. At St Momelin the detachment held out, repulsing all enemy attempts to cross, until relieved by French troops on 25 May. Eleven panzers attacked the gun at Hazebrouck which was sited to cover the road from St Omer. This followed an earlier engagement in which that gun had stopped the German column, knocking out the leading vehicles. In the unequal engagement, the 18-pounder knocked out one or possibly even two tanks before four enemy shells wrought havoc in the detachment. The first round wounded the layer who was relieved by Sergeant Mordin who, although wounded in the eye by the second shell, carried on in spite of his pain. Shell number three killed Sergeant Godfrey Woolven,[50] the Number 1, and seriously wounded the other detachment member while the fourth hit the ammunition limber which exploded. Consequently, the now useless gun was withdrawn with its detachment. Sappers were blowing the bridge at Arques when the second gun arrived to deploy about a mile east of the bridge. As advancing enemy troops neared the 18-pounder, 12th Lancers arrived and provided covering fire for withdrawal. There was no cover for the gun at Renescure which was also in action against tanks. Two of the detachment were wounded, but the gun continued to fire, knocking out a panzer before enemy mortar fire allowed the position to be overrun; the gun and detachment were captured. The gun at Wardrecques was under French command and knocked out enemy positions in nearby buildings as well as silencing a machine gun. However, the French officer was killed and his men withdrew. Although the 18-pounder remained in action it was knocked out by a direct hit shortly afterwards. Blaringhem's detachment was heavily engaged supporting both British and French infantry and repulsed an enemy attack, hitting a tank and two troop carriers. A second attack forced the gun back but it remained in action until enemy infantry began closing in. Although the order to limber up was given, an enemy shell broke the connection and the 18-pounder had to be abandoned. Contact was lost with the detachment at Wittes which, it was learned later, had been captured.[51]

Such was the lot of the field gunners as the BEF withdrew. Their story alone would take a complete volume but is told here through these examples which show the tenacity demonstrated by Regular and Yeomanry Gunners, all of whom lived up to their Regiment's traditions. But they were not the only Gunners in France and Flanders. Their comrades in medium and heavy regiments also fought gallantly, providing critical support for the BEF on many occasions.

On 10 May, 1st Medium Regiment moved into Belgium, passing through Brussels two days later. Its guns were in action at Neeryssche on the 13th with OPs sited on the Dyle. Next day the position of D Troop 5/22 Battery came under enemy fire and was placed under temporary command of 67th (South Midland) Field Regiment. Three days later the Regiment began the long trek to the coast, staging at Acsemberg and then Hoegstrop, near Ninove, before crossing the Escaut to take up positions at Froidmont. There the Regiment came under heavy and continuous enemy fire on the 18th. In spite of some unwelcome attention from the Luftwaffe it remained in action for some days with 1/3 Battery at Guignies and 5/22 Battery at Wez Velvain, the latter supporting 48th Division although remaining under I Corps command. The Regiment lost two officers, one NCO and three Gunners to enemy action on the 21st with several others wounded.[52]

Also in action near Froidmont was 5th Medium Regiment whose 20/21 Battery was engaged at only 1,200 yards on 20 May. With no infantry to their front the Regiment suffered many casualties before being ordered to withdraw to cover the bridges over the Lys canal on the 23rd. Still on iron-tyred wheels, the 6-inch guns of 65th Medium Regiment fired 1,800 rounds at attacking panzers on 19 May near Cazeau-le-Cornet on the Escaut while, two days later, 61st (Carnavon and Denbigh (Yeomanry)) Medium suffered seventeen casualties during a German attack north of Calonne; the enemy troops were beaten off by artillery fire.[53]

Among the anti-tank regiments with the BEF was 57th (East Surrey), a TA unit born out of 5th East Surrey Regiment. On 24 May the regiment's 228 Battery was in action, as part of an improvised force, near Morbecque on what one of its officers described as its 'finest day'. In spite of an initial setback when two guns had been destroyed by tanks, the battery held out well with a detachment of J Troop putting two enemy tanks out of action: 'two German tanks were caught and blew up in a great sheet of flame and clouds of smoke'. Unfortunately the gun that knocked both tanks out was then targeted by further tanks and was itself damaged but not before it had accounted for a third panzer; however, the detachment commander, Lance Bombardier Henry Bosman was wounded fatally. Lance Bombardier Stredwick was awarded the Military Medal while the BC, Captain P G Hampton, received the Military Cross. The regiment fought throughout the day, at the end of which they had lost five dead, sixteen wounded and twenty-seven missing.[54]

The BEF's anti-aircraft (ack-ack from the contemporary British phonetic alphabet) Gunners had seen action before the German attack on 10 May. On many occasions, guns had fired on Luftwaffe reconnaissance aircraft, although this was no real preparation for the intensity of action to come. Typical of the AA units was 8th (Belfast) HAA Regiment.[55] Part of 3 (Ulster) AA Brigade, the Regiment had been raised in Northern Ireland in early 1939 as part of the Supplementary Reserve. As such, it had been destined for the field army and was posted with 3 AA Brigade to the BEF; the brigade was less 9th (Londonderry) HAA Regiment which had been sent to Egypt in late 1939.

Following the German attack, ack-ack Gunners often found themselves playing several roles, including infantry. The Belfast Regiment's three heavy batteries[56] – 21, 22 and 23 – were eventually evacuated from France via three different ports and with three very different tales to recount.[57] Sergeant (later Lieutenant Colonel) Harry Porter, of 21 HAA Battery, recalled that everything had to be abandoned, save the uniforms that the soldiers wore and their rifles. Evacuated through Dunkirk, 21 Battery had fought hard but was eventually surrounded by German tanks. Under intensive enemy machine-gun fire, the 3.7s were destroyed and their breech blocks removed. After that the Gunners took up small arms and fought as infantry until they were taken off.[58]

Cherbourg was the point of evacuation for 22 HAA Battery which managed to save two of the Regiment's precious 3.7s when the BC persuaded a ship's captain that the guns weighed only 3 tons each, whereas, in fact, they were three times as heavy.[59] Whether the seaman was really taken in or whether he was happy to rescue the guns is not recorded. The Regiment's third heavy battery (its light battery, 5 LAA, had gone to Egypt with 9th HAA Regiment) escaped through St Malo after a series of adventures. Sergeant (later Major) Cunningham Fowler recalled that 'We first met the Germans along the Seine between Paris and the coast'. A Number 1, Fowler recalled that 23 HAA Battery had overnighted in a wood, knowing that enemy troops were across the river. When dawn broke, they stood to, but heavy mist prevented them from seeing the opposition. However, 'One of my detachment was a former field Gunner and I can still remember him saying to me "Sergeant, when that mist lifts, we're for it", and he was right'.[60]

As the morning sun burned away the veil of mist, the Germans could be seen across the river. They opened fire on the ack-ack Gunners and a light aircraft appeared overhead as the Germans prepared to throw a pontoon across the river. In the first burst of fire from the enemy positions two of Cunningham Fowler's detachment were hit and killed. (Sixty years later, Major Fowler returned to the scene for the first time and not only found the graves of his two Gunners in a small French cemetery but also met a Frenchman who remembered the day the men died.) Before the Germans could make their crossing, 23 HAA Battery received orders to withdraw and eventually reached St Malo whence, minus its guns, it was evacuated to Britain.[61]

Also in 3 (Ulster) AA Brigade was 3rd (Ulster) Searchlight Regiment of four batteries – 9, 10, 11 and 12 – which had been deployed around Arras, Béthune and Dunkirk. The latter was the destination for the Regiment when the order to retreat was received.[62] The withdrawal was confusing for the ordinary soldier. Gunner Bert Sterling, a despatch rider, or Don R, with 10 SL Battery, recalled that 'We kept being pushed back and back. The ordinary soldier really didn't know much about what was happening and it was a worrying time.' When the Regiment reached Dunkirk orders were given to destroy all equipment and vehicles. The searchlights were smashed, lorries sabotaged by various means and 'I had to take a sledgehammer to my motorbike'. That motorcycle was a 500cc side-valve Norton which, as a keen motorcyclist, Bert Sterling hated having to destroy.[63]

Many of the Gunners were deployed as infantry, some to guard bridges across a canal until engineers could destroy the structures. Then it was on to the beaches where many were issued with Lewis machine guns on AA mounts to defend the troops awaiting evacuation from attacks by German aircraft. By this stage the Regiment's CO had been charged with defending part of the Dunkirk perimeter. Gunner Abbey Rusk recalled this as a dangerous episode during which several of his comrades were killed and others wounded as Luftwaffe aircraft strafed and bombed the lines of soldiers.[64] However,

> Their bombs made many holes in the sand and we were grateful for that. It gave us somewhere to hide whenever the planes came over. We were very scared.[65]

Other AA and searchlight regiments had similar stories. The TA Gunners of 60th (City of London) HAA Regiment were engaged initially at Villers-Bretonneux before deploying between Béthune and Seclin. There 169 Battery was attacked by tanks and aircraft and was eventually forced to destroy its guns. The other two batteries, 168 and 194, went to Béthune and Merville respectively; 168 then deployed to St Omer. On 21 May the Regiment was ordered to Merville in an AA role. By then it had only eight 3-inch guns and four 40mm guns, although there were also two troops from 5 SL Battery. At St Omer 168 Battery had a similar complement of 3-inch and 40mm guns plus some machine guns on AA mounts while at Clairmarais the Regiment had another four 3-inch guns, four 40mm guns, a troop of AA machine guns and two searchlight troops. On 25 May the Regiment deployed to protect the evacuation beaches at Dunkirk and was in constant action. The war diary noted that heavy smoke over the area made observation difficult.[66] Nonetheless, the Gunners remained at their tasks until ordered to destroy their guns and join the men awaiting evacuation. The CO of 1st HAA Regiment was

> ordered to collect all the AA guns I could find and report to General Alexander at the Mole by dawn 1st June … I found four heavy and three light guns and about 500 rounds per gun. We drove out of la Panne after dark through the infantry and entered Dunkirk. I was told to put the four heavy guns into action by the Bastion and the three light guns on the Mole itself. I ordered the fire to be concentrated

over the Mole to force the enemy to fly across it, thereby reducing their chance of a hit.[67]

Throughout the brief campaign, many German aircraft had fallen to the guns of the Royal Artillery. As shown by the men of 1st HAA Regiment at Dunkirk, they had kept up their task until the very end, covering the evacuation from Dunkirk's mole and beaches. The CO, Lieutenant Colonel Thuillier received the DSO, two of his officers were awarded the MC and three DCMs and three MMs were also awarded to the Regiment.[68]

Several TA divisions arrived in France without artillery, their initial role being to provide labour parties. As the BEF expanded to become two armies, these formations would have been joined by their Gunners, but that was not to be. In some cases, ad hoc arrangements were made to provide artillery support for such divisions as illustrated by the remarkable story of A Field (Anti-Tank) Regiment, known as 'Burns' Tigers', formed in France on 17 May and disbanded in the UK on 26 June.[69] In between, the regiment accounted for a significant number of German tanks and played a major part in several actions while never deploying more than nineteen guns.

The regiment's CO Major E R V Burns was commanding the RA Instructional Wing at the BEF Base when he was appointed CRA to 23rd (Northumbrian) Division, one of those without artillery. Although a detached battery was to join the division, this unit was destroyed by enemy action and another battery moving to join 23rd Division was cut up by the Germans. Burns, now an acting lieutenant colonel, had expected forty-eight guns but found that he had only nineteen. Most had sights but little else in the way of technical stores; one weapon could be sighted only through the open bore. Ordnance depots had supplied the assorted guns while the personnel came from the Royal Artillery Base Depot. In all, there were twelve 18/25-pounders, five 18-pounders of differing vintage and two 4.5-inch howitzers. These were 'roughly sorted' into A, B, C and D Batteries with two captains, a lieutenant and a second lieutenant as battery commanders. The GOC 23rd Division deployed A Regiment on the line of the Canal du Nord at Cambrai in an anti-tank role.[70]

The Regiment did not remain long with 23rd Division which was reported 'scattered by Panzers' at Locon on 21 May. By then A Field Regiment had been cut off and had retreated behind the Béthune canal. At Fôret de Nieppe, on the 22nd, the Regiment came under command of another division and occupied positions to deny the crossings of the Canal d'Aire to the enemy. Then came a sudden order to move south to Béthune under command of 46th Division, and later 2nd Division, with the guns deployed along the canal about 200 to 300 yards from the bridgeheads. Once again their role was to deny the crossings to the enemy. At Vieille Chapelle on the 24th and 25th the detachments were machine gunned and mortared heavily but continued to fight courageously. In particular, Second Lieutenant C W J Kaye-Shuttleworth's battery fought a 'very gallant action' when the position of his gun, covering the bridge at Chequeaux, was pinpointed by the enemy and came under heavy fire. With the position no longer tenable, Kaye-Shuttleworth reconnoitred a route for withdrawal and, with the bridge demolished, destroyed his gun and withdrew his detachment, himself carrying a wounded Gunner. For this action he was awarded the MC.[71]

Although two 18-pounders were captured one was recovered by a party under the CO. As the group closed on the captured gun they spotted broken roof tiles scattered across their line of approach and stopped to lay a carpet of hay to prevent the inevitable crunching noise of army boots on tiles. On reaching the gun, almost under the noses of a German patrol, they had to free the split trail before manhandling the weapon some 300 yards to a lorry. This was fraught with danger as a second German patrol appeared, but fortune was with the Gunners as one German kicked a petrol can and the patrol fled.[72]

During its defence of the Béthune–Merville area, A Regiment destroyed seven panzers and damaged five. Three were knocked out by Lieutenant H J Willis's isolated gun position at Merville, thereby stopping a German attack that had already broken through the infantry. However, the Regiment paid a heavy price, with a battery all but wiped out, two gun detachments killed to a man and six guns destroyed or lost. A particular tribute was paid by the infantry commander when he commented that the Regiment had provided 'the best artillery support he had ever received'. Some of that support was improvised hastily with Second Lieutenant Shankland using cardboard and coat-hangers to produce quadrants for the 4.5-inch howitzers. With such rudimentary instrumentation, the 4.5s fired some 200 rounds on a concentration of enemy troops in the Hinges area; this was the fire that drew such praise from the infantry.[73]

Eventually the Regiment received an order from the GOC 2nd Division to deploy at night at Neuf Berquin where there was severe fighting with panzers in the village. The Regiment was cut off as the infantry withdrew through a flank. However, A Regiment was able to withdraw, although in close contact with the Germans, with almost no casualties. At la Couronne on the night of 27/28 May, the CO was trying to contact HQ for orders when he learned, from his counterpart of an army field regiment, of the order to retreat to Dunkirk. Although there was a panzer brigade between A Regiment and the BEF, and the area was flooded with French soldiers trying to surrender, some very anxious recce'ing uncovered a gap through which the Regiment passed to rejoin the BEF rearguard near Bailleul. Then it was on to the beaches, guns and vehicles having been destroyed, where the Gunners were subjected to heavy bombing and used their mess tins to dig slit trenches. Everyone was hungry since the Regiment was on no one's ration strength and no food was available.[74]

In spite of A Regiment's outstanding performance, it was disbanded soon after returning to the UK. Subsequently Lieutenant Colonel Burns was required to refund the difference between a major's pay and that of a lieutenant colonel as he had not commanded any more than nineteen guns.[75]

When the BEF returned to the United Kingdom, it was a much-depleted force. Many were left behind, either dead, wounded or in captivity, and much equipment had been abandoned. For the Royal Artillery, with its proud tradition of serving the guns until the end, it had been especially painful to have to destroy so many of those guns, the 'colours' of the Royal Regiment.

In total, 2,732 guns were lost at the end of the campaign in France, including 2,472 field guns and 260 anti-aircraft guns; 300 searchlights were also lost. Of these, 518 guns were destroyed in action or accidentally. Losses for field guns include not only the 18-pounders, 18/25-pounders and 4.5-inch howitzers of the field regiments but also the mediums, heavies and super-heavies, plus the anti-tank guns.[76] It was a scale of loss that was difficult to contemplate and which would have to be made good even as Britain prepared to defend itself against the threat of invasion.

Notes

1. Gailey et al, *The Territorials in Northern Ireland*, p. 32
2. Clements, *Defending the North*, p. 87; NA Kew, WO166/1727, war diary, 525 Coast Regt, Aug 1939–Dec '41
3. Farndale, *The Years of Defeat*, p. 16
4. Ellis, *The War in France and Flanders*, p. 17
5. Farndale, op cit, p. 17
6. Ibid, pp. 9–10
7. Ellis, op cit, pp. 6–7
8. Farndale, op cit, p. 7
9. Ibid, p. 9
10. NA Kew, WO197/39, composition of the BEF
11. NA Kew, WO167/495, war diary 75 (H'ld) Fd Regt, 1939–40
12. NA Kew, WO167/677, war diary 2 SL Regt, Jan–Jul 1940
13. Bidwell, *Gunners at War*, p. 108
14. These were Regular formations except for 3 (Ulster), which was the sole Supplementary Reserve formation not only in the Royal Artillery but also in the entire Army. It had arrived in France minus one of its regiments – 9th AA – which had been sent to Alexandria to defend HMS *Nile*, the naval base. Another noteworthy aspect of this brigade was that its two AA regiments each included three heavy and one light AA batteries. However, neither light AA battery – 5 or 6 – went to France.
15. Farndale, op cit, p. 16; The divisional history notes that 'the artillery regiments 'existed in cadre only'. (Williamson, *The Fourth Division*, p. 3)
16. The AASF was not part of the BEF but represented, as its name indicates, a mainland-based element of RAF Bomber Command. The French bases placed the Command's forward strike force closer to targets in Germany.
17. Farndale, op cit, p. 12
18. RUSI *Journal*, August 1933 ; Parham & Belfield, *Unarmed into Battle: The Story of the Air Observation Post*, p 10; Bidwell, *Gunners at War*, p. 110
19. Farndale, op cit, p. 11
20. Ibid, p. 12
21. Ibid, pp. 32–3

22 Ibid, p. 27; Derry, *The Campaign in Norway*, p. 62
23 Naval Staff paper to Hitler, October 1939, quoted in Adams, *The Doomed Expedition*, p. 6
24 Adams, op cit, p. 7
25 Farndale, op cit, p. 27
26 Ibid
27 Adams, op cit, p. 155; Derry, op cit, p. 207; Farndale, op cit, p. 28; NA Kew, WO168/45, war diary 3 LAA Bty, Sep '40
28 Adams, op cit, p. 81
29 NA Kew, WO167/468, war diary 7 Fd Regt 1940
30 Farndale, op cit, p. 30
31 Ellis, op cit, p. 325. For a more recent analysis of the campaign see Thompson, *Dunkirk: Retreat to Victory*.
32 Farndale, op cit, p. 31
33 Quoted in Mead, *Gunners at War*, p. 16
34 Bidwell, op cit, p. 135
35 Maj R R Opie MBE, 'Hondeghem: 51 Years On', *Gunner*, Oct 1991
36 Hughes, *Honour Titles of the Royal Artillery*, p. 184; Farndale, op cit, p. 66
37 Duncan, *The RA Commemoration Book*, p. 13
38 Ibid, p. 13
39 Farndale, p. 66; Hughes, p. 185
40 www.cwgc.org.uk
41 Bidwell, op cit, p. 133
42 Farndale, op cit, p. 66; Hughes, op cit, p. 185; Mead, op cit, p. 18
43 Farndale, op cit, p. 66; Hughes, op cit, p. 185
44 Farndale, op cit, p. 66; Mead, op cit, p. 17; Hughes, op cit, p. 185
45 Farndale, op cit, pp. 66–7; Hughes, op cit, pp. 185–6
46 Hughes, op cit, p. 186
47 Farndale, op cit, p. 67; Hughes, op cit, p. 184
48 Quoted in Farndale, op cit, p. 60
49 Ellis, op cit, p. 129
50 Ibid, pp. 129–30
51 Ibid
52 NA Kew, WO167/534, war diary 1 Med Regt, 1940; Farndale, op cit, pp. 41–2
53 Goodacre, *The Story of the 57th (East Surrey) Anti-Tank Regiment, Royal Artillery (TA)*, pp. 70–7
54 NA Kew, WO167/538, war diary 5 Med Regt, 1940; Farndale, op cit, p. 42
55 According to Frederick's *Lineage Book of British Land Forces* the change in designation from AA to HAA occurred on 1 June 1940. However, the war diary of RHQ, 9th (Londonderry) HAA Regiment (NA Kew, WO169/303) indicates that the Regiment received notification of the change on 14 May and that the official date of the decision was 9 May.
56 Both 8th (Belfast) and 9th (Londonderry) Regiments had an order of battle that included three heavy and one light battery. The only TA regiment raised in Northern Ireland – 102nd HAA Regiment – also had three heavy batteries but included two light batteries.
57 NA Kew, WO167/616, war diary 8 (B) HAA Regt, 1940
58 Lt Col H J Porter, interview with author; Farndale, op cit, p. 44
59 Lt Col H J Porter, interview with author
60 Maj C Fowler, interview with author
61 Maj C Fowler, interview with author

62 NA Kew, WO167/676, war diary 3 (U) SL Regt, 1940

63 Mr B Sterling, interview with author

64 Mr A Rusk, interview with author; Doherty, '3rd (Ulster) Anti-Aircraft Brigade, RA (SR)' in *The Irish Sword*, Vol XVIII, No. 71, p. 122

65 Mr A Rusk, interview with author

66 NA Kew, WO167/618, war diary 60 (City of London) HAA Regiment, 1940

67 NA Kew, WO167/611, war diary 1 HAA Regt, 1940; Farndale, op cit, pp. 78–9

68 Farndale, op cit, pp. 78–9

69 Duncan, op cit, p. 23; Farndale, op cit, p. 74

70 Duncan, op cit, pp. 23–4. Farndale, op cit, p. 74, notes the BCs as a major, an acting major and two captains.

71 Duncan, op cit, pp. 23–6

72 Ibid, p. 24

73 Ibid, p. 26

74 Ibid

75 Ibid

76 Farndale, op cit, p. 264

Chapter Three

Learning Lessons

The catastrophic campaign in France and the Low Countries led to much analysis and self-examination in all the services, not least in the Army which had experienced the full fury of the Wehrmacht. The Gunners faced their problems with equanimity although, to many, the future must have seemed bleak. Since the war such emphasis has been laid on the 'Dunkirk spirit' that it has become almost an article of faith to believe that Britain's forces and public were imbued with a deep faith that they would win in the end. This was not always so, and it is easy to see how a typical Gunner might have contemplated a bleak future when reflecting on what had been lost in France – not just huge amounts of equipment but the very many regular officers and soldiers, some of whom would certainly have become officers, who were now confined to prison camps.

There can be little doubt that the leadership of the Royal Family and Winston Churchill were invaluable in ensuring that morale did not crumble. Shelford Bidwell comments that while

> There was no actual defeatism or loss of morale, nothing on which a finger could be placed ... there was the beginning of a sense of hopelessness. One wondered what path could possibly lead the country out of its difficulties.[1]

Regular officers, accustomed to the peacetime Army, faced a great influx of citizen soldiers – cast from a very different mould than the regulars – and the problems of making them into a viable self-confident army that could step off on the long march to victory. There seemed little of that resourcefulness for which the regular British soldier and his Indian counterpart were famed. Studying one British unit of conscripts, an Indian officer commented that 'if you left such men in a field with a sheep and a bundle of sticks they would starve to death'. Such was the task facing the trainers.[2]

However, there were resourceful men in the Army's upper echelons who believed that the new citizen army could be turned into field armies comparable to those which had won the Great War. They included Alan Brooke, a Gunner, who became Commander-in-Chief, Home Forces, and his successor in that post, Bernard Paget. They commanded some remarkable trainers, including he whose note of thanks to the Gunners of 21 Army Group opens this book – Bernard Montgomery. Perhaps Monty's greatest strength – apart from his PR flair – was his skill at motivating men. When he gathered all V Corps' field officers in a Maidstone cinema, he told them that 'I have never allowed the Germans to interfere with my plans and I do not intend to start now'.[3]

That opening remark gained everyone's attention. The speech that followed held that attention. This strange little man – who instructed his audience to concentrate their coughing into one minute before he started speaking – spoke positively of his intentions and of their role.[4] There was no defeatism in Montgomery. Some may have amended their views of him when he began inspecting formations and units under his command. Having complimented 4th Division on creating sector defences, he then commented that their general standard was unsatisfactory and that the 'artillery is definitely below standard'. Montgomery considered that 4th Division included much 'dead wood' which would have to be cut out, including the CRA and two field regiment COs, together with the CRASC (Commander, Royal Army Service Corps) and GSO II. He recommended that these men 'should be removed at once'.[5]

However, the Gunners were examining themselves with an equally ruthless eye, as were others who viewed the artillery's performance in the recent campaign as a failure. The apostles of fast, mobile warfare even argued that the division, as a fighting formation, was obsolete and that the brigade was the largest formation a single commander could handle. Such a reconstruction would remove the post of CRA and substitute advisers at each command level. Not until 1941 was this argument resolved with the completion of the major anti-invasion exercise, BUMPER, which demonstrated that the best way of employing artillery was to concentrate their firepower, a lesson already known to Gunners. Montgomery, one of the chief umpires for this exercise, had chosen as his artillery adviser Brigadier Sydney Kirkman who held strong views on the correct employment of artillery. When Montgomery assumed command of Eighth Army in August 1942 he asked for Kirkman as his Brigadier, Royal Artillery (BRA).

The flaws demonstrated in BUMPER led to increased professionalism through the restoration of a proper artillery chain of command, while the *Artillery Training and Field Service Regulations* were also restored to their proper place (the post of medium artillery commander, exercising tactical command under the Corps Commander, RA, eliminated in 1940, was restored). Emphasis was placed on the infantry cooperating in making fireplans with their affiliated Gunners while 'a determined effort was made to streamline the fire-control system'. Commanders and HQs to control reserve artillery outside divisions were also reintroduced; such units were brigaded into Army Groups, Royal Artillery (AGRAs). Why this title was chosen is unclear: the formation was certainly a brigade of artillery and AGRAs were used as brigades, their massive firepower deployed at the point of a corps', or army's, main effort. Alternatively an AGRA could provide striking power for a counter-battery organisation, or deploy its medium and field batteries to reinforce divisional artilleries.

In Chapter Two we noted the deficiency in communications created, at least partially, by the French ban on using radios in the BEF during the 'Phoney War'. This was among the first problems to be tackled as the Royal Regiment applied the lessons from the continent. Efficient and effective field radios were critical in modern warfare and among the requirements for a Gunner radio set were portability and that it should work in a moving vehicle. Between the wars the impetus for developing radios that worked in moving vehicles came, not surprisingly, from the armoured school, whence came the initiative of employing a gifted electrical engineer called Fuller. As a result of the efforts of Fuller and others, the application of radio to military communications began slowly to evolve.[6]

In 1928 the Gunners received some morse-only sets for experimentation and within five years demonstrations of conversations on the move were being given using battery staff vehicles. This was considerable progress for the time although it would be another five years, in 1938, before radio sets efficient enough for fire control became available. Although such sets were issued to the BEF's Gunners, a peculiar paranoia then made itself felt. While some Gunners saw radio as the main means of communication and embraced it enthusiastically, others saw only its disadvantages, especially the possibility of enemy interference with radio signals. Thus both direction finding and radio transmissions were set about with strict regulations and even discouraged, an attitude underlying that ban on using radios in training.[7]

No one below a certain age today can be aware of the proclivities of the radios of the 1930s and 1940s. Not for the operators of that era the simple task of switching on a set that 'thought' for itself as do today's digital examples. Instead Royal Signals personnel and Royal Artillery signallers operated crude sets that could go out of tune following a knock or a simple jolt. The signaller needed considerable dexterity to operate his set, and much practice in its use. Tuning was achieved by turning knobs and dials between a finger and thumb and was much more difficult in a moving vehicle; needless to say, the operator required a delicate touch, defined by Bidwell as the equivalent of green fingers. But the difficulties did not end with tuning: conversations had to be conducted against a background of roaring static that made mutual understanding difficult. To overcome this, operators developed a special 'voice' that could be heard over that background; this 'high *castrato* tenor' became the hallmark of wartime radio operators and was imitated by a range of actors.[8]

The need for robust, reliable radios was being tackled by British industry and sets meeting most of the Gunners' needs became available to help make Britain's artillery a war-winning weapon. Seemingly endless training and practice played important parts as 'one-to-one' circuits gave way to networks as frequency bands became more crowded and signallers learned to handle such traffic. Rather than creating a problem, as the earlier paranoia might have perceived it, this had the tactical advantage of allowing battle information to be circulated to many stations simultaneously. Great pride was taken in ensuring that stations did not jam each other, something demanding considerable discipline, skill and practice. In action, it became unforgivable for 'a set to fail through any other fault than a shell fragment going through it'. Techniques were adopted to ensure effective networks: stations were moved if they were not 'through', perhaps due to signals being masked by high ground, or 'in case there was some kind of electrical shadow'. Aerials grew taller and relay stations were established, often with sets that had been acquired additional to a unit's official entitlement. The Gunners and their Royal Signals' colleagues made sets work effectively at distances well beyond those intended by their designers.[9] As Major General Sir Campbell Clarke KBE CB, wartime Director of Artillery at the War Office, wrote later, 'It was to radio technique that we chiefly owed the striking improvement in the flexibility of artillery fire-power'.[10]

Efficiency and effectiveness were also sought in other fields, not least in the field regiment organisation. As already noted, the 1938 re-organisation left the field regiment, with its twenty-four guns, as a two-battery unit. Since each infantry division included three brigades, each of three battalions, the Gunner orbat did not chime with the formation it supported and so eight-gun batteries were formed, each of two linked troops, thus allowing allocation of a field regiment to each brigade with a battery per battalion. These allocations became such a regular feature of active service life that Gunners felt an allegiance to their affiliated brigades and vice versa. In 78th Division, 17th Field Regiment became the supporting artillery unit for 38 (Irish) Brigade and such was the camaraderie between Gunners and Irish infantry that 17th Field adopted the entirely unofficial style of Royal Hibernian Artillery. Elsewhere, 9th Royal Lancers referred to their affiliated battery of Honourable Artillery Company as their 'fourth squadron' while even a medium regiment could develop a similar happy alliance, as with 2nd Medium which supported 6th Armoured Division so often that it became known, with affection, as the 'siege train'.[11] The best example of this spirit known to this author came in Italy in June 1944 when, following the battles at Lake Trasimene, the CO of 1st Royal Irish Fusiliers, his Intelligence Officer and their affiliated BC of 17th Field, Major Duffy Anderson, went forward in the CO's command tank to visit the companies. When the driver took a wrong turn and ended up in German lines, the party were all made prisoner. Commenting on this over fifty years later, the Fusiliers' then Adjutant, Brian Clark, told the author that Duffy Anderson was the only real loss that day because he was a superb Gunner; the CO and IO were not missed.[12]

Under this revised organisation, troop commanders were given the manpower to form OPs in addition to those of the battery commander and battery captain. Thus OP officers, especially the battery commander with his two OP officers, could become part of the fabric of the battalions they supported. This proved most successful and many accounts from infantry veterans of the subsequent campaigns emphasise the importance of the Gunners. When ill health forced Brigadier Nelson Russell to relinquish command of the Irish Brigade in Italy in February 1944 he wrote in glowing terms of the officers in the brigade group, commenting on 17th Field Regiment and its CO, Lieutenant Colonel Rollo Baker.

> There may be as good Field Regiments in the Army as the 17th Field – but this I doubt. There is, however, only one Rollo Baker. We fought together in many battles – and Rollo ensured our 'Perfect Fire Plan' – and I was always pernickety about fire plans. I would have felt half dressed if I'd had to face a battle without Rollo.[13]

Russell's praise for the Gunners of his brigade group was not restricted to 17th Field for he also had similar comments for his anti-tank and light AA battery commanders:

> And Arthur Weldon – eager to drive his Anti Tank guns in front of the leading Infantry – if need be.
>
> And Bell – with his Anti-Aircraft guns in position before you gave him the order to move.[14]

The trust between this Brigade and its Gunners was typical of the field armies. Not only did the Gunners provide a battle-winning weapon for commanders but they also saved the lives of many infantry and armoured soldiers in so doing. The respect was not all one-way: Gunners felt that they became part of the regimental families of the battalions with which they worked. Shelford Bidwell recounts the story of one battery commander at a conference opining that his CO 'wouldn't like that'. His CO, of his Gunner regiment, was present, as were his fellow BCs, but the CO to whom he was referring was he who commanded the BC's affiliated infantry battalion. The comment caused a quizzical moment of silence before his fellow Gunners burst out laughing as they realised exactly what he meant.[15]

Of course there was much more than good fellowship in the trust and confidence that developed between artillery and infantry. For the latter there was the certain knowledge that the guns were there to support them, to shoot them onto their objectives, to fire defensive tasks when necessary and to silence the enemy's artillery as far as possible. British infantry knew that their artillery was accurate, effective and concentrated sufficiently to make the foe keep his head down. And such a state of affairs did not happen simply because Gunner OPs lived with their infantry battalions. It happened because the Gunners trained to reach a high pitch of effectiveness and developed the ability quickly to drench an area with concentrated fire. The work that led to that happy state began before the war as Gunner officers applied themselves to the problem of bringing concentrated fire to bear as quickly as possible.

During the Great War the Royal Artillery had fired bombardments of colossal strength but, generally, from static positions after careful planning. As the war progressed the Gunners' skills and technical knowledge developed to levels hitherto undreamt of, but the problem for the Second World War field Gunners was to produce similar bombardments in minutes rather than hours of preparation and calculation. Two men deserve special mention for solving this problem. One has already been mentioned in these pages, Jack Parham. The other was Brigadier A J T Farfan, a veteran of the Great War, during which he commanded 27 Indian Mountain Battery.[16] As Commandant of the Indian School of Artillery, Farfan studied the problem of quickly concentrating the fire of several batteries and, inspired by an article in *The Royal Artillery Journal*, adapted the writer's thoughts to develop 'a system of such simplicity that the School at Larkhill adopted it in its basic form and it was used until 1956'.[17]

Farfan proposed deploying pairs of batteries about a quarter of a mile apart thereby reducing the essential calculations to one distance measurement, one angle measurement and reference to a set of tables.[18] Allied to modern methods of surveying, made much easier by mechanical transport and radio, this created a foundation for thinking Gunners, such as Parham, to build on. In Chapter Two we noted Parham's regimental concentration in France on 15 May with 10th Field Regiment. This had wrought terrible havoc on a German tank battalion that had been refuelling, unaware that their presence had been spotted by one of Parham's FOOs. Within ten minutes, Parham's guns had hammered the wood in which the Germans thought they were concealed with some 500 rounds, setting tanks and fuel lorries ablaze.

In the aftermath of Dunkirk, one proposal arising from the post mortems had been that the RAF should introduce a Ju87 Stuka-equivalent for close support of ground forces, which indicated the effect of the Stukas on morale. However, rational analysis of their performance showed that good field artillery would do the job even better. Parham was among those who recognised that the Stuka's days were numbered since the RAF would increase its fighter strength and such slow machines could not survive in a sky dominated by more and faster Spitfires. Furthermore, the field armies would have their own light AA regiments in numbers sufficient to ensure that Stukas would suffer many losses.

The clinching argument, as espoused by Parham, was that the field artillery could do all, and more, that the dive-bomber could. In fact, the latter was restricted by weather conditions and could operate only in daylight hours: no dive-bomber pilot would put his plane into a near-vertical dive when he was unable to see the ground. Targets sought by dive-bombers also lay within the area that field guns could dominate: some 7–8,000 yards of the line of contact. Since the 25-pounder had a range of 11,000 yards, placing these weapons about 3,000 yards behind the forward defended localities, and allowing each gun an arc of 90 degrees, gave it a target area of about thirty square miles. The two dozen 25-pounders of a field regiment, firing three rounds per gun per minute, could drop almost a ton of metal and explosive on a target in one minute at any time of day or night. In every respect the field gun was much more effective than the dive-bomber. In the years that followed the wisdom of this thinking was demonstrated time and time again when fighter-bombers were grounded by sandstorms in the desert, muddy landing grounds in Tunisia, foul weather in Italy and north-west Europe, or were too far away to give urgent support, as in Normandy. On all such occasions, the guns were still on call. The only question that needed answering was: could mass artillery react to orders quickly enough?[19]

In Parham's mind there was no doubt: the answer was a simple 'yes'. Possessed of a sharp, analytical mind, and no respecter of dogma, Parham identified a basic essential for rapid communications. The contemporary 'drill' was for communication from troop to battery to regiment to divisional HQRA and then back via the same chain. Each link required re-transmitting which placed a brake on the speed achievable but, if the chain of command could be circumvented, the process of bringing down fire would be accelerated. By 1941, Parham, now a brigadier, was CRA of 38th (Welsh) Division, based in the south-west of England. In his new post he had much more scope to develop his ideas, one of which was to establish a master OP, manned by himself. With this OP on the HQ radio frequency, he could speak directly to his regiments, thereby reducing delay.[20]

Another established practice was to seek extreme accuracy, a doctrine Parham also decided to forgo. This call for extreme accuracy was due to at least two factors. Anxious to ensure that field units would not resort to their own approaches, the Gunnery Staff had insisted on the doctrine and enforced it though IGs' inspections. Those Gunnery Staff officers had spent much of their service in that era when everything was at a premium, including shells, and analysing firing exercises, after the event, had always included a cost calculation. With ammunition in short supply, every shell that failed to hit its correct target was money wasted and so predicted fire was not permitted except when guns and targets had been surveyed in, or the firing unit had an adequate supply of large-scale maps.[21]

But, argued Parham, why seek such extreme accuracy with a weapon that could not provide pinpoint accuracy with every round fired? Fire a hundred rounds from a 25-pounder, or any field gun, and they would land in a 'beaten zone' in the shape of an elongated oval. As Bidwell comments 'a battery commander whose salvo fell much within the area of, say, a football ground, either had the laws of probability working on his side or some uncannily accurate gunlayers'. By now, survey methods had advanced to the stage where guns could quickly be brought on to the grid and accuracy would improve after deployment. With large-scale maps of Europe available, it would be possible to spot targets with a degree of accuracy sufficient for battlefield conditions; Britain was well served with 1-inch Ordnance Survey maps that allowed spotting with accuracy down to about a hundred yards. By deploying the firepower of three or four regiments any inaccuracy in spotting would be compensated for by the spread of shot; the target would certainly be within the beaten zone of such a concentration.[22]

To prove his point, Parham organised an exercise in Dorset that required 38th Division's artillery – 102nd, 132nd and 146th Field Regiments[23] – to advance to the coast. Once there, the guns came into action, allowing a brief pause for survey and, under command of Parham's divisional OP, established on the cliffs, fired a series of test shoots at buoys anchored offshore. The results proved encouraging with compact, well-grouped bursting patterns, while response time had been only four or five minutes. Under the existing system of 'brigade control' the response time might have been as long as an hour.[24]

It was now time for Parham to move on to the next phase: a major demonstration for senior officers. Fortunately, he had the wholehearted support of the School of Artillery at Larkhill where Brigadier Fitzgibbon believed firmly in Parham's methods. This led to arrangements for a demonstration at Larkhill for Home Forces' officers and other VIPs, employing 144 guns, the artillery of two divisions. Although successful, the demonstration almost ended in disaster. Paradoxically, that near-disastrous conclusion added to its effectiveness by proving how quickly Parham's system of control could stop a bombardment.

So that spectators would appreciate that nothing had been rigged in the demonstration, a randomly-selected spectator was asked to direct the fire of a mortar onto any part of the range. The mortar fired a smoke bomb as the target indicator for the 144 guns. In less than five minutes the target area was drenched with fire. So far, so good. Then came phase two: showing that fire could be switched from one target to another, or adjustments made for greater accuracy. At this stage disaster almost befell those present. To ensure speed and simplicity in fire control, a method of switching fire had been chosen that was inherently inaccurate; but it was considered that the error 'would be unnoticed inside the large spread of such huge concentrations'. However, when the third or fourth switch was being ordered, a correction was applied that was so large that it exceeded the parameters within which the error was insignificant. As the guns roared, their shells fanned out and fell around and within the VIP enclosure. But the single fire order 'Stop', over the radio, was obeyed immediately and all firing ceased.[25]

Such an end to a demonstration in normal times would have written 'finis' to the subject of the demonstration and, probably, the career of the officer concerned. But this did not happen. The value of Parham's system was recognised and those who had developed it were told simply to apply the necessary corrections. The system was ordered into use. Correction proved relatively simple as Bidwell noted.

> Conventional fire-control orders told the battery concerned to shoot more left or right or shorter or longer: they were very quick because the order could be applied directly to the sights of the guns of the battery. In other batteries compensating corrections had to be calculated. The Farfan system simplified these corrections; the Parham system ignored them. A special type of fire-order was now introduced using compass points; e.g., 'shift your fire 400 yards north-east of where it is now' abbreviated to 'Go NE 400'.[26]

Every battery involved in a concentration could apply this order without correction, irrespective of its location, or that of its OP. Furthermore, should the OP officer be knocked out the infantry unit he was working with could understand and apply the system. This was a great strength.[27]

Although the system was adopted without a title, it employed letters to describe levels of fire, using the contemporary phonetic alphabet. A target for the twenty-four guns of a regiment was a Mike Target, while an Uncle Target was for the guns of the divisional artillery. At corps level, the call was for a Victor Target; Yoke Targets were for AGRAs and a William Target brought in all the guns of a field army. Only the simple, but urgent, radio call 'Mike Target! Mike Target! Mike Target!' was needed to initiate a concentration; the code was always called three times. In practice the system proved easy to use and very effective.[28]

In the years ahead the term 'Stonk' was to be used to describe a standard concentration and was even to be used as a verb, especially by infantry calling for an enemy position such as a machine-gun post or mortar position to be 'stonked'. Ian Hogg suggests that the word 'stonk' derived from a contraction of 'standard regimental concentration', a description of 'a 525-yard block of fire that could be rapidly calculated ... and quickly fired to relieve pressure where needed'. The block's dimension derived from the lethal area of shell bursts from a regiment of guns, eg twenty-two 25-pounders or eighteen 5.5s.[29] However, Niall Barr suggests that the term derived from the development of a concentration by all seventy-two guns of a division on a single target area, 'a rectangle 1,200 yards long and 600 yards deep whereby the coordinates of the centre point and the grid bearing of the perpendicular axis could be used to lay in every gun'. This was refined in training in Syria by 2nd New Zealand Division's artillery and the CRA, Brigadier Charles Weir (later GOC of 46th Division), who discussed its use as a standard operational procedure with the BRA of XIII Corps, Brigadier Standford. Barr comments that the term 'stank', as 'a convenient code name', was proposed by Weir since it was 'closest to Standford's name'. However, this was changed to 'stonk, apparently after 'stink' had been rejected.[30]

While there is no doubt that both the term 'stonk' and the tactic originated in the Middle East, Colonel Will Townend, Secretary of the Royal Artillery Historical Society, believes that the origin of the term 'stonk' may be somewhat different. 'I suspect that Brig Weir may have chosen STONK (as a contraction of Standard Concentration) as the codeword, amended it to STANK as a private joke with Brig Standford, suggested STINK as a bigger joke, and then gone back to STONK.'[31]

Whatever the origin of the word 'stonk', there is no doubt that the tactic was developed by Weir and adopted by Gunners of Eighth Army. It became a valuable tactic that could be applied rapidly but the widespread use, or misuse, of the term to cover almost any call for fire became an irritation with many Gunners.[32]

Jack Parham's contribution to the development of British firepower was not restricted to creating this system. As noted in Chapter Two he was an enthusiastic exponent of the aerial OP and had played a significant role in developing air observation, as had Charles Bazeley. The latter's dedication to this concept had led him to seek a secondment to the RAF and he had commanded the trials' flight that went to France in 1940 but which had been unable to complete its task due to the German attack. However, Bazeley persevered, in spite of reservations expressed not only by the RAF but also by some senior Army officers. Since RAF Lysanders had suffered horrifically at the hands of the Luftwaffe in France – to avoid further losses, the Lysander squadrons were brought back to England before the campaign ended – senior air officers believed that the slow-flying aircraft the Gunners proposed to use would suffer likewise.

Bazeley's trials flight, D Flight, had officially been disbanded after returning from France, but unofficially Bazeley kept it in being at Knighton Down on Salisbury Plain. He was able to report on the trials held in France as D Flight had worked for three weeks at the French artillery ranges at Mailly in cooperation with A/E Battery 1st Regiment RHA, 1 LAA Battery and French units. Although no operational trials had been held, thanks to the German attack, considerable practical work had been done and Bazeley noted that an AOP, flying only 6–700 feet above a battery position, could engage enemy positions as far away as 7,000 yards (almost four miles), if those positions were visible. When D Flight was officially re-established at Larkhill in July, Bazeley was able to carry on his work with official backing. The Vice Chief of the Imperial General Staff (VCIGS), Lieutenant General Sir Robert Haining, himself a Gunner, wrote to his counterpart in the RAF, the Vice Chief of the Air Staff (VCAS), seeking pilots for further trials; a course was organised at Old Sarum in Wiltshire for four more Gunner officers to train as pilots.

Definite progress seemed to be being made when, at a meeting on 2 August, the VCIGS and VCAS agreed to continue Bazeley's trials. There were even suggestions that the concept be widened 'to include active co-operation with all ground troops in answering calls for fire, in reconnaissance, in counter-battery work and in photography'.[33] Pilot training was also progressing with the Air Ministry accepting an Army request for fifty Gunner officers to begin training courses, six weeks long, began in September. And the search for the most suitable aircraft was also narrowing. Although the Comper Fly looked suitable, its designer, Flight Lieutenant Comper, was killed, reducing the choice to the Taylorcraft and Stinson Voyager.

The requirements for an AOP aircraft were demanding.

> [It] would have to be capable of operating from small, hastily constructed air strips close to the guns it served; it should have short take-off and landing capability, be robust and easily maintained and have, relatively speaking, a good rate of climb as well as good all-round [vision] and stability in flight; on top of all this it would be required to have the capability of carrying a pilot, an observer and a radio.[34]

The Stinson O-74 Vigilant seemed the better option, being 'an aircraft in many ways comparable to the German Storch, whose remarkable slow speed characteristics had made a big impression just before the war'.[35] Although a hundred were ordered in July 1940, the Americans were reluctant to provide these machines to Britain quickly. The first did not arrive until December 1941, seventeen months after the order had been placed, but most had been crushed by 300 tons of cheese that had been loaded with them.[36] In the interim, D Flight, having to improvise with what it could lay its hands on, used a collection of machines, including the Taylorcraft. The Taylorcraft's manufacturers proved most cooperative and contact was maintained with them to introduce improvements that made the plane more suitable for AOP duties; a more powerful engine was fitted and the solid cabin roof was replaced with a clear roof to enhance all-round vision. This proved fortunate as the Ministry of Aircraft Production 'appeared to have cancelled the [Stinson] order in error'.[37] Four Vigilants received for training proved that the machine would have been too big for its role.[38]

Between September and December 1940 trials continued apace, co-ordinated by the Chief Instructor at the School of Artillery, Colonel Hilton, and No. 22 (Army Co-operation) Group, RAF. These trials were thorough and intensive as those involved sought to develop effective operating procedures. During this period, Captain Merton of D Flight invented what became known as the Merton photograph, a gridded print that became standard for use by AOPs, the RAF and Gunners and which allowed identification and fixing of targets from photographs. Bazeley was busy organising the flying and operational training of new pilots as they arrived from Elementary Flying Training Schools and in maintaining contact with the Director of Military Training. He had also to attend exercises and present lectures to all arms on the nascent AOP system and what it would be able to do for the soldiers on the ground.

Some hiccoughs appeared in early 1941 with the Air Ministry suggesting that the Air Staff would be 'opposed to recommending the creation of special air units for artillery observation or reconnaissance unless it can be shown that there is an urgent requirement for such units which cannot be met by Army Co-operation Squadrons.'[39] In fact, those squadrons, with their Lysanders, had been shown to be incapable of this task in France. But the intervention of two group AOCs made it clear that the RAF could not fulfil the Army's requirements in addition to their many other tasks. One former Gunner, Sir Arthur Barratt, now an air marshal and AOC-in-C Army Co-operation Command, expressed scepticism about the AOP proposals, even suggesting that a tethered balloon could do all that an aeroplane could. That was in January 1941 and, two months later, he was expressing 'the gravest doubts' about the survival chances of AOP pilots when opposed by enemy aircraft. Fortunately, by April 1942, Barratt had become a supporter of the AOP concept. Although General Haining also began to have doubts about AOPs, the support of General Sir Alan Brooke, then C-in-C Home Forces and a Gunner, ensured the concept's survival. Brooke wrote to the Director of Staff Duties on

5 July requesting that the first squadron be established by 1 September. Little over a month later the Air Ministry asked the War Office for fifteen pilots and eight batmen for the new No. 651 Squadron RAF, which was to begin forming at Old Sarum on 1 August. During September agreement was reached on command of these squadrons: this would be by Royal Artillery officers seconded to the RAF. Not surprisingly, Major Charles Bazeley was appointed to command No. 651 Squadron, which had another fifteen pilots, all captains.[40]

Bazeley's work had borne fruit and AOPs would prove a valuable Gunner asset from Tunisia onwards. By 1943, twelve squadrons were in existence; all saw active service.[41] Among procedures worked out during D Flight's trials – it later became 1424 Flight – was a new system for controlling gunfire from the air. Since the Great War, Gunners had used a clock code system, referring to the hands of a clock with 12 o'clock being directly in front of the gun positions, but this was now replaced by the AOP pilot giving orders to the guns by reference to line of fire and distance between guns and target.[42]

Bazeley's No. 651 Squadron was the first to see action for which credit goes to Brigadier Jack Parham. By now BRA, First Army, the expeditionary force to Tunisia, Parham argued for the inclusion of two flights of No. 651 Squadron in the first follow-up convoy to Tunisia. Although the aircraft were Mark Is, he made a strong case that these should be deployed to Tunisia where they could increase by a large factor the effectiveness of the guns, especially as artillery would be in short supply in the early stages. The new Mark III aircraft would not be available until 1943 and would come out with the rest of No. 651 Squadron in spring 1943.[43]

The development of Parham's ideas on gunnery and the concentration of fire, and of Bazeley's aerial observation posts had not been in isolation, but had occurred alongside other developments in the artillery world. Some of these we shall see when studying Anti-Aircraft Command and when examining the anti-tank units. But there were also developments in the tools of the Gunner's trade with new weaponry being tested and approved for use.

In Chapter One we saw how obsolete Great War guns had had to soldier on due to government parsimony so that many were still in service in 1939. When the BEF was despatched to France, such antiques as the 9.2-inch howitzer remained in use; two dozen were lost in France and the remainder were deployed as anti-invasion defences on England's south-east coast. A replacement had been sought before the war but it was 1941 before the first proof model was fired; this had a split trail, 50-degree traverse and fired a 315lb shell to a range of 16,000 yards. Trials showed that a trained detachment could bring the new howitzer into action in an hour and out again in thirty minutes but, in spite of such great improvements, the new development was stopped in October 1942. There seems no clear reason for that decision other than the possibility of the United States supplying the 240mm howitzer MI before the new 9.2 could be produced. It is also possible that no great need was seen for such a weapon; certainly only a few American 240mm howitzers entered British service.[44]

The shortage of heavy artillery in 1940 led to a demand for a new weapon of about 8-inch calibre but with greater range than the veteran 8-inch howitzer. As the same type of carriage was required, trials were held to determine the maximum stress that the existing carriage and recoil system could tolerate. Following this, it was decided to develop a 7.2-inch howitzer, firing a 200lb shell with 1,700 feet per second muzzle velocity, by relining existing barrels and modifying breech mechanisms. Thus was created the 7.2-inch howitzer Mark 1, approved for service in April 1941. A similar procedure was adopted with American 8-inch howitzers, built to the British design during the Great War.

However, the recoil system of the 7.2 could not fully absorb the recoil forces and the carriage, two-wheeled with a box-trail, moved backwards on recoil. Since this could be dangerous on wet ground, detachments had to stand well clear when the weapon fired. As a solution, wedge-shaped 'scotches', or quoins, were placed behind the large balloon-tyred wheels allowing the recoiling gun to run up the scotch before returning to the level. Even so, the 7.2 remained a weapon demanding more than usual respect; with Charge 4, it was not considered to be under sufficient control for an acceptable rate of fire and so, in early 1943, a project began to produce a new carriage. The result was a piece mounted on the multi-wheeled carriage of the American 155mm gun M1 which became the 7.2-inch howitzer Mk 5. When this led to questions about mounting such an elderly weapon on a modern carriage, a new piece was designed that, coupled with the American carriage, became the Mk 6, which entered service in time for Operation OVERLORD in 1944 and became the standard weapon for heavy regiments until the 1960s.[45]

The dangers posed by the early 7.2 are illustrated by the story of the first meeting between two of the, retrospectively, most famous Gunners of the Second World War, Gunner 'Spike' Milligan and Lance Bombardier Harry Secombe. The latter was serving with 321 Battery 132nd Field Regiment, a Welsh TA unit, and he and his comrades were deployed in a Tunisian wadi when a 7.2 rolled over the bank of the dried-up river and landed amongst them, fortunately without causing injury or damage. Milligan then leant over the edge and called 'Has anybody seen a gun?', to which Secombe replied 'What colour?' Having fired its first round from a new position, the 7.2 had run back so far that it plummeted into the wadi; it was one of the guns of 56th Heavy Regiment which Brigadier Peter Mead, in his book *Gunners at War*, mischievously dubbed 'Spike Milligan's Own'.[46]

Development continued on modern weapons already in service, including the 25-pounder and 3.7-inch heavy AA gun with both equipments improving to meet the many situations that faced them. Attempts were made to provide a more mobile 25-pounder which could serve with armoured divisions, the first practical application of this concept coming with the marriage of a 25-pounder to a Valentine tank chassis. The result, dubbed Bishop, was far from revolutionary. With the tank's turret removed, a high, armoured barbette housing a modified 25-pounder top carriage and gun was fitted. Since the gun compartment restricted elevation to 15 degrees, range was reduced to 6,400 yards. In October 1941 an order was placed for a hundred Bishops which entered service in North Africa in early 1942. Detachments fought in close, cramped, very hot conditions; Bishop was a stopgap that provided useful service and was certainly valuable in training regiments in the basics of self-propelled gun handling and tactics.[47] Bishop was succeeded by the American 105mm M7 howitzer motor carriage, known as Priest,[48] although some Bishops fought in Sicily and the opening phase of the Italian campaign. Later, Priest would be joined, and superseded, by another ecclesiastically named SPG, Sexton, with a 25-pounder on a Canadian Ram tank chassis. This equipment would continue to serve for many years after the war.[49]

Trials took place with the 3.7-inch heavy AA gun in an anti-tank role but, although proving highly effective, demands for the AA role were so great that none could be spared for anti-tank work. Development was carried out on a 3.7-inch anti-tank gun with a 37lb shell, but trials, in June 1944, fell far short of expectations; it was superseded by the 32-pounder, which never came into service, although some were built and trials completed in 1946.[50]

While much thought was given to developing anti-tank artillery during the war, a great mistake was made in 1940 with the decision to maintain 2-pounder production on the grounds that it was better than no anti-tank gun at all. Such had been the losses of 2-pounders in France that it was proposed that it was opportune to put into production its successor, the 6-pounder. This gun, of 57mm calibre, had been designed in 1938 with the first example test-fired in 1939. However, it was argued, starting 6-pounder production would mean stopping production of the earlier gun with the inevitable hiatus before new weapons began flowing from the factories creating a severe shortage of anti-tank weapons. Furthermore, it was felt that the 2-pounder was a weapon with which its users were familiar but a new gun would require retraining. Thus the 2-pounder continued in production and, although an order for 400 6-pounders was placed in June 1940, none were built until November 1941; six months later ordnance factories were producing 1,500 6-pounders each month.[51]

When it became available, the 6-pounder was issued to Royal Artillery anti-tank units, allowing 2-pounders to be transferred to infantry anti-tank platoons, a process accelerated in 1943 when 17-pounder anti-tank guns began reaching Gunner regiments. The latter weapon resulted from a discussion on the eventual replacement for the 6-pounder, a discussion held before the 6-pounder even went into production. Although some favoured an 8-pounder as the next step, since it would be the same size as the 6-pounder, other counsels argued, and won, for an even heavier weapon, a 3-inch gun firing a 17lb round. The decision to go for this weapon was made on 21 November 1940. Four pilot guns were ordered in July 1941, tested in early 1942 and, the final production pattern chosen, the 17-pounder, was approved for service on 1 May 1942. While carriage design delayed the final version entering service, an interim gun, mounted on a 25-pounder carriage, was tested in September 1942 and issued for service in North

Africa.[52] One veteran told this author of returning to his AA unit in Tripoli in early 1943 and seeing examples of this new gun in the convoy on which he travelled from Egypt.[53] Self-propelled anti-tank guns were also to become part of the Gunners' inventory, beginning with the portée 2-pounder, followed by Deacon, a 6-pounder mounted on a Matador lorry with minimal armour protection. American M10 self-propelled anti-tank guns entered Royal Artillery service under the name Wolverine although the M10 was also upgunned with the 17-pounder to become Achilles. Archer was the name chosen for the 17-pounder on a converted Valentine chassis, with the gun facing to the rear; the driver had to quit his seat before firing to avoid decapitation. Archer had a lower profile than Achilles and remained in service post-war.[54]

Among 1940's lessons for anti-tank Gunners was the necessity for more officers in each regiment as troop commanders dealing with company commanders needed to be of commissioned rank. It was also realised that more internal communications were necessary, that some self-propelled anti-tank guns were essential and that an anti-tank regiment was also required in the corps artillery.[55] Although there were delays, all these changes were implemented.

Thus it was that the Royal Artillery used the post-Dunkirk period to best advantage by developing its tactics, command and control systems and weaponry. The Royal Regiment continued growing in size with AA Command absorbing a substantial proportion of the Army's overall manpower (in 1941 one British soldier in nine served in the Command),[56] while more field regiments – including medium and heavy units – were added to the orbat. Such was the call on the Gunners' services that many also went to sea to defend merchant ships. What started in February 1940 as a request for some manpower to supplement the shipboard gunners – 1,000 soldiers from Home Forces – turned into a major contribution and led to the creation of Maritime AA Regiments, which saw service across the globe and eventually numbered over 11,000 men, the figure peaking at 14,200 in September 1942.[57]

Notes

1. Bidwell, *Gunners at War*, pp. 137–8
2. Ibid, pp. 136–7
3. Ibid, p. 138
4. Ibid, p. 138
5. Hamilton, *The Making of a General*, p. 422
6. Bidwell, op cit, pp. 107–8
7. Ibid, p. 108
8. Ibid, p. 108
9. Ibid, p. 144
10. Duncan, *RA Commemoration Book*, p. 33
11. Bidwell, op cit, pp. 142–3; Doherty, *Clear The Way!*, p. 233
12. Lt Col B D H Clark MC GM to author, 1990

13 Doherty, op cit, p. 114
14 Ibid, p. 114
15 Bidwell, op cit, p. 144
16 Farndale, *The Forgotten Fronts and the Home Base, 1914–18*, p. 316
17 Bidwell, op cit, p. 98
18 Ibid, p. 127
19 Ibid, p. 145
20 Ibid, p. 146
21 Ibid, p. 146
22 Ibid, p. 146
23 Joslen, *Orders of Battle*, p. 65
24 Bidwell, op cit, p. 146
25 Ibid, pp. 147–8
26 Ibid, p. 148
27 Ibid, p. 148
28 Ibid, p. 148; Mead, *Gunners at War*, pp. 85–6; Evans, http://members.tripod.com British Artillery in World War 2
29 Hogg, *Barrage*, p. 8
30 Barr, *Pendulum of War*, pp. 292–3
31 Col W A H Townend to author
32 Hogg, op cit, p. 8
33 Farndale, *The Years of Defeat*, p. 112
34 Ibid, p. 112
35 Parham & Belfield, *Unarmed into Battle*, p. 22
36 Farrar-Hockley, *The Army in the Air*, p. 137
37 Ibid
38 Ibid, p. 53
39 Quoted in Farndale, op cit, pp. 112–3
40 Farndale, op cit, pp. 112–5
41 Bidwell, op cit, p. 115
42 Farndale, op cit, p. 114
43 Bidwell, op cit, pp. 116–7
44 Hogg, *British & American Artillery of World War 2*, p. 143
45 Ibid, p. 138
46 Obituary Sir Harry Secombe, The Gunner, May 2001; Mead, op cit, p. 64
47 Hogg, op cit, p. 30; Hogg & Weeks, *The Illustrated Encyclopedia of Military Vehicles*, p. 158
48 Hogg, op cit, p. 61; Hogg & Weeks, op cit, p. 161
49 Hogg, op cit, p. 30; Hogg & Weeks, op cit, p. 158
50 Hogg, op cit, p. 81
51 Ibid, p. 75
52 Ibid, pp. 79–80
53 Mr Tom Moore, 26 HAA Bty, to author
54 Hogg, op cit, p. 80 (Archer), pp. 88–9 (M10 Wolverine/Achilles)
55 Duncan, op cit, p. 572
56 Cooper, *Anti-Aircraft Command*, p. 115
57 NA Kew, WO32/10373, 'Maritime Royal Artillery 1943–45'

Chapter Four

Defending Britain

Not since November 1688 and William of Orange has Britain been invaded successfully. However, it has faced many invasion threats, the worst of which was in 1940 after the fall of France when it appeared that the United Kingdom faced Germany alone. Although the Commonwealth and the Empire stood alongside, there was little immediate support that countries as far away as Canada, Australia and New Zealand could give should the Germans invade.

With invasion expected in the summer of 1940, priority was given to beach and coast defences with guns deployed to cover stretches of coastline that were considered vulnerable and at small ports around the coast. This was all in addition to the existing coast artillery, which protected the major ports; these were termed Class A and the newer sites Class B. In Chapter One we have already noted the engagement of a ship entering Belfast Lough by 188 (Antrim) Heavy Battery in the opening days of war. Whatever the circumstances of the engagement – it was what today would be called 'friendly fire' – this battery certainly fired the first shot by a coast defence unit during the war.

Coast defence was entrusted to the former Coast Brigades of Royal Garrison Artillery (TF) which, from 1921, adopted consecutive battery numbers as Coast Batteries RGA (TA). Redesignated Heavy Batteries RA (TA) in June 1924, these provided the nucleus of the Coast Batteries that were formed in considerable numbers from 1940.[1] Examples of that re-organisation include the Clyde Heavy Regiment RA (TA) which became 538th (Clyde) Coast Regiment on 12 January 1941; the Devonshire Heavy Regiment RA (TA) which became 566th, 567th and 568th (Devon) Coast Regiments on 14 April 1941; and the Princess Beatrice's (Isle of Wight Rifles) Heavy Regiment RA (TA) which became 530th The Princess Beatrice's (Isle of Wight Rifles) Coast Regiment from 14 July 1940.[2]

This massive expansion and re-organisation of coast defence artillery placed a heavy burden on the training system which included two elements: the Coast Artillery School, at Shoeburyness in Essex at the mouth of the Thames estuary, and 70th Coastal Training Regiment, at the Royal Citadel, Plymouth. Matters were exacerbated when the skies over the School became the scene of air battles that restricted training so much that it was decided to seek a new location. Suitable sites were examined, with a War Office proviso that there should be no need to build new accommodation, and Llandudno was chosen. The move to Llandudno began

> with a visit to Woolworth's, the object being to purchase flags for markers. Only toy balloons were available, so, decorated with a car load of these, the CIG, the SMIG and an armament artificer repaired to the gunsite, where, under the direction of the CIG, the flags were moored in positions representing OPs, guns, radars and searchlights – a harmless and colourful scene.[3]

The increasing number of Gunners, or gambardiers in the case of coast artillery, being trained led to the formation of the Coast Artillery Training Centre (CATC), under Colonel R C Gill, with 69th Training Regiment in Devonport, 70th at the Citadel, 71st at Staddon Heights and the Officer Cadet Training Unit (OCTU) at Plymouth and Brixham. When the Luftwaffe bombed Raglan Barracks, Devonport, 69th Regiment moved to a holiday camp at Paignton and HQ CATC to Ivybridge. A radar wing for the Centre was also established, in an old fort at Whitsand Bay, on the Cornish side of Plymouth Sound.

Of the regiments under the aegis of the Training Centre, 69th was intended for basic training while gunnery training was carried out by 70th and 71st Regiments. When primary training centres were introduced across the Army, 69th Regiment became redundant. Two other coast artillery training regiments were formed: 72nd was created at Norton Camp, Isle of Wight, by expanding 1 Coast Training Battery while 73rd was formed at East Blockhouse Fort, Milford Haven, by expanding 2 Coast Training Battery. Both were short-lived; their roles, respectively, were to train 6-inch and 12-pounder Gunners, and Gunners for twin 6-pounders.[4]

By the autumn of 1941, however, the invasion threat had virtually disappeared, allowing coast defences to be re-assessed. On 22 December 1941, Major General W J Eldridge, Director of Anti-Aircraft and Coast Defence, issued a letter outlining a re-organisation of UK coast defences. This would see the formation of two HQs Corps Coast Artillery, Class A in V and VIII Corps and five HQs Corps Coast Artillery, Class B in I, II, IX, XI and Canadian Corps. HQs Fixed Defences, Class A at Portsmouth, Plymouth, the Humber and the Tyne would be disbanded, as were the HQs Fixed Defences, Class B at Portland, Falmouth, Yarmouth & Lowestoft, Tees & Hartlepool, Cromarty, Clyde, Milford Haven, the Mersey and Harwich. However, a new HQ, Class A was formed for the Severn Defences.[5]

A major problem in this redeployment was the shortage of guns after the evacuation from France. Additional weapons were obtained from the United States and the Royal Navy. The latter supplied a variety of guns that had been removed from scrapped warships during the 1920s and 1930s and 'mothballed': these included 6-inch, 5.5-inch, 4.7-inch, 4-inch, 3-inch, 12-pounder and 3-pounder guns. Legend has it that some were discovered under 'a mountain of coal' but this was probably a myth created by Gunners.[6] In all, 510 equipments were handed over although a proper accounting, and official transfer, did not occur until October. Since most of the guns had been mounted on ships, it was necessary to make holdfasts to allow them to be fitted to a variety of pedestals and set into quick-drying concrete. Gunshields were manufactured locally although, where no local workshop was available, the nearest Royal Ordnance Factory would produce these from patterns made at the gunsite. Of the 4-inch naval guns supplied, forty-nine were on mobile mountings fitted to suitable lorries to be used as a mobile reserve.[7]

> Unmartial America, however bemused with her fantasies of perpetual peace through the League of Nations, had nevertheless kept her guns in grease, and was already, as the arsenal of democracy, packing for Britain 500,000 rifles, 80,000 machine guns, 900 field guns.[8]

Thus, from the United States, came hundreds of 75mm guns of three discrete types. The oldest were French 75s of 1897 vintage while the youngest were modern US weapons. In between were examples of the venerable British 18-pounder, converted to 75mm by the US forces. While these were a welcome additional to the Royal Artillery's inventory, suitable ammunition was in short supply. However, they came with a development that allowed older carriages to be converted quickly from wooden to pneumatic wheels. These guns allowed an expansion in coast defences with fixed defences augmented by the addition of defence batteries of Royal Artillery, assigned to the coast defence role but equipped with mobile weapons, allowing re-deployment to meet immediate or developing threats.[9]

An altogether different form of coast artillery was deployed in the Dover area in the form of heavy guns that could dominate the Channel and fire across the strait. Included in their number as the war progressed were 9.2-inch, 14-inch and 15-inch guns as well as super-heavy railway guns. The 14-inch equipments, of which there were two, nicknamed 'Winnie' and 'Pooh', were manned by Royal Marines since they were naval weapons taken from the reserve stock for the King George V-class battleships, but the other weapons were manned by Gunners.[10] Their role was to engage any enemy shipping attempting to pass through the Dover straits; counter-battery fire was carried out against targets on the French coast. Also deployed to the Dover area to join the anti-invasion defences was a Great War vintage railway howitzer. Based at Bekesbourne on the line from Dover to Canterbury, this was HM Gun 'Boche Buster', an 18-inch howitzer on the mounting of a scrapped 14-inch railway gun that had been used in France in the earlier conflict. Since it was a howitzer its range was restricted and it could not hit the French coast; its rounds would reach barely halfway across the Channel. It did, however, prove a morale booster, being photographed in various warlike poses although never firing in anger.[11] By 1943 this weapon was serving with 11 Super Heavy Battery of the Super Heavy Railway Regiment, together with three 13.5-inch guns, also fitted to old 14-inch mountings. These weapons were HM Guns 'Scene Shifter', based at Lydden on the Dover-Canterbury line, 'Gladiator', at Martin Hill on the Dover-Deal line, and 'Peacemaker', at Guston Tunnel on the same line. All three had originally been manned by Royal Marines but were handed over to the Royal Artillery in November 1943 on formation of the Super Heavy Railway Regiment.[12]

By the time that regiment was formed coast artillery was being scaled down and the role of the Super Heavy Railway Regiment was to support the planned invasion of France. Allied air superiority rendered the role redundant in June 1944 with aircraft performing the tasks that might have been assigned to the guns which were declared obsolete in 1945 and scrapped.[13]

As the war progressed and the threat of invasion receded, the primary role of coast artillery reduced in importance, although many guns on the south coast were used offensively against enemy positions in occupied France, and against enemy shipping in the Channel. The Gunners of the coast artillery units

> waited day after day eagerly and confidently, and in vain, for a chance to show their prowess. It was an irksome life indeed to keep keyed up for days, months and eventually years, knowing that they must be ready, yet gradually losing faith in the appearance of the enemy, whom at first they had expected almost nightly. It was also extremely difficult to convince them that their very presence acted as a deterrent and in itself prevented attack. However, they remained watchful and ready until they were no longer required and eventually departed to fight in other spheres.[14]

Hitler's planned invasion of the United Kingdom, Operation SEALION, was scheduled to take place from mid-August. However, prerequisites for success were control of the Channel, denied to the Germans by the Royal Navy, the coast defence units and the Royal Air Force, and air supremacy over the invasion area, denied to the Luftwaffe by RAF Fighter Command in the Battle of Britain. Under Fighter Command's operational control was the Army's Anti-Aircraft Command, which also played its part in defeating the Luftwaffe during the Battle of Britain.

Anti-Aircraft Command was a unique organisation, the only major headquarters of the Army commanded by one individual throughout the war. Elsewhere, 1939's most senior commanders generally paid with their jobs for the failure of successive governments to provide the Army with modern equipment. General Sir Frederick 'Tim' Pile, a Dubliner, earned his jacket with the Royal Horse Artillery in India before the Great War, in which he served on the Western Front. In the inter-war years Pile transferred to the newly-formed Royal Tank Corps before returning to the Royal Artillery. He commanded a brigade in Egypt and provided a salutary lesson in infantry night fighting to the future Field

Marshal Montgomery. Pile's interest in matters scientific and technical was one of his command's greatest assets during the war; his eagerness to work closely with scientists almost certainly accelerated technical developments that allowed AA Command to meet the threat from the Luftwaffe, especially the flying-bombs which first appeared in 1944.[15]

Anti-Aircraft Command was formed in April 1938 with Lieutenant General Sir Alan Brooke as commander-in-chief. When Brooke was succeeded by Tim Pile, on 28 July 1939, the Command was still woefully short of equipment. As early as June 1936, the Reorientation Committee had assessed national AA needs at seventy-six batteries, each of eight heavy guns, with searchlight companies to provide 2,500 lights at a time when there were only sixty effective guns and 120 searchlights.[16] Yet, on 3 November 1938, only 126 guns were 'ready in all respects for action'.[17] The modest 1936 gun requirement of 608 weapons was increased to 1,274 heavy guns, 2,000 light guns and almost 4,728 searchlights, a target still not reached when war broke out.[18] However, Pile thought that the position was improving at that point 'because production was at last beginning to assume a reasonable size and there were no extraneous demands for equipment which would inevitably reduce the number of guns available for ADGB'.[19]

In the war's early months there were growing demands for more guns and searchlights. The Admiralty wanted guns to defend dockyards and anchorages, the RAF to defend airfields, and industry to defend centres of production. From France came demands from the BEF for more AA guns, and for 3.7s to supplement the 3-inch guns with which the Force was equipped in the main. Pile noted the number of equipments necessary to meet all defensive requirements at 3,744 heavy guns, 4,410 light guns, 8,000 single or twin-barrel rocket projectors, 160 multi-barrelled projectors and 8,500 searchlights.[20] The rockets were 'a possible substitute for the 3.7-inch gun' and 'a much cheaper proposition', although in 'the first instance, [they were] intended for thickening the defence of those vulnerable points which, although chosen for light anti-aircraft defence, had not yet been allocated any heavy anti-aircraft weapons'.[21]

At the beginning of the war, Anti-Aircraft Command's heavy guns included the vintage 3-inch, the 3.7-inch and the 4.5-inch weapons (although, strictly, the first two were medium, units equipped with 3.7s were classified as 'heavy'). The 3-inch was being replaced and plays little part in the Command's wartime story. Of the other two weapons, the 3.7 was destined to be a classic that served in both mobile and static versions with the Command and with the field armies, becoming a valued multi-role weapon. Firing a 28lb shell at a muzzle velocity of 2,600 (792 metres) feet per second, the 3.7 had an effective ceiling of 23,500 feet which, as the weapon was modified and improved, increased to 32,000 feet; in its Mark VI version the effective ceiling was 45,000 feet but this was a 4.5-inch gun with its barrel relined to reduce the calibre to 3.7. Alongside the 3.7, AA Command deployed 4.5-inch guns on static mounts. The Royal Artillery had wanted a 4.7-inch heavy gun that fired a 50lb shell at just under

2,500 feet per second to a height of 45,000 feet[22] but financial restraints led to the 4.5-inch naval gun being adopted instead as its 'ballistics were close to the proposed 4.7in design, the ammunition was in production, and, since most of the heavy guns would be close to naval bases and dockyards, the supply of ammunition by the Admiralty supply system would be simple'.[23] Since the naval gun fired a 54lb shell at 2,400 feet per second to 44,000 feet a compromise was easy to accept and the 4.5-inch gun Mk II entered service in 1938. Although it could be moved on a custom limber, there was no mobile version. It fired a 53lb shell to a maximum 44,000 feet at a muzzle velocity of 2,400 feet per second and could also be used in coast defence; positions close to the sea, on the Mk IA mounting, could depress the piece by 9.5 degrees; it had a maximum horizontal range of 22,800 yards, or almost thirteen miles. Armour-piercing shells were provided for this purpose.[24] Later in the war, another naval gun, the 5.25-inch, was adopted as both an AA and coast defence gun although the first examples did not reach the Army until 1942.

For light AA weapons, the Royal Artillery had ruled out the Swiss Oerlikon 20mm gun, adopted by several other nations and by the Royal Navy as a shipboard weapon, since its 20mm shell was considered too light. The naval 2-pounder 'Pom-Pom' automatic gun was also evaluated, as was the Swedish Bofors 40mm automatic. Both were purchased, the 2-pounder as a static weapon, on a modified naval mount, and the Bofors for mobile defence of the field armies. On its modified naval mount, the 2-pounder was very heavy, almost eight tons, for a twin-gun installation, and with each gun firing sixty rounds per minute to a 6,000 feet ceiling it was quickly realised that the Bofors could fire as many rounds in a minute, with one barrel, while tipping the scales at a quarter of the weight. That meant the end of the twin 2-pounder. The Bofors became the standard light AA gun, not only for field armies but also for AA Command.[25]

Bofors had put their 40mm on the international market as far back as 1931 and it was a well-tried piece of equipment by 1937 when Britain ordered 100 guns and 500,000 rounds of ammunition. Thereafter, a licence was agreed for production in Britain and Canada, although further guns were purchased off the shelf from Hungary and Poland, who were also building them under licence. Modifications were made to British-manufactured guns to improve production, or the handling of the gun, while the adoption of the Kerrison – or No. 3 – predictor increased accuracy. The Bofors was fitted with an auto-loader operated by the gun's recoil, allowing a rate of fire of 120 rounds per minute from four-round clips fed into a hopper. In theory a round could reach 23,600 feet although, in practice, shells burst at 5,000 feet, triggered by the burning out of a self-destroying tracer. A versatile weapon, the Bofors could even be used in the anti-tank role although Pile had problems securing anti-tank ammunition, which he requested in May 1940, realising that the guns could be used against enemy armour should an invasion occur.[26]

No matter how good the guns, they were only part of the air defence equation. While they shared that role with the RAF's fighters, there were other factors in the equation, including warning and control. It had been planned to use sound locators, parabolic walls to pick up the sound of approaching aircraft and reflect it via microphones, 'but they were hopeless owing to the extraneous noises'.[27] Early warning of enemy aircraft was critical, since bomber speeds had increased greatly in the inter-war years. Fortunately, radar came along at just the right time. Known at first as RDF, radio direction finding, which had been in use almost since the invention of radio, this not only gave the direction of a target but also its range, and hence 'radar' for radio detection and ranging. Although Britain was not alone in developing radar, what made British work unique was the creation of 'a coherent defensive system of radars, observers, communications and control rooms which ensured that the information ... extracted was sent to ... where it would do the most good'.[28] In other words, Britain developed a radar-based defence system whereas other nations simply produced radar sets.

In 1940 the British system could give early warning of Luftwaffe attacks long before the bombers had crossed the Channel, allowing Fighter Command to have fighters airborne awaiting the enemy's arrival. Without this system the Luftwaffe might well have overwhelmed Fighter Command. The guns also benefited from such early warning and it was realised that radar could be used to lay guns on to their targets although many refinements were needed before that became practical.

Each gunsite also had fire-control equipment, including a predictor and a heightfinder. Before gun-laying radar became a practical proposition there was also a spotter, a telescope manned by two Gunners, which picked up an approaching plane and reported its bearing and angle of elevation. This information was passed to the predictor and heightfinder teams which then picked up the target and 'laid on' to it through telescopes. The heightfinder team's task was to work out the target's height as soon as possible and relay this to the predictor team who fed the information into their machine which had also been provided with data such as wind speed and direction. The predictor then calculated where the target would be when the shells reached it and indicated the fuse setting so that each shell would explode at the correct altitude. Electrical cables carried bearing and elevation data to each gun where it appeared on dials on either side of the weapon. Two layers then adjusted pointers on the dials to match the predictor's information and, in doing so, swung the gun into the right position for bearing and elevation. Only when the officer commanding the gunsite received the report 'Predictor steady' did he give the order 'Fire'. As may be imagined, this was a continuous process with information being updated and bearings and elevations revised by the minute.[29]

The gun is actually the projector of the real weapon, the shell. Anti-aircraft shells had presented the problem of developing a time fuse to burst them in the right area at the right time and every time. This had taken most of the Great War to solve but by the 1930s the standard AA shell was a high explosive device with an accurate clockwork fuse. Before the war, Britain bought fuses from Switzerland but the fall of France ruled out this source. British industry tried to perfect an indigenous clockwork fuse but this took time and many defective fuses found their way to guns where some exploded prematurely, killing or injuring many Gunners. However, wartime developments in Britain and the USA would see great improvements in this sphere.[30]

When Britain went to war, its AA units had a strength of 8,720 regular officers and men, plus 3,331 Supplementary Reservists; but the largest proportion of AA Gunners was in the Territorial Army, at 118,799 officers and men. Therein lay the bulk of AA Command's strength; the TA was, therefore, committed very heavily to the UK's gun defence. Of course, AA units had also to be found for field armies wherever they might be deployed although, in 1939, no one could have foreseen that more than 200 AA regiments would be needed outside the UK.[31]

Although there had been no major German air raids on Britain, the Luftwaffe began mine-laying during the 1939–40 winter, especially in the Thames estuary. So much damage was caused to shipping that novel measures were adopted, especially as mine-laying aircraft flew so low that fighters had difficulty intercepting them while land-based AA guns could not engage them. Thus was born the Nore Flotilla, an extemporised floating AA unit of three paddle steamers – *The Queen of Kent*, *The Queen of Thanet* and *The Thames Queen*. Each carried a single Bofors and two searchlights, manned by Gunners, and deployed in the estuary where they proved effective in dealing with the mine-layers.

> This flotilla very seriously hampered any mine-laying activities. They illuminated many targets, which were engaged by Bofors and Lewis guns, and they destroyed a lot of floating mines, besides rescuing survivors from sinking merchant ships. The troops enjoyed this new role greatly. They were better fed by the Navy than they were on shore, and as their leave periods were in excess of those of their comrades on shore, the job was a popular one.[32]

It also presaged a role that Gunners would undertake in great numbers in the years ahead, that of maritime AA artillery on board merchant ships across the globe. The minelaying operations led, in part, to another counter-measure, the building of the Maunsell forts in the Mersey and Thames estuaries. (A more important reason for the forts was to close the gaps in AA defences caused by wide estuaries.) When the V1 campaign began the Thames forts played 'their part in the defence of London ... Had we had the Maunsell forts in the Mersey in the winter of 1940, the damage done to Merseyside ... would have been much reduced'.[33] Supported on steel legs sunk into the seabed, and presaging oil-drilling platforms, each Maunsell fort could accommodate a troop of 3.7s 'using separate towers connected by walkways'. Also included were LAA guns for local defence and living accommodation for the detachments.[34]

AA Command had a much quieter time than expected during the war's first winter and could concentrate on creating defences, emplacing guns and ancillary equipment, and training its Gunners. Manpower posed yet another problem since the Command was seen as a pool of men for other duties and often lost personnel as a result. Many conscripts sent to the AA defences 'were the leavings of the Army intake after every other branch of the services had had their pick', according to Pile, who noted that his Command's first intake in December 1939

> had had extensive medical examination, but many ... were quite unsuited for any military duty, let alone the highly technical duties of AA. Out of twenty-five who arrived at a fairly representative battery, one had a withered arm, one was mentally deficient, one had a glass eye which fell out whenever he doubled to the guns, and two were in the advanced and more obvious stages of venereal disease.[35]

Solutions to this problem included employing female personnel in AA Command while, in spring 1941, Pile would tackle vigorously the low standard of some of the Command's recruits.[36]

AA Gunners also faced the difficulty of tracking targets in conditions other than clear daylight. While RDF stations could give early warning of the approach of enemy aircraft across the Channel, once hostile planes had crossed the coast there was, initially, no electronic method of tracking them. At that point the defence fell back on visual spotting by the Observer Corps (Royal Observer Corps from 1941) from whose reports the hostiles' courses were plotted. This left room for many errors and Winston Churchill had commented, in June 1939, that a raider, on crossing the coast, moved from 'the middle of the 20th Century to the Early Stone Age'.[37] Moreover, whenever bombers arrived over their targets the guns relied on visual sighting by day and searchlights and sound location by night. Aware of all these problems, Pile was already expending considerable energy in ensuring that the guns would have more modern detection and fire-control equipment.

An example of the early problems faced by Gunners was witnessed by Pile at RAF Hawkinge during a Luftwaffe raid when 'literally, until the bombs began to fall no one had any knowledge that enemy aircraft were in the neighbourhood'.[38] The raiders, aware of the British early-warning system of radar stations, had flown low, using valleys as cover, until they were close to the airfield, at which time they popped above the trees to attack before employing a similar tactic to escape. Strengthening the Observer Corps and posting lookouts on high towers to watch possible approach routes helped to deal with that tactic. This soon paid dividends with both fighters and guns able to inflict damage on the attackers.

Luftwaffe raids on Britain began shortly after the declaration of war. AA Command was on the alert even before that September Sunday when Chamberlain made his broadcast. Sadly, the first occasion on which the guns fired was against RAF aircraft, one of which was shot down at Sheerness on 6 September. In mid-October, as noted in Chapter Two, heavy guns in the Forth area fired 104 rounds at German bombers, damaging two.[39] However, a surprise raid on the Scapa Flow anchorage on 16 March 1940 saw the guns perform poorly. The raiders, about fifteen Junkers Ju88s, struck as darkness was falling and above half of their number dive-bombed the Home Fleet while the others hit at the nearby airfield. Scapa was well defended with sixty-eight guns in place, although of fifty-two that could fire at the attackers only forty-four did so;[40] the others had just been emplaced. However, the heavy guns could not tackle the dive-bombers which task fell to the light guns. These failed completely. Several jammed while the detachments on others were blinded by the flashes from their own discharges, made even brighter by the gloaming, and could not observe their targets. Of 108 searchlights at Scapa, only thirty were in action and the radar station had not detected the raiders until too late for adequate warning to either fighters or guns. Although fighters took off, the bombers escaped with neither casualties nor damage.[41]

Many lessons absorbed from these encounters proved valuable in the months ahead. However, AA Command's first real test came in summer 1940 with the Battle of Britain, in the initial phase of which the Luftwaffe attacked shipping in the Channel as well as ports and airfields. Although causing much damage at several ports, the bombers did not get away lightly. Guns downed several with those at Dover claiming half of the first twenty-six German planes shot down over Britain. The work of 75th HAA Regiment, under Lieutenant Colonel N V Sadler, was especially effective with 'concentrations over individual points in the harbour and shipping channel'. Supported by light guns this led to seven Ju87s being shot down in one day, as well as two Bf109s and a Dornier Do215.[42]

Since these were mainly daylight raids, gun detachments could see their targets. The problems of night-time and poor visibility target acquisition remained to be solved with the first gun-laying (GL) radar sets experiencing considerable teething problems. Pile was working to improve the guns' effectiveness, a task on which he worked closely with scientists and industry. With the cooperation of men such as Professor Paddy Blackett, the father of operational research, the Command's problems were analysed and resolved.

Before the war training had been based

> on certain assumptions, the only ones possible with the equipment then available. These were that hostile aircraft would fly at a constant height and speed (200mph), that they would be visible by day and illuminated by searchlights at night. Moreover it was held that a plane must keep to a steady height and course, if its bombs were to be released accurately on its predetermined target, for at least half a minute.[43]

These were assumptions not shared by the Luftwaffe which varied tactics to include, as noted, dive-bombing and low-level approaches. Furthermore, clear weather could never be assumed over the United Kingdom and spotters were often frustrated by cloud or mist. As a result, Gunners had to relearn their trade as the Battle of Britain developed. Considering the fire-control equipment available before the war, it would have been difficult to have taken any other approach to training. Even then Pile recognised a problem from the assessment of training exercises: Gunners tended to fire below and behind the target-towing planes used for practice. All those aircraft had been flying straight and level. He realised that better fire control meant reducing, as far as possible, the human factor. The quest to do so was underway as the Battle of Britain raged.

Throughout those summer days of 1940 AA Command's guns played their part in fighting the Luftwaffe but then, and ever since, the focus of public attention was on Churchill's 'Few' – the pilots of Fighter Command. The role of the guns was often overlooked and, worse, Gunners were criticised by members of the public, councillors and MPs. Pile had to accept a degree of criticism almost unprecedented for a British general; his guns were fighting their war in full view of the British public with some close to Westminster and the Houses of Parliament. He took a sanguine view of the credit given to Fighter Command.

> There is no doubt that the RAF played the predominant part … nor is there any doubt of the heroic fighting qualities of the pilots who took part in that battle. It is, therefore, not unreasonable to expect that the lesser role played by the ground defences should, first of all, fade into the background, and then into complete obscurity. Yet without the ground defences the Battle of Britain could not have been won by the fighter pilots, any more than the Battle of El Alamein could have been won by the infantry and tanks without the Gunners.[44]

He was not alone in this view: at the battle's height, Sir Hugh Dowding, supremo of Fighter Command, demanded additional guns and searchlights, thus indicating his appreciation of the value of the ground defences.

With grave shortages still plaguing his Command, Pile was making every effort to fill the gaps. He was especially concerned about the shortage of Bofors 40mm guns and Kerrison predictors. These guns, 'the most efficient killing-weapons' in his inventory, were critical in combating low-level raiders. In cases such as this, Pile's ability to make friends and gain their confidence came into play. He now numbered among his friends and confidants Lord Beaverbrook, Minister for Aircraft Production in Churchill's Cabinet, to whom he explained his problem. Beaverbrook undertook to do all that he could to increase production both of Bofors and their fire-control equipment. Beaverbrook was so impressed with Pile's performance as C-in-C, AA Command that he suggested that Pile should succeed Sir John Dill, the incumbent CIGS.

Pile also gained Churchill's friendship and confidence and the Prime Minister took a keen interest in AA Command; his daughter, Mary, later served in an anti-aircraft battery while Duncan Sandys, his son-in-law, was a liaison officer with the Command. Friendship did not protect Pile from the occasional Churchillian sideswipe; in one note to Pile's chief of staff the premier commented that the low expenditure of 40mm ammunition indicated that Bofors guns could be replaced by rockets; Churchill failed to appreciate that such low expenditure was attributable to a shortage of 40mm guns. Nor did friendship mean that Pile could always get his point across to Churchill. Once, while on a night-time guided tour of London gunsites, Churchill expressed excitement as the guns at Richmond Park opened fire, telling Pile that the sound of the cannon, as he insisted on calling them, exhilarated him. But Pile commented that 'he was always more interested in questioning me as to the number of cannon I had in action in the various areas than in the other equipment so necessary to make those cannon useful'.[45]

Scientists were endeavouring to improve radar so that it might be employed to control the guns, thereby reducing the rounds needed to bring down an aircraft. That this was an urgent priority was emphasised in September as the Luftwaffe, having lost the daylight battle, switched to night attacks on Britain's cities. Such attacks brought devastation throughout the United Kingdom in that following winter's 'blitz' while AA Command became the first line of defence since fighter pilots were blind during the hours of darkness. Airborne-interception (AI) radar was in its infancy and the only aircraft in which the early sets could be fitted, the Bristol Blenheim, was too slow to catch the bombers. As an interim measure, Hurricane fighters controlled by ground radar stations were deployed alongside Blenheims until the faster and more effective Bristol Beaufighter entered service in numbers sufficient to create a true nightfighter force. AA Command searchlights provided another element in the nightfighter battle. One tactic was to trap an enemy aircraft in a cone of three searchlight beams with a new light taking over as each light in the cone fell out of range: fighters could then be directed on to the aircraft or it could become a target for AA guns. By 1941 searchlights had their own special radar, SLC, codenamed 'Elsie'.

AA Command now had some GL Mk I radar sets although too few in number and not sufficiently advanced for radar control of the guns during night raids. Pile and his staff were forced to revert to a method born in the Great War: the barrage; this was a curtain of shellbursts in the path of attacking aircraft, forcing them to turn away, take avoiding action that would put them off their aim, or risk being shot down. To some the system was as scientific as a shotgun blast. Consuming vast quantities of ammunition, it prompted a caustic Churchillian note on the heavy expenditure of 260,000 rounds for September and demanding weekly returns of ammunition fired.

Although barrage tables were drawn up, Pile considered London's gun defence a 'policy of despair' rather than a true barrage since guns were ordered to fire as many rounds as possible on approximate bearings and elevations. In truth, the barrage was intended as much to bolster civilian morale as to deter the Luftwaffe. And yet it succeeded to a very large extent in both respects: morale was sustained and up to 48 per cent of bombers turned away. Nonetheless, large numbers of bombs were still falling: between 23 August 1940 and 1 January 1941 there were only eight nights on which London was free of bombers. Not surprisingly, the morale of many did suffer and, with the guns highly visible, many Londoners vented their frustrations on the Gunners. Letters arrived at Pile's HQ at 'Glenthorn' at Stanmore which made clear that frustration: one told him that he did not 'understand the meaning of the word barrage' while another suggested that the 'anti-aircraft defence of London [was] the biggest scandal since Nero'. Pile was keenly aware that just over half the bombers were getting through the defences; that 48 per cent turned away was little consolation for those suffering the attention of their more determined fellows.[46]

Was the barrage system of any value? Professor A V Hill criticised it severely, using mathematics to support his argument. Since a cubic mile of space measured 5,500 cubic yards while the lethal zone of a bursting 3.7-inch shell was no more than a few thousand cubic yards, and only for about one-fiftieth of a second, Hill opined that it was nonsense to talk about a barrage since, to have a one-fiftieth chance of shooting down an aircraft flying at 250mph through a ten-mile-wide and four-mile-high vertical rectangle required 3,000 shells a second.[47] In strict mathematical terms, Hill was right but he did not include the human element in his calculation, a failing of many scientists. No pilot calculates the mathematical probability of being hit when he sees an ack-ack barrage in front of him but, instead, sees something he knows can destroy his aircraft and kill him. Faced with this, he will either swerve to avoid the shellbursts or even drop his bombs in the wrong place. One former RAF bomber pilot told this author that he remembered seeing an ack-ack barrage over Germany which was so thick that 'it looked like you could have got out and walked on it'.[48] Luftwaffe pilots attacking Tripoli in early 1943 described the city's gun defences as a '*wand aus stahl*', or wall of steel.[49] Professor Hill may have been unaware of this human factor but Tim Pile and his Gunners knew about it and exploited it to the full.

Although Pile had 'a few brilliant scientists, under Professor Blackett, [working] to solve the problem for him … he could not wait for them to formulate a plan as the situation was looking black for London'.[50] The author of *Roof Over Britain* describes how, after raids on the nights of 8 and 9 September, all GPOs from London sites, with battery, brigade and divisional commanders, were called to a conference at which all the schemes that the scientists could devise were explained. So, too, was the final option: should all else fail, every gunsite would be notified of a height after which those on the ground should use their ears to estimate the attackers' location before firing the barrage in front of the intruders.[51] In short, they were told that 'the guns had got to fire, and fire like hell, that night, even if the only method was the GPO's 'flappers''.[52]

> The result was remarkable. Punctually to time the German bombers arrived – and were met by a roar of guns which must have astonished them as much as it heartened the Londoners. The enemy had been flying at 12,000 feet; as soon as the barrage opened they climbed to 22,000 feet. Many turned back and at least nine 'planes were shot down by AA fire. Guns were in action all night; and at dawn, as the ammunition

> lorries moved into the sites to replenish the unprecedented number of rounds which had been fired, the Gunners were washing out the hot bores of their guns.[53]

Next morning's papers carried headlines extolling the barrage and it was said that morale in the city jumped by 100 per cent. The barrage had given civilians an assurance that London, in the form of its AA defences, was fighting back. This was another factor missed by Professor Hill when expounding his theory on the ineffectiveness of barrage fire.

The blitz ended as 1941's spring brought shorter nights that increased the danger to bombers over Britain while preparations were also underway to send many of those bombers eastwards for the attack on the USSR. With no quick victory over the Soviets, Luftwaffe bombers did not return to France for a renewed offensive against Britain in autumn 1941. They were not seen in large numbers in British skies for another three years although there would be 'tip-and-run' attacks by fast fighter-bombers and raids by small formations. Thus the people of Britain found relief.

There had been some positive developments during the blitz including progress with gun-laying radar. The new GL II set had been installed experimentally at Burnt Farm gun-site in London where Cossor's, the equipment manufacturer, had a facility. This unofficial link-up between producer and user produced such good results that Pile believed that, had forty GL II sets been available during the winter of 1940-1, the skies over London would have become a death trap for the Luftwaffe.[54] The Burnt Farm trials symbolised clearly how AA Command and its chief could co-operate with manufacturers. As Pile later wrote:

> I doubt if there has been a Command in war which had so much influence on the type of equipment it was eventually armed with. The producers heard once a month ... what we required and why. I am also in no doubt that a similar committee ... would have resulted in far better tanks and anti-tank guns than we possessed. ... If Sir Robin Sinclair had done nothing else in the war, and he did a lot, his work as DGAR [Director General of Army Research] would have been sufficient to earn him a place in history.[55]

In spite of the many difficulties of those early days, AA Command achieved considerable success. When the Ministry of Information published *Roof Over Britain* in 1943, it noted that

> In the first two years of the war ... AA guns were responsible for destroying nearly 600 enemy aircraft ... Many more were damaged by AA fire and of these a fair proportion failed to reach their home bases. This is not purely conjecture, but inference from a number of factors, such as the condition of damaged aircraft when last seen and the examination of wreckage and bodies washed ashore.[56]

Although GL Mk II proved much more effective than its predecessor, it still had shortcomings. GL Mk I had been ineffective until the appearance of the Bedford E/F (elevation finding) attachment, a 'gadget ... designed to fit onto GL Mk I to enable continuous following of the unseen target ... and its appearance caused a wave of optimism to spread through AA Command. Here, at last, we thought, is a piece of equipment that will enable us to shoot straight at night'.[57] (This was named for one of the scientists working for Cossors.) It was not quite so simple: the E/F attachment proved a temperamental fitting that, according to one officer, 'required stroking every hour to keep [it] in a good temper' and also needed a large wire mat around it. This mat, of netting wire, was critical as it helped to ensure a 'clean' return from the target. However, the 'provision and erection of a mat for every GL in AA Command was a major feat. Practically the entire stock of wire netting in the country was required for the purpose.'[58] Such mats also aroused curiosity from the general public. In some areas, at least, Gunners spread the story that they were intended to represent water to high-flying aircraft.[59]

Not only did the mats require almost all Britain's netting wire, but they also used about 3,500 miles of stay wiring as supports. By the end of January 1941, about one in ten GL sites had been provided with mats at a time when the average number of rounds needed to shoot down each unseen aircraft had reduced to 4,087, more than 2,000 fewer than the previous average. However, it was considered that this reflected improvements in gunnery rather than being attributable to the mats; it was too soon to claim credit for the latter.[60]

There was no respite for AA Command in early 1941 with shortage of resources continuing to plague it. This was exacerbated by calls for additional guns for Coventry, the western ports and Northern Ireland; the last had assumed significant strategic importance after the fall of France. A continued shortage of guns meant that not all demands could be met and both Belfast and Coventry suffered especially heavy raids with great losses. When the Luftwaffe targeted Belfast on Easter Tuesday night 1941 they inflicted on that city the heaviest single night's casualties of any city outside London, yet not until the autumn of that year did Belfast have its full gun complement.[61]

Rockets have already been alluded to and it will be recalled that a requirement for 8,000 single or twin-barrel rocket projectors and 160 multi-barrelled projectors had been set. Known as UPs – unrotated projectiles – to keep the nature of the weapon secret, rockets were much favoured by Winston Churchill who, at one stage, wanted them to replace Bofors guns. However, rockets were less effective than the Premier believed; they were inaccurate, had a relatively short range and were not very lethal. However, they had one 'great asset': in common with the barrage, they had a tremendous deterrent effect against piloted aircraft. Throughout the war, efforts were made to control rockets in flight by means of radar and considerable progress had been made by 1945, at which stage further development was handed over to government scientists.[62] In time, such research and development led to the end of the heavy gun as a projector of AA missiles and saw guided missiles, such as Thunderbird, assume the heavy role with other systems replacing the light AA guns.

We have already seen that AA Command faced a manpower problem that worsened as demands on it increased. Even as equipment levels were being brought up to what was required, Pile learned, in September 1941, that another 50,000 men were to be taken 'for the Field Forces' with 30,000 to be drawn from searchlight units.[63] With reinforcements needed for Britain's only field army, in the Middle East, a partial solution was found by using Home Guard personnel, although these were available only when not involved in their everyday civilian jobs. Nonetheless, Home Guard soldiers were organised into watches to man AA guns, as well as coast and defence battery weapons. The real solution to the manpower problem lay in woman-power, although there was an initial reluctance to assign Auxiliary Territorial Service (ATS) personnel to anything more warlike than administration, driving and cooking. Before long, however, women were trained in technical duties, such as operating telescopes-identification, predictors, height-finders, GL radar and on plotting tables.

This was no solution of last resort for Pile but one to which he had given consideration. As early as 1938 he had invited Caroline Haslett CBE, later Dame Caroline, founding secretary of the Women's Engineering Society, to visit a battery in Surrey and give him 'her opinion about women's capacity to do the work' that she would see on the gunsites.

> She spent several Sundays there and assured the General that women could do the job. The event has proved her right. Women man everything except the guns themselves in Heavy AA units, and man them extremely well.[64]

The first mixed battery started training in early 1940 with ATS volunteers and men who were recent recruits, it being felt that the latter would have had no other experience of service life and thus 'would not find the atmosphere of a mixed battery so hysterically unorthodox'.[65]

At a meeting with Churchill on 7 October 1941, Pile was told that there 'was no possibility that we could be given more than the 280,000 men … agreed upon'. Churchill told him that he would have to leave weapons unmanned but Pile, unwilling to accept this, told the Prime Minister that, given the guns, he, Pile, would find the manpower, either regular soldiers, ATS or Home Guard.[66]

> This greatly appealed to Churchill, and he said that could it be achieved it would be at least as valuable as a major victory. The Prime Minister had rapidly added up in his mind the figures involved. 'Forty thousand men saved,' he said, 'equals a major victory for this country'.[67]

Thus, by the end of 1941, Pile was recommending 'that members of the Auxiliary Territorial Service should be employed in searchlight operational duties', a proposal the operational, administrative and medical aspects of which had been discussed at a War Office conference where both he and the C-in-C Home Forces were represented. Implementing this proposal would lead to sixty-seven searchlight batteries being manned by ATS personnel with the remaining 117 continuing to be manned by men with ATS administrative personnel. The sixty-seven batteries would employ about 40,000 ATS personnel, of whom 32,000 would be operational, thus allowing redeployment of 30,500 male personnel. With that ceiling of 280,000 men for ADGB there was no other way of meeting the figures required.

This was only the beginning. ATS personnel proved efficient and effective, and rose above considerable prejudice from their male counterparts and the protective, but patronising, attitude of many in public life who felt that women should not engage in such roles. On 2 December 1941, Pile wrote to the Under Secretary of State at the War Office stating that ATS searchlight regiments 'should … be composed almost entirely of ATS, although to begin with I recommend that a percentage of the officers should be male'. He further pointed out that in a recent experiment with ATS personnel in a searchlight regiment, the women soldiers had shown that they

> were capable of performing all other ranks duties including that of the number 9 on a Lister generator. It may however be necessary to provide a self starter for this Generator in winter months or, alternatively, to arrange that the engine is kept warm.[68]

The inclusion of ATS personnel in searchlight regiments was so successful that the scheme was broadened to allow them to take on an even wider range of duties, although questions were asked in parliament about women handling 'lethal weapons' and whether this meant that women would be forced to operate such weapons. On 2 December 1941, Churchill responded

> We do not propose, when once they have joined the ATS, to compel them to serve in the lethal or combatant branches. Women will have the right to volunteer, but no women in the ATS will be compelled to go *to the batteries*. It is a matter of quality of temperament, of feeling capable of doing this form of duty, which every woman must judge for herself and not one in which compulsion should be used. I want to make it clear that a woman may be compelled to join the ATS but only volunteers from within the ATS will be allowed to *serve with the guns*.[69]

There followed a steady stream of ATS volunteers for AA Command. When Churchill provided that assurance in the House of Commons, the first mixed heavy AA regiment had already opened fire – on 1 November. A week later another mixed HAA regiment shot down its first German bomber at Newcastle.[70] So many ATS personnel volunteered that, eventually, fifty-one mixed HAA regiments were formed;[71] the first was 131st (Mixed) HAA Regiment, formed at Bitterne, Hampshire on 25 August 1941 with 251, 310 and 368 Batteries.[72] Eventually, mixed regiments served in North-West Europe. The inclusion of so many ATS personnel in AA Command was described by Churchill as one of the greatest experiments ever tried in the British Army.[73] It proved a resounding success.

No account of the role of women in AA Command would be complete without mentioning two individuals: Nora Caveney and Violette Szabo. The name of the latter will be known to most readers but that of the former may not be so familiar. Nora Caveney was an 18-year-old ATS soldier from Walsden, Todmorden in Yorkshire who volunteered for service with the AA guns. Trained as a predictor number, she was posted to 505 Battery in the recently-formed 148th (Mixed) HAA Regiment.[74] On 17 April 1942 she became the first fatal operational casualty in the ATS Gunners when she was hit by a bomb splinter while operating her predictor. When she collapsed her place was taken by a spotter and the engagement continued without a break. W91467 Private Nora Caveney is buried in Netley Military Cemetery, Hampshire.[75]

Violette Szabo was born in New South Wales, the daughter of Charles George and Reine Blanche Bushell. Also a predictor number in the ATS, attached to 137th (Mixed) HAA Regiment, she 'was a keen and efficient 'Gunner' and popular with her fellows'.[76] She married Lieutenant Etienne Szabo, of the Fighting French Forces, and left the ATS on becoming pregnant. Violette Szabo gave birth to a baby girl but her husband was killed in action at El Alamein on 24 October 1942. Later she rejoined the service and subsequently volunteered for special operations. By now, she had been commissioned and later volunteered for a dangerous mission in occupied France.

> In her execution of the delicate researches entailed she showed great presence of mind and astuteness. She was twice arrested by the German security authorities, but each time managed to get away. Eventually, however, with other members of her group, she was surrounded by the Gestapo in a house in the south-west of France. Resistance appeared hopeless, but Mme Szabo, seizing a Sten-gun and as much ammunition as she could carry, barricaded herself in part of the house and, exchanging shot for shot with the enemy, killed or wounded several of them. By constant movement, she avoided being cornered and fought until she dropped exhausted. She was arrested and had to undergo solitary confinement. She was then continuously and atrociously tortured, but never by word or deed gave away any of her acquaintances or told the enemy anything of any value. She was ultimately executed. Madame Szabo gave a magnificent example of courage and steadfastness.[77]

Her exact date of death is not known but was probably during late January or early February 1945. Violette Szabo was awarded posthumously the George Cross while the French government also awarded her the Croix de Guerre.[78]

As the blitz came to an end in spring 1941, the Wehrmacht was preparing to invade Russia, which had to be delayed until June due to the operations in Greece. For the invasion, codenamed BARBAROSSA, the Luftwaffe's bomber fleets were transferred to the eastern front. Hitler hoped to overrun the Soviets in a rapid campaign but his armies became bogged down in a Russian winter; had they attacked in the spring it might have been a different story. As a result the bombers remained in the east, thus giving Britain a further respite.

There was no renewed blitz in the winter of 1941–2. However, the Luftwaffe was not entirely quiescent, as we shall see, while AA Command suffered further losses, including many of its Bofors. When the Japanese attacked the US Pacific Fleet at Pearl Harbor on 7 December 1941, US forces were 'desperately short of light guns and had nothing in any way comparable in effectiveness with the Bofors'. Thus British guns were supplied to US forces, in a little known gesture of solidarity. In December, Pile lost 192 light guns to the Americans, as well as sixty-six heavy guns, followed in January by a further twenty-two light guns.[79]

Added to this transfer to the Americans was the need to send equipments to the Far East and, worst of all, falling production in factories making the Bofors. It seemed as if even the minimum requirements for light guns would not be met at a time when the prospect of invasion could not be ruled out entirely. Invasion did not come, but the Luftwaffe did, in 'tip-and-run' raids dubbed the Battle of the Fringe Targets. During the latter part of 1941, some coastal towns suffered fleeting attacks by German aircraft. Although not much damage resulted, Luftwaffe activity was increasing and the decision was made to provide 'such defences as we could raise' for towns such as Yarmouth, Lowestoft, Falmouth, Skinningrove, Bridlington, Skegness, Fraserburgh, Peterhead, Montrose and Penzanze.[80]

The idea of mobile gun circuses was dismissed; there were not enough guns and it would be a matter of chance if guns were in the right place when needed. While it had been suggested that there might be low-level attacks in 1942, the Joint Intelligence Committee concluded that these were 'unlikely to differ materially from those experienced during the latter half of 1941'.[81] Once again the Germans did not act as expected.

On 27 March 1942, Torquay had an unwelcome and unexpected Luftwaffe visit. Four Messerschmitt Bf109s roared in at about 150 feet to bomb the town, which had no military value. Little notice was taken of this raid but, four days later, two fighter-bombers raided Brixham and another six bombed Bognor almost a week after that. Then came further attacks by small numbers of aircraft on Swanage, targeted twice on successive days, Portland, Exmouth, Bexhill, Folkestone and several other coastal towns. No serious damage was caused and when, after a series of such raids, the Luftwaffe 'suddenly struck again by night it was felt that this night attack was what we had really been waiting for'.[82]

When the Luftwaffe returned to night bombing, the choice of targets was very different. Each town or city bombed had little or no military significance, beginning with an attack on Exeter by twenty-five bombers on the night of 24/25

April. Next night a force twice that size raided Bath, which had no gun defences. Bath was targeted again the following night, this time by sixty-five planes, one of which was shot down when it flew too close to Bristol's guns. There was considerable anger in Britain that cities such as Bath and Exeter should be bombed, although Bath, now a major Admiralty centre, had military significance. But the Germans were seeking revenge for RAF raids on historic centres such as Rostock and Lübeck and had begun what were termed 'Baedeker Raids' on targets of historical significance.

Since these had been the heaviest raids for many months, Pile redeployed AA defences to defend 'such places as Penzanze, Truro, Hayle, Exeter, Bath, Basingstoke, Salisbury, Aldershot, Andover, Winchester, Taunton, Guildford, Maidstone, Tunbridge Wells, Ashford and Canterbury'.[83] However, the next target was Norwich where twenty-five bombers caused significant damage. As a result, a dozen guns were deployed there immediately while Ipswich, Cambridge, Colchester, Chelmsford, Lincoln, Peterborough and York were selected for AA defence; Oxford, Chicester and Brighton were added days later. Rocket projectors of the multi-barrelled variety were included in this deployment 'to be used freely, even at the expense of accuracy' as it was felt that this would cause the bombers to fly as high as possible. This had echoes of the London barrage.

When over thirty bombers bombed York on 28/29 April this deployment had not been completed but, next night, forty raiders over Norwich received a hotter reception than they had anticipated as newly-emplaced guns fired some 780 rounds to claim two 'probables' and two damaged. It seems that the Luftwaffe were chastened by this experience as four nights passed before another raid, this time on Exeter where night-fighters took priority over the guns which fired but a dozen rounds on a night that the city sustained heavy damage. Because of this Pile protested to Fighter Command to allow the guns to play a greater role. The next raid, over Cowes, saw four bombers shot down by the AA defences.

A further spate of Baedeker raids during May included attacks on Norwich, Hull and Poole. The month ended with a firebomb raid on Canterbury which was visited again the following night, as were Ipswich and Bury St Edmunds. During a raid on Canterbury on a third successive night three bombers were shot down. Raids on Nuneaton, Great Yarmouth and Weston-super-Mare at the end of June brought the Baedeker campaign almost to an end although it was August before the last attacks occurred.[84]

The Baedeker raids had seen the first real operational test of a new searchlight technique planned in late 1941. Hampered to some extent by shortage of equipment, this technique involved the SLC radar, known as Elsie, and it was the shortage of Elsie sets that was the problem, coupled with incomplete operator training. Nonetheless, although continuous illumination of aircraft was not achieved, it was clear to the Luftwaffe that the searchlights were improving from the old system in which 'lights were controlled from the depths of an Operations Room'. As a result, bombers were less inclined to venture far inland; they also flew faster, made more changes of course and raids were also less concentrated.[85]

As Baedeker raids were taking place by night so, too, were 'tip-and-run' raiders continuing the Battle of the Fringe Targets. Early May saw only forty-three Bofors guns deployed along the south coast, half the allocated number. Even so, this was a significant proportion of AA Command's Bofors for, across the UK, there were only 884 under Pile's command. Most new Bofors were allocated to the field armies, while many were deployed on merchant ships, manned by the Royal Artillery. Thus Pile had to obtain the necessary guns by stripping small quantities, usually one or two, from inland vulnerable points. This gave him another thirty-eight guns. Some new guns were allocated but these totalled only thirty-four. No more were available immediately. With this shortage of guns AA Command had to wage this most difficult campaign.[86]

The raids were usually mounted by four aircraft, Messerschmitt Bf109s or Focke Wulf FW190s, coming in low and fast from the sea to machine-gun and bomb targets 'from Deal to Dawlish and beyond'. Trains were among their targets, which were usually south coast towns and, although the number of raids reduced in June and July, by August there were three every two days.

> The dwellers in the South Coast towns were beginning to be critical. The raids were awkward to meet; the guns achieved so few successes as to cause morale to flag rapidly.[87]

Pile gave an example of the suddenness of such a raid. He visited one south coast town and described the everyday scene that he met – albeit a wartime everyday scene – including people sitting in cafes gazing 'wistfully at the pier broken in the middle'. Yet the very next day, those townspeople saw Luftwaffe fighter-bombers race in over that pier, all guns firing, before dropping bombs near the gasworks and railway station and turning rapidly out to sea again. The intruders were gone before the Gunners could bring their weapons to bear and even before warning sirens had sounded. In truth there was little warning: of thirty-nine attacks in August, warning was received in only eight cases. September was worse with one warning in twenty-four raids. The planes were coming in under the radar with guns and fighters almost always taken unawares. Along the south coast there were only 219 Bofors guns by 24 September while 130 attacks had been made on fifty-seven different targets by 323 enemy aircraft. The guns had managed to destroy only five intruders although a further nine were damaged.[88]

As usual AA Command rose to the challenge with the support of Fighter Command and with several innovations while its own signals' system played a critical role. Major General Basil Hughes, then a brigadier on Pile's operations staff, provided an account of how this was done.

> The most important step taken was to connect the low-looking radar directly both to the fighter-aircraft's dispersals and to the LAA Troops; this, of course, provided only 'raw' information, unfiltered and unidentified, but it was coupled with a rule prohibiting friendly aircraft from crossing the coast below 1,000 feet and giving the guns freedom to engage below 500 feet without recognition.
>
> Ultimately, 543 40mm guns were deployed on the 'Fringe targets', reinforced by 304 20mm Oerlikons manned by the RAF Regiment, 506 Vickers twin .5-inch machine guns and 340 2-inch rocket-projectors.
>
> There was, however, still scope for improvement in ways of alerting the LAA defences. The strain of continuous manning throughout the hours of daylight, while gazing into a mixture of haze and sun over the sea, called for frequent reliefs and physical exercises to maintain alertness. But it was in the sphere of 'local warning' that the greatest advances were made; Brigadier E S Lindsay of 2nd AA Group was foremost in devising these, which included detached OPs, connected to the guns by radio, and a simple, but most profitable, system of colour code to indicate the direction of approach.
>
> As a result of these improved arrangements the reinforced gun defences showed a marked improvement in performance during the autumn of 1942, 34 aircraft casualties being caused between October and January. There was a slight drop in … attacks during the bad weather of February 1943, and then the guns really started hitting, 13 aircraft casualties being inflicted in 12 attacks. The great day, however, was on 30 May when of 15 FW 190s which flew into Torbay 6 were put straight into the sea and, of another 20 which attacked Frinton, 4 were brought to an untimely end. With 3 more destroyed, 1 probably destroyed, and 3 hit and damaged on the next three days the German air force had had enough and the attacks ceased completely.
>
> From first to last the guns had destroyed 56 aircraft with another 8 probably destroyed and 49 damaged, an overall casualty rate of 9.2%. During the last three months the German casualties from guns had risen to 15.7%, 9.9% having been destroyed or probably destroyed over the targets. To these losses must be added the casualties inflicted by … Fighter Command – an overall figure of 51 destroyed, 4 probably destroyed and 25 damaged over the whole period, and it will be clear, as it was to the Germans, that low altitude attacks on the coasts of England had been unmistakably defeated.[89]

The low-level radar referred to was the faithful Chain Home system which had proved so valuable in the Battle of Britain. Since the beginning of the war, it had been improved with Chain Home Low (CHL) and Chain Home Extra Low (CHEL) stations added to Chain Home High and it was the CHL and, especially, CHEL stations that were so important in defeating the tip-and-run raiders. Normally, their information was fed through RAF fighter group filter rooms, which meant a delay in it reaching AA GORs, but direct lines were laid from these stations to local LAA control centres so that the guns should have an immediate picture. Allied aircraft returning over the south coast were also directed to use safe 'lanes', to fly, as noted, above 1,000 feet and not to approach in line-astern, a favoured Luftwaffe tactic.[90] Pile ordered his Gunners to fire at anything below 500 feet, rather than the RAF's 1,000 feet, to allow for bad estimates; anything at such heights would be fired on automatically unless it had its undercarriage lowered as a distress signal. Unfortunately, in late October, LAA guns shot down a Beaufighter, with undercarriage lowered, at Rye.[91]

While AA Command had defeated both Baedeker and 'tip-and-run' raiders, the price for those successes, in redeploying guns, left thirty-nine gun defended areas (GDAs) and 236 vital points (VPs) in the Midlands and North of England without defences, which alarmed the Chiefs of Staff and illustrated, yet again, how limited were the resources available to the Command.[92] On the plus side, there had been a great improvement in Bofors production which allowed the increase to the 543 guns referred to by Brigadier Hughes. The further use of smaller calibre weapons, including Oerlikon and Hispano 20mm guns, was also a critical factor: some Gunners, including General R F E Whittaker, argued that these were more effective against tip-and-run raiders; they also needed less manpower with the Hispano being a one-man weapon.[93]

Brigadier Hughes' reference to Brigadier Lindsay of 2nd AA Group indicates that AA Command had been re-organised. Built on a typical army structure, with regiments assigned to brigades that, in turn, formed divisions, it included, between divisions and HQ AA Command, the AA Corps, formed in November 1940. HQ I AA Corps, at Uxbridge, had been responsible for southern England and much of Wales, while II Corps, with HQ in Nottingham, covered the Midlands and North plus north Wales, leaving Scotland and Northern Ireland to the Edinburgh-based III Corps. When the corps had been created, five new divisions and six new brigades were also added to the order of battle.[94]

By late 1942, Pile had decided that re-organisation was necessary to make best use of manpower, improve efficiency and provide greater operational flexibility, a decision that was, no doubt, influenced by the new Luftwaffe offensives. AA Command's new shape reflected its close alliance with Fighter Command through the adoption of the RAF group system which removed both divisional and corps levels of command. With six Fighter Command groups covering the UK, AA Command now followed the same pattern, although with one additional group: 1st AA Group covered the London area and was surrounded by 2nd AA Group covering the South-East and East Anglia; 3rd AA Group controlled the south-west and south Wales; 4th had the Lincolnshire–Yorkshire area; 5th the north-east and Scotland; and 7th Northern Ireland. Implemented in October 1942, this new structure remained until preparations for Operation OVERLORD in early 1944 required modifications; later, the V1 campaign of 1944–5 called for further drastic revisions of gun defences and consequent restructuring of the Command.[95]

This re-organisation prompted one battery commander to confide to his diary that 'Pile is self-critical enough to do an enormous redeployment. He has cut out the Corps altogether and formed … Groups to conform to RAF boundaries.

A senior Civil Servant is said to [have] congratulated him on having got rid of nine generals'. The same civil servant added that it would have been better still if Pile had also been able to get rid of an equal number of politicians. [96]

For a time Pile's principal problems were in manpower, especially as planning went ahead for the liberation of Europe and personnel were transferred to field armies.

> From time to time the Chiefs of Staff used to lay down minimum scales of defence which were always just out of reach. First, shortage of equipment had been our trouble, now it was shortage of men. The situation had gone from bad to worse. We had provided practically all the AA regiments for overseas: we had had none sent back to us. Except for a small number of Regular regiments which were already overseas when war broke out and those infantry battalions converted to an AA role, every British AA unit in every theatre of war had come from AA Command, either in the form of complete units or as cadres. We had sent 170 regiments overseas. We were the AA nursery for the British Army, and this role had cost us the cream of our manpower.[97]

Even the use of ATS personnel could not solve the manpower problem since, by June 1942, the supply of ATS had dried up and some planned mixed units had to be forgone. In July 1942 AA Command was cut from 280,000 to 264,000 men – with 170,000 ATS – but 58,000 of those were assigned to the field armies and, involved heavily in training for that role, unavailable to the Command. Then, in October, Churchill proposed cutting the Command to 180,000 men and 76,000 women. It was then that the Home Guard began providing significant assistance. The latest cuts meant that it was possible only to man 2,400 heavy and 1,700 light guns, which could be achieved only by reducing the number of searchlight regiments. Thus it became impossible for Pile to implement his scheme for ATS-manned searchlight regiments and only one – 93rd (Mixed) SL Regiment – was formed.[98]

The Ministry of Labour directed men into AA Home Guard units as there was a shortage of Home Guardsmen for AA Command. Initially there was friction between newcomers and established personnel but 'the queer mixture of soldier and civilian succeeded' in the long term. Some drafted personnel were of little use, being men 'who were doing nothing else, and who in many cases were determined to continue to do nothing else'. Many never turned up for duties or were so poor in attending that the annual wastage rate was so high that numbers could be maintained only by transferring personnel from Home Guard ground defence units.[99]

This personnel problem persisted until almost the end of the war, although it was alleviated to some extent by the arrival of American AA units which deployed in the air defence of Britain, the first element to do so being 54 Anti-Aircraft Brigade. That brigade fired its first shots against the Luftwaffe on 15 January 1944; two weeks later an American battery at Stansted in Essex claimed a 'probable'.

Fourteen US AA battalions deployed with ADGB in that month, totalling some 10,500 personnel but their numbers declined from then until June when they had all left the UK; they had been in action fifty-three times.[100]

The reduction in Luftwaffe strength and its inability to mount a sustained bombing campaign against Britain was used by the War Office to reduce further AA Command. Britain was, said the Chiefs of Staff, over-defended in some areas, especially in the north, which now faced very little threat. Pile had told them that, if he could have the units assigned to the field force back, he could accept a cut of 35,000 men. Those units were not returned but the Chiefs of Staff went ahead with a preliminary redeployment of 17,500 men from the Command. It was felt that, even though the Germans were experimenting with pilotless aircraft, there would be sufficient manpower to meet any threat.[101]

Since 1942 there had intelligence reports of German experimentation with pilotless aircraft and, in a speech at the Mansion House in November 1943, Churchill hinted at the expected use of new enemy weaponry. In December AA Command was told to expect the arrival of pilotless aircraft at the rate of about 200 an hour. Although Churchill's principal scientific adviser, Professor Lindemann, later Lord Cherwell, thought this, and other German secret weapons, to be a hoax, AA Command began planning to meet the threat.[102] However, before the pilotless aircraft, better known as the V1s, appeared, there was another brief campaign against manned Luftwaffe aircraft. This was a night-time repeat of the 'tip-and-run-raids, again using fighter-bombers, dubbed 'scalded cat' raids by the press.

Although the intruders gained an early advantage by coming in low and fast under cover of darkness, it was not long before AA Command had their measure. Tactics were again refined and co-operation with Fighter Command, now under Air Marshal Roderic Hill, improved even more. Control of searchlights was handed over to the RAF and individual gunsites began directing the fire of their guns rather than relying on information from the Gun Operations Rooms. After a particularly heavy raid on London on 7/8 October, Pile held a conference of gunsite officers, as he had done in 1940. It was clear that they wanted more information about height, direction and identification of approaching enemy aircraft.

New equipment was coming into use in the form of GL Mk III, which was more sophisticated and accurate than previous gun-laying radars. This proved invaluable when the Luftwaffe adopted the RAF tactic of using 'Window' – dropping strips of metallic foil – to confuse the radar. In doing so, Luftwaffe fighter-bombers acted as pathfinders to Junkers Ju88 bombers. 'Window' did not affect GL III although it caused interference on older radars, many of which were still in service.

> But the ATS operators stood up to it marvellously: they worked with the utmost determination, and, in spite of all their difficulties, managed to defeat the enemy's

> object by keeping their instruments working. Less than 25 per cent of the attackers ever got inside the London defences.[103]

It seemed that the Luftwaffe might be building up to a major raid. This proved to be the case when some 200 bombers in two waves, the biggest effort in almost three years, attacked London on 21/22 January. The first wave came in with returning RAF bombers, dropping 'Window' while crossing the coast. Unknown to the Luftwaffe, they had another unexpected factor assisting them: this was the night chosen for a major AA exercise involving large numbers of British bombers. Even so, the defences coped. 'Window' affected the Ground Control Indicator stations but not the GL sets and searchlights were only affected slightly. A heavy barrage was fired, aided by the new automatic fuse-setters, which increased the rate of fire, and most bombers turned away. No more than a fifth of the force reached London, whose gun defences fired over half the 33,824 heavy rounds discharged that night. Guns destroyed eight raiders with a further eight brought down by fighters, half of those following searchlight-aided interceptions. In another raid at the end of the month, about one in three of some 130 bombers reached London and about fifty incendiaries fell around a radar set on a gunsite in the Thames estuary. Although surrounded by flames, the ATS operators continued at their task. Lance Corporal G C Golland, in charge of the set, was awarded the British Empire Medal for her courageous example that night.[104]

Once again the Luftwaffe had been defeated and AA Command had shown its adaptability. GL III had proved invaluable but an even better system was in train with American BTL electrical predictors becoming available; some were being installed on gunsites by REME technicians while the raids were going on. REME also converted manually-operated GL III sets to automatic working and the combination of these and BTL predictors led to a great improvement in gunnery. Even greater improvements would come as the guns faced the flying-bomb campaign.

On 13 June 1944, D-Day+7, as the Allied bridgehead in Normandy was expanding, AA Command faced a new enemy weapon. In the early hours of that day, Pile was 'awakened by an unusual uncertainty on the part of our local air-raid siren'. Almost as soon as an 'Alert' signal had ended, it was followed by an 'All Clear' and then another 'Alert'. When Pile's phone rang not long after this he learned that 'Diver had at last arrived'.[105]

Diver was the codename for the first of Hitler's secret, or vengeance, weapons, the V1 (*Vergeltungswaffe* 1) flying bomb. This had been expected for some time and the threat of a V-weapons offensive had been codenamed CROSSBOW. The V1 was a pilotless aircraft, the Fieseler Fi103, which had been in development for some time. It was not a precision weapon but could be used for area bombing. A simple airframe with short straight wings, fitted with a single pulse-jet engine mounted above the fuselage, it carried a 1,870lb warhead. Flying at just under 400mph, it was controlled by a gyrocompass-based autopilot with a nose-mounted vane anemometer determining when it had reached its target area. A countdown timer linked to the anemometer began the final dive sequence which had been intended to be a powered dive, attaining an impact speed of almost 500mph. However, the effect of tipping into the dive cut off the fuel supply and hence the popular memory that the engine stopped before the V1 dived. In time, this problem was solved and later V1s dived under full power as intended.[106]

That first attack by flying bombs included seven weapons, one of which reached London where it plunged into a railway viaduct, blocking the lines from Liverpool Street station. At first the public were allowed to believe that this was a conventional aircraft shot down by the defences, which may have been partially true as the fuse of a heavy AA shell was discovered in the wreckage. Less than an hour after this first group of V1s, another thirteen were plotted, followed by a further pair which seemed to have come from the Cotentin peninsula.[107]

Initial reaction in AA Command was cautious. Intelligence had assured Pile and his staff that they would have up to a month's warning to prepare for the flying-bombs' arrival. These had come without any such warning, leading to the conclusion that this was a German final fling, 'an attempt to test the possibilities of the flying-bomb before the War was ended'.[108] This proved a very mistaken conclusion as the arrival of even more V1s on the night of 15/16 June proved. It was time to implement the measures planned to deal with the flying-bombs.

AA Command had estimated that redeployment to meet the V1s would take eighteen days. It was accomplished in one day, a remarkable tribute to the quality of Pile's staff and the efficiency of the units involved. Forty batteries, with 192 heavy and 192 light AA weapons, carried out the initial redeployment which, by the end of June, had increased to 376 heavy and 576 40mm guns. These guns were placed in 'Diver Belt', from East Grinstead to Maidstone, under the flight path of the V1s from the Pas de Calais to London. There were also 560 RAF Regiment light AA guns along the south coast.[109]

Flying bombs that reached London posed a difficult problem. If guns hit a V1 causing it to explode in mid-air the menace from that bomb was reduced, although falling fragments could cause damage. However, if a shell or shells hit a bomb without exploding it then the V1 would plunge immediately to earth and the AA Gunners would have done the Germans' job for them. Once this was appreciated it was decided to restrict the London guns which led, inevitably, to claims from the public, and many public representatives, that the guns were doing nothing. Questions were even raised in the House of Commons on 13 July, a month to the day after the first V1s landed.[110]

At this stage the Gunners' contribution to the battle of the V1s was, in Pile's own words, 'not very impressive'. It became essential to maintain secrecy so that the Germans would not learn the extent of the strain on British resources, nor that areas north of London were open to attack. Although the V1s posed a theoretically ideal target for AA guns, by flying at a steady speed, at constant height and in a straight line, Pile reckoned that his guns were shooting down only about 13 per cent. In fact, the Germans were sending their missiles over at a height that presented the greatest difficulties for the guns: just too high for effective engagement by light guns and too low for the heavies.[111]

But there was an answer to this problem. Pile had already asked for the new American SCR 584 gun-laying radar but none had been delivered so far. Coupled with the electrical predictor, SCR 584 would provide 'a robot defence against the robot weapon' with no manual operation either at the radar set or predictor once the target had been picked up. With the guns also remotely controlled the entire operation was automatic.[112] In the meantime further redeployments, aimed at obtaining the best possible results from the radar sets, were tried although this was complicated by RAF Balloon Command's decision to redeploy their balloon barrage. With ground and air defences overlapping, there was a need for a re-appraisal. It was then that Churchill took a direct hand and called a series of conferences, held every second night, at which he cross-examined those involved on what they were doing and what they intended to do.[113]

The redeployment had also presented a major engineering problem. Since the static 3.7 was better suited to engaging the V1s, as it had a smoother traverse than the mobile equipment, fixed gun positions had to be prepared. Previously, this had been a lengthy procedure as the gun was bolted into a concrete platform, the creation of which had been time-consuming. There was no time to build such platforms but Pile's technical staff provided a solution. Brigadier John Burls, AA Command's Deputy Director Mechanical Engineering (DDME), designed what became known as the 'Pile platform', a lattice of steel rails and railway sleepers. Filled with ballast, a Pile platform was as steady a gun platform as concrete and had the great advantage of being movable.[114]

In spite of what Pile regarded as an uncertain start, it was not long before the guns were exacting a heavy toll of the robot bombers. Once they were given first priority in engaging the V1s, AA Command's detachments demonstrated their effectiveness in spite of being worked harder than at any time in the past. In their first week of operations in the new deployment, guns destroyed seventeen per cent of all missiles entering the gun area, a proportion that increased to fifty-five per cent by the fifth week. Although gun detachments were often called on to man their guns twenty-four hours per day, their kill rate continued rising. By 23 August the guns were claiming sixty per cent of targets shot down which increased to seventy-four per cent by 1 September. On one night alone, eighty-two per cent of V1s fell to the guns. Of those that escaped the guns, many were destroyed by fighters which were often guided on to their targets by searchlights of AA Command.[115]

With 21 Army Group breaking out of Normandy and overrunning the launch sites in the Pas de Calais, the first phase of the V1 campaign was brought to an end. Since 13 June the guns had brought down over 1,550 V1s with searchlights helping fighters shoot down a further 142.[116] Churchill signalled Pile to congratulate his Gunners on the 'brilliant work of the anti-aircraft batteries which has more than borne out what we did hope for them'.[117] However, that 'brilliant work' was not made public. As far as the average British civilian knew, the V1s had been shot down by aircraft of the RAF. No radio news bulletin or newspaper article ever told the public that AA guns had shot down even one V1 in those summer months. There was, of course, a sound reason for this. Had the Germans been aware of the effectiveness of the AA guns they could have taken effective measures to combat the guns. As long as the Luftwaffe believed that fighters were the main cause of V1 losses then there would be no countermeasures aimed at the guns. Unfortunately, the long-term effect of this necessary ruse has been that there remains a public perception that fighters shot down most V1s.

It was not long before the V1 offensive was renewed with bombs coming in over the east coast. The first arrived on 6 September. In this new phase of the campaign, some V1s were launched from bombers over the sea. A redeployment of the defences was set in motion with guns removed from the southern Diver Belt into Diver Strip, which stretched from Diver Box, around the Thames estuary, northwards to Yarmouth and Lowestoft. Not only did the kill rate increase to eighty-two per cent by the end of November, but the average kill rate for the three months was sixty-five per cent while each V1 destroyed needed only 156 rounds of ammunition.[118] This latter achievement was due to the introduction of the VT fuse, an American development of a British invention. Often referred to as proximity fuses, these ensured that the shell burst close to the target. Pile recalled that it was the work of Mr B J Edwards, of Pye Radio, that produced the first valve 'small enough to go into a fuse and robust enough to stand up to the shock of discharge'.[119] It was the US Navy's development of this work that led to the VT fuse. Although often referred to as the 'variable time' fuse, the letters VT did not denote this at all but simply indicated that the fuse derived from the US Navy Bureau of Ordnance's Department V's Project T.[120] By the end of 1944, the VT fuse was also in use for field artillery and proved its effectiveness with US artillery in the Ardennes.

While AA Command was fighting the flying-bombs, it was yet again being used as a manpower pool for the field armies. Some 50,000 men were transferred to reinforce 21 Army Group on the continent while 23,000 ATS personnel were also taken and regiments were deployed to Belgium to counter the V1s being launched against Antwerp. Thus other areas of the UK had to be stripped of guns to maintain the Diver defences which were extended even further by the establishment of Diver Fringe from Skegness to Whitby. However, Diver Fringe was set up only in skeletal form as the V1 menace seemed to be all but over. In the closing months of 1944, Pile was asked to provide another 40,000 men for the mainland but, by that time, the battle against the V1s was nearing its end. It had been a battle in which AA Command had played the major part and which more than justified the tremendous resources invested in the Command during the war years.[121]

The war was not quite over. Although only a shadow of its former self, the Luftwaffe could still strike and did so on 3 March 1945 in Operation GISELA, the last major raid by enemy bombers on Britain. On this occasion, Luftwaffe fighter-bombers infiltrated RAF bombers returning from raids on Cologne and the Ruhr. It was impossible for the guns to engage as there was too much danger of shooting down RAF aircraft. Luftwaffe machines shot down twenty-four RAF bombers as they landed at their home bases and attacked airfields, roads and other targets with some even striking at London. Pile wrote that it 'was almost impossible to distinguish friend from foe in the confusion', on this most frustrating night for Gunners. Next night there were some more attacks but on a much reduced scale; some guns did fire on this occasion; 24 and 25 HAA Batteries engaged enemy aircraft with a total of eighty-eight rounds. These were the last significant operations by the Luftwaffe over Britain although there were at least three small raids later in March.[122]

March was also the month in which the last V1s landed in Britain; the final missile exploded in a sewage works near Hatfield, Hertfordshire on the 29th. This had been one of a salvo of twenty-one launched over a twelve-hour period from a site in The Netherlands; most had been shot down by AA Gunners on the coast or by fighters over the Channel.[123] But the V1 had been joined by a more sophisticated weapon, the V2, the world's first ballistic missile. V2s arrived with no warning since the weapons were supersonic and followed a ballistic trajectory. However, Pile and his scientists were not dismayed. They believed that they could create a defence against these weapons. Pile wrote

> But we were determined to have a crack at finding the answer, for we knew that, even if we failed to get a complete answer, our labours would help in the development of counter-measures in the future. It was some measure of the seriousness of the situation that Fighter Command agreed that if I could produce scientific data to support an outside chance of 100–1 against hitting any rocket my proposals might go forward to higher authority.[124]

A small party of Gunners and scientists was formed in December 1944 with the remit of producing a scheme to blow up the rockets in the air. They came up with a theoretical scheme that involved special radar stations and a sophisticated method of prediction. But the problems facing them included adapting radar sets designed to detect aircraft at heights up to 30,000 feet and ranges of about 30,000 yards to detect rockets at ten times those heights and almost five times the range. Much modification was needed, especially when it was found that the sets were picking up meteorites and were even having problems with the Milky Way.[125]

By February 1945 the team had come up with a new scheme that looked hopeful and, by mid-March, 'we were confident that we were within measurable distance of some considerable success'. Following over 25,000 complex calculations, it was believed that the rockets' point of impact could be predicted allowing AA guns to fire a barrage of shells in their path. But there were only two seconds in which to make that prediction and the guns had to fire when their targets were some thirty miles from the point of impact. Finally, all was ready to set up a trial but before permission could be obtained from the war cabinet Germany had surrendered. The V2 menace was over.[126]

Tim Pile retired from the Army in April 1945, just before the war ended in Europe. During his time as the head of Anti-Aircraft Command, he had taken it from being a makeshift defensive organisation to being one of the most effective elements of the Allied forces in the Second World War. His Gunners, male and female, had played a critical part in the defence of Britain. Some measure of that success was seen in the tally of 1,972 V1s shot down, 822 enemy aircraft destroyed, 237 probably destroyed and 422 damaged.[127] It was probably the most scientific of arms as shown by its defeat of the flying bombs and eagerness to take on the V2s. The story of the Command is very much the story of Tim Pile who was one of Britain's greatest and most successful commanders of the Second World War.

Notes

1 Frederick, *Lineage Book of British Land Forces*, p. 601
2 Ibid, pp. 613–7
3 Duncan, *RA Commemoration Book*, p. 487
4 Ibid
5 NA Kew, WO32/9758, 'Army Organisation: Royal Artillery'
6 Mead, *Gunners at War*, p. 20; Hogg, *British & American Artillery of World War II*, p. 193
7 Hogg, op cit, p. 193
8 Johnston, *Regimental Fire*, p. 20
9 Mead, op cit, pp. 20–1; Duncan, op cit, p. 47
10 Hogg, op cit, pp. 200–01; Mead, op cit, p. 21
11 Hogg, op cit, p. 172
12 Ibid, p. 170
13 Ibid
14 Duncan, op cit, p. 487
15 Doherty, *Ireland's Generals*, p. 94
16 Fraser, *Alanbrooke*, p. 123
17 Pile, *Ack-Ack*, p. 85
18 Ibid, p. 86. He gives the date for approving these numbers as 9 February 1939, although he quotes only heavy guns and searchlights.
19 Ibid, p. 106. ADGB was the Air Defence of Great Britain, the umbrella organisation for RAF Fighter and Balloon Commands as well as AA Command.
20 Ibid, p. 131
21 Ibid, pp. 87–8
22 Hogg, *Anti-Aircraft Artillery*, p. 70
23 Hogg, *Allied Artillery of World War Two*, pp. 106–7
24 Ibid, pp. 107
25 Ibid, pp. 108–10
26 Pile, op cit, p. 127
27 Duncan, op cit, p. 524
28 Hogg, op cit, p. 95
29 Reckitt, *Diary of Anti-Aircraft Defence*, p. 17; Hogg, *Allied Artillery of World War Two*, pp. 96–7

30 Doherty, *Wall of Steel*, p. 209
31 Routledge, *Anti-Aircraft Artillery 1914–1955*, p. 74
32 Pile, op cit, p. 111
33 Ibid, p. 217
34 Routledge, op cit, p. 395; NA Kew, WO32/9751, 'Mounting of AA equipment in towers in narrow waters'
35 Pile, op cit, p. 115
36 Dobinson, *AA Command*, p. 265
37 Quoted in Dobinson, *AA Command*, pp. 284–5
38 Pile, op cit, p. 137
39 Ibid, pp. 101–2; Routledge, op cit, p. 374
40 Routledge, op cit, p. 375; Pile, op cit, p. 103
41 Routledge, op cit, p. 375; Pile, op cit, p. 103
42 Routledge, op cit, p. 383
43 Reckitt, op cit, p. 18
44 Pile, op cit, pp. 132–3
45 Doherty, *Ireland's Generals*; Dobinson, op cit, p. 265 (in which the site is identified as ZS20); Pile, op cit, p. 169
46 Pile, op cit, p. 172
47 Ibid, pp. 172–3
48 Sqn Ldr D H Cooper DFC to author
49 Doherty, *Wall of Steel*, p. 112
50 Duncan, op cit, p. 524
51 Ministry of Information (MoI), *Roof over Britain*, p. 49
52 Duncan, op cit, p. 524
53 MoI, *Roof over Britain*, op cit, pp. 49–50
54 Pile, op cit, p. 159
55 Ibid, p. 165
56 MoI, *Roof Over Britain*, op cit, p. 22
57 Duncan, op cit, p. 524; Routledge, op cit, pp. 98–9
58 Duncan, op cit, p. 524
59 McCusker, *Castle Archdale and Fermanagh in World War II*, p. 32
60 Pile, op cit, p. 183
61 Doherty, *Ireland's Generals*, p. 99
62 Duncan, op cit, p. 526
63 Pile, op cit, p. 222
64 MoI, *Roof over Britain*, op cit, p. 58
65 Ibid, p. 58
66 Pile, op cit, p. 222
67 Ibid, p. 222
68 NA Kew, WO32/9752, 'Intake of women into ATS on SL duties'
69 From column 1047 of Hansard, quoted in NA Kew, WO32/9752, op cit
70 Mead, op cit, p. 25
71 Frederick, op cit, pp. 785–798
72 Ibid, p. 785
73 Mead, op cit, p. 24
74 Formed at Debden Manor, Hythe, Southampton on 16 February 1942 (Frederick, op cit, p. 788)
75 Mead, op cit, p. 25; www.cwgc.org.uk
76 Mead, op cit, p. 25
77 *The London Gazette*, 17 Dec '46, GC citation

[78] www.cwgc.org.uk
[79] Pile, op cit, p. 229
[80] Ibid, p. 231
[81] Quoted in ibid, p. 232
[82] Pile, op cit, pp. 232–3
[83] Ibid, p. 233
[84] Ibid, p. 236
[85] Ibid, p. 237
[86] Ibid, pp. 237–8
[87] Ibid, p. 238
[88] Ibid, pp. 238–9
[89] B P Hughes, quoted in Mead, op cit, pp. 26–7
[90] Routledge, op cit, p. 404
[91] Pile, op cit, p. 241
[92] Routledge, op cit, p. 404
[93] Pile, op cit, p. 241
[94] Dobinson, op cit, pp. 287–8
[95] Ibid, pp. 363–4
[96] Clark, *Five Years on Full Alert*, p. 53
[97] Pile, op cit, pp. 254–5
[98] Ibid, pp. 255–6
[99] Ibid, pp. 257–8
[100] Ibid, pp. 293 & 296
[101] Ibid, pp. 289–90
[102] Ibid, pp. 324–5
[103] Ibid, p. 304
[104] Ibid, p. 306
[105] Ibid, pp. 326–7
[106] Wood & Gunston, *Hitler's Luftwaffe*, p. 155
[107] Pile, op cit, p. 327
[108] Ibid, p. 327
[109] Ibid, pp. 327–8
[110] Ibid, pp. 328–9
[111] Ibid, p. 329
[112] Ibid, pp. 330–1
[113] Ibid, pp. 313–4
[114] Doherty, *Ireland's Generals*, p. 100
[115] Ibid, pp. 100–1
[116] Ibid, p. 101
[117] Pile, op cit, p. 344
[118] Doherty, op cit, p. 101
[119] Pile, op cit, p. 340
[120] Hogg, *British & American Artillery of World War 2*, p. 16
[121] Doherty, op cit, p. 191
[122] Doherty, *Wall of Steel*, pp. 175–6; NA Kew, WO166/16705, war diary 9 (L) HAA Regiment
[123] Doherty, op cit, p. 176
[124] Pile, op cit, p. 386
[125] Ibid, p. 387
[126] Ibid, pp. 387–8
[127] Ibid, p. 397

Chapter Five

War in North Africa

In September 1939 a small British force was stationed in Egypt to defend the Suez Canal and the Royal Navy base at Alexandria, HMS *Nile*, under the terms of the Anglo-Egyptian Treaty of 1936. Although the force was also involved in training the Royal Egyptian Army, and helping defend Egypt in time of war, no more than 10,000 British troops, plus auxiliary personnel, were permitted.[1]

When war broke out Egypt faced no immediate threat since Germany had no presence in the Mediterranean although its Axis partner, Italy, had a North African empire, including Libya, Egypt's western neighbour, Abyssinia, Eritrea and Italian Somaliland. Italy did not join Germany in military alliance in 1939 but the possibility remained that Italy's dictator, Benito Mussolini, would recognise the opportunity to expand the Italian empire by attacking Egypt, especially as Italy had a large navy with modern ships, including battleships. Mussolini had declared the Mediterranean to be *Mare Nostrum*, 'our sea' but his own short-sightedness had left the *Regia Marina* without aircraft carriers; according to *Il Duce*, Italy was a huge aircraft carrier dominating the Mediterranean.

With bases at Gibraltar and Malta as well as Alexandria, the Royal Navy appreciated the dangers posed by Italy. One of the first requests to the War Office for reinforcements for Egypt came from the Admiralty, seeking additional anti-aircraft guns for HMS *Nile*, which was already defended by a small force of Royal Marine AA gunners. That request led to the deployment of a heavy AA regiment from the UK with 9th AA Regiment detached from 3 AA Brigade in Northern Ireland to join the Alexandria defences. Arriving at the end of November 1939, the regiment took over gun positions from the Royal Marines and took 20 AA Battery under command. No one in 9th Regiment would have claimed that it was fully trained on arrival in Egypt but when war came to the region it was ready for action and in the succeeding years built an enviable reputation.[2]

On arrival in Alexandria, 9th AA Regiment encamped at Sidi Bishr on the city's eastern outskirts. The previous occupants, 7th Medium Regiment,[3] had been part of the pre-war force in Egypt: 25/26 Battery was equipped with 60-pounders and 27/28 Battery with 6-inch howitzers. Unfortunately, these still had wooden, iron-tyred wheels, thus reducing the unit's mobility.[4] Nonetheless, 7th Medium played a significant part in the campaign in North Africa, serving in Operation COMPASS in December 1940 before deploying to Greece for the ill-fated campaign there, at the end of which the Regiment had to destroy all its equipment before being evacuated to Crete. Eventually evacuated from Crete, 7th Medium arrived back in Alexandria to be given accommodation by 9th (Londonderry) HAA Regiment. The Regiment's meanderings continued with service in Syria against the Vichy French and then in Libya during Operation CRUSADER.

The units in Egypt concentrated on training until 10 June 1940 when Italy declared war on Britain and France. Since Italian military commanders were more sanguine about the preparedness of their forces than was Mussolini, there was no immediate invasion of Egypt, although *Il Duce* pressed Marshal Balbo, Libya's governor, to attack. When Balbo was killed at the end of June he was succeeded by Marshal Rodolfo Graziani who was also reluctant to show aggression. Not until 13 September did Tenth Italian Army, under General Italo Gariboldi, cross the frontier. It then stopped at Sidi Barrani and dug in.[5]

Italian armies were much less mobile than their British counterparts and Tenth Army was no exception.[6] By digging in around Sidi Barrani, Gariboldi created a tempting target for the British who, although numerically weaker, had much greater mobility. General Wavell, the Commander-in-Chief, Middle East, resolved to evict the Italian army from Egypt and Western Desert Force, under Lieutenant General Richard O'Connor, was ordered to undertake that task. Western Desert Force, including 7th Armoured and 4th Indian Divisions, began preparations for Operation COMPASS, intended as a raid in force and scheduled to begin in early December.[7]

Western Desert Force included seven Gunner regiments in its corps troops: 1st and 104th (Essex Yeomanry) Regiments Royal Horse Artillery, 51st Field Regiment (Westmoreland and Cumberland Yeomanry), all with 25-pounders, 7th Medium Regiment with 6-inch howitzers and 60-pounder guns, 64th Medium Regiment with 4.5-inch guns, 37th Light AA Regiment with Bofors 40mm guns and 6th Survey Regiment. Two batteries of 2nd HAA Regiment were also available: 1 LAA and 16 HAA Batteries.[8] In 7th Armoured the divisional artillery included 3rd Regiment RHA, less J Battery, with 2-pounder anti-tank guns, 106th (Lancashire Yeomanry) Regiment RHA with a mix of Bofors 37mm anti-tank guns and 20mm Breda anti-aircraft guns, and 4th Regiment RHA with 25-pounders; 4th Indian Division disposed three field regiments – 1st, 25th and 31st – each with 25-pounders – and J Battery from 3 RHA with 2-pounders. The latter division was commanded by Major General Noel Beresford-Peirse, a Gunner, and its artillery was trained to a fine pitch, although 25th Field Regiment had joined only days earlier.[9]

Operation COMPASS was launched on the night of 8/9 December; the corps artillery opened fire at 8.00am on the 9th, preparing the way for an attack by Matilda tanks of 7th Royal Tanks. The fireplan, involving 4th Indian's three field regiments and 7th Medium, was completely successful, in spite of some command and control difficulties. For the Gunners the task was 'to demoralise and neutralise the defenders and cover the tanks on to their objectives with their new 25-pounders'.[10] Air observation was provided from Lysanders, flying with fighter escorts. Fifteen minutes was allowed for registration before, at 7.30am, the guns fired concentrations on Nibeiwa fort on the south-east of the Italian positions at the same time as 7th Royal Tanks and two infantry battalions, supported by 31 Field Battery, attacked the north-west corner. The guns of 31 Battery deployed to fire at close range at the last pockets of opposition and by 10.30am the battle for Nibeiwa was over.

It was a similar story at Tummar West where 5 Indian Brigade, supported by 25th Field less 31 Battery, continued the attack. At 11.00am 7th Royal Tanks joined 5 Brigade and the Gunners began registering, in spite of a sandstorm. At 1.00pm the attack was launched and although the Italian artillery showed tremendous courage the battle was over in three hours, allowing the attackers to switch attention to Tummar East which was finally mopped up next morning. C Battery 4 RHA had also fought a brisk engagement with Italian gunners near Sidi Salim where the battery had come under accurate fire while crossing a broad wadi. B Troop covered the Battery's withdrawal and, firing at 4,500 yards over open sights, suffered several casualties.

> [O]ne gun was hit and a tracer [round] hit the ammunition which caught fire; expenditure and damage caused ammunition to run short. More was brought up and, with one section firing 'HE Rapid' and another smoke, the third got out to cover the other two. In one hour the troop fired 478 rounds ...[11]

During this action, eleven men were wounded, among them Sergeants Cooper and Jerrold and Gunner Rogers, whose conduct, in spite of injury, was described as exemplary.[12]

The next objective for Western Desert Force was Sidi Barrani itself which was isolated from possible Italian reinforcement. Both 1st and 31st Field Regiments supported 16 Brigade's advance and when Italian artillery was directed on the infantry, those two regiments, with 7th Medium, knocked out the enemy guns. Some of 7th Medium's equipments were showing their age with the trails of several 60-pounders developing cracks. While Sidi Barrani was attacked – an operation supported by 4th Indian Division's guns – several smaller objectives were also taken by 4 Armoured Brigade using not its own units but 3rd and 106th Regiments RHA with some light tanks. Although COMPASS had achieved its initial aim, O'Connor decided to pursue Tenth Army and deployed his armoured brigades on that task. Once again Gunner units were in support with 1 RHA joining 7th Support Group while 13th LAA Regiment came under command of 7th Armoured Division. On 15 December the Chestnut Troop A/E Battery was in action with 3rd Hussars at Fort Capuzzo while B/O Battery was approaching Bardia.[13]

The pursuit took Western Desert Force across the Cyrenaican bulge to engage the remnants of Tenth Army at Beda Fomm. However, 4th Indian Division was withdrawn to be sent to the Sudan, although 16 Brigade remained, and was relieved by 6th Australian Division under whose command were placed 104th Regiment RHA, 51st Field and F Battery RHA, in addition to the division's two Australian field regiments. As the Australians were to take Bardia they also had both 7th and 64th Medium Regiments under command and could call on 1 and 4 RHA from 7th Armoured Division, plus 3rd and 106th Anti-Tank Regiments RHA. In total the Australian commander had 120 guns, of O'Connor's 154 total. Royal Australian Artillery surveyors ensured a masterly fireplan and at 5.30am on 3 January 1941 the guns fired, without any previous registration, along a front of 800 yards. That fireplan played a major part in capturing Bardia, although it took three days' fighting in all. It will be noted that the artillery produced a heavy concentration of fire, probably the heaviest thus far in the war. Once more Italian gunners had shown superb courage and discipline and inflicted many casualties on their attackers. There were more cracked trails in the 60-pounders of 7th Medium, which also had eight 4.5-inch howitzers from 234 Battery 68th Medium Regiment under command.[14]

The pursuit of Tenth Army ended in early February when Combeforce, under Lieutenant Colonel J F B Combe, 11th Hussars, was despatched across the chord of the Cyrenaican bulge towards the coast road. Combeforce included two squadrons of Combe's own regiment, 1st King's Dragoon Guards, with armoured cars, and the Green Jackets of 2nd Rifle Brigade. Its Gunner strength came from C Battery 4 RHA, with 25-pounders, but only 160 rounds per gun, and nine 37mm Bofors anti-tank guns of 106 RHA (Lancashire Yeomanry), the latter carried portée; the Lancashire Yeomen also disposed a number of Breda 20mm anti-aircraft guns.[15]

Combeforce reached the coast road at about midday on 5 February to deploy near Sidi Saleh, south of Beda Fomm. Combe established a roadblock with anti-tank guns deployed to engage any Italian tanks that might venture down the road. The 25-pounders were also sited to good effect and engaged the first Italian vehicles to appear. Several uncoordinated Italian attacks were beaten back. Late in the afternoon, 4 Armoured Brigade appeared and was soon engaged. Before long 4 RHA's guns were down to thirty rounds each with no immediate resupply available. The battle continued into the following day with a thin British cordon around the Italians. Fortunately for the former, the Italians believed they were surrounded by much stronger forces which did their morale no good whatever. Nonetheless, many Italian soldiers continued fighting determinedly, few more so than their artillery men. Italian tanks crews also proved their valour in persistent attacks on the British positions.[16]

In the course of the battle an Italian 75mm field gun and a portée 37mm of 106 RHA fought a duel at a distance of a kilometre – each gun was beside a kilometre marker. No hits were scored on the portée but 106's Gunners put two 37mm rounds through the shield of the Italian gun at which point the Italian gunners decided to end the duel.[17] The 37mms of 106 RHA were also in action against Italian M13 tanks in their final effort to break through the British cordon. Firing while underway, which was not the common practice of the day, the Italian tanks took a heavy toll of the Bofors. For their part, 106 RHA's Gunners immobilised many of their tormentors but the Bofors were being knocked out one by one. Meanwhile, the Green Jackets of 2nd Rifle Brigade were overrun by Italian infantry and, to save the day, the 25-pounders of 4 RHA were asked to put down fire on the Rifle Brigade positions.[18]

Major R S Burton, the anti-tank battery commander, later wrote of the engagement.

> All our anti-tank guns did very well ... Sergeant Gould knocked out six tanks at extremely close range – he handled [his portée] very cleverly – getting some tanks in the rear as they ran down the road past his position.[19]

For his courage, Gould was awarded the Distinguished Conduct Medal. Major Burton also took a hand in the battle. With his batman and a cook, he took over a portée that had been damaged the day before and drove it to a position from which he could engage the Italian tanks from the flank. With five rounds he accounted for five M13s. Other tanks were knocked out by Green Jacket anti-tank rifles – emphasising the vulnerability of the Italian armour – and 25-pounders. The last M13 was stopped within yards of the officers' mess tent.[20] The Battle of Beda Fomm was over. Tenth Army had been destroyed. Western Desert Force, now renamed XIII Corps, expected to advance on Tripoli and bring the war in North Africa to an end. Instead it was ordered to remain in Cyrenaica while troops were pulled out for the abortive expeditionary force to Greece.[21] With the German Afrika Korps arriving in Tripoli in February, there would be many more battles to fight.

Among Western Desert Force's prizes was Tobruk, the port that was to become a valuable link in the logistical train of British forces in the desert war. With the despatch of the expeditionary force to Greece, XIII Corps, re-designated Cyrenaica Command, was stripped of troops. It was anticipated that it would be some time before the Axis forces would feel strong enough to attack in the region. Thus only a small force guarded Cyrenaica. However, Middle East Command had reckoned without Afrika Korps' commander, Major General Erwin Rommel. A veteran of the Great War, who had written a textbook on infantry warfare, Rommel had seen service in Poland and France, commanding, in the latter campaign, 7th Panzer Division which had earned the soubriquet the Ghost Division from its habit of appearing where it was least expected. Rommel had a keen eye for the battlefield and believed in taking risks. Although instructed not to take the offensive – his orders were to form a *Sperrverband*, or blocking force – he reconnoitred the front and became convinced that the British could be easy prey. An attack was a risk worth taking and Rommel decided that he would take it. Before long he had persuaded his immediate superior, General Gariboldi, to agree.

The resulting offensive, launched on 23 March, pushed the British back over all the ground gained only months before. By 10 April Rommel was at Tobruk but his attempt to 'bounce' the port failed and the siege of Tobruk had begun. The officer commanding the attack, General Heinrich von Prittwitz und Gaffron, was killed when an anti-tank round hit his car.[22] A storm of fire from 1st and 107th Regiments RHA had been one of the major contributors to the rebuff.[23]

Garrisoning the port was 9th Australian Division under Major General Leslie Morshead – 'Ming the Merciless' to his men. Also present was 3 Armoured Brigade, from 2nd Armoured Division, with various groups of British and Indian soldiers who had made their way into Tobruk and whom Morshead integrated into his defensive plans. The Royal Navy had confirmed that Tobruk could be maintained and reinforcements came by sea while 107th Regiment RHA (South Notts Hussars) arrived just before Rommel, having crossed the desert from Egypt. This was but one of several Gunner regiments to serve in Tobruk and earn the soubriquet 'Rats of Tobruk' from Josef Goebbels' scoffing comment that they were trapped like rats in the fortress port.

Other Royal Artillery units included 3 RHA, with its anti-tank guns, 1 RHA, 104 RHA (Essex Yeomanry) and 51st Field, all with 18/25 or 25-pounders, as well as 4 AA Brigade with batteries from both 51st (London) and 89th HAA Regiments, RHQ 13th LAA Regiment and RHQ and detachments from the Royal Wiltshire Yeomanry Searchlight Regiment. Elements of both 13th and 14th (West Lothian Royal Scots) LAA Regiments were deployed in the perimeter area. The AA units had two dozen 3.7s, of which sixteen were mobile, although two were unserviceable, four Italian heavy AA guns – two 102mm and two 149mm – as well as eighteen 40mm guns, forty-two Italian 20mm guns and ten searchlights, of which two were Italian. There were also light machine guns and two gun-laying (GL) Mark I radar sets. In addition, there were a field regiment, an anti-tank regiment and a LAA regiment of Royal Australian Artillery as well as anti-tank companies in infantry battalions. Not least, there were also 'Mr Clarke's guns', a collection of captured Italian howitzers with plentiful ammunition for which RSM Arthur Leonard Clarke MBE DCM of 1 RHA devised sights and 'gradually developed such an effective organisation that [his guns] became an extremely important factor in the defence of [Tobruk]'.[24] RSM Clarke's detachments were inspired by his enthusiasm, leadership and bravery and their actions mirrored those qualities. Sadly, RSM Clarke was killed at El Alamein on 25 October 1942 and is buried in the Commonwealth War Graves Commission's cemetery there.[25]

Having failed to bounce Tobruk, Rommel made a determined attack on 13 April, Easter Day. This began with a heavy artillery bombardment at 5.00pm, followed an hour later by infantry and armour. Rommel was trying to bite out a bridgehead across the anti-tank ditch west of the El Adem road but met determined resistance from an Australian battalion and drew back. A renewed attack in the small hours of the morning created a bridgehead, allowing tanks to pass through northwards. But the Australian infantry did not budge and inflicted many casualties on the German infantry. As the tanks moved on in the grey light before dawn they were engaged by the 2-pounders of M Battery 3 RHA and veered off to seek an easier way through, but not before several had been knocked out or disabled. They then came on A and E Troops 1 RHA with 25-pounders.

> Peter Hemans, commanding A/E Battery, ordered 'Tank Alert', but although we could hear the rumbling of tanks it seemed an age before anything happened. At last six black objects huddled together in groups of three appeared to the right front of the Troop. It was still very dark and difficult to judge the range, but we set our sights at 400 and opened fire.
>
> The first shot from No. 1 gun set the leading tank on fire. No. 2's first round lifted the turret clean off another tank – a good start, but we had stirred up a hornets' nest. Soon there were 15 or more tanks firing at us with 75mms and machine guns. We scored hit after hit, but I fancy we put a number of shells into tanks that were already dead. During this period two officers – the only officers with the guns – and four other ranks were hit. The tanks were now working round our right towards E Troop. Just as our No. 1 gun swung round to engage them, a 75mm shell landed on the trail, killing all the detachment and setting fire to a box of cartridges. At the same time a gun of E Troop received a direct hit on the shield, disabling the whole detachment. The Battery Sergeant-Major (Batten), although wounded, manned the gun himself and continued to fire.
>
> Nos. 2, 3 and 4 guns were in great heart, and every time a tank was hit a cheer went up. For perhaps half an hour the battle continued thus; then gradually the firing slackened till all was quiet. The surviving tanks had pulled back.[26]

Throughout Easter Monday and into Tuesday the attacks continued but made no impression on the defenders. The final attacks, on Wednesday, were also stopped. The pattern had been set for the siege which would last until November.

The Royal Navy kept its promise to supply Tobruk – and even effected a changeover of the garrison in September – although at a high cost in ships and men. Rommel may have thought that those within Tobruk were only waiting to be rounded up but the aggressive defence of the port became a major thorn in his side.

Rommel's advance took him into Egypt where, by the end of April, having taken Halfaya Pass and captured Sollum on the frontier, he had forced the British back to Mersa Matruh. However, Wavell was determined that Rommel would be repulsed and, on 15 May, launched Operation BREVITY. But Rommel had been bringing fresh troops up to the front and these ensured that BREVITY failed, although Halfaya Pass was again in British hands. British attempts to take

Fort Capuzzo were beaten off by well-sited defences which took a heavy toll of British tanks while a breakdown in communications clouded matters even more. Ten days later, Halfaya Pass was back in German hands, captured by a combined infantry/armour force despatched by Rommel. Fresh defences were then prepared, including 88mm guns dug in to leave only their barrels visible. Not for nothing did British troops rename the pass 'Hellfire Pass'.[27]

Winston Churchill, impatient for Wavell to knock Rommel out of Egypt, risked sending a convoy carrying tanks through the Mediterranean to Alexandria. Over 200 tanks were sent in this 'Tiger' convoy[28] and additional Hurricane fighters were also promised for the Middle East. Having provided this largesse, Churchill began prodding Wavell to attack and Operation BATTLEAXE was launched at dawn on 15 June. In spite of all the hopes invested in it, BATTLEAXE was a total failure with more than half the British tanks knocked out by the end of the day. At the end of three days' fighting, Wavell called off the operation, reporting to Churchill 'I regret to report the failure of BATTLEAXE.' XIII Corps' losses were heavy: almost 1,000 casualties, including 122 killed, were suffered, nearly a hundred tanks had been lost completely – others were recovered for repair – and the RAF had lost thirty-six aircraft.[29] Gunner losses had been low, with only four weapons lost but the Germans had demonstrated how to fight an all-arms battle. Those 88s dug in on Halfaya had taken a heavy toll of British tanks as their crews had pursued panzers into the trap presented by the 88s. German thinking was not that tanks should fight and destroy tanks but that anti-tank guns should do the destroying while the panzers dealt with enemy infantry.

The Gunner contribution to BATTLEAXE was 3 RHA, an anti-tank unit, 4 RHA, the former 106 RHA, now converted to 106th LAA Regiment (Lancashire Hussars), 1st, 8th, 25th and 31st Field Regiments and 27/28 Medium Battery. However, the guns were not concentrated but concentration might have compensated for their paucity of numbers for this operation. It seemed that some senior officers believed that since tanks carried guns they were self-sufficient in firepower; that belief ignored the fact that 'all battles are in the end some form of fire and movement and that firepower, not manoeuvre, comes first.' Although XIII Corps suffered heavily before being withdrawn, the Germans had also suffered to the extent that they were unfit for pursuit or any immediate further operations.[30] For the Gunners there had been one highlight of the battles on 16 June when 8th Panzer Regiment of 15th Panzer Division attacked Capuzzo at dawn, an attack met by 4 Armoured Brigade, supported by 31st Field's 25-pounders. The intense fire that met the panzers stopped the German attack. Later in the day, 8th and 31st Field, 'spread out in the open plain between Bir Nuh and Pt 207', provided sterling service that saved 22 Guards Brigade from being overrun, their boldness keeping the enemy at bay.[31]

During the battle, an OP party of 31st Field recovered from Fort Capuzzo a 25-pounder that had been lost to the enemy earlier. However, the BC of 116/118 Battery refused to have thirteen guns in his battery and the weapon was sent to the wagon lines. It was later brought into action when one of his guns was damaged badly by shellfire.[32]

The failures of BREVITY and BATTLEAXE cost Wavell his post as C-in-C, Middle East since Churchill assigned the blame to him. In an exchange of posts, Wavell moved to India to become C-in-C there while General Sir Claude Auchinleck, the C-in-C, India, moved to Cairo, assuming his new post on 7 July. Wavell had shouldered an exceptionally heavy burden during his time in Cairo: not only had he responsibility for the desert campaign but he also had to engage Italians in East Africa, Vichy French in Syria, Italians, and then Germans, in Greece and Germans again in Crete. He had worked wonders with stretched resources but had been unable to turn the Axis tide in Greece and North Africa, although he could look back on success in Syria, East Africa and Iraq, where a pro-Nazi coup had been defeated. In each campaign, the Royal Artillery had lived up to its motto. Even the campaign in Syria, largely an Australian affair, had included units of the Royal Regiment, in addition to the Royal Australian Artillery, with 1st and 4th Field Regiments as well as 57th LAA Regiment and an additional LAA troop taking part.[33] There, also, an Australian Gunner, Lieutenant Roden Cutler, 2/5th Field Artillery, gained a Victoria Cross.

The other successful campaign fought by Wavell's men had been in East Africa where there was a large Gunner element: 1st, 25th and 31st Field Regiments with 4th Indian Division; 4th, 28th and 144th Field Regiments with 5th Indian Division; 68th Medium Regiment, which deployed 212 Medium Battery of 64th Medium, 41 LAA Battery 15th (Isle of Man) LAA Regiment, and a detachment of P Anti-Tank Battery RHA.[34] This campaign was fought to liberate Ethiopia, now Abyssinia, against determined and very professional Italian troops. Nowhere was that determination better demonstrated than at the two battles of Keren.

In the first battle, in early February, the Gunners had a very difficult task in mountainous terrain. Their positions in the valley below the Italian fortress meant that 'every shot was visible to the enemy and his counter-battery fire was accurate'. The steep ridges, their reverse slopes providing good cover for Italian guns and infantry, meant that the 25-pounders had to fire at very high angles, thus reducing their accuracy. Although some progress was made, an alternative approach had to be taken during which the infantry were caught 'between the strong enemy defences and the bare and fire-swept basin of the Happy Valley and were constantly shelled, mortared and dive-bombed'. What gains were made were lost to an Italian counter-attack and the attack was abandoned.[35]

The second battle for Keren opened at 7.00am, half an hour after sunrise on 15 March, with a ninety-minute bombardment by ninety-six guns on the mile of crests northwards from Mount Sanchil. Four squadrons of bombers – Blenheims, obsolescent Wellesleys and obsolete Hardys – had also made their contribution, bombing Italian positions along the Dongolaas Gorge and the rear areas. Then, from 10 o'clock until noon, the guns of 4th and 5th Indian Divisions fired continuously on the infantry's objectives. Although the defenders of Sanchil held firm, the Hog's Back, a mile away, was taken, thus allowing observation of the Keren valley, which permitted more effective counter-battery fire. Spirited defence and counter-attacks by Italian troops continued and it was not until the 25th that the British force broke through the gorge; Keren was entered two days later.[36]

This marked the beginning of the end of the campaign which was concluded in mid-May when the Duke of Aosta surrendered at Amba Alagi. Emperor Haile Selassie returned from exile in London, via Alexandria where he inspected a Royal Artillery guard of honour found by 9th (Londonderry) HAA Regiment en route to reclaiming his throne in Addis Abbaba. During the sixty-six days of the campaign, the Gunners provided effective support for their infantry comrades with 31st Field's historian noting how that effectiveness had been demonstrated: 'the hills were littered with dead, the houses in the town [Keren] were full of wounded'.[37]

The Italians had threatened the Anglo-Egyptian Sudan and there was even fear that the vital port of Aden might be attacked, especially after Italian troops overran British Somaliland in August 1940. Reinforcements despatched to the Sudan included 25 HAA Battery 9th (Londonderry) HAA Regiment from Alexandria. At first only two sections deployed to Port Sudan but the other two followed soon afterwards.[38] As the only HAA unit in the region the Gunners were kept busy fighting off Italian air raids on Port Sudan itself but also contributing a section to General Platt's force engaged in the liberation of Eritrea; this was G Section which was ordered to Kassala on the Sudan/Eritrea border where it saw no action but suffered intense heat of up to 152°F, flies and white ants.[39] The only Italian aircraft spotted turned out to be a Caproni 133 in RAF hands. F Section had been ordered to British Somaliland but was diverted to Aden where it seemed the presence of two 3.7s was sufficient to encourage any bombers to drop their bombs out at sea.[40] These detachments can probably permit 9th HAA Regiment to lay claim to the title of the most-widely dispersed regiment in the Royal Artillery.

Just as 25 Battery was preparing to return to Alexandria in April 1941, news was received that a flotilla of *Regia Marina* destroyers had sailed from Massawa to attack Port Sudan. G Section was deployed almost on the beach with B Section 23 HAA Battery, Hong Kong and Singapore RA and Wingate Battery, a coast defence unit, to engage Italian naval or air units; E, F and H Sections were ordered 'to engage any attacking aircraft or, in the event of a seaborne attack only, any naval targets on which they could bear'.[41] Their services were not needed. Early on 3 April, Fleet Air Arm Swordfish torpedo-bombers took off from Port Sudan to engage the attackers. Throughout the morning there was a shuttle of Swordfish, Blenheim and Wellesley aircraft taking off and heading out to sea from where many explosions could be heard. The destroyers had been intercepted by the planes and all six were sunk; many survivors were later landed at Port Sudan.[42]

Some of 9th HAA Regiment's men also took part in the Greek campaign. The Regiment had taken 20 HAA Battery under command and when this unit was ordered to Greece volunteers were sought from 24 and 26 HAA Batteries to strengthen 20 Battery which deployed with a dozen 3-inch guns.[43] Many of those volunteers were fated to spend the rest of the war as prisoners although some escaped from Greece and then Crete to rejoin their Regiment in Egypt. They were but a small part of the Gunner contingent that went to Greece which also included other heavy and light AA batteries, among them the batteries of 106th LAA Regiment RHA, now converted to the light ack-ack role with three dozen Breda 20mm guns. Both 7th and 64th Medium Regiments also went to Greece, as did several field and anti-tank regiments, both British and Australian.

The story of the Greek campaign is a sad one but the Gunners made a major contribution to the successful withdrawal and evacuation of so many British and Commonwealth troops from the country. Major C I W Seton-Watson MC, then a subaltern in H Troop 2 RHA, wrote of his experiences as H/I Battery provided fire support for Greek, British and Australian troops.

> About 3pm the pace quickened. We could see infantry retiring from the ridge to our right front, and a stream of vehicles moved back past our guns. The Rangers [9th King's Royal Rifle Corps] kept us busier than ever with targets. Then both they and the Australians were forced off the ridges overlooking the mouth of the [Veve] pass. One of these ridges showed over a feature immediately in front of us, and so, to discourage its use by the enemy as an OP, Sergeant Souter's gun registered it over open sights. But the Germans were pressing hard. At about 4.30pm the Colonel of the Rangers told us he had given his companies five minutes to get off the ridge immediately in front of our position. We hadn't had time to do more than give the order 'Prepare to withdraw' when a shower of white Very light success signals went up from the ridge in question and enemy infantry came over the top, about 600 yards away. Captain Scott Plummer ordered F and G sub-sections out of action while the other two guns took on the infantry over open sights, with himself in the layer's seat of H gun. It was not an easy position to get out of in a hurry, for the ground was thick in mud and slush. Rifle bullets were by now singing past our ears, and as Sergeant Panton brought his E sub-section out of action, a machine gun opened up somewhere from the left. At that moment the last rifle platoon were passing us. H sub-section went on firing till the rest of the Troop was out of sight, and for the moment this stopped the enemy's advance … Some minutes later, when the rest of the Troop was safely round the corner and down the road, H sub-section followed, with a few shells pursuing it harmlessly for the first half-mile. And then there was time to think what a narrow scrape it had been.[44]

Later, at Ptolemais, the regiment's guns were again fighting over open sights while the 2-pounder anti-tank guns of 104 RHA stopped a German tank attack, immobilising eight attackers. In three days' fighting, 2 RHA fired 3,100 rounds and suffered only two men wounded. Meanwhile 64th Medium had also been busy. Withdrawing to Servia on 12 April a gun tractor and gun were lost when the road collapsed under its weight. Recovery efforts were abandoned due to German shelling of the road and the gun was destroyed by Captain McClure.[45]

And so it continued with Gunners fighting hard along the weary roads that led to evacuation for many but captivity for others. Churchill authorised evacuation to Crete but stressed that that island should be held in force. On St George's Day, 2 RHA received orders to evacuate and, next day, arrived at Vaya where some enemy attacks were beaten off, including an armoured thrust; there was also constant air attack. H/I Battery destroyed its guns and, with RHQ and B Echelon, embarked on HMV *Glengyle*. L/N Battery deployed to cover the beaches at Marathon but was picked up late on the 26th. Alexandria was reached on 29 April and the personnel of the regiment, 352 in all, were encamped alongside 102nd LAA/Anti-Tank Regiment RHA and 149th (Lancashire Yeomanry) Army Field Regiment[46] in the Canal Zone by May Day.

The story of the brief campaign on Crete is well known although the part played by Gunners is probably not so familiar. Once again it was a case of the Royal Regiment living up to its motto and performing its duty. Around Maleme airfield, where German paratroopers and gliderborne troops were landing, 156 LAA Battery had deployed its Bofors on high ground to obtain all-round fields of fire.

> The battle raged furiously, the Gunners firing for all they were worth, including their few small arms, but the toll was heavy and casualties high. Soon a heavy pall of dust and smoke hung thickly over the area as the guns and machine guns fired at the attacking aircraft which flew ultra-low and in large numbers to confuse and swamp the defences. Next, gliders were seen swooping down to the west of Maleme and on each side of Canea. Then came the parachute troops en masse. The enemy dominated the skies. The guns were saturated with targets but kept on firing, many parachutists fell on top of the defences and many were killed.[47]

A troop of 234 HAA Battery was overwhelmed when enemy troops landed on their gunsite early on 20 May, although, later in the day, the site was recaptured. German troops also landed close to 151 LAA Battery's positions and 156 LAA Battery's HQ. The AA guns remained in action and shot down 'very considerable' numbers of enemy aircraft although no accurate log was maintained. Next day the assault continued despite the many transport planes that were being shot down. So furious was the fire of the AA guns that 'many 3.7-inch barrels burst through [the] strain of excessive firing'. But the AA Gunners also had to deal with infantry attacks, as with 234 HAA Battery which lost its BC, Major L Hakins, captured among the 245 casualties sustained by the battery, of whom thirty-seven were killed in action. Only twenty-nine Gunners of 234 Battery returned to Egypt.[48]

The battle for Crete lasted over a week with some Gunners, such as those of the much-travelled 7th Medium Regiment, serving as infantry. In spite of their heavy losses, the Germans gained the upper hand and British forces on the island were fighting a losing battle. Once again, evacuation proved necessary and, once again, the Royal Navy played a valiant role in rescuing so many from Crete. On 28 May, 7th Medium, then fighting as infantry at Heraklion with 14 Brigade, was ordered to embark that night. Moving to the docks the Regiment boarded destroyers and cruisers which took them, in spite of the Luftwaffe's worst efforts, to Alexandria, where their old friends of 9th HAA provided accommodation for them.[49]

Losses in Greece and Crete were many, both of personnel and equipments. Every effort was made to replace those losses but these were still felt throughout the Middle East. In some cases equipments were provided from other regiments to make good the losses of recent campaigns as with 64th Medium Regiment, reborn in Egypt in June with eight 6-inch howitzers from 68th Medium Regiment.[50] Although Allied losses were heavy, the Germans had also lost heavily in men and equipment. Such were the losses on Crete that Hitler never authorised another airborne assault, which may well have saved Malta from similar attack. Likewise, the time spent by German forces in Greece and Crete delayed the launch of the invasion of Russia from March until late June and thereby probably contributed to the failure to take Moscow that year and eventual German defeat in Russia.

Of the honour titles awarded to Gunner batteries during the Second World War, two were for actions in the desert war, including one which also resulted in a posthumous Victoria Cross for a young Royal Horse Artillery officer. The honours were to J Battery 3 RHA, which earned its title at Sidi Rezegh, where Second Lieutenant Ward Gunn also earned his posthumous VC, and 105/119 Field Battery 31st Field Regiment, honoured for its distinguished service at Alam Hamza. Sidi Rezegh also brought the Gunners another Victoria Cross, to Brigadier Jock Campbell, commander of 7th Armoured Division's Support Group.

Both battles took place during Operation CRUSADER, launched by the newly formed Eighth Army on 18 November 1941. This operation led to a series of clashes that represent some of the most complicated fighting of the war. One of the principal objectives was to relieve Tobruk, to which end it was planned to capture the area around Sidi Rezegh, with its airfield, since this was close enough for the Tobruk garrison to break out and link up with the attacking force. On the 18th and 19th, Eighth Army moved forward until, by the evening of the 19th, 7 Armoured Brigade had reached Sidi Rezegh. At that stage Support Group of 7th Armoured Division was to relieve the Brigade and effect a junction with the troops from Tobruk.

No plan survives first contact and this was no exception. When 7 Armoured moved on Sidi Rezegh its action provoked strong reaction from the German 90th Light Division which counter-attacked. The target of the German attack was 7 Support Group which retaliated with an attack of its own. Although initially successful, this was brought to a standstill by anti-tank guns. The situation became more serious as 15th and 21st Panzer Divisions were brought in from the Axis left flank and assaulted the defenders of Sidi Rezegh on their eastern flank.

There followed a battle in which tremendous courage was shown on both sides, many gallantry awards were earned and during which J Battery RHA gained its honour title. Four portée 2-pounder guns of the Battery, under Second Lieutenant Ward Gunn, were supporting 2nd Rifle Brigade when sixteen Panzers attacked the battalion's Support Company. Although the first German assault was beaten off, with several tanks damaged, it was obvious that another would follow. Moreover, two 2-pounders had been knocked out. The next attack was met with every weapon that could be brought to bear, including 25-pounders from 4 RHA and 60th (North Midland) Field Regiment.

The Rifle Brigade's historian described what followed:

> The enemy tanks were now being engaged by the 25 pounders of the battery of 60th Field Regiment and some guns of 4th RHA which had come into action behind them. Apart from those, unsuitable but brilliantly fought, there were three weapons capable of taking on the enemy tanks – two 2 pounders on their unarmoured portees under Ward Gunn ... and one Bofors anti-aircraft gun commanded by Pat McSwiney. These three engaged the enemy as best they could, outranged and unarmoured as they were .... The small party round the [Rifle Brigade's] blazing pick-ups watched these three guns firing away at the enemy, watched the crews, completely composed, completely undaunted, picked off one by one. The enemy gave everything they had: machine-gun fire from the tanks and the supporting infantry, mortars, shells from the Mark IVs and the field guns. One 2-pounder was destroyed, the Bofors was set on fire. All the crew of the remaining gun were either killed or wounded, and the driver not unnaturally began to drive it out of the battle. Ward Gunn, at battalion headquarters, was joined at that moment by Bernard Pinney, the commander of M Battery. He said to Ward: 'Go and stop that blighter', and even then it seemed hard to be so described for driving a useless gun and dead crew out of action. Ward immediately ran out and stopped him and together they dragged the bodies off the portée and got the gun into action, Bernard Pinney joining in. No one could gauge the effect of his fire because to look over the edge of a slit trench was suicidal ... The Germans concentrated their fire on the one remaining gun. But at least the two nearest enemy tanks were blazing. In a matter of seconds the portée was on fire, the offside front wheel had been hit and the tyre was blazing; two boxes of ammunition held in brackets behind the passenger seat were also in flames. Pinney took the fire extinguisher and got the fire in the tyre under control; but the ammunition boxes continued to burn. Ward Gunn, who had kept on firing throughout, was hit in the forehead and died instantly. Pinney pushed his body out of the way and went on firing until further hits on the gun made it unusable.[51]

A correspondent to *The Gunner* pointed out that Ward Gunn was laying the gun but that Gunner Haverson, the driver, was the loader while Pinney was fighting the fire on the vehicle. When Gunn was killed both Pinney and Haverson 'continued to fight the gun until it was put out of action by a direct hit'.[52]

The Victoria Cross was awarded to Ward Gunn but not to Bernard Pinney, which seems strange as they had worked as a team. Pinney was later killed by an airburst.[53] Pat McSwiney, the Bofors commander, was awarded the Military Cross for his actions that day.[54] McSwiney, actually John Murray McSwiney but 'Pat' because he was Irish, belonged to 1st LAA Regiment and this was but one of many actions in which that Regiment distinguished itself.

As the CRUSADER battles raged on, an Allied counter-attack eventually forced an Axis withdrawal and Tobruk was relieved at last. It seemed as if the Axis forces were beaten as they began withdrawing from the battle area. Advancing northwards towards Alam Hamza* was 4th Indian Division with two brigades up with, on the right, 1st Buffs and C Squadron Central India Horse (CIH) supported by 105/119 Field Battery. Unknown to them, their column had penetrated the boundary between two Italian divisions. Worse still, they were also unaware that much of the two German armoured divisions – 15th and 21st Panzer – was on their left flank.

On 13 December the column reached Point 204, on the western end of Alam Hamza* ridge while the rest of 5 Indian Brigade attacked the eastern end. Since this was held strongly, the attack was beaten off, leaving 1st Buffs, CIH and 105/119 Battery in a tenuous position on the far end of the ridge. Next morning the column took up defensive positions with the 25-pounder troops deployed in the anti-tank role. It was not long before the Germans attacked, preceded by heavy shelling and dive-bombing. Their assaults lasted throughout the day, during which many panzers were accounted for. Then came a heavy artillery bombardment followed by an attack by some forty panzers and infantry. Several guns were knocked out as the enemy tanks advanced and D Troop was overrun. Attacked from both the south and west simultaneously, E Troop suffered the same fate. Although B Troop fought on it was quickly reduced to one 25-pounder. In some cases gun detachments had been down to two men who continued to serve their guns until killed or captured.

> This gallant action of 105/119 Field Battery exemplifies a fact which was of the greatest significance in the war in the Desert at that time. For, though it was not of course designed primarily for that purpose, the 25-pounder gun was the only weapon in the Allied armoury ... capable of defeating the German tanks. The skill, courage, and endurance of these 25-pounder batteries, their refusal to be beaten against any odds, and the toll that they took of the German tanks proved therefore to be the one really effective means of preventing the Axis forces from driving their way into Egypt.[55]

---

* The honour title was awarded as '*Alem* Hamza'.

The war diary of 31st Field Regiment summarises the action:

> 105/119 Battery were overrun and the enemy then turned his attention to the soft vehicles and personnel causing casualties to both with MG fire. B Troop continued to engage until … forced to evacuate the position and the order was given to withdraw. Three of B Troop's guns were limbered up but only one eventually got away. All vehicles and men that could, made their way back to Brigade HQ where they were … sorted out into a composite Battery to man 6 new guns that had just arrived, in case the tank attack was followed up. About one third of the Regiment was left after the action. 105/119 Battery suffered the most severe losses, only one officer and a small number of personnel returning. It is not known how many enemy tanks were knocked out, but that the enemy withdrew after this can be directly attributed to the Regiment's magnificent fight.[56]

Of course, 3 RHA and 31st Field were not the only Gunner regiments involved in the CRUSADER battles. In addition to 4 RHA, 60th (North Midland) Field and 1st LAA Regiments, were 25th Field, 65th Anti-Tank and 57th (King's Own Yorkshire LI) LAA Regiments, all of whom performed gallantly and left their foes with a grudging admiration for British Gunners. They had taken a heavy toll of the German tanks: 57th LAA Regiment destroyed or damaged twenty-two panzers in the period from November 1941 to March 1942, as well as destroying 130 enemy aircraft and damaging a further 301. In one action, while supporting 7 Indian Brigade in early December, a troop of the Regiment disabled sixteen enemy tanks. On 4 December, A Troop 3 Battery 1st LAA Regiment fought off seventeen Ju87 Stuka divebombers before engaging three Bf109s that were pursuing Hurricanes. Of these, five Stukas were seen to be on fire and at least one Bf109 was shot down. For its part, 25th Field was credited with saving 7 Indian Brigade from being overrun in a German attack when the Regiment's 25-pounders tackled the panzers at close range. Although 31/58 Battery was overwhelmed, its BC, Major William Lyell Newell, firing the last gun single-handedly to the end, 12/25 Battery still stood in the way of the attackers. (Newell had also rallied a group of infantrymen from 1st Royal Sussex and led them in a successful attack on their objective; he received an immediate DSO.)[57] On the left, 31 (Kirkee) Troop opened fire but the guns were knocked out. To the right, 58 (Maiwand) Troop waited to fire until the range was down to 500 yards. Two tanks were disabled quickly as the 25-pounders fired AP ammunition into them at ever shortening range; one gun was reckoned to have fired when 'a tank [was] only a few yards from its muzzle'. It was a desperate battle in which a 2-pounder troop of 65th Anti-Tank Regiment and a troop of 57th LAA Regiment also took part, together with a platoon of 7 Indian Brigade's anti-tank company. But, having overrun 31/58 Battery, the German tankmen were confronted with the eight fresh guns of 12/25 Battery which now engaged them.

> Such Bofors and 2-pdr portées as had survived the earlier fight, together with the Valentines, added to the fire from flank positions. The Germans continued to advance. Was 12/25 Battery to be overrun as well?'[58]

By now the strain on the Germans was approaching breaking point. With many of his tanks blazing, the German commander could afford to lose no more. The threat from 12/25 Battery's guns guaranteed that such losses were inevitable and so, deciding not to take on those eight 25-pounders in pitched battle, he turned away.[59] Behind them the Germans left fourteen tanks blazing but the price was high for 25th Field: seven officers and fifty-eight men were dead or wounded but their actions 'had saved 7 Brigade. The day was won, and next day the advance rolled westward again'.[60]

Let us now look at that other VC earned by a Gunner at Sidi Rezegh. Brigadier John Charles 'Jock' Campbell was commanding Support Group, 7th Armoured Division. The group's role was to provide artillery and infantry support to 7th Armoured Division which included 4 and 7 Armoured Brigades. Campbell's command included 3rd and 4th Regiments RHA, 1st LAA Regiment and two motor battalions: 1st King's Royal Rifle Corps and 2nd Rifle Brigade. The senior of the RHA regiments (Ward Gunn's unit) had been converted to the anti-tank role and its part in the battle has already been noted, as has that of 1st LAA Regiment.

With the British armour under severe pressure, Support Group HQ being shelled and enemy troops only 1,000 yards away, Campbell led 6th Royal Tank Regiment's surviving tanks in an attack on the Germans.

> ... riding in an open unarmoured staff car ... hanging on to its windscreen ... he shouted, 'There they come. Let them have it'. When the car began to fall behind, he leaped on to the side of a tank ... and directed the battle from there. He turned aside through the enemy barrage to his own twenty-five pounder guns and urged the men on to faster loading and quicker firing. He shouted to his gunners, 'How are you doing?' and was answered, 'Doing our best, sir.' He shouted back, grinning, 'Not good enough'.[61]
>
> Advanced HQ was still at the SE end of the LG with Battle HQ, 7 Support Group. The whole of this area then became a tank battleground. Our own and enemy tanks were engaging each other at short range, 25-pounders were firing over open sights and 2-pounders on Portees were being switched from place to place to meet the nearest threat. Fine work was done by the Gunners and great gallantry displayed. ... Brig Campbell ... was away performing the most brilliant deeds of gallantry leading various tank squadrons into battle, himself standing in his open staff car holding a blue flag in the air as a signal for them to follow.[62]

Such was Campbell's courage and inspiring leadership that he turned the tide of the battle around Sidi Rezegh. For this he was awarded the VC, the ribbon of which he later received from General Sir Claude Auchinleck. But he never lived to receive the

Cross itself: by then promoted to major general, and commanding 7th Armoured Division, Campbell died when his staff car crashed on 23 February 1942.

While Eighth Army prepared for the offensive to take the airfields in the Cyrenaican bulge and help relieve Malta, an attack was organised on an Axis airstrip at Martuba 'to divert Luftwaffe attention from a vital convoy sailing to relieve Malta'. This expedition, mounted by elements of 150 Brigade from their 'box' in the Gazala Line, included a company of infantry, 285 Field Battery, 171 LAA Battery and some Sappers. They were to make a night march of about thirty miles, behind enemy lines, and shell Martuba airfield. At first light the guns were in position and a scaffolding OP built for the BC but rocky ground prevented the digging of slit trenches. When 285 Battery's 25-pounders began shelling their target the enemy reacted violently and, before long, Luftwaffe aircraft appeared. At long range these were mistaken for RAF machines, as air support had been promised, but Lance Bombardier O H Perks, using a self-made monocular, identified them as the crank-winged Ju87s. Perks was wounded in the first bombing attack on his troop but the Stukas did not have it all their own way as the Bofors Gunners engaged them sharply and 'Several planes were shot down, others were damaged'.

> As the action continued barrels got so hot that there were prematures. Ammunition supply was difficult and hazardous. Tractors and trucks were shot up. Our casualties grew. One gun received a direct hit. Another was finally manned by the No. 1, a wounded Gunner, the BC and the Troop Commander.

The enemy attacks continued throughout the day, ceasing only at dusk and the raiding column slipped away under cover of darkness, the guns towed by the surviving roadworthy trucks. Eight of 171 Battery's nine Bofors were rescued and were soon back in action in the Gazala Line but almost half the LAA Gunners had been killed or wounded.[63]

Another light AA unit gained the unusual distinction of capturing intact a German aircraft. The unit was 6 LAA Battery which relieved 5 South African LAA Battery of the task of defending the Western Desert Railway at the end of March 1942. Equipped with captured Breda 20mm guns the battery's detachments were mounted on railway wagons and on portées to patrol the railway, which had been extended almost to Tobruk. All the Bredas were carried portée, including those on the railway flats. (These were disposed one at the front of the train, one in the centre with the engine and one at the rear.)

During April and May the battery fought off a number of attacks and at least one attacker, a Messerschmitt Bf109, was shot down. However, on the night of 28/29 May a road convoy of RIASC lorries was travelling alongside the railway when an explosion was heard. An officer went to investigate at much the same time as two portées of 6 LAA Battery arrived. Sergeants John Hunter and Alan Elliott, the detachment commanders, also went to investigate. What they found was an abandoned Fieseler Fi156 Storch with its engine ticking over. One of the NCOs switched off the engine and the battery claimed the Storch. However, the RAF had other ideas and the machine later became a 'hack' for the Desert Air Force commander. (It was still in service in Normandy in July 1944 as the personal plane of the commander of 2nd Tactical Air Force, Air Vice Marshal Harry Broadhurst.)

The Storch had been one of two carrying a sabotage party intent on blowing up the railway. Disturbed at their task it was believed that the Germans had made off in one of the machines, abandoning the other. Some damage was caused but this was soon repaired and a trainload of tanks for Eighth Army was delivered safely. This sabotage operation may have been part of Rommel's plans for the attack along the Gazala Line.[64]

Before Eighth Army could complete its preparations for an offensive, Rommel made his move. Launching a feint attack on the Gazala line, he wheeled armoured forces south into the desert to outflank Eighth Army. When his forces swept around Bir Hacheim, held tenaciously by Fighting French troops, they ran up against a British outpost at 'Knightsbridge'. Marked by a noticeboard bearing the name 'Knightsbridge' and its map reference – 37984118 – this was little more than the junction of two desert tracks on a small plateau on which there was also a shallow depression, no more than 600 yards square. 'Knightsbridge' had been garrisoned by a strong force including 2 RHA, with 25-pounders, C Battery 102nd Anti-Tank Regiment (Northumberland Hussars), under Major R I G Taylor, with recently-issued 6-pounder anti-tank guns – dubbed Roberts as a security cover[65] – and two troops of 43rd LAA Regiment, with Bofors 40mms.[66]

Rommel's first attacks, made by infantry with artillery support, were driven off by 2 RHA's 25-pounders while subsequent tank attacks were met and beaten off by the Northumberland Hussars' 6-pounders which proved very effective. Following this initial aggressive flurry, the Germans left 'Knightsbridge' alone save for some dive-bombing attacks. However, about five miles west-south-west was another much larger depression, some two miles by four in area. Into this depression Rommel's armour moved and to it was applied the description 'Cauldron'. Although the British minefield lay west of the Cauldron, between the German armour and their main force of artillery and infantry, Rommel's engineers quickly created gaps through the minefield to enable the armour to be refuelled and replenished with ammunition.

Recognising the danger of the Cauldron, Eighth Army's commander, Lieutenant General Neil Ritchie, planned to take the Cauldron and deployed 10 Indian Brigade to pass through the German anti-tank screen at night, with 22 Armoured Brigade then passing west of the Cauldron while the main body of 7th Armoured Division and 9 Indian Brigade destroyed the German armour within it. A heavy artillery bombardment was to support the first element of the operation. Unfortunately, the attacks were not co-ordinated properly. While 22 Armoured was to support 9 Indian Brigade's infantry, its orders made clear that its first priority was 'destroying the enemy's tanks' and infantry action 'was to depend on any armoured engagement that might occur'; the infantry were not to 'hamper the movement' of 22 Armoured.[67]

All went well at first as, on the night of 4/5 June, the attackers took their first objectives. Tragically, the main objectives were farther west than had been believed and had, therefore, not had to endure the main weight of the artillery bombardment. Thus 22 Armoured Brigade, which reached the western edge of the Cauldron by dawn, suffered heavy fire from enemy artillery as the new day broke. To this fire, the brigade's supporting 107th Regiment RHA (South Notts Hussars) replied with its 25-pounders, enabling 22 Armoured Brigade's tanks to move on to meet enemy armour farther west. Also with the brigade were Northumberland Hussars' 6-pounders.

With their OPs having a clear view of the enemy positions in the Cauldron, the South Notts' 25-pounders rained a heavy bombardment and caused many casualties. However, the infantry attack into the Cauldron met tough resistance and 2nd Highland Light Infantry had to withdraw after many losses. Elsewhere, 3/9th Jats, of 9 Indian Brigade, moved to assist 2/4th Gurkhas, both supported by 28th Field Regiment, in the north-east corner of the Cauldron. Meanwhile, south of the Cauldron, 4th Field was supporting 4/10th Baluchis while 157th Field was west of 4th Field and supporting 10 Brigade.

That evening 22 Armoured Brigade withdrew to refuel and refit. The tanks were to return to the fray next day but did not appear. It seems that they had been unable to locate their maintenance areas, such was the prevailing chaos. Command and control, inadequate to begin with as already noted, now seemed non-existent. During that night the Gunners took the opportunity to emplace their guns 'as well as possible, although all the batteries found themselves on hard rock [that was] very difficult to break up'.[68] Thus many guns were exposed when the enemy renewed the battle on the morning of 6 June. Concealed 88s began firing at the 25-pounders of 4 Battery 4th Field Regiment at 7.00am. The Battery soon began suffering casualties with two guns lost to direct hits and the battery commander wounded and evacuated, leaving the battery captain, Captain Melville Milner, in command. The Gunners had already been ordered to hold fire until German tanks came within 1,500 yards, the range at which the 25-pounder could kill a tank.

When the tanks appeared Milner ordered 'gun control', allowing each of the five surviving guns to choose its own targets when the panzers were at 1,500 yards. At the same time the concealed 88s were still sniping at the 25-pounder positions. It was a one-sided battle although 4 Battery managed to inflict considerable damage on the enemy before being overrun. By mid-morning the struggle was over. Elsewhere, 28th Field, 167th Field and the South Notts Hussars were having similar experiences. On the north side of the Cauldron, 28th Field was fighting desperately, as was 167th to the south-east. But the heaviest pressure was on the South Notts Hussars and their Northumberland Hussar comrades to the west.

Under command of Lieutenant Colonel E P A des Graz, of 50th Reconnaissance Battalion, this group had been in action since early morning. The first attack had seen ten crippled German tanks lying only a few hundred yards from the guns of the South Notts' 425 Battery. In their next attack the Germans overran a position to the Battery's left, exposing a flank. When Stukas arrived it became clear that the British position was surrounded. Shelling continued and casualties mounted. In one location three gun detachments had all become casualties although their 25-pounders were still intact. BSM James Hardy, who was killed later that day,[69] and a driver used a quad to tow the guns back 400 yards, a feat achieved under heavy machine-gun fire.

The Northumberland Hussars' anti-tank guns fired valiantly to protect the 25-pounders but all were eventually knocked out. As detachment members died or were wounded severely, other soldiers risked enemy fire to take their place so that drivers and signallers were often manning the guns. The Commanding Officer, Lieutenant Colonel William E Seely, provided example and inspiration to his Gunners as he drove around their positions in his Honey command tank. In the early afternoon he was at 426 Battery's command post when he spotted three lorryloads of German infantry appear over the escarpment about 1,000 yards from F Troop's positions. Fire was brought to bear on them by F Troop and 6-pounders of the Northumberlands as well as small-arms fire from the Recce men. The German attack was brought to a stop.

There could be but one end to this story. Attack after attack was launched by the Germans but still the South Notts' Gunners held out. By evening the Indian infantry had been overrun and still the guns defied the enemy armour. Then it was decided to move E Troop's guns to the rear and four quads drove up to hook up the guns for the move. They had not moved 200 yards before all four were hit by enemy shellfire. When Major Gerry Birkin, 520 Battery's commander, went to assess the situation BSM Hardy was killed as Birkin's armoured car was struck by a German AP shot. Before long, both 425 and 520 Batteries had been overrun. Gerry Birkin was also among the dead.[70]

Guns of 426 Battery were still firing as German tanks neared their positions. Even when the command post was overrun, F Troop managed to score two direct hits at 800 yards' range on enemy tanks. The troop commander, Captain Alan Chadburn, died later that day from wounds received during his Troop's gallant stand. Also among 107th Regiment's dead of that day was their gallant CO, Lieutenant Colonel Seely, killed with his driver when their Honey took a direct hit. In the final moments of the battle, the Gunners of 426 Battery destroyed their gun sights and made their 25-pounders inoperable. They could do no more. It was the end of their battle and the end of their regiment as they had known it. Although reinforcements were drafted in to join the survivors, they formed 107 Battery. Not until 1944 did the Regiment reform as 107th Medium Regiment.

The loss of all the Gunner units in the Cauldron prompted the official historian to comment that

> This day was both a splendid and a tragic episode in the history of the Royal Artillery, for the Gunners fought their guns to the last and died where they stood.[71]

Brigadier Raymond Briggs, commanding 2 Armoured Brigade, was impressed greatly with the support his formation received from 11th (HAC) Regiment RHA. He wrote to Lord Galway, Colonel Commandant of the Honourable Artillery Company, describing how the Regiment had fought continuously and 'magnificently' between 27 May and 15 June under Battery Commanders and Troop Leaders 'worthy of the best tradition of the RHA'.

> The determination to win was never missing and the example of F Troop, on 14 June, who kept in action till every piece was hit, will go down in the annals of your Company history.
>
> I am more than proud to have had them under my command and their comportment has been an example to the Brigade Group.[72]

Rommel's offensive rolled on, Tobruk fell to Panzer Armee Afrika and Eighth Army withdrew, at first to Mersa Matruh and, then, when General Auchinleck sacked Ritchie and took direct command, to the El Alamein line. Gunners played critical roles in that retreat and in the battles that raged on that line during July. One example of how pivotal the guns were is provided by Robcol at Deir el Shein on 1 July when an unfinished British position, with no supporting armour, had to be abandoned in the face of a tank attack. The Deir el Shein battle was fought mainly by 18 Indian Brigade which suffered heavy losses, including Brigade HQ and all but a dozen men of 2/5th Essex.[73] Rommel had been attempting to penetrate between the South Africans at El Alamein and the New Zealanders to the south. This area, about fifteen miles from north to south, was dominated by 'a long finger of high ground [that] rose gradually out of the west until it overlooked both the sea coast and the deep desert'.[74] That long finger, ending in an abrupt promontory at its eastern end, was Ruweisat ridge, key to the El Alamein position.

The German attack was however blunted by Robcol, named for Brigadier R P Waller, CRA of 10th Indian Division, which included 11th Field Regiment, Lieutenant Colonel A O McCarthy, A Battery 11th (HAC) Regiment RHA, Major G Armstrong, 265 Anti-Tank Battery and a troop of 155 LAA Battery, with infantry of C Company 1/4th Essex Regiment. As recently as 15 June, 11th Field had been in Iraq but had been rushed to Egypt and thrown into battle at Mersa Matruh before withdrawing to El Alamein and joining Robcol.

On 2 July Robcol was strengthened by elements of 104th (Essex Yeomanry) Regiment RHA with three machine-gun platoons and an anti-tank company of 4th Royal Northumberland Fusiliers. Further reinforcement came from a composite Guards battalion, 9th Rifle Brigade with the balance of 104 RHA, and 3 RHA.[75] On that same morning, shortly after 11 o'clock, 11th Field's 25-pounders 'began to hammer masses of enemy transport in the Deir el Shein area'. Retaliation came in an attack by a lorried infantry group, followed by an artillery bombardment and then an armoured attack.[76]

Eleventh Field plays a central part in the story of Robcol on 2 July, for it was the 25-pounder Gunners

> ... who all day long bore the brunt of the tank assault. In E Troop, Sergeant Keenan (who had become separated in the retreat from Matruh from his unit 515 Battery 165th Field Regiment and had joined the troop two nights before) found himself the only man in his detachment who was not a casualty. He continued to fight his gun alone under intense fire, and was given an immediate award of the DCM for his gallantry. It was Sergeant Keenan, too, who under a hail of machine-gun bullets gave RSM Clark a lecture on the new no. 29 telescope. The RSM proved such an apt pupil that he stepped into the layer's seat and scored three successive direct hits. But of all that devoted band, none displayed more shining and indomitable gallantry than Bombardier Johnson. Early in the day, his left arm was shot off, but he continued to lay and fire with his single arm, refusing all attention. As a result this very gallant soldier died in hospital two days later.[77]

In this bitter, hard-fought engagement the Gunners lost twenty-one 25-pounders, twenty-one 6-pounders and fourteen 2-pounders, although three, five and seven of these equipments respectively were saved. The price had been high, but Panzer Armee Afrika had been stopped in the campaign's last close engagement between 25-pounders and enemy tanks. Although an effective tank killer *in extremis*, and then at short ranges, the 25-pounder had never been intended for that role and its use really was a case of desperation. The 6-pounder, now entering service in the desert, was much more effective. Indirect concentrated fire by 25-pounders on tank formations was always effective in breaking up such formations.[78]

Over the years many writers and commentators have questioned why the 3.7 was not used as an anti-tank gun. The simple answer is that it was, but only on occasion since most 3.7s were protecting areas well removed from enemy tank attacks. However, some were deployed in the desert and opportunities for training in field and anti-tank roles were taken with derelict enemy tanks – German Mark IIIs and IVs and Italian M13s – as targets, and the results were 'most successful'.

> Although no hits were actually scored on the front of a turret, SAP penetrated the 60mm armour in the front of the hull with ease. HE fired at Fuse 4 caused damage to tracks and hull, and 4 rounds HE fired at an M13 scored hits and severely damaged one track and blew in the front part of the hull and the lower part of the turret. Further practice is being held and a full report will be submitted at the conclusion.[79]

Shortly after that report was written, in June 1942, there were at least three examples of 3.7s engaging tanks. The first was in the Knightsbridge Box whither four 3.7s deployed to act both as field and anti-tank guns. However, their appearance was not greeted with delight by the Gunners already present; they wondered how these large weapons could be concealed. Such concern appeared justified since, every time the 3.7s fired, they raised a pillar of sand and dust about 100 feet into the air and drew the attention of enemy artillery.[80] During the 1942 Axis assault on Tobruk, 3.7s of 68th HAA Regiment engaged enemy tanks from their AA positions. On the morning of 20 June, the Gunners had been in action against enemy aircraft.

> The 3.7s had been deeply dug in for protection from dive-bombing attacks but found themselves faced, at short notice, with a duel with Mark III and Mark IV tanks. Stripping the walls of their emplacements to obtain low-angle fire, the positions engaged with armour-piercing and high explosive rounds until overrun and mopped up by swarms of enemy infantry. The 3.7s, in this brief action, emulated the German 88mm; one position held up an armoured battalion for four hours and killed four tanks. The outcome was inevitable; Tobruk was isolated, co-ordinated defence collapsed and the South African force commander gave up the struggle. HQ 4th AA Brigade and 68th HAA Regiment were wiped from the AA Order of Battle ... [81]

The third example of 3.7s engaging enemy tanks occurred in the initial clashes along the El Alamein line. H G Harris, an Operator Fire Control (OFC), recorded how his troop of 3.7s had deployed before a small rise with the GL set being used as a rangefinder. The guns were not dug in, nor was there any form of defence, although camouflage nets were employed. Ordered to engage ground targets, the Gunners spotted German trucks towing 88s, the range was calculated using the GL set and fire was opened, with the vehicles as the first targets. With the vehicles destroyed, the 88s were then hit and the entire unit wiped out. At no time did the 3.7s come under fire. The 3.7 detachments then engaged two German tanks, identified as Mark IVs, which were knocked out using shells with fuses set to 'safe' to produce solid shot. Over several days the troop engaged both tanks and enemy infantry. Solid shot was used against tanks but for the infantry the Gunners developed a new technique, 'skipping' rounds by firing them at the ground in front of the target. The rounds then skipped above the target and exploded in the air, creating an airburst effect, which was devastating to infantry in the open. That the 3.7s saw considerable action is demonstrated by all four weapons needing barrel changes; new barrels were fitted one at a time so that the troop could remain in action.[82] The recommended time for a barrel change was after every 700 rounds. Perhaps it was such experience with 3.7s, or simply the realisation that what one heavy AA gun could do, so could another, that led to plans to adapt the 3.7 for field and anti-tank roles with 'special scotches being made so that 3.7s could fire from their wheels against ground targets'.[83]

It is a common perception that the principle of concentrating artillery was not applied in North Africa until Montgomery arrived in mid-August 1942. In truth, as we have seen, the principle was already in practice before that worthy made his appearance. Auchinleck had established a higher war course at Sarafand to train officers likely to become divisional commanders as part of his efforts to improve the effectiveness of leadership and training in the Middle East, and bring about closer co-operation on the battlefield. At the same time the Staff College at Haifa had been expanded with an RAF element added to encourage better inter-service co-operation while all tactical and weapon training schools in Middle East Command were ordered to 'ensure that a uniform doctrine, which took account of the characteristics of all three arms and was attuned to modern conditions, was taught under a single direction'.[84]

With this work going on in the background it is not surprising to find that artillery was being concentrated. As early as 1 July Frido von Mellenthin, of Rommel's headquarters, had noted how 90th Light Division, trying to bypass the El Alamein box

> … ran into a crescent of fire from the 1st, 2nd and 3rd SA Brigades and their supporting artillery, and was thrown into confusion not far removed from panic. Rommel himself went up to 90th Light to try and urge the division forward but the volume of fire was so heavy that even he was pinned down.[85]

Although 90th Light was much reduced it speaks volumes for the artillery fire from the El Alamein box that this formation could be brought almost to a state of panic. That 'crescent of fire' was the effect of the South African artillery units bringing down a heavy concentration of fire on the battlefield from all the guns of the divisional artillery. It was something that 90th Light had not experienced before; but it was an experience with which Axis troops would become very familiar. It is not entirely accurate to describe this fire as the work of the South African artillery alone as 11th Field Regiment had 'responded to an urgent call from the South Africans for additional artillery support'.

> Deploying south of the coastal highway, the guns were laid on a bearing of 270 degrees. Throughout the morning we brought down harassing fire on enemy armour moving south on the Rahman Track. A khamseen or dust-storm developed later in the morning and by 1500 hours observation became impossible. As the sun dipped to the bottom of the horizon … we came out of action, limbered up and withdrew into leaguer between El Alamein and El Imayid.[86]

Three weeks later, on the night of 21/22 July, Eighth Army launched an attack supported by 200 guns, an even more impressive concentration of artillery that presaged the famous bombardment that would open Operation LIGHTFOOT in October. In this attack 6 New Zealand Brigade reached the El Mreir depression but came under German counter-attack in daylight with panzers catching the New Zealanders in an exposed position. The New Zealand anti-tank guns were knocked out as, unfortunately, were the armoured vehicles carrying the liaison officers who were maintaining contact with the guns.

The July battles along the El Alamein line stopped Rommel, forcing him on to the defensive. With Eighth Army so close to its supply bases, the British forces could only get stronger. The build-up for Eighth Army's offensive had already begun with 300 Sherman tanks being despatched across the Atlantic from the United States. Needless to say, Eighth Army's artillery was also gaining in strength with more guns arriving in Egypt and much more ammunition. Some re-organisation had also taken place with the disbandment of 25th, 72nd, 157th and 164th Field Regiments, 67th Medium Regiment and RHQ 68th HAA Regiment as well as 277 and 282 HAA Batteries. Also axed were 5, 81 and 107 LAA Batteries, a troop of 135 Z AA Battery, 202, 206 and 432 Coast Batteries. These disbandments, which took effect from 1 August, were attributed to heavy losses in recent fighting; most of the units had been lost at Tobruk. Auchinleck was also told that he could only have forty field regiments, 120 field batteries.[87]

Before long the war would enter a new phase.

Notes

1. Playfair, *The Early Successes against Italy [to May 1941]*, pp. 5–10; Roskill, *The Navy at War*, p. 24; Ireland, *The War in the Mediterranean*, pp. 13–17
2. Doherty, *Wall of Steel*, pp. 29–30; Maj Gen B P Hughes, letter to author
3. NA Kew, WO169/303, war diary 9 AA Regt, 1939; WO169/280, war diary 7 Med Regt, 1939–40
4. Farndale, *The Years of Defeat*, p. 118
5. Playfair, op cit, p. 209
6. Playfair includes this statement from Tenth Army's Intelligence Summary of 19 October 1940: 'As is well-known, the enemy has units more manoeuvrable in the desert than ours.' (p. 209)
7. Raugh, *Wavell in the Middle East*, pp. 88–93; NA Kew, WO169/53, HQ Western Desert Force GS, 1940
8. NA Kew, WO169/56, war diary CRA Western Desert Force, Sep–Dec 1940; Latimer, *Operation Compass 1940*, p. 25
9. Latimer, op cit, p. 25; Farndale, op cit, pp. 132–5
10. Farndale, op cit, p. 132
11. Ibid, p. 134
12. Ibid
13. Ibid, pp. 132–5
14. Ibid, pp. 135–8; Playfair, op cit, pp. 282–7; Latimer, op cit, pp. 41–54; NA Kew, WO169/56, op cit; WO169/280, op cit
15. Latimer, op cit, p. 74
16. Ibid, pp. 75–6; Farndale, op cit, pp. 141–3; NA Kew, WO169/1429, war diary, 4 RHA, 1941
17. Latimer, op cit, p. 84

18 Ibid, pp. 84–5; NA Kew, WO169/1434, war diary, 106 RHA, Jan–Feb '41
19 Quoted in Latimer, op cit, p. 85; NA Kew, WO169/1434, war diary, op cit
20 Latimer, op cit, p. 85
21 Playfair, op cit, pp. 364–5
22 Playfair, *The Germans come to the help of their Ally*, pp. 35–6
23 Farndale, op cit, p. 166
24 Duncan, *RA Commemoration Book*, p. 183; Farndale, op cit, p. 165
25 Duncan, op cit, p. 183; www.cwgc.org.uk
26 Duncan, op cit, pp. 184–5; NA Kew, WO169/1426, war diary, 1 RHA, Jan–Nov '41
27 Playfair, op cit, pp. 160–2
28 Ibid, p. 162
29 Ibid, pp. 168–171
30 Farndale, op cit, p. 191
31 Roberts, *31st Field Regiment RA. A Record* p. 14
32 Ibid
33 Farndale, op cit, p. 270
34 Ibid, pp. 273–4
35 Roberts, op cit, pp. 10–11; Glover, *An Improvised War*, p. 81
36 Glover, op cit, pp. 111–22; Roberts, op cit, p. 11; Brett-James, *Ball of Fire*, pp. 56–80; Stevens, *Fourth Indian Division*, pp. 46–50
37 Roberts, op cit, p. 12
38 NA Kew, WO169/303, war diary, 25 HAA Bty, 1940; Doherty, op cit, pp. 69–72
39 NA Kew, WO169/303, op cit, G Sec narrative; interview with George Lapsley; Doherty, op cit, p. 75
40 NA Kew, WO169/303, op cit; Doherty, op cit, p. 70
41 Doherty, op cit, p. 76
42 Ibid
43 Ibid, p. 55; NA Kew, WO169/1573, war diary, 9 HAA Regt, 1941; WO169/1591, war diary 20 HAA Bty, 1941; Farndale, op cit, p. 170
44 Duncan, op cit, p.
45 Farndale, op cit, p. 172
46 This regiment converted to an anti-tank role on 1 July 1941 and claimed the territorial title Cheshire but this was not approved and the former title of Lancashire Yeomanry was adopted from 30 May 1942. (Frederick, *Lineage Book*, p. 929; NA Kew, WO32/9659, 'Middle East. Re-organization of Artillery Regiments')
47 Farndale, op cit, p. 178
48 Ibid, p. 180
49 Ibid, p. 183; NA Kew, WO169/1491; war diary 7 Med Regt 1941; WO169/ 1573, op cit
50 Farndale, op cit, p. 184
51 Quoted in Hughes, *Honour Titles*, pp. 190–1
52 A B Marvin, *Gunner*, Jan 2008
53 Maj Michael Lacy, *Gunner*, Jan 2008; www.cwgc.org
54 Doherty, *Irish Volunteers in the Second World War (IV)*, p. 112
55 Hughes, op cit, pp. 192–3
56 NA Kew, WO169/1451, war diary 31 Fd Regt, Nov-Dec 1941
57 Doherty, op cit, p. 111
58 Duncan, op cit, p. 194
59 Ibid, p. 194
60 Ibid
61 Moorehead, *The Desert War*, pp. 94–5
62 NA Kew, WO201/355, 'Action at Sidi Rezegh, 1st King's Royal Rifle Corps'

63 O H Perks, Martuba – 21 March 1942, *Gunner*, April 1992 and Lt Gen Sir Edward Howard-Vyse, Martuba – 21 March 1942, *Gunner*, June 1992

64 Doherty, *Wall of Steel*, p. 188; NA Kew, WO169/4913, war diary, 6 LAA Bty, 1942; Doherty, 'The Ultimate Souvenir', *Britain at War*, July 2008

65 Duncan, op cit, p. 202

66 The account that follows is based on those in Hart, *To The Last Round*, pp. 190–219 and Mead, *Gunners at War*, pp. 44–9

67 Playfair, op cit, p. 232

68 Mead, op cit, p. 46

69 www.cwgc.org.uk

70 The CWGC gives his date of death, incorrectly, as 27 May. www.cwgc.org.uk

71 Playfair, op cit, p. 234

72 Johnston, *Regimental Fire*, p. 86

73 NA Kew, CAB44/98, p. 340

74 Stevens, op cit, p. 181

75 Duncan, op cit, p. 224

76 Stevens, op cit, p. 182

77 Duncan, op cit, p. 224; www.cwgc.org Bdr John Robert Johnson died on 3 July and is buried in El Alamein war cemetery.

78 Henry, *The 25-pounder Field Gun 1939–72*, p. 34

79 NA Kew, WO32/9805, 'Experience gained in the employment of RA units, 1941–1943' This report is dated June 1942.

80 Duncan, op cit, pp. 204–6

81 Routledge, *Anti-Aircraft Artillery, 1914–1955*, p. 140

82 H G Harris, IWM 84/44/1; quoted in Doherty, *The Sound of History: El Alamein 1942*, pp. 22–3

83 NA Kew, WO201, 'Defensive Planning in the Western Desert, 24 Aug to 6 Nov 1942'

84 NA Kew, CAB44/97, p. 10

85 Von Mellenthin, *Panzer Battles*, p. 125

86 E A Oates, 'The First Battle of El Alamein: The Action on the Ruweisat Ridge', *Gunner*, Dec 1991

87 NA Kew WO32/9659, 'Reorganisation of Artillery Regiments, Middle East, 1941–43'

Chapter Six

Far to the East

While the Luftwaffe ranged over Britain and the desert war surged back and forth, life for servicemen in the Empire's eastern outposts remained much as it had been before the war. News from North Africa was listened to eagerly but it seemed as if the war was in a different world. All that changed when Japan launched its surprise attacks on the US Navy's Pacific Fleet at Pearl Harbor in Hawaii and on British possessions in Malaya on 7 December 1941. (In fact, the Japanese attacked Malaya before their aircraft reached Pearl Harbor but the intervention of the International Date Line means that the invasion of Malaya is recorded as beginning on 8 December.)

The attack on the US Fleet brought America into the war but only against Japan. Four days later the situation changed completely when Hitler and Mussolini, in one of the war's greatest strategic blunders, declared war on the United States. Truly, this was now a world war. British attention focused, initially, on Malaya where a small but determined and very well trained Japanese army began pushing down the peninsula from Kota Bharu, often outflanking through the jungle those British strongpoints intended to stop or delay them. The great prize that beckoned was the naval base on Singapore Island. As their soldiers advanced remorselessly, on 10 December the Imperial Japanese Navy sank the Royal Navy's *Prince of Wales* and *Repulse*, which had put to sea without an aircraft carrier to provide air defence.

In spite of the gallant efforts of the defending troops, the Japanese had pushed them back to the Perak river by 17 December, on which day Japanese troops invaded North Borneo. Next day, more Japanese troops landed on Hong Kong Island, having attacked the colony's mainland territory ten days earlier. One week later the colony surrendered; it was Christmas Day. Hong Kong's defences had included some naval vessels but no combat aircraft while ground forces included five Gunner units:[1]

The Hong Kong Volunteer Defence Corps (HKVDC), numbering over 1,600 personnel, included light armour, artillery, engineer, signals and infantry plus service troops and medical units; its Gunner element was 400-strong. Its AA

Regiment	Batteries
8th Coast Regiment	12, 30 and 36 Batteries
12th Coast Regiment	20 and 26 Batteries
5th HAA Regiment	7 RA; 17 and 18 HK-SRA Batteries
1st Hong Kong Regiment HK-SRA	1 and 2 Mtn; 3, 4 and 25 Med Batteries
	965 Defence Battery, HK-SRA
Hong Kong Volunteer Defence Corps	1, 2, 3, 4 (Coast) and 5 (AA) Batteries

battery was under command 5th HAA Regiment which thus had one British battery, two from the Hong Kong–Singapore Royal Artillery (HKSRA) and one from the HKVDC; the regiment deployed twelve semi-mobile 3-inch guns, four 3.7s, six 40mms and a variety of light machine guns. This woefully weak AA defence was exacerbated by the absence of modern combat aircraft; only a few obsolete Vickers Vildebeeste torpedo-bombers, used for target-towing, and Supermarine Walrus amphibians were available, none of them capable of action against modern bombers and fighters.[2]

Hong Kong was defended by a brigade-sized infantry force, including two British and two Indian battalions. In November 1941 two Canadian battalions arrived but neither was trained properly, and both lacked transport. It was accepted that, in the event of an attack, it would be impossible to defend the frontier with mainland China; this was too long for the troops available. Instead an eleven-mile line on the mainland would be defended until it became necessary to withdraw to Hong Kong Island; from Gin Drinkers Bay to Port Shelter by Tide Cove, this was dubbed the Gin Drinkers Line. Its defence was assigned to the Mainland Brigade – 2nd Royal Scots, 2/14th Punjab and 5/7th Rajputs – with artillery support from 2 Mountain Battery with four 4.5-inch and four 3.7-inch howitzers, a troop of 1 Mountain Battery with four 3.7-inch howitzers, and 25 Medium Battery with four 6-inch guns. The mediums deployed along the entire front while the mountain guns deployed with a troop to each battalion; three 6-inch howitzers and two 60-pounders on Stonecutters' Island could also engage mainland targets. As with the AA defences, this was inadequate. Likewise with the Island Brigade – 1st Middlesex, the Royal Rifles of Canada and the Winnipeg Grenadiers – there was a weak artillery component: eight 6-inch guns of 3 and 4 Medium Batteries and a troop of four 4.5-inch howitzers from 1 Mountain Battery; 965 Defence Battery's 18-pounders deployed for beach defence.[3]

By November it was known that the Japanese Twenty-third Army, four divisions strong with the artillery of three divisions, was massing across the Chinese border. And it was only then, when the Canadians arrived, that serious work began on the defences. In early December, many non-combatants were evacuated to Singapore and war preparations were stepped up. On 7 December, twenty-six merchant ships departed for Singapore and the Gunner units reported that they were ready for action. The first Japanese attacks came with air assaults on Kai Tak airfield at 8.00am on 8 December which destroyed all the military aircraft, plus eight civilian machines. Other targets included Shamsuipo Barracks while reports were received that two Japanese columns were crossing the Sham Chun river to advance into the colony. Guns at Stonecutters and Mount Davis registered target zones on the mainland while OPs took up position. Then, at 10.00am, 30 Coast Battery's 6-inch guns at Bokhara, near Stanley, shelled a Japanese destroyer. Before the day was out the same guns were engaging Japanese infantry on the Tai Po–Sha Tin road.[4]

It is worth mentioning that a contemporary rumour held that Hong Kong's coast artillery could not engage mainland targets. This was untrue: 'Arcs of fire of the coast batteries at Stone Cutters, Mount Davis, Jubilee, Devil's Peak and Pakshawan between them could and [did] engage the enemy advancing upon Hong Kong.'[5] In fact, the guns inflicted considerable harm; one Japanese officer later described as 'extremely effective' the British 'long range fortress artillery bombardments'.[6]

As the Japanese worked their way into the Leased Territories, Gunners began engaging them; 2 Mountain Battery reported firing on an enemy light gun and a working party at Lo Wai before noon on 9 December.

> More targets were engaged at 1437 and 1740 hours. Seldom in the next three days were the guns of these mountain Gunners silent. No call for fire went unanswered, and by all accounts they were splendid. The 60-pounders on Stonecutters Island were by then within range and opened up effectively, controlled from an OP on Shing Mun with A Company, 2nd Royal Scots.[7]

Shing Mun was the site of a small but desperate struggle later that night when the Japanese launched a surprise attack on the redoubt, south of the Shing Mun (Jubilee) reservoir. This guarded the approach to Smuggler's Ridge, and was also the location of 2 Mountain Battery's OP, manned by Second Lieutenant W J Willcocks; the redoubt was held by a Royal Scots' platoon. Recognising the danger, Willcocks called for fire onto the Shing Mun river. However, the enemy closed on the OP itself, throwing grenades into it. There followed a two-hour battle before the position was overrun; two Indian Gunners died as the Japanese charged in. Although the others were captured they escaped later. Fire was then brought down onto the redoubt itself, and in front of both the Royal Scots and the Rajputs, inflicting many casualties on the attackers. Later, the 9.2- and 6-inch batteries fired concentrations on the reservoir approaches. Although the brigade commander wanted the Royal Scots to counter-attack at dawn, they were unable to do since about half of their reserve company were victims of malaria. When General Maltby, Hong Kong's commander, learned that Shing Mun redoubt had been taken by the enemy he realised that the Gin Drinkers' Line was in serious difficulties.[8]

Fifteen minutes before 8 o'clock on the 10th came a fresh attack, preceded by a heavy bombardment, on the Rajput company on Smuggler's Ridge. Although this was beaten back after a tough close-quarter battle, the brigade commander decided to shorten his line. Throughout that day both sides' artillery maintained steady fire. The heavy guns on Stonecutters' Island hit Shing Mun redoubt with a heavy concentration at noon and were, in turn, shelled by Japanese guns and attacked by enemy aircraft, causing both casualties and damage. By now, Maltby was planning to evacuate the mainland and it was during that night that Hong Kong Island was hit for the first time by Japanese shellfire. At the same time, the two 60-pounders on Stonecutters and the battery on Mount Davis were shelled by a Japanese 5.9-inch howitzer battery. When Mount Davis was bombarded, its 9.2-inch guns were shelling enemy troops on the Castle Peak road.[9]

This was a prelude to the desperate fighting that continued until Christmas Day when Maltby was forced to advise the Governor that the garrison could no longer hold out. At that stage only nine guns were still in action in the colony, including two 6-inch howitzers and four 4.5-inch howitzers. The Gunners had served their guns with determination, great courage and skill. On Christmas Eve, 1 Battery HKVDC defended Barton's Bungalow in what Farndale suggests 'must go down as one of British artillery's finest hours'. Attack after attack was beaten off and even when the enemy brought up flamethrowers and mortars the Gunners continued to hold out, although reduced greatly in numbers. In the fury of the battle there was no quarter as the Japanese 'rushed in regardless of casualties and bayoneted everyone they found, alive or dead'. Only one outcome was possible. The band of some thirty Gunners was wiped out but the Japanese had suffered hundreds of dead. Lieutenants H S Jones and K E Muir, with thirty-three Gunners, were killed while Captain F G Rees and three others were wounded. Later that day, a 2-pounder knocked out three enemy tanks on South Bay Road but was overrun in the darkness. Individual detachments fought gallant actions, the details of which were lost with their lives.[10] After the war, a posthumous Mention in Despatches was awarded to Lance Bombardier John Bullen, 1st Hong Kong Regiment, HK-SRA who

> ... displayed great courage and outstanding leadership at a difficult time. In the absence of officers or senior NCOs, he inspired his comrades to prolong their resistance to a Japanese attack and finally lost his life whilst enabling some of the survivors to withdraw from an untenable position.[11]

Such courage was typical of those who defended Hong Kong, not least those manning the guns. Noting that, of its 568 pages, the first volume of the official history of the war in the Far East, *The War Against Japan*, only forty-four covered the fall of Hong Kong, Field Marshal The Lord Bramall wrote:

> This tended to obscure the fact that unlike some other defeats suffered, in those early years, by the Allies at the hands of the Japanese, no shame or disgrace whatsoever could be ascribed to the inexperienced, ill-equipped and often untrained British, Canadians, Indians and local Hong Kong garrison, when they heroically held up the overwhelming Japanese attack for nearly three weeks.[12]

In those three weeks of fighting, Gunners had, as ever, lived up to their regimental motto: Quo Fas et Gloria Ducunt.

In Malaya, Gunners fought in the delaying actions in the peninsula as the Japanese closed on Singapore. The island's defences included three 15-inch guns sited to deal with attacks from the sea and with ammunition intended for use against ships. As with the guns of Hong Kong, there has been a persistent myth that Singapore's guns could not engage landward targets, in spite of the fact that they fired at the Japanese in Malaya. On 16 January 1942, General Wavell told Churchill that these guns had 'all-round traverse, but their flat trajectory makes them unsuitable for counter-battery work. Could certainly not guarantee to dominate enemy siege batteries with them'.[13]

Major Jim Nelson, then brigade major to Brigadier E W Goodman, the senior Gunner in Malaya Command, related how he had been told that the guns could not fire landwards but all that was needed was a re-routing of the power supply and the guns traversed to engage mainland targets. Nelson was disappointed not to be allowed to shell the Sultan of Johore's palace since, it was said, that worthy had paid for the guns.

> So I selected a railway yard in the same area. An Australian Gunner officer was appointed to observe the fire and a telephone link established direct from him to me in Fort Canning.
>
> The first three-gun salvo of 15-inch shells was quite something – like three express trains roaring overhead – most impressive, but for quite a time no reaction from the observer. After what seemed an interminable wait a highly excited Australian reported to the tune, 'It's terrific – magnificent – those shells must have burrowed deep into Johore before the fuses went off. Whole chunks of land have now come up, hurling trains, engines and trucks high in the air. More, please! It's marvellous.'[14]

However, as Peter Mead noted,

> These guns, and the other coast artillery guns which also engaged landward targets, were not, nor could they have been, a decisive factor in the defence of Singapore under the prevailing conditions. The field artillery which had fought in Malaya

> continued to fight on the island and were almost out of ammunition when, on 15 February 1942, the garrison had finally to capitulate.[15]

The garrison of Malaya included two Indian and one Australian divisions, each of two brigades, two fortress brigades in Singapore, and single battalions in Penang and Sarawak. Later 18th (East Anglian) Division would arrive but too late to make any difference to the outcome of the campaign; it took part in the final battles for Singapore island. When the Japanese attacked, Malaya was defended by some 88,600 men, of whom about 19,600 were British; there were 4,612 Gunners. There were only seven field regiments, two coast artillery regiments, two anti-tank regiments, a mountain regiment and a light battery of the Federated Malay States Volunteer Force. Anti-aircraft artillery included 1st and 2nd HAA Regiments HKSRA, 3rd HAA Regiment RA, 1st Indian HAA Regiment, 3rd LAA Regiment HKSRA and 5th SL Regiment RA.[16] When 18th (East Anglian) Division arrived in late January it brought 118th (8th London), 135th (Hertfordshire Yeomanry) and 148th (Bedfordshire Yeomanry) as its divisional artillery; the division also disposed 125th Anti-Tank Regiment which was on HMT *Empress of India* when that ship was sunk on 5 February; all but four of the regiment's 2-pounders were lost.[17] An earlier (mid-January) redirecting of a convoy bound for the Middle East had brought several other Gunner units to Malaya: 77th HAA, 21st LAA and 48th LAA Regiments. Although their equipment, on a separate convoy, went to the Middle East, the regiments were re-equipped from stocks held in Singapore.[18]

The first artillery round of the campaign was not fired by a Gunner unit but by an infantry battalion, 3/17th Dogras, with an 18-pounder saluting gun commandeered for beach defence. With it they claimed the sinking of a landing craft at Kota Bharu. Before long 21 Mountain Battery was also in action, sinking further enemy landing craft. With further Japanese attacks at Singora and Patani and air attacks on Singapore – the first against the British in the Far East – it was soon clear that the Gunners would be stretched. Much reliance had been placed on airpower to defend Malaya but the RAF lost half its aircraft – and there had been but 110 to begin with – in the first twenty-four hours. Nor did the AA defences have any early-warning radar; and there were not enough guns anyway. With more Japanese landings being reported Force Z, HM Ships *Prince of Wales* and *Repulse*, escorted by four destroyers, sailed to engage the invasion fleets. When the Japanese learned that the two capital ships were at sea, a Saigon-based air flotilla, which was preparing to bomb Singapore, was re-armed with torpedoes to attack the Royal Navy vessels. By early afternoon *Repulse* and *Prince of Wales* had been sunk.[19]

As the attacks continued, the RAF began evacuating airfields. Engagement followed engagement in a remorseless advance and the story of 155th (Lanarkshire Yeomanry) Field Regiment is typical of the experience of Gunner units in the campaign. The regiment fired its first rounds at Jitra on 11 December, on which day D Troop claimed to have shot down a Japanese aircraft with machine-gun fire.

Next day, the regiment put a barrage down in front of a battalion of Leicesters 'who said it was very effective and stopped the enemy closing up on them'. That same day batteries from 137th Field and 22nd Mountain Regiments came under command, C Troop's OP with the Leicesters was attacked by Japanese infantry and Captain Forster and his assistant were killed. Late that night the regiment had moved to Alor Star airfield but F Troop had lost two guns during the move.

The Lanarkshire Yeomanry Gunners had also supported a counter-attack by 1/8th Punjabis and, at noon, had beaten off a Japanese attack on D Company of 2/9th Jats. As the enemy maintained pressure, ammunition stocks were dwindling; finally, the order was given to withdraw. Major General Murray-Lyon's 11th Indian Division had been forced from its positions by an attacker that numbered no more than two battalions of infantry and a company of tanks. Morale suffered badly.[20]

With retreat underway, AA Gunners were kept busy, being 'under constant attack'. At Port Swettenham, 9 HAA Battery shot down seven attackers but there were no AA guns or aircraft to defend Penang island, which was evacuated on the 17th. Gunners of 8 Coast Battery HKSRA had the sad task of destroying their 6-inch guns to deny them to the enemy. Throughout the rest of December the story remained the same. Although General Percival knew that reinforcements were en route, he also knew that their convoys would come under Japanese attack but the further north he could hold the enemy the more the threat to the ships would be reduced. And so orders were issued to the forces in Malaya to maintain their delaying actions.[21]

When the Japanese attacked on 31 December, 155th Field Regiment was again in the thick of the fighting. The main assault followed early on 1 January but was held by the 'tenacity of the infantry and deadly accuracy of the Scottish Gunners'. Next morning, Troop Sergeant Major Harold Hugill, acting as a FOO with the Leicesters at Kampar, earned the Distinguished Conduct Medal.

> A party of enemy got into the position but Hugill from a forward trench continued to engage them and alone defeated them just as they looked likely to succeed. His OP line was cut so he traced it back to his main OP and met a party of enemy in one of our machine gun posts. Hugill took charge of some infantry and led a bayonet charge which destroyed them. He then reported to battalion headquarters. It was mainly due to the skill and tenacity of this Warrant Officer that a heavy attack was beaten off.[22]

Also decorated for his actions at Kampar was Gunner Harold Walker who received the Military Medal for taking, single-handedly, an enemy machine-gun post which he held until relieved. Gunner Walker had been bringing rations forward when he came under fire from the Japanese machine gunners.[23]

Other field regiments engaged included 88th (2nd West Lancashire) and 137th, the latter being the duplicate of 88th (although due to adopt the subtitle 2nd West Lancashire, it was wiped from the order of battle before this could happen). Over a three-day period 88th Field fired off all their ammunition but when a fresh Japanese attack was launched the enemy was hit hard by the guns of 137th Field.[24] In spite of the courage of infantry and Gunners the retreat continued with no air support at all and with Japanese aircraft roaming almost at will. En route from India were some reinforcements, including two anti-tank regiments, one without its guns, 6th HAA Regiment, with two batteries, and 35th LAA Regiment; 21st LAA and 77th HAA Regiments were diverted to Java for airfield protection there when the RAF quit Singapore, as was 6th HAA Regiment, less 3 HAA Battery.[25]

There could be only one outcome to the campaign. Gunners might delay the Japanese, as 155th Field did again at the Slim river and at Batu Pahat, or 137th Field at Trolak but the advance could not be stopped. BSM Roadnight of 155th Field led six Gunners in a bayonet charge that routed an enemy platoon and gained some valuable time for the regiment while Captain Sewell and Bombardier Shone of 115th Field earned the MC and MM respectively after recapturing an OP from the enemy and engaging the Japanese with a mortar, which Shone had never used before. Roadnight was later awarded the DCM. By the end of January, however, the long retreat was all but over and the Japanese were pressing hard on the road to Singapore.[26]

We have already seen that the 15-inch guns of Johore Battery on Singapore fired at mainland targets with great effect. They were not alone: a 6-inch coast gun of the Pasir Laba Battery harassed Japanese forces at possible embarkation points between Sungei Pendas and Tanjong Tuan until so badly damaged that it could no longer fire. The BC, Captain J R Asher, was killed while evacuating wounded and the gun was destroyed by some gunners from another party. Johore Battery and Connaught Battery – three 9.2-inch guns – also kept firing although under constant air attack; had they had more HE ammunition they would have done more damage than was achieved by armour-piercing rounds. However, the Buona Vista Battery could not engage the attackers and was demolished on 11 February.[27]

Until the end Singapore's Gunners manned their equipments and withstood dreadful punishment from Japanese artillery and aircraft. British and Australian Gunners, with their comrades of the Hong Kong-Singapore RA, performed sterling service, often saving the day in a myriad of engagements. The final factor in the decision to capitulate came on 15 February with a report that water supplies were at a very low level since the reservoirs were in enemy hands. Low, too, were stocks of food, artillery ammunition and fuel. At 11.30am the process of surrender began although fighting did not finish immediately.[28] What were probably the last shots of the campaign were fired at about 1.00pm by a troop from 272 Anti-Tank Battery 80th Anti-Tank Regiment, which went to support the Malay Battalion. In that final action the troop commander, Lieutenant Francis Fosbery, was killed and Lance Sergeant Tuck earned the MM for his courage.[29]

Japanese forces in Siam invaded Burma in January 1942. The pre-war Burma garrison was pitifully small since invasion from the east had never been considered. That garrison included a small Gunner complement of 2 (Derajat) Mountain Battery, Indian Artillery, with four 3.7-inch howitzers, 5 Field Battery, Burma Auxiliary Force (BAF) with six 18-pounders and the Rangoon Coast Battery with two 6-inch guns. Writing of this time, Brigadier G de V Welchman CBE DSO, successively CRA of 17th Indian Division, CCRA of I Burma Corps and BRA Fourteenth Army, noted that there were only thirty-six guns in Burma in December 1941, a figure that increased by twenty in January 1942. When Welchman became CCRA I Burma Corps he had 150 guns, of which seventy-four were withdrawn over 900 miles – and some over 1,000 miles – although only twenty-five guns were brought back into India. Of these, ten were 25-pounders, eleven were 3.7-inch howitzers and four were 2-pounders.[30]

Although a heavy AA regiment of the BAF was formed when war broke out, it had no guns until 1941 when four 3.7s and eight 40mms arrived. These were in action with 1 HAA Battery and 3 LAA Battery against Japanese aircraft over Rangoon on 23 December in the city's first air raid. Over 2,000 civilian casualties were sustained and the two batteries claimed three enemy aircraft shot down for the loss of two 3.7s and a 40mm. On the last day of 1941 the AA defences were strengthened by the arrival of 8 Indian and 3 Indian LAA Batteries, followed by 8 HAA Battery. Confusingly, this meant that there were two 8 HAA Batteries, one British and one Indian, and two 3 LAA Batteries, one Indian and one BAF. Other Gunner reinforcements included 27th Mountain Regiment. When the Japanese invaded Burma on 15 January 1942, there were about 150 guns in Burma, as Brigadier Welchman noted, of which only twenty-five would survive the subsequent disastrous campaign.

As in Malaya, the Japanese again outmanoeuvred the opposing British and Indian forces who, before long, were on the retreat. This was a retreat that would end only when the survivors of what had been re-styled the Burma Army reached Assam in north-east India in May. Although Rangoon was pivotal to any defence of Burma it was vulnerable to attack by land, sea and air. Both the city and Moulmein airfield, across the Bay of Martaban, came under air attack and the AA Gunners were engaged heavily. They behaved with great courage as did their mountain gun comrades. A troop of 3 Indian LAA Battery was lost when Japanese troops dressed as Burmese landed and mingled with retreating Burma Rifles personnel to attack the Gunners and seize their guns. The Gunners fought a fierce hand-to-hand battle but the outcome was predictable and the guns were lost. However, an exceptionally courageous subaltern, Second Lieutenant Mehar Dass, learning that the enemy were not guarding the captured guns, led a small party of Gunners in a raid to disable the guns. Unable to disable one Bofors, they tried to bring it back but could not get it on board a steamer and thus had to leave it behind. However, Mehar Dass

> … could not bear to leave his guns and so many of his men, and this gallant young Indian officer dived off the boat and swam ashore under heavy fire to disable the gun

> and save his men. He was not seen again, surely an action in the finest traditions of the Regiment.[31]

Although this was the first occasion on which 3 Indian LAA Battery had been in action its Gunners had fought with resolute courage and determination and caused many casualties in the Japanese ranks. Their conduct inspired one Japanese officer to describe their stand as 'a fierce resistance by a determined enemy'.[32] Not surprisingly, the last guns in action in the retreat to Assam were those of this same battery.[33]

The mountain batteries' guns also saw action: 5 Mountain Battery fought at Martaban and then at Pa'an to the north where a section supported 7/10th Baluchs on the night of 11/12 February. This became a close-quarter battle with the Japanese closing on the British positions but the Baluchs and Gunners stood firm, although more than half their number were dead or wounded. The last stand of the Baluchs and Gunners was made by the survivors of the battalion HQ following a defiant burst of machine-gun fire in response to a call for surrender. Eventually, the enemy advanced into the gun lines where they began bayoneting the Gunners and the guns were finally lost. Of those who had faced the initial Japanese attack, only seventy officers and men, both Gunners and Baluchs, escaped.[34]

When the survivors of 5 Mountain Battery reached Bilin, they received two new 3.7-inch howitzers, still in grease, while 28th Mountain Regiment, newly arrived from Madras, increased Gunner strength in Burma by eight guns, four 3.7s in each of two batteries. A plan to stand along the Bilin river was made redundant by a Japanese outflanking move. Nonetheless, there was a battle as British and Indian troops counter-attacked their foe with Gunner support.[35]

Before long, however, the retreat was again underway, although the action on the Bilin had delayed the enemy by four days and allowed the deployment of 7 Armoured Brigade. The next action was on the Sittang river where three 3-inch AA guns of 8 Indian HAA Battery and four Bofors of B Troop 3 Indian LAA Battery defended the bridge. They were soon in action against Japanese aircraft while, during the night, 5, 12 and 28 Mountain Batteries 'were continuously engaging targets at point blank range in the moonlight'.[36] That night and the following day, the mountain Gunners took a heavy toll of the attackers. Tragically, the Sittang bridge was demolished prematurely, leaving many British troops on the wrong side of the river. Many Gunners were among those lost, a number of whom drowned while trying to swim the river. Lieutenant Gilmour of 5 Mountain Battery, with two Gurkha officers, helped many wounded across the river under fire, for which he received the Military Cross.[37]

The subsequent redeployment saw 8 Indian HAA Battery and 3 Indian LAA Battery with 17th Indian Division at Pegu where they saw much action, shooting down six Japanese planes in one day. With 7 Armoured Brigade had come veteran Gunners from the desert: 414 Battery 104th Regiment RHA (Essex Yeomanry), with 25-pounders, and A Battery 95th Anti-Tank Regiment. Another new arrival was 1st Indian Field Regiment, also with 25-pounders, but such reinforcements could only help fight rearguard actions; there was no stemming the Japanese advance. In this type of fighting the newly-arrived Gunners showed considerable skill with 414 Battery enabling units of 7 Armoured Brigade to escape on several occasions through the accuracy of their shooting while Captain Shorter, their FOO, showed 'complete disregard for his personal safety'.[38]

When it became clear that it would be impossible to hold Rangoon, 8 HAA Battery destroyed most of its equipment and moved its remaining guns, with those of 3 Indian LAA Battery, to Hlegu bridge to join 8 Indian HAA Battery. By 7 March the retreat from Rangoon, the final phase of the campaign was underway. En route, there were many battles and Gunners did sterling work against both ground and air targets; on one occasion 8 Indian HAA Battery went rapidly into action off the line of march to shoot down two of six planes attacking their column.

Along that weary line of retreat, Gunners did their utmost to support their comrades. What they achieved is demonstrated by the actions of two units: 414 Battery RHA with its 25-pounders and 3 Indian LAA Battery with its 40mm Bofors guns. In the closing days of the withdrawal, 414 Battery and the few remaining tanks of 7 Armoured Brigade provided the rearguard, remaining in action through the daylight hours before trekking after the infantry under cover of darkness. Waypoints included Kalewa, Imbaung, Yezago, Khampat, Witok and Tamu, where the monsoon broke. At last, on 18 May, they reached Palel and relative safety. On 11 June 414 Battery arrived at Dhond near Poona to rest and refit. Some weeks later, at the end of August, the battery was ordered to expand to become 14th Regiment RHA, its BC, Major Pereira, being promoted to lieutenant colonel to command this new regiment.[39]

For its part, 3 Indian LAA Battery had also done magnificent work. Under its BC, Major Charles McFetridge, its guns fought their last action in Burma on 10 May at Shwegyin, some five miles south of Kalewa, on the east bank of the Chindwin river. The battery was supporting the rearguard of 16 Indian Brigade and engaged not only enemy aircraft but also Japanese artillery, infantry and mortar teams. The firing was often over open sights as the Gunners covered the embarkation of casualties, troops and tanks on vessels that would ferry them over the Chindwin. Finally, those vessels could no longer operate and McFetridge's guns provided cover as the last rear parties made for a crossing place farther north. With that option not open to the guns, McFetridge ordered the destruction of the equipments but not before they fired a final 'tremendous concentration', described in one war diary as 'a cheering sound, the like of which we had not heard during our time in Burma'.[40] The Japanese failed to follow up the retreating rear parties. This was out of character. Perhaps it was a direct result of that final concentration fired by the Gunners?

Since it first went into action as an untried unit, 3 Indian LAA Battery had destroyed twenty-two enemy aircraft, a gun and a mortar and had probably destroyed many more, as well as inflicting heavy casualties on the Japanese. Eight guns were lost in action and the dead totalled forty-one with another seventeen wounded. The battery received two MCs, a DCM, an Indian Order of Merit, three Indian Distinguished Service Medals and five Mentions in Despatches. (In the post-war era the battery became 14 LAA Battery Pakistan Artillery.)[41]

In India, the Gunners began preparing for fresh operations and much training was undertaken while guns and ancillary equipment were replaced. The prospect was of jungle fighting in which the 3.7-inch howitzer was to be one of the most useful weapons. A proven equipment, the 3.7 had been designed to be 'broken down' and carried by mules or porters, but it could also be towed by jeeps, the light, versatile American four-wheel-drive vehicles then coming into service (designated officially, 5cwt 4×4 car). Although the 25-pounder was also to be used in Burma, the 3.7 remained the principal weapon. A short-axled 25-pounder was produced for use in jungle conditions and the 3-inch mortar was also introduced into some Gunner batteries, those regiments with a mix of guns and mortars being styled 'jungle field'.[42] Both medium and heavy artillery were also used against the Japanese although in smaller numbers than in other theatres; they were to prove useful in dealing with Japanese bunkers.

To operate effectively in jungle conditions, field artillery had to find gun positions with an effective field of fire, which was often much more difficult than in European or desert battlegrounds. Moreover, such positions had to be defended against parties of Japanese soldiery who would infiltrate the Allied lines to attack gunsites. This added another dimension to the choosing of gun positions. Back in Britain, and in the Middle East, Gunners were evolving methods of bringing to bear quick concentrations of artillery fire and, although there were limitations in dense jungle country, such methods were also to be used in the Far East. However, the problems and terrain conditions met in Burma were unique in the history of the Royal Artillery.

> As experience was gained proficiency improved. The movement of guns of all natures, from 2-pounders to 7.2-inch howitzers, by raft, country boat and landing craft of all types along rivers and creeks, their deployment into action over mud and mangrove swamps (occasionally by motor transport, but mostly by manpower), their maintenance and ammunition supply, were successfully accomplished by British, Indian and West African gunners. The old Gunner tradition carried us though: to get into action on time to support our infantry. More than once, we were there first.[43]

In September 1942, 14th Indian Division launched an offensive into the Arakan, the north-western coastal area of Burma, to push down the Mayu peninsula as part of a plan to wrest from the Japanese Akyab Island with its port and airfields. While 14th Indian Division drew the attention of the Japanese, 29 Independent Brigade was to land on Akyab, in which action it would be joined by 6 Brigade Group, crossing from the Mayu peninsula. Circumstances conspired against this plan from its earliest days with monsoon conditions hitting 14th Division as it trudged towards the Mayu and then the news that neither 29 Brigade nor its landing craft would be available. Nonetheless, the plan went ahead. By early February 1943, two brigades of 14th Division, 47 Indian and 6 British, had reached Donbaik and were facing the final Japanese positions north of Akyab.[44]

At the end of March the Japanese attacked, advancing up the Mayu valley and pushing aside parties of 47 Brigade to cross the Mayu. There, on the coastal plain, 6 Brigade had established positions, no more than a mile deep, along a seven-mile strip of coast. At the north end, the brigade's lay-back position was manned by 1st Royal Berkshires and twelve 25-pounders of 130th Field Regiment (Lowland) (TA). In Indin area were the brigade's other three battalions – 1st Royal Scots, 1st Royal Welch Fusiliers and 2nd Durham Light Infantry – as well as 130th Field's remaining 25-pounders, those of 494 Battery. Four jeep-towed 3.7-inch howitzers of 472 Battery, attached from 99th Field Regiment (Buckinghamshire Yeomanry), a company of Durhams and a party of machine gunners from the Jats were a further three miles south, in the Kwason area. Brigadier Cavendish's HQ was in a copse between the artillery and infantry, a strangely isolated position for any HQ.[45]

On 5 April, in the afternoon, the Royal Welch Fusiliers and Durhams attacked the Japanese to their east. The Gunners awaited the call to action. Early on the 6th, Lieutenant Colonel Ronald Nicholson, commanding 130th Field, was awoken to receive a telephone message from the brigade commander. Cavendish's HQ had been surrounded and he was handing command of all troops south of the HQ to Nicholson, who was to instruct the Durhams' CO to take command of the infantry, clear the Brigade HQ area and force a way north for the guns.[46]

Having passed on the orders to the Durhams' CO, Nicholson made a dawn reconnaissance during which he spotted enemy troops in the Brigade HQ area and the brigade commander being held by the Japanese. (It is believed that Brigadier Cavendish 'suffered a particularly barbaric death at the hands of his captors'.)[47] Then the commander of 472 Battery, Major Awdrey, arrived and established an OP alongside Nicholson. The 3.7s of 472 Battery shelled the area around the HQ forcing many Japanese to make for the hills to the east. It was probably at this time that one mountain battery FOO who found himself engaging Japanese positions only thirty yards from his OP, and between his position and the guns of his battery, nonetheless maintained his OP for several days before slipping away unseen through the jungle.[48]

> It says much for the laying and accuracy of the dear old 3.7 howitzer that although many hundreds of rounds were fired in defensive shoots and in observed fire, the OP party suffered no casualties.[49]

However, there were still enemy present while others in the foothills were trying to outflank Nicholson's position to the right. To combat this, a company of Durhams with an OP from 494 Battery moved out to delay the Japanese. Meanwhile, plans were being made for the break-out to the north from Indin, scheduled for 3.00pm, the earliest time they could cross a stream; by then a smokescreen would have been laid. The guns in the lay-back position, and the crews of each vehicle, were to fire as they passed at the former Brigade HQ copse.[50]

The break-out operation went to plan, the smokescreen provided cover and the vehicles and guns made for the stream. Although the first vehicle, a carrier, stuck, the next found the crossing place and made it over in spite of mortar bombing. By 4.15pm, the final vehicles were underway. The last guns, under Major Mike Lawrence, which had kept firing until the Japanese were within 1,500 yards, limbered up and drove off at the convoy's tail.

> Having passed the former Brigade HQ the guns of A Troop of 315 Battery and P Troop of 494 Battery, now in view of the Japanese in the foothills 800 yards to the east, came into action. Firing over open sights, the Gunners engaged the enemy with every kind of ammunition, including smoke and armour-piercing shell. Men, mules and vehicles moved on to the north under cover of this fire.[51]

Ronald Nicholson recalled what he described as 'the great moment of this hectic day' which occurred as the infantry moved out to the beach in columns and began filing past the guns, which were bombarding the enemy.

> The sight of the Gunners, now under fire from the Japs, sending shell after shell in retaliation was too much for the magnificent discipline of the Infantry. Taking off their helmets they broke ranks and rushed up to the guns. As in 1811 "An English shout arose", but on this 6th April 1943, it was a British cheer – from Englishmen, Scotsmen and Welshmen – which rolled out over the Bay of Bengal above the din of battle. Cheering the Gunners again and again and clapping them on their backs the infantry showed, in this spontaneous action, their appreciation of the co-operation given by the men of the Royal Regiment.[52]

As the infantry marched away the Gunners continued to fire, preventing the Japanese from interfering with the withdrawal. This operation could not have succeeded without artillery support, as the Gunners

> In their dirty begrimed khaki drill battledress (jungle green was still unheard of) swearing as only a British soldier can swear, grinned and went on loading and firing. The infantry reformed and marched on, the RWF leaving some carriers to protect the guns. When the last shell had been fired the Gunners, revving up the Quads, limbered up and went on their way rejoicing that they had at last defeated Colonel Tanahashi and his redoubtable troops of 112 Japanese Regiment, and lived again to fight another day with the 25-pdrs they had brought through to safety.[53]

The first Arakan expedition may have been a failure but the Gunners could hold their heads high: by doing their job well, they had prevented a major tragedy for 6 Brigade.

Let us now review the situation at the end of 1942. The Japanese had advanced as far as the Chindwin, to the southern end of the Kabaw valley, and to Fort White in the Chin Hills. This pause on their part allowed the rebuilding of British forces in India to get underway in earnest and, during 1943, new divisions were formed whose training reflected the many lessons learned about the Imperial Japanese Army. Lieutenant General Bill Slim was overseeing training and inspiring all those he met with a confidence that a resurgent British/Indian force would beat the Japanese. Above all, Slim challenged the myth of the Japanese soldier as a superman. Soldiers learned that their foe could be beaten through learning the rules of jungle fighting, active patrolling and making the jungle a friend.[54]

Slim's efforts were to bear fruit in the work of Fourteenth Army which was created in 1943 with Slim as C-in-C. For the army's badge, Slim chose a sword pointing downwards. Heraldically, this may have been incorrect but it symbolised how the new army, which was to be Britain's largest, would strike down from the frontiers of India into Burma to defeat the Japanese. The badge was designed by Slim personally.[55]

> A difficult time this for Gunners, both in the Arakan and in Assam, a period of frustration and terrible weather conditions, with green mould spreading inside all the instruments; a period without movement but with much sickness; a period of acute shortage of manpower and material; a period of desperate deficiency of Allied air power and of frequent attacks by Japanese aircraft (19 enemy planes were destroyed by our anti-aircraft guns in the Digboi area on 2 October 1942 alone).[56]

This difficult period was, however, coming to an end. Fourteenth Army made its first appearance in the field in the winter of 1943 with 5th and 7th Indian and 81st West African Divisions under command, charged with reducing the threat of an invasion of India by driving the Japanese from the Mayu peninsula and the Kaladan valley. This operation began in January 1944 with the occupation of Akyab island as a main objective.

Fifth Indian had little real difficulty clearing Maungdaw, on the right flank, while 7th Indian pushed on for Buthidaung. The latter division was on the left, operating between the Kalapanzin river and the Spine, the lofty, narrow ridge running the length of the Mayu peninsula. Meanwhile, 81st West African Division first of all cleared, 'through the worst jungle covered hills you could find', a road that was later made fit for jeeps and 15cwt lorries before coming up against Japanese forces in the Kaladan valley. By this time the divisional artilleries of both 5th and 7th Indian Divisions were complete; the corps artillery consisted of 6th Medium, 8th (Belfast) HAA and 36th LAA Regiments.[57]

While 5th Division made good progress, the country across which 7th Division was fighting was very difficult and the advance on the left flank had not reached the Maungdaw–Buthidaung road when, in February, the Japanese counter-attacked. The end result was the famed stand of 7th Division in the 'Admin Box' at Sinzweya, which began on 7 February and lasted until the 23rd. Having occupied the east–west Ngakyedauk Pass, Japanese forces infiltrated between brigades of the division. Gunners were prominent in the battle: a battery of 6th Medium, a troop of 8th (Belfast) HAA, 24th LAA Regiment, two batteries of 24th Mountain Regiment, and a mortar battery of 139th Jungle Field Regiment, all inside the Box, as well as 7th Division's artillery were engaged.[58]

As 5th, 26th and 36th Divisions moved to relieve Sinzweya, the defence of the box, lying in open paddy fields, was organised by Brigadier Geoffrey Evans. Control of 7th Division was passed to the CO of 24th LAA Regiment in the Admin Box by the CRA, Brigadier A F Hely, who later wrote of this battle:

> Gunners soon showed their versatility. HQ 24th LAA Regiment became HQ 7th Indian Division. Gunner signallers and sets were soon working to all brigades and as our communications with outside regiments had never been broken we were in a comfortable position. Ammunition for the guns in the Box was there for the taking, since the corps ammunition dump was in the centre of the valley.
>
> Outside the Box 136th Field Regiment, under Geoff Armstrong, and Harry Hall's 139th Field Regiment were safely with 33 Brigade; 25th Mountain Regiment, under Lewis Pugh, were with 114 Brigade; and 7th Indian Field Regiment were rather isolated some distance away, while 24th Mountain Regiment, under Humphrey Hill, were on the Box perimeter. The first two regiments had tremendous tasks. Not only did they shoot for their own brigade, but also, turning their guns round, they shot day after day and night after night for the beleaguered Box. They were particularly useful for counter-battery tasks, of which there were many.
>
> The Japs soon consolidated their positions around the Box. They occupied the hill features and could look down at all the activities of the garrison. Battle took place daily for the immediate hills, and it was with great difficulty that these were held. Cole's LAA boys, moving their Bofors around, shot Japs off many hill positions over open sights and supported infantry counterattacks.[59]

The 3.7s of 21Battery 8th (Belfast) HAA Regiment provided the Japanese with a considerable shock as, with the Bofors, they engaged and shot down or damaged many attacking aircraft. But the heavy AA guns were also used extremely effectively in a ground role. Two-one Battery's troop earned two MCs, two MMs and several Mentions in Despatches. Typifying the Gunner role in the Box is the citation for the MC awarded to Captain Robin Reade for 'courage and devotion to duty above the average'. The citation noted that Reade's troop

> ... was singled out for attack by enemy bombers, and enemy guns engaged the detachments over open sights. Despite 40% casualties Capt Reade continued to keep his guns in action and by his coolness and leadership set a fine example to his men. Disregarding his personal safety he attended to the wounded during the period of shelling, and after the air attack, turned his guns onto the fd guns which were shelling over open sights and assisted in silencing them.[60]

Not only was this the first – and only – occasion on which the Japanese air force was seen in any numbers in the Arakan but it was also the first occasion on which Gunners in Burma had the support of AOPs. Major Denis Coyle's No. 656 AOP Squadron, less one flight, arrived just after the Japanese offensive began and the little Austers proved their worth in the later battles. Hely reckoned that without their assistance the effectiveness of the artillery in this and subsequent battles would have been halved.[61] At least one pilot made a lasting impression on a Gunner in the Box.

> [He] was a big Scottish bloke with a black moustache ... and in this Auster ... he had a radio, a revolver and a bottle of Scotch. His job was to take off from this strip ... identify targets and then radio back to our command post whatever height or distance was required. And he told us that on one occasion about eighty-odd Japs were killed, lining up at their cookhouse with their bowls of rice.[62]

Gunners who were not needed on the gun positions were formed into infantry companies and undertook aggressive patrolling during the sixteen days of siege. Thus surveyors, battery clerks, cooks and other men whose skills were not needed constantly on the guns 'became grim, determined infantry soldiers' who took a severe toll of the Japanese.[63]

Although the siege of the Admin Box was raised at the end of February, fighting continued in the Arakan until the monsoon broke in May. While the corps artillery and other divisions withdrew to better monsoon billets in the Chittagong area, 25th Indian Division remained in the line where the divisional artillery, reinforced by a battery of 3.7-inch HAA guns and two 5.5-inch mediums, known to everyone as Gert and Daisy, kept up persistent shelling of the Japanese. The CRA of 25th Division, Brigadier T O'Carroll-Scott, 'was full of ingenious ideas for harassing fire and novel fireplans for the support of patrols'.[64]

In September 1943 the Gunners of 51st (Westmorland & Cumberland) Field Regiment were surprised to learn that they had been chosen for a new role. Probably even more surprised were their comrades of 69th (Duke of Connaught's – Hampshire) LAA/A-Tk Regiment, who had been through a very recent re-organisation: on 6 August RHQ 285 and 292 Anti-Tank Batteries of 69th Anti-Tank Regiment had been amalgamated with 132 and 523 Batteries of 33rd LAA Regiment (the other two batteries of each regiment formed 33rd LAA/A-Tk Regiment).[65] On 18 October a further amalgamation took place when 51st Field and 69th LAA/Anti-Tk Regiments merged to become 51st/69th Regiment RA.[66] Although retaining the Gunner title the regiment was to serve as infantry, in a long-range penetration role behind Japanese lines in Burma. They were to become part of Major General Orde Wingate's Special Force, or Chindits, serving with 16 Brigade as 51 and 60 Columns. Specialists from both regiments were transferred to the RA Base Depot which left the new unit short of the total of 800 men needed to form two columns. As a result, 51st/69th Regiment was brought up to strength with a squadron from 45th Reconnaissance Regiment, and a company from 2nd Queen's. A platoon of Sappers, a section of five RAF personnel, a Royal Signals' section and a detachment of Burma Rifles completed each column.[67]

Also selected for conversion to the Chindit role was 60th (North Midland) Field Regiment in which the feeling, when told of the proposal, was one of anger. Attempts were made to have the decision reversed but to no avail and the Regiment became 60 and 88 Columns; 237 Battery and half of 442 Battery would form 60 Column with 238 Battery and the other half of 442 forming 88 Column. They would not take part in the early phase of operations but were deployed late in April, 'the very last two columns of the last Chindit brigade to go into action'[68] The story of their time behind Japanese lines is told in *All The King's Enemies*, a history of 60th Field.

Orde Wingate was a Gunner who had organised anti-guerrilla operations with his Special Night Squads in Palestine before the war and had added to his reputation for irregular warfare in Abyssinia. It was on that basis that General Wavell, the C-in-C, India, sent for him to come to India to organise a campaign behind Japanese lines in Burma in 1943. This, at brigade strength, was the first Chindit expedition. It had limited military effect but far-reaching beneficial effects on morale. Wingate so impressed Winston Churchill that he was given permission for a second expedition in 1944: Operation THURSDAY. This was to be at divisional strength but the Chindits were kept behind enemy lines for so long that they suffered horrendously and the military dividend of their operations was not commensurate with the scale of the undertaking or the level of sacrifice.[69] The men of 51st/69th Regiment RA performed as well as any others in this new role. Having marched in from India, the only brigade to do so, 16 Brigade deployed 51 and 69 Columns to take the Japanese-held village of Lonkin. Both columns fought a sharp battle there, evicted the small Japanese garrison and created an airstrip from which light aircraft evacuated the wounded. Then it was on to 'Aberdeen', a stronghold, which the Gunner columns reached two weeks behind their comrades. However, 'Aberdeen' was not to be held as long as the other strongholds and was abandoned in early May after an unsuccessful attempt to take Indaw, the brigade's true objective. Already suffering from exhaustion and illness, the men of 16 Brigade returned to India, having left many of their number behind.[70] They were fortunate not to be kept in Burma as long as the other brigades which were all but destroyed by their experiences. Among the men to suffer were the Gunners who supported and protected the strongholds.

The strongholds established by the Chindit columns were garrisoned by, among others, R, S and U Troops 160th Jungle Field Regiment and W, X, Y and Z Troops 69th LAA Regiment (these were some of the Gunners of the latter unit who had not been re-roled as infantry).[71] Y and Z Troops served at Aberdeen where, before leaving, they 'had a field day on 4th May when they destroyed five out of 12 attacking aircraft'. From 'Aberdeen' they moved to 'Blackpool', commanded by Major John Masters, acting commander of 111 Brigade. Also moving to 'Blackpool' was U Troop 160th Field, with 25-pounders (these were the jury, or short axle, 25-pounders with which all four troops were equipped). On the Gunners' first night at 'Blackpool' they were attacked, coming under fire from a Japanese 105mm. The casualties included the Chindit CRA, Major Richard Duxbury, who was killed by a shell splinter from the 105. No fire was returned as U Troop's guns had yet to arrive.[72]

Three guns of U Troop were flown in by C-47 Skytrains, the plane carrying the fourth gun having been forced to return to base. The guns were assembled and in position by dawn on 14 May and were shelled not long after that. Further shelling occurred at 9.34am. By 9.50 the guns were ready and a land line had been laid to the OP. Retaliatory fire was put down around the enemy 105 and other targets were registered. However, an attempt to free-drop ammunition, that is, without using parachutes, failed as all the shells were damaged on hitting the ground. There were further casualties from enemy shelling and the troop commander, Captain Philip Young, was killed by mortar fire on OP Hill.[73]

Constant enemy shelling and infantry attacks led Masters to conclude that 'Blackpool' was untenable and he decided to evacuate the stronghold. The guns were stripped of their sights and breechblocks and those who were still fit were detailed to help carry the wounded. Only eighteen Gunners returned. It may seem that U Troop made little contribution to the defence of Blackpool but its effect on the morale of the infantry was tremendous. Those who were present and survived retained a deep admiration for their Gunner friends. Colonel Desmond Whyte DSO, then the senior medical officer of 111 Brigade and who was recommended for the VC for his service in Blackpool, told the author that he had the utmost respect for all Gunners because 'I watched brave men die at their guns' in the 'Blackpool' block.[74]

While Operation THURSDAY was getting underway, the Japanese were continuing their advance towards India with the launch of Operation U-GO on 8 March. This was intended to push into India on its north-east frontier. On 16 March Japanese troops crossed the Chindwin en route to the Kohima–Imphal road and British forces were withdrawing to Imphal. Two Japanese divisions, 15th and 31st, were closing on Imphal and Kohima respectively while a major threat was developing about six miles north-east of Imphal towards Sangshak. Lieutenant General Scoones, commanding IV Indian Corps, deployed forces to cover the Imphal–Kohima road, keep open the Dimapur–Imphal road and hold, at all costs, Kohima. At Sangshak was 50 Indian Parachute Brigade with 152nd (Indian) and 153rd (Gurkha) Parachute Battalions, 4/5th Mahratta Light Infantry of 49 Indian Brigade, half the Nepalese Kaki Bahadur Regiment, 15 (Jhelum) Mountain Battery 28th Mountain Regiment, under Major R J P Lock, and D Troop 583 Battery 158th Jungle Field Regiment, which was equipped with mortars.[75]

Japanese troops making for Kohima were diverted to deal with the Sangshak garrison but their first attack cost them heavily. However, the defenders' outposts fell back towards the gun positions which were in a confined area, a 'small feature about 100 yards by 50 on the highest part of the position'. Two OPs, one in the church and the other with the Mahrattas, had been established. All through the night of 22/23 March, the Japanese attacked the position. No. 1 gun of 15 Mountain Battery, being more exposed than most, received special attention but the mortars of D Troop defended the position vigorously. Over the next few days there were many more attacks, accompanied by aircraft and Japanese artillery while snipers were a constant threat. At one point the OP in the church came under attack but this was beaten off and a Japanese officer was wounded and made prisoner. Jhelum Battery's guns wreaked havoc amongst enemy troops gathering at Sanjing village for an attack while No. 2 gun fought a duel with an enemy artillery piece and silenced it, receiving applause from the infantry for so doing.[76]

On the 26th the enemy penetrated the positions and a new perimeter was formed around No. 2 gun and

> A very strong resistance was put up by Havildar Surwan Dass of 15 Mountain Battery, some officers of 152nd (Gurkha) Parachute Battalion and some Gunners from No. 3 Gun under Naik Ali Akbar. Gunners Gheba Khan and Ayub Khan fought like tigers with small arms and grenades and, with the encouragement of the wounded Major Lock, somehow this splendid little band held on.[77]

Although wounded in the face the previous day, Lock remained at his post and with Major John Smith, BC of 583 Mortar Battery, a former mountain Gunner, led a charge to clear No. 1 gun's position, in the course of which he bayoneted three enemy soldiers. Sadly, both Lock,[78] who had been twice Mentioned in Despatches, and Smith[79] were killed while clearing a trench beyond the gun position. The battle continued and the infantry used the gun positions as their rallying point for a final attack alongside the Gunners. Eventually only No. 3 gun was in a position to fire and loosed off seventy rounds at Japanese guns at Lingshang even as enemy snipers fired at the detachment. The Japanese guns were knocked out and the Sangshak garrison was ordered to withdraw. The guns were destroyed to prevent them falling into enemy hands and the garrison made for Imphal.[80]

The battles at Imphal and Kohima were to be the turning point of the war in Burma, marking the high tide of Japanese success. In particular, the stand of the Kohima garrison, which included 24th Indian Mountain Regiment, ensured that the Japanese could not invade India and, in turn, the efforts of the defenders of Sangshak in slowing the enemy advance ensured that Kohima could be held. During these pivotal battles Gunners were to the fore with mountain, jungle field and medium units battering the attackers. When 3/9th Jats were beaten off Point 3833, Nungshigum Hill, on 7 April, the position was regained quickly with the aid of an air strike and the guns of both 4th Field and 28th Jungle Field Regiments. Recognising the value of the position, the Japanese attacked and regained it but were once more evicted by infantry supported by Gunners, tanks of 3rd Carabiniers and air strikes. Within days, 8th Medium Regiment had arrived – it had been engaged along the Tiddim road – to deploy 246 Battery, less B Troop, under 23rd Indian Division while 247 Battery, less C Troop, joined 20th Indian Division; B Troop was with 5th Indian Division on the Ukhrul road while C Troop was in 'Sardine Box', west of Imphal airfield. In thirty days, 246 Battery fired 2,885 rounds. The longer the battle raged the fewer were the chances of the Japanese breaking through to India as British muscle was increasing while the Japanese were on the end of a long logistical tail. In fact, they had intended to sustain their onward advance by plundering the British dumps.[81]

On 12 April Japanese troops were forced off 'Nippon Hill' in an attack by 80 Indian Brigade supported by the divisional artillery of their parent 20th Indian Division which included 9th Field, 114th Jungle Field, 23rd Indian Mountain and 55th LAA/A-Tk Regiments. Their guns and mortars smashed the subsequent counter-attack but, on the night of the 16th, Japanese infantry, with heavy artillery support, recaptured the hill although failing in their subsequent effort to push through the Shenam Pass. In spite of some local gains, this was the sum result of their efforts although fighting continued for three months.[82]

Elsewhere, on Bishenpur Hill, a series of battles was fought, beginning in mid-April. During the second battle, on the night of 20/21 May, a Japanese column struck at the junction of the main road and the Silchar track, having gained complete surprise in its advance. When day broke, a gun of A Troop 88 LAA Battery 82nd LAA/A-Tk Regiment fired at enemy infantry who were digging in east of the road. At least four Japanese were killed and the column was finally overrun early on the 24th. Next day the enemy attacked Bishenpur again. Their objective seemed to be the gun box and at 3.50am, a party of about fifteen soldiers, led by a captain, attacked A Troop HQ and A4 gun, north-west of the main road and Silchar track. Penetrating the wire, the party attacked with the officer charging at the sentry, Gunner Skelly, who parried the man's sword stroke and then shot him before raising the alarm.[83]

This began a skirmish that lasted until first light. A Japanese warrant officer charged the gunpit with a grenade in his hand but was brought down on the edge of the pit.

> By this time all A Troop personnel had taken post in the weapon and gun pits, where they came under fire from a light machine gun and a grenade discharger used at short range.
>
> The troop commander, Lieutenant W Widdup MM, accompanied by Troop Sergeant J B Palmer, made a reconnaissance to ascertain the enemy's strength and location. It was found that they occupied a position outside the perimeter, dominating the box and threatening the security of the gun area. Lieutenant Widdup immediately organised six men to throw grenades over the crest on to the position.[84]

In daylight Widdup organised an attack on the enemy position during which the last-surviving Japanese blew himself up with a landmine, injuring Sergeant Palmer and his men. A Troop suffered two dead and four wounded in this engagement but twelve Japanese had been killed and two wounded and captured. William Widdup was awarded the Military Cross and John Palmer the Military Medal.[85]

Despite all the Japanese efforts, and reinforcement of the attacking formations, their advance was finished. The 'march on Delhi' was over and the Gunners had played a major role in stopping it. By late April the entire Kohima battlefield was overseen by Gunner OPs of 10th, 16th and 99th Field Regiments, the divisional artillery of 2nd British Division. These regiments knew each other so well, having trained together since 1940, and also knew their infantry, that they provided a giant battery that could deploy guns wherever they were needed and to whomsoever needed them.

As 1944 neared its end, the campaign in the Arakan was still underway with strong British forces pushing down the Kaladan valley where, on 15/16 December, near Tinma, the fourth Gunner VC of the war was earned. The laureate was Havildar Umrao Singh, of 30 Battery 30th Indian Mountain Regiment, who was commanding a gun in an advanced section of his regiment when it came under heavy fire from enemy 75mm guns and mortars. This bombardment was maintained for ninety minutes before two companies of Japanese infantry attacked. During the ensuing engagement, Umrao Singh 'so inspired his gun detachment by his personal example and encouragement to fight and defend their gun that they beat off the attack with losses to the enemy'.[86]

But the Japanese came back and Umrao Singh, although wounded twice by grenade splinters in the earlier encounter, continued rallying his detachment. This time he directed their small-arms' fire with considerable skill while himself manning a Bren gun which he fired over the shield of his gun. Once again the Japanese were beaten off and once again they suffered considerable losses. Undaunted the enemy returned, to be met with the same stubborn defiance and the inspiring example of Havildar Singh. A third attack was beaten off, as was a fourth.

A fifth time the Japanese attacked. The other gun in the section having been overrun and all his ammunition exhausted, Singh seized a gun bearer – a steel bar – and called on the other survivors to follow him as he took the fight to the foe, striking down at least three Japanese soldiers in desperate hand-to-hand fighting. Eventually the gallant havildar was overwhelmed and knocked unconscious beside the gun he was trying so desperately to save. It seemed that the enemy had won the day. However, six hours later, a counter-attack evicted the Japanese from the position and Umrao Singh was found beside his gun. He was still alive, although exhausted and all but unrecognisable due to having sustained seven wounds. The bodies of ten Japanese were found beside him.[87]

Havildar Umrao Singh became the sole other rank in the Royal Artillery or the Indian Artillery to receive the Victoria Cross in the Second World War. On 15 October 1945 he was decorated with the VC by King George VI at Buckingham Palace.[88] Such had been the service of the Indian Gunners that the King-Emperor also conferred the title Royal on the Indian Artillery.

To destroy the Japanese hold on central Burma, Slim planned a bold strike in which XXXIII Corps would clear the region between the Chindwin and Irrawaddy rivers. With that accomplished, crossings were to be made of the Irrawaddy: 19th Indian Division, which had first seen action as recently as December, would cross north of Mandalay with the British 2nd Division on its right and 268 Independent Indian Brigade between them; these formations were to seize airfields at Yeu and Shwebo and make ready to attack Mandalay from the north. Meanwhile 20th Indian Division would cross the Irrawaddy west of the city and attack from the south. While the Japanese focused their attention on Mandalay, IV Corps would advance through the Gangaw valley to cross the Irrawaddy near Nyaungu before striking out across Burma's central plain to take the communications' centre of Meiktila and its airfields.[89] For this operation IV Corps would also create the impression that it was a much smaller formation. A corps artillery group, including eighty guns from 25-pounders up to 7.2-inch howitzers, was formed to support the advance on Mandalay.[90]

Unit	Equipment
1st Medium Regiment (less one troop)	12 × 5.5-inch medium guns
Battery 134th Medium Regiment	8 × 6-inch howitzers
101st HAA Regiment	4 × 7.2-inch howitzers (from 6th Medium Regiment) 16 × 3.7-inch HAA guns
10th Field Regiment (from 2nd Division)	24 × 25-pounders
18th Field Regiment	16 × 105mm SPGs (Priests)

On 14 and 15 January 1945, 19th Division crossed the Irrawaddy at two points, fifty and seventy miles north of Mandalay, and began advancing down the river's eastern bank towards the city.[91] Thirty-five miles west of Mandalay, 20th Division began crossing on 12 February[92] using vessels that the divisional engineers had 'conjured out of nothing'[93] The Gunners' contribution to the operation was memorable.

> Every night at dusk the Corps artillery, 120 guns, threw a tremendous barrage across at the opposite bank. This was a new experience for us and the mighty roar of 25-prs and 5.5s gave us tremendous encouragement, [as] up to then we had had no front line and had not taken part in co-ordinated artillery fire.[94]

The writer, Sergeant Ralph Billings of 114th (Sussex) Field Regiment, was one of the first Gunners across the river, although, as he waded from his boat to the bank, the batteries for his wireless set were destroyed by immersion. The situation was saved by using the infantry's lightweight sets to pass orders to the guns which, as day dawned, fired to break up Japanese counter-attacks on the bridgehead. Guns were later rafted over but remained close to the riverbank with all their equipment, and even their cooks, dug in in front of the gun positions. Alongside 114th Field was 9th Field Regiment and so close were the pair that, on one occasion, the latter opened up on their SOS lines after hearing the signal for such fire come into the former's position.[95] At this stage the Japanese air force appeared in much more strength than had been seen for some time. Casualties from air attack included several C-47 Skytrains, hit while on the ground, and some men and vehicles of 99th (Buckinghamshire Yeomanry) Field Regiment.[96]

When the attackers broke out of their bridgehead, Gunner FOOs were in the van of the advance. Among them was Captain Fred Maller, of 232 Battery, who 'stood up in full view of the enemy and urged forward not only his own party but also the leading platoon'. His Regiment's war diary noted that Maller 'pursued enemy south'. His actions led to his second recommendation for a decoration in two weeks. So quickly did XXXIII Corps advance that it was outrunning its supply chain and was ordered to pause. The corps commander then amended the original plan by ordering 2nd Division to take Sagaing while the two Indian divisions attacked Mandalay. When warning of a possible Japanese counter-offensive was received from Slim, 20th Indian Division was ordered to take Monywa and Myinmu as soon as possible, for which task it was reinforced with, inter alia, a troop of 1st Medium Regiment and 101st HAA Regiment, less one battery. At the same time additional forces allotted to 19th Indian and 2nd British Divisions included a battery of 1st Medium and the third battery of 101st HAA to the former and another troop of 1st Medium to the latter; a 7.2-inch howitzer troop was held in corps reserve.[97] However, the counter-offensive came to naught and the advance was resumed.

For its part, IV Corps had also made steady progress with 7th Indian Division seizing a bridgehead through which 17th Division passed en route for Meiktila. Leading the advance was 255 Indian Tank Brigade Group, which included 59 Battery of 18th Field Regiment, equipped with eight M7 Priests. This group took the first of the Meiktila airfields, having had only one sharp encounter on the way, after which another brigade was airlifted in. Soon Meiktila was surrounded, which sparked a furious Japanese reaction. The Priests of 59 Battery took part in a brisk battle on 3 March during which a strong enemy force, including artillery, was evicted from its positions on the road to Mandalay; four Japanese guns – two 37mm and two 75mm weapons – were captured. Meiktila fell on the 4th. Thus the Japanese 15th and 33rd Divisions were entrapped; 19th Indian and 36th British Divisions were approaching to close the trap.[98]

During 2nd Division's advance on Mandalay there occurred what must be a unique incident when men of 99th Field Regiment uncovered a telephone cable into which they tapped and were able to listen, with the aid of interpreters, to a Japanese railway transport officer (RTO) in a village further along the road. The RTO was giving details of his timetable for that evening, which included a train that was then in the station. Armed with this information,

> 394 Battery shot up the station and was disappointed to hear the RTO announce that the rounds were falling near a pagoda 200 yards away. The pagoda was marked on the map and the battery commander corrected his fire. The train was found burning next morning.[99]

As one Gunner officer commented wryly, this must have the sole occasion on which a Japanese officer, 'and an RTO at that, ranged a British battery'.[100]

On 11 March, 19th Division, having advanced from the north-east of the Irrawaddy, captured part of Mandalay Hill. This was achieved by Stiletto Force, which included 240 Battery 115th (North Midland) Field Regiment and a troop of 82nd LAA/A-Tk Regiment; 240 Battery opened fire on Mandalay Hill and also broke up a Japanese counter-attack.[101] Following this there began a protracted struggle for the remainder of the hill, the city itself and Fort Dufferin. When air attacks using bombs and rockets failed to smash the fort's walls, the attackers had recourse to the age-old weapon for use against such defences – heavy artillery. In the days of siege warfare the optimum range for the bombarding guns had been between 600 and 200 yards and it was within these parameters that 6-inch howitzers of 134th Medium Regiment and 5.5-inch guns from 5/22 Battery 1st Medium Regiment began to pound at the old but robust walls. Deployed at ranges of from 300 to 500 yards the guns hammered at the walls until, on the afternoon of 20 March, six Burmese, with a Union flag and a white flag, came out from the east gate to tell the Gunners that the Japanese had gone. Soldiers of 62 Brigade were the first to enter the fort.

> At 1.30pm a Gunner of the Medium Regiment, a detachment of which went in with the infantry, nailed a Union Jack to the fort flagstaff. Kipling himself, who immortalised Mandalay, could not have thought of a more suitable ending to the battle.[102]

The British soldier had come back to Mandalay.

Fighting still raged around Meiktila where the Japanese were determined to retake the airfield where 9 Indian Brigade was being flown in by USAAF C-47s. Enemy artillery was handled with great skill during these battles but the Japanese attackers were eventually repulsed, the guns of two Indian artillery regiments making a major contribution; these were 1st Indian Field and 21st Indian Mountain Regiments. For the first time, also, a cab-rank system of air support gave added striking power to the Allied troops.[103]

> The Japanese reacted strongly to the capture of Meiktila and moved up towards it from all directions, so that during the first two weeks of March the garrison was out-numbered and the only course to adopt was to take constant and vigorous offensive action to ensure that the initiative was not lost. The method employed was to organise offensive sorties of very strong infantry and tank columns that set out from the area of the defensive harbours and boxes in the town with the aim of engaging and destroying the Japanese wherever they might be found. Many of these actions took place in the area of the air-strip which, although in allied hands, and in use from 5th March, was continually attacked by Japanese ground forces so that supplies on many days still had to be dropped by air, and it was not until 31st March that supply-dropping was discontinued and the planes began to land once more.[104]

Also engaged were the Priests of 59 Battery from 18th Field Regiment whose history, quoted above, notes that the OP parties, working with those infantry/tank columns, bore the brunt of the action as the battle developed.

> Each day a different sortie would be made by a column which ... generally consisted of a squadron of tanks, an infantry battalion and a tank OP. It was during one of these sorties, to the south of Meiktila that Francis Allam, B Troop Commander, was severely wounded, dying in hospital in Meiktila later before he could be evacuated.[105] His place as B Troop Commander was taken by Lieutenant Peters. Similarly, during one of the attacks to clear the airfield, which encountered heavy artillery and mortar fire, Captain Preston was slightly wounded, and thereafter, A Troop was commanded by Lieutenant Birch ... The two Troop Tank OP crews, although under severe strain, insisted on remaining in their teams and once again it was one of these, L/Bdr Lillis, who suffered, losing an eye whilst supporting an assault to clear the airfield.[106]

By this time, 59 Battery had been fighting with 255 Indian Tank Brigade since leaving Gangaw at the end of January. The brigade had been at the head of

Fourteenth Army for most of that time and 59 Battery had been spearheading the brigade's advance. Thus for nine weeks this SP battery had been in the forefront of the fighting against a very determined and still strong enemy.[107] Not surprisingly, 59 Battery was awarded an honour title as Meiktila Battery. Today the Battery is 148 (Meiktila) Commando Forward Observer Battery of 29th Commando Regiment RA.

The CO of 129th (Lowland) Field Regiment, Lieutenant Colonel Charles Younger, testified to the ferocity of the Meiktila fighting in a report to the BRA, Allied Land Forces, South-East Asia (ALFSEA) when writing of his regiment's experiences in April. 'Tree snipers have recently gone out of fashion and in recent attacks I have noticed that the majority of enemy snipers have been in positions on the ground such as tree roots' which indicated how unhealthy the practice of climbing into a tree had become for any enemy sniper due to the airburst rounds fired by the Gunners.[108] But the Japanese infantry remained a real danger to gun positions, which were always prime targets, and Gunners became expert at local defence as 'the number of times when one can sit back and say that the infantry will hold the fort for you are few and far between these days or in our experience in the past.' Younger also commented on the number of fireplans in the previous two months and on how the Regiment was always able to respond quickly:

> with our communications and a little foresight this presents no difficulties. They require control by an FOO with the lead infantry ... because the infantry can never be sure of their speed across the ground in a jungle against a resolute foe.[109]

At the beginning of April, with its pre-monsoon heat, Fourteenth Army stood ready for the next phase of operations in Burma – the advance to Rangoon. With Main HQ Fourteenth Amy and HQ No. 221 Group RAF at Meiktila, IV Corps advanced to Pegu en route to Rangoon while XXXIII Corps pushed down the valley of the Irrawaddy. Meanwhile, an amphibious landing – Operation DRACULA – saw XV Indian Corps' 26th Indian Division make a seaborne landing while 50th Indian Parachute Battalion of 44th Indian Airborne Division dropped south of the city at Elephant Point; the seaborne troops had travelled in their transports from Ramree and Akyab islands. Rangoon was abandoned by the Japanese and foul weather conditions created more problems for the attackers than did the enemy.[110]

However, the Japanese had remained tenacious. As Fourteenth Army advanced, news was received at its HQ that Japanese forces were assembling for a counter-attack near Toungoo. Slim immediately flew there to assess the situation since there was only one brigade of 19th Division to guard the army's lines of communication against attack. Slim found Rees, the GOC, confident that he would defeat the Japanese, even though he was outnumbered and his men were already on half rations.

> I visited some of his units and stayed to watch a battery firing at Japanese reported to be collecting for an attack. One of the gunners, stripped to the waist, his bronzed body glistening with sweat, was slamming shells into the breach of a twenty-five-pounder. In a lull in the firing I stepped into the gun pit beside him. 'I'm sorry,' I said, 'you're got to do all this on half rations.' He looked up at me from under his battered bush hat, 'Don't you worry about that, sir,' he grinned, 'Put us on quarter rations, but give us the ammo and we'll get you into Rangoon!'. I did not doubt it; with men like that who could?[111]

No one episode illustrates better the morale of Fourteenth Army than the comment by that unidentified Gunner. His battery, and every unit of Royal Artillery and Indian Artillery in the campaign, was showing the same determination to bring to an end the Japanese occupation of Burma. As Rangoon fell, so the forces fighting in the Arakan also pushed their foe out and were able to deploy elements to link up with the main body of the army, thus trapping remaining Japanese forces in Burma. There was still fighting to be done in which Gunners played their part but this tended to be smaller engagements involving not large numbers of guns but troops, batteries and regiments. Then, on 6 and 9 August, the USAAF dropped atomic bombs on the Japanese cities of Hiroshima and Nagasaki. On 14 August the Japanese government surrendered unconditionally and, before long, Fourteenth Army's soldiers witnessed the almost unbelievable sight of Japanese forces laying down their weapons. It is difficult to summarise Fourteenth Army's achievements but it should be remembered that it was the largest of Britain's field armies, with almost a million men in its ranks at one point, covered a frontage of 750 miles – twice the distance from London to Glasgow – and its HQ moved forward over 800 miles during the Burma campaign. That this chapter has considered only a very few of its Gunners can be gleaned from the simple fact that, in July 1944, Fourteenth Army disposed 2,148 guns. Fourteenth Army had won the longest land campaign of the Second World War and had inflicted on the Imperial Japanese Army its greatest defeat of that war, in which the Royal Artillery had, as always, been instrumental in bringing about victory.

Notes

1 Farndale, *The Far East Theatre*, pp. 3–4
2 Ibid, pp. 12–13
3 Ibid, pp. 14–15
4 Ibid, p. 15
5 Lindsay, *The Battle for Hong Kong*, p. 31
6 Ibid, p. 100
7 Farndale, op cit, p. 16
8 Ibid, p. 16
9 Ibid

10 Ibid, pp. 26–7
11 Quoted in Farndale, op cit, p. 26
12 Bramall, in Lindsay, op cit, p. xiii
13 Churchill, *The Second World War VII, The Hinge of Fate*, p. 42
14 Quoted in Mead, *Gunners At War*, pp. 67–8
15 Mead, op cit, p. 68
16 Farndale, op cit, pp. 30–1 See also p. 330 for the information on 125th A-Tk Regt.
17 Joslen, *Orders of Battle Second World War*, p. 60
18 Farndale, op cit, p. 53
19 Lindsay, op cit, pp. 86–7 (A recent and excellent account of the fate of Force Z is to be found in *Hostages to Fortune* by Arthur Nicholson (Sutton, 2005)
20 Farndale, op cit, pp. 37–8
21 Ibid, p. 39
22 NA Kew, WO373/35; *London Gazette*, 13 December 1945. In the Supplement to the Gazette of 27 June 1946 Hugill's rank is corrected from WOIII to Sergeant.
23 NA Kew, WO373/35
24 Frederick, *Lineage Book of British Land Forces*, p. 523 & p. 532; Farndale, op cit, p. 41
25 Farndale, op cit, p. 42
26 Ibid, p. 47
27 Ibid, p. 55
28 Ibid, p. 65
29 Ibid; Frederick, op cit, p. 924; www.cwgc.org
30 Duncan, *RA Commemoration Book*, p. 86
31 Farndale, op cit, p. 83
32 Quoted in Farndale, op cit, p. 83
33 Ibid, pp. 83–4
34 Ibid, p. 84
35 Ibid, pp. 85–7
36 Ibid, p. 89
37 Ibid, p. 90
38 History 414 Bty RHA, quoted in Farndale, op cit, p.
39 Farndale, op cit, pp. 89–92
40 Mead, op cit, p. 69
41 Farndale, op cit, p. 106
42 www.members.tripod.com British Artillery in World War 2 (March 2008); Farndale, op cit, p. 173
43 Duncan, op cit, p. 91
44 Allen, *Burma: The Longest War*, pp. 91–100
45 Farndale, op cit, pp. 129–30; Mead, op cit, pp. 69–70
46 Mead, op cit, p. 70
47 Pitt, *The Military History of World War II*, p. 170
48 Ibid
49 Duncan, p. 91
50 Mead, op cit, p. 70
51 Ibid, p. 71
52 Nicholson, *Royal Artillery Journal*, Jan 1949, quoted in Mead, op cit, p. 71
53 Ibid
54 Hickey, *The Unforgettable Army*, pp. 91–4
55 Cole, *Formation Badges of World War 2*, p. 25
56 Duncan, p. 87
57 Ibid, pp. 91–2

58 Farndale, op cit, pp. 151–3; Hickey, op cit, p. 108
59 Duncan, p. 103
60 NA Kew, WO373/35
61 Duncan, p. 92
62 Tom Reynolds, interview with author, Feb 1989
63 Duncan, p. 103
64 Ibid, p. 92
65 Farndale, op cit, p. 174; Frederick, op cit, p. 845
66 Farndale, op cit, p. 166; Frederick op cit, p. 515
67 Chinnery, *March or Die*, pp. 102–4
68 Bartlett & Benson, *All The King's Enemies*, p. 237
69 Accounts of Op THURSDAY may be found in Bidwell *The Chindit War*, Chinnery *March or Die*, Masters, *The Road Past Mandalay* and Rooney *Wingate and the Chindits*.
70 Bidwell, *The Chindit War*, pp. 134–55
71 Farndale, op cit, p. 166
72 Farndale, op cit, pp. 185–6; www.cwgc.org, Major Duxbury had been Mentioned in Despatches
73 Farndale, op cit, pp. 185–6; www.cwgc.org Captain Philip Young is commemorated on the Rangoon Memorial.
74 Farndale, op cit, pp. 186–7; Col D G C Whyte DSO, interview with author, April 1989
75 Seaman, *The Battle at Sangshak*, p. 139; Farndale, op cit, p. 180
76 Farndale, op cit, p. 180
77 Ibid
78 www.cwgc.org Major Lock is buried at Imphal War Cemetery
79 www.cwgc.org Major Smith is also buried at Imphal War Cemetery
80 Farndale, op cit, pp. 180–1
81 Ibid, p. 201
82 Ibid, p. 202
83 Goodacre, *With the Fighting Cock and the Black Cat in India and Burma*, p. 40
84 Ibid
85 Ibid, pp. 40–1; *The London Gazette*, 3 Oct '44
86 Farndale, op cit, p. 241; Supplement to *The London Gazette*, 29 May 1945
87 This account is based on the citation published in *The London Gazette*
88 Farndale, op cit, p. 240
89 Slim, *Defeat into Victory*, pp. 373–406; Allen, op cit, p. 389; Hickey, op cit, pp. 203–8; Mead, op cit, pp. 120–1
90 Duncan, op cit, p. 118
91 Slim, op cit, p. 417
92 Ibid, p. 420
93 Sgt Ralph Billings, 114th Field Regt, quoted in Mead, op cit, p. 121
94 Ibid
95 Mead, op cit, p. 122
96 Farndale, op cit, pp. 250–1
97 Ibid, pp. 251–2
98 Mead, op cit, p. 122; Farndale, op cit, p. 274
99 Duncan, p. 100
100 Ibid
101 Farndale, op cit, p. 276; Mead, op cit, p. 122
102 Kirby, *The War Against Japan*, Vol IV, pp.300–1
103 Farndale, op cit, p. 280
104 Quoted in Hughes, *Honour Titles*, p. 203

105 www.cwgc.org His father, a major in the Royal Engineers, died on active service on 4 October 1941. Captain Allam's name is shown as Allom in several published works. Captain Allam had been Mentioned in Despatches.

106 Quoted in Farndale, op cit, p. 281

107 Farndale, op cit, p. 281

108 Ibid, p. 281

109 Ibid, p. 281

110 Slim, op cit, pp. 506–7; Hickey, op cit, pp. 224–5

111 Slim, op cit, p. 504

Preparing for war: a 2-pounder anti-tank detachment with their gun on Epsom Downs. The car in the background has white-painted mudguards, indicating that the blackout has already been imposed. (Wimbledon News/Newsquest via Ray Goodacre)

(Left) During the Phoney War, a Gunner of 3rd (Ulster) Searchlight Regiment prepares one of the unit's searchlights in France. (Private photo)
(Right) Among the first Gunners to be decorated for gallantry in the Second World War were men of 57th (East Surrey) Anti-Tank Regiment RA (TA). Bombardier E Stredwick was awarded the Military Medal for his part in an action near Morbecque on 24 May. The ribbon of the MM may be seen on his battledress blouse. (Ray Goodacre)

Aftermath of war: 2-pounders lie wrecked in the ruins of a village street along the route to Dunkirk. (Dominique Faivre/ARHAM via Ray Goodacre)

(Left) Also decorated was Captain P G Hampton of 228 Battery 57th Anti-Tank Regiment. Hampton was awarded the Military Cross for his role in the action at Morbecque. (Ray Goodacre)
(Right) On 17 April 1942 W91467 Private Nora Caveney, 505 Battery 148th (Mixed) HAA Regiment, became the first fatal operational casualty in the ATS Gunners. Nora was struck by a bomb splinter while operating her predictor. ATS personnel in AA Command were allowed to wear the Gunners' bursting grenade badge which can be seen above the left pocket of Nora's tunic. She was the first female British soldier to be killed in action against the enemy and is buried in Netley Military Cemetery, Hampshire. (David Griffiths via Halifax Evening Courier)

As the Germans prepared to invade Britain, air raids were launched on strategically important towns and cities, including Dover. During the attacks on Dover, 75th HAA Regiment RA (TA), under Lt Col N V Sadler, took a heavy toll of the attackers. Three of the regiment's mobile 3.7s may be seen in this photograph as well as one of the balloons of the local barrage. (IWM H 4726)

Anti-aircraft command spotters were provided with special chairs which swivelled and reclined. Here two ATS personnel pose at a site near Londonderry in Northern Ireland. Immediately behind them may be seen a height and rangefinder with a gun in the middle background. However, the gun appears to be a dummy. (9th HAA Regiment Archive)

Coast Defence artillery around the United Kingdom remained on high alert in the early years of the war. This 6-inch BL Mk VII naval gun of D, later 381, Coast Battery is emplaced on LO 7, a mixed AA/Coast site at Magilligan in County Londonderry. The water in the background is Lough Foyle and the hills behind are in Éire. (IWM H 5519)

On a cold gunsite 'somewhere in England' these Gunners of 117th (Royal Ulster Rifles) LAA Regiment man their Bofors 40mm. Greatcoats, scarves, gloves and balaclavas are worn to fight off the cold. (Museum The Royal Ulster Rifles)

During the 'tip-and-run' raids of the Battle of the Fringe Targets, LAA guns were redeployed rapidly to defend possible targets. In this photo a Bofors detachment of the Royal Canadian Artillery are ready to meet intruders in their position on the west pier in Brighton. (Alexander Mackenzie Stirton/National Archives of Canada/PA3223277)

Three sea forts in the Solent estuary guarded the approaches to Portsmouth harbour and were manned by Royal Navy and Army personnel. This is Horse Sands Fort in the eastern Solent which was built in the late nineteenth century. The fort, about 200 feet in diameter and fully armour plated, had a complement of thirty men. During the war, a more modern variation on these forts, the Maunsell forts, were built in the Thames and Mersey estuaries. (IWM H 4611)

'Boche Buster', a 14-inch howitzer of Great War vintage mounted on a railway carriage, is pictured at Catterick, Yorkshire in 1940. It was later moved to Kent where it operated near Dover. As a howitzer it could engage targets in the Channel but did not have enough range to bombard France. However, it was good for morale and many photographs of it were published. (IWM H 6089)

The V1 offensive, which began in June 1944, led to a major redeployment of AA defences. With its smoother traverse, the static 3.7 was better suited to the role of engaging the flying bombs but this created a real difficulty that was resolved quickly by AA Command. The static gun was bolted down to a concrete holdfast that took much time to construct but Brigadier Burls came up with a design for what became known as the 'Pile Platform', which could be transported and on which the 3.7s could be mounted. This photo shows a battery of static 3.7s on Pile platforms on the promenade of a south coast town in August 1944. (IWM H 39807)

In November 1939 9th (Londonderry) HAA Regiment RA (SR) became the first reserve forces unit to deploy overseas when it arrived in Alexandria for the defence of the Mediterranean Fleet's base, HMS *Nile*. The MT Section of 25 Battery were still in service dress when this photograph was taken at Sidi Bishr in December 1939. Included are (front: L-R) Gnrs Bobby Simpson, J J Doherty (the author's father), Sgt Tommy Gamble, Gnrs Bertie Porter and Bobby McFeeters and (back: L-R) Gnrs Bertie Monteith and Jimmy (Toby) McFeely. (9th HAA Regiment Archive)

There was always time for sport. Two Gunners train for a tournament in Alexandria involving 7th Medium, 9th HAA Regiment and 3rd Coldstream Guards. (A W Hogg)

And sometimes for relaxation. 'Big Bill' Irwin, later killed in East Africa, runs the 'tot' at a race meeting for his fellow Gunners. There were no horses, the betting being on imaginary mounts, the names of which often showed considerable imagination. (A W Hogg)

Almost as soon as Mussolini's declaration of war on Britain Italian bombers raided Alexandria, the first of many raids on the city and its harbour. British and Egyptian searchlight detachments illuminated the skies for the AA guns. (9th HAA Regiment Archive)

One of the gunsites in Alexandria was at Ras el Tin where four guns of 24 HAA Battery were deployed. Their arcs of fire were limited by the presence of the Ras el Tin lighthouse, from the top of which this photograph was taken. It shows clearly all or part of the four heavy gun positions, the predictor, height and rangefinder and the spotter's platform. A light gun position is also visible. (A W Hogg)

In the desert battles the 25-pounder played a major role, being used as both a field gun and an anti-tank gun. This detachment, of 11th Field Regiment, is operating in the field role during the first Battle of El Alamein in July 1942. The blast from the gun muzzles raised large quantities of sand and dust to be added to the fog of war. (IWM E 14114)

(Left) The campaign in North Africa flowed back and forth between El Alamein and El Agheila from mid-1940 until early-1943. In June 1941, these AA Gunners of 25 HAA Battery were at Sidi Barrani where the ruins of a building served as an improvised gunpit. (9th HAA Regiment Archive)

(Middle) Eighth Army held the Gazala Line during the early months of 1942 and Tobruk was a major supply base. As well as its sea connections, Tobruk was also linked to the Nile Delta by the Western Desert Railway which was guarded by Gunners with LAA guns on portées, some of which were carried on the trains using the railway. This portée of 6 LAA Battery mounts an Italian Breda 20mm gun. (6 LAA Bty OCA/Ronnie Gamble)

(Below) North Africa also saw the introduction of self-propelled guns to the Royal Artillery. The first SPG to see action was Bishop, a 25-pounder mounted on a Valentine tank from which the turret had been removed. A compromise, the end result looked clumsy and neither the 25-pounder nor the tank body operated at full effectiveness. Nonetheless, Bishop provided experience with the SPG concept and some were still in use early in the Italian campaign. (9th HAA Regiment Archive)

On the night of 28/29 May 1942, 6 LAA Battery captured this Fieseler Storch, which was one of a pair that had brought in a sabotage party to blow up the Western Desert Railway. The Storch was taken over by the RAF and was still in use in Normandy in 1944 as Air Vice Marshal Harry Broadhurst's personal hack. (6 LAA Bty OCA/Ronnie Gamble)

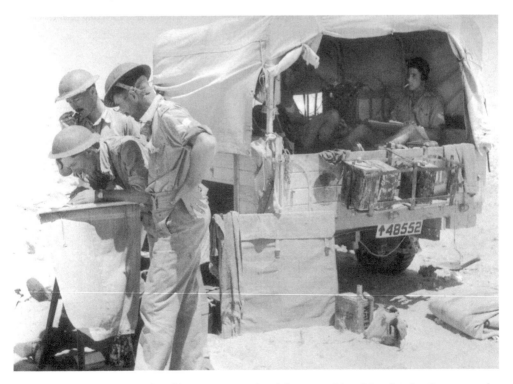

Rushed from Iraq to Egypt, 11th Field Regiment joined Eighth Army at Mersa Matruh in late-June 1942 and took part in the first Battle of El Alamein. With 2nd South African Divisional artillery, it broke an attack by 90th Light Division on 1 July. The photo shows the command post of 83/85 Battery during the battle. (IWM E 14109)

The 5.5-inch medium gun first saw action in the desert in May 1942. During the final El Alamein battle 5.5s were among the forty-eight medium guns available to Eighth Army and they gave good service throughout the remainder of the campaign and the war. Three members of this detachment are protecting their ears from the gun's blast. (9th HAA Regiment Archive)

En route to Tripoli in January 1943, these members of 25 HAA Battery have stopped for a rest close to the sea. On the left mudguard of their vehicle may be seen the regimental tactical number, 2021, under the symbol of the Sudan Defence Force; the Battery had served in the Sudan in 1940/41. (A W Hogg)

General Montgomery visits members of 24 HAA Battery at Tripoli and insisted on having photos taken with the Gunners when he discovered that they came from Londonderry which, he told them, was also his family's home. His mother then lived about eighteen miles from the city, at Moville in Donegal. (Thomas McCready via J A McCready AFM)

The spoils of war between El Alamein and Tripoli included a number of enemy AA guns among which were 88s. Four of these equipped Mac Troop, formed from 9th (Londonderry) and 51st (London) HAA Regiments, which served with 2nd New Zealand Division until the end of the campaign. Two Gunners of Mac Troop load their weapon in Tunisia where the 88s served in several roles. (9th HAA Regiment Archive)

The damaged tanker *Ohio* is helped into Grand Harbour, Valletta, by HM Ships *Penn* and *Ledbury*. Maritime RA Gunners on board *Ohio* had shot down or damaged many of the enemy aircraft that attacked the tanker and at least one aircraft crashed on *Ohio*'s deck. Her master, Captain Dudley Mason, was awarded the George Cross. (IWM GM 1505)

From North Africa the Allies moved into Sicily where the terrain proved particularly difficult. At times, batteries had to deploy their guns along the road as no suitable off-road firing points were available. The photo shows a troop of 25-pounders of 5th Division so deployed. (Private photo)

Operations in Sicily were difficult but the Gunners answered every call. This 5.5 of 66th Medium Regiment is in action on the slopes of Mount Etna on the morning of 11 August 1943. One can only imagine the difficulties that had to be overcome in deploying these guns in such locations. (IWM NA 5854)

While Eighth Army landed in Calabria, Fifth Army went ashore in Operation AVALANCHE in the Bay of Salerno. Although initial opposition was light the situation soon changed and Gunners were pressed into service as infantry. HAA Gunners also deployed as field artillery and this photo shows 3.7s of 25 HAA Battery firing in a counter-battery programme in the beachhead. (9th HAA Regiment Archive)

Allied troops soon learned that Italy was not always sunny. A 75mm howitzer of a mountain regiment is emplaced on a snow-covered mountain with ammunition supply by mule train. This photo, of 461 Battery, was taken in February 1945 but similar conditions prevailed in the winter of 1943/4. (IWM NA 22051)

Canadian Gunners were a vital asset in Italy. This detachment of B Troop 5 Battery 5th Field Regiment RCA is pictured in action in the mountains during the winter. (Michael M Dean/NA of Canada/PA 3192317)

Canadians also manned 17-pounder anti-tank guns. This detachment of 57 Battery 1st Anti-Tank Regiment RCA is ready for action at Campobasso on 25 October 1943. Left to right are Gnr F S Steel, L/Bdr R V McKeachie and Gnr W O Jorheim. (Jack H Smith/NA of Canada/PA 3599876)

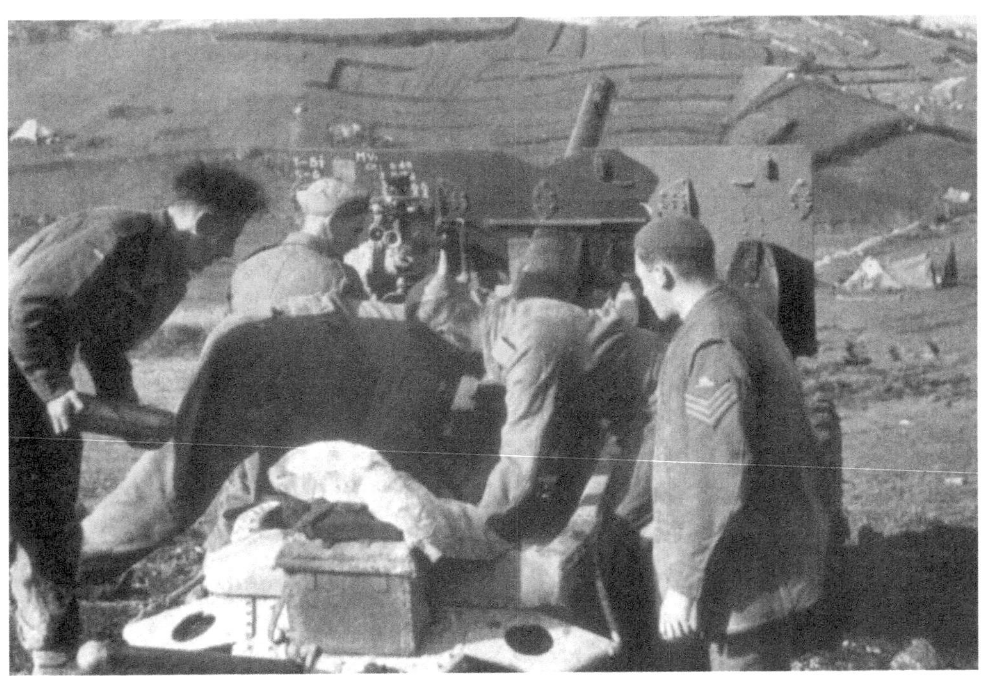

Also in the mountains is this 25-pounder detachment, probably of 92nd Field Regiment, deployed north of Rionero in October 1943 with 5th Division. (Private photo)

Bombs and shells land on Cassino town in a bombardment by US aircraft and Allied artillery. In the background are the slopes of the mountain on which sits the monastery of Monte Cassino, the pivot of the Gustav Line. Gunners fired one of their largest fireplans of the war in the opening of Operation HONKER, Eighth Army's attack on the night of 11 May 1944. (US Official, via Ken Ford)

A second Italian winter awaited the Allies. Conditions in the northern Apennines were no better than they had been further south. The difficulties of re-supply are shown clearly in this photograph in which a Gunner unit is trying to move up to the front while a convoy is travelling in the other direction. (Private photo)

In spite of all the difficulties, Gunners could still get their guns into the most unlikely places. This American 155mm 'Long Tom' of 33 Battery 61st Heavy Regiment was ready for action at Vergato in February 1945. (IWM NA 22470)

HM King George VI, Captain General of the Royal Artillery, inspects 2nd Medium Regiment RCA in Italy in July 1944. A considerable amount of time has been spent polishing boots. (Alexander Mackenzie Stirton/ NA of Canada/PA 3191934)

(Left) Malta was crucial to Allied success in the Mediterranean region and the island depended on convoys for supplies. Maritime Royal Artillery Gunners manned AA guns on the ships in those convoys as shown by this Gunner at his Bofors on board a merchant ship in the Mediterranean. (Frederick G Whitcombe/NA of Canada/PA 193881) *(Right)* AOPs came into their own in Italy, having proved their value in Tunisia and Sicily. At Castel Frentano, in February 1944, Bdr Barney Little, L/Bdr Aby Castel and Lt David Armour of 17th Field Regiment RCA receive signals from an Auster AOP III. (Alexander Mackenzie Stirton/NA of Canada/PA 3524497)

And this is one of the Austers just returned from a mission. The ground crew check the machine while the pilot, Captain N H Chase RA, reports to Major E M D McNaughton. (Alexander Mackenzie Stirton/NA of Canada/PA 137424)

Preparing for OVERLORD. US pilots, using Spitfires, were briefed for their role in spotting for VCS-7 (Cruiser Squadron 7) by this inter-service and international team of (L-R) W/Cdr Robert J Hardiman, RAF, Commander Allied Spotter Pilots, Ensign Robert J Adams, USNR, Maj Noel East, British Intelligence, Lt Harris Hammersmith Jr, USNR and Capt John Ruscoe RA, Gunnery Liaison Officer, (standing with pipe in hand) (US Navy Official. US Navy Photo Archives 80-G-302115)

First shots. 'Arras', one of the M7 Priests of 9 (Irish) Battery 7th Field Regiment fired Second Army's first shots at the Normandy coast at 06.55 on 6 June as the Regiment's LCTs steamed towards the beach in the run-in shoot. (Courtesy of the artist, David Rowlands; the original painting is held by 24 (Irish) Battery RA)

A 7.2-inch howitzer detachment of an unidentified heavy regiment firing in support of an attack by 9 Canadian Brigade in Normandy on 28 June 1944. (Ken Bell/NA of Canada/PA 3520587)

(Left) At Gouy in France, on 30 August 1944, a 6-pounder of 3rd Anti-Tank Regiment RCA is towed by a Universal carrier. The demeanour of the detachment suggests that they are moving out for a rest. (Donald I Grant/NA of Canada/PA 3203098)
(Right) Canadian infantry of the Stormont Dundas and Glengarry Highlanders cross the Orne on a Bailey bridge under the protection of a triple LAA gun of 93rd (Loyals) LAA Regiment RA. (Ken Bell/NA of Canada/PA 130170)

In the battles for the Odon and Hill 112, the 25-pounders of 112th (Wessex) Field Regiment RA (TA) were worked hard. The photo shows guns of the Regiment firing smoke in support of Operation JUPITER. That the smoke shells were effective is clear from the photograph. (Major Douglas Goddard MBE, late 112th (Wessex) Field Regiment)

As the Allies raced out of Normandy to the Low Countries, the port of Dunkirk was among several to be masked. The forces besieging Dunkirk maintained a bombardment of the German garrison and turned some of their own weapons on them, including this 155mm gun. X Battery RCA, based at Adinkerke in Belgium, is seen preparing the gun for action. Gunners are digging a breech pit to allow the weapon to be brought into use. (Ken Bell/NA of Canada/PA 3378347)

The much-improved 7.2-inch howitzer in action with a heavy regiment in late-1944. (Private photo)

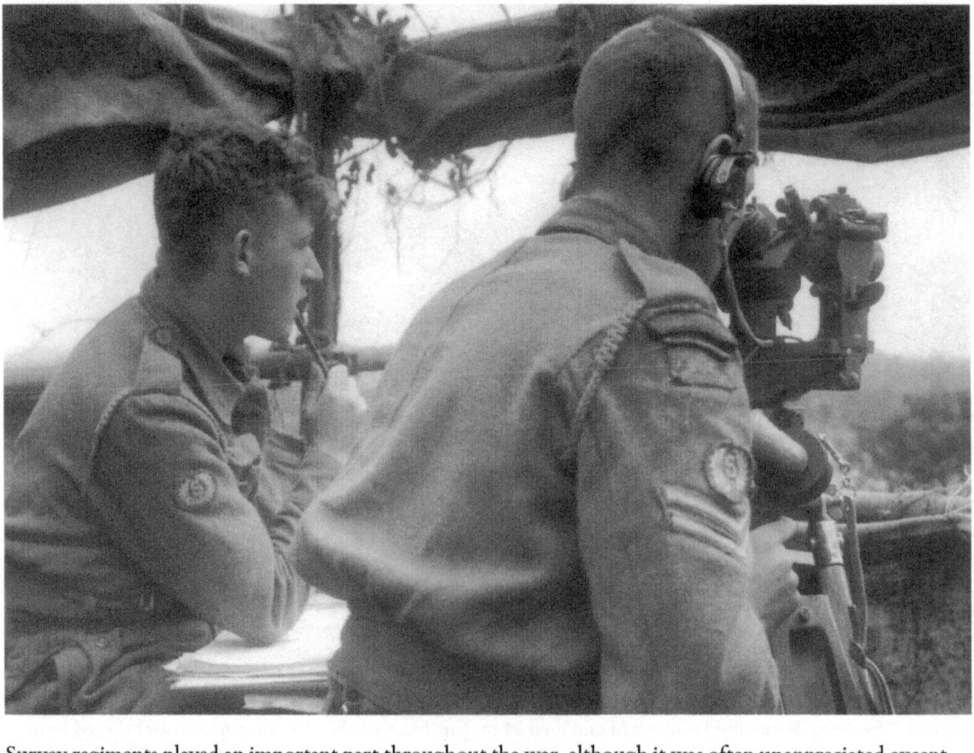

Survey regiments played an important part throughout the war, although it was often unappreciated except by other Gunners. These two flash spotters of 10th Survey Regiment RA are operating from a 66-foot-high platform north of Cheux in July 1944. (IWM B 7041)

During the North-West Europe campaign many anti-tank regiments were equipped with self-propelled equipments. The American M10s, Wolverines in British service, had been upgunned with the 17-pounder to produce the Achilles, one of which is seen using its gun against pillboxes on the German frontier in October 1944. The Achilles is from 75th Anti-Tank Regiment RA, one of the units of 11th Armoured Division. (IWM B 10773)

In March 1945 Montgomery's 21 Army Group crossed the Rhine in Operation PLUNDER. The fireplan involved 3,500 guns, including these 5.5s of 235 and 336 Medium Batteries, which have been lined up wheel-to-wheel for the bombardment. That line-up is a clear sign that the Luftwaffe has all but ceased to exist and that German artillery no longer poses a real threat. (IWM B 15767)

A self-propelled Bofors of 366 Battery 112th LAA Regiment RA being ferried across the Rhine near Xanten on 24 March. These were the first guns of the corps to cross the river. (V J Emery, late 112th LAA Regiment)

There was still unfinished business in The Netherlands where First Canadian Army was operating. The photo shows a 5.5 detachment of 2nd Medium Regiment RCA in action on 2 April 1945. From left to right are Sgt E F Noyes, Gnr A Marriner, Bdr R W Findlay, Gnrs J P Otto and W E Grasse McDougall. (Colin Campbell/ NA of Canada/PA 3209132)

Sexton SPGs of 86th Field Regiment (Hertfordshire Yeomanry) engage enemy positions in April 1945 during the closing weeks of the war when the mobility of the self-propelled equipments was especially appreciated. (IWM BU 3576)

'A terrifying weapon.' The Landmattress rocket launcher had come into service in late-1944 and was used to devastating effect on many occasions. This photo shows Gunners of 1 Rocket Battery RCA loading their Landmattress at Helchteren in Belgium in October 1944. It was said that one equipment produced the firepower of fifteen medium regiments. (Frank L Dubervill/NA of Canada/PA 3204964)

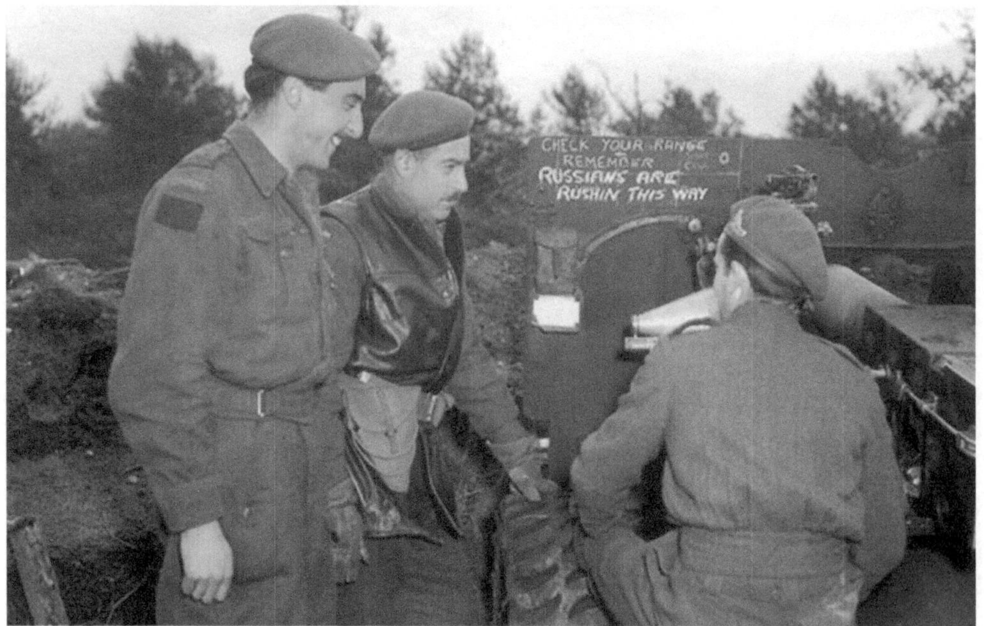

In The Netherlands in early-1945 Lt W P Kennedy, Maj Dick Walker and Gnr Bill Ballantyne are seen with a 25-pounder of 5th Field Regiment RCA on which someone – Gnr Ballantyne? – has painted the inscription 'Check your range – Remember Russians are rushin' this way'. (Michael M Dean/NA of Canada/PA 3240700)

Another example of inscribing. This time it was Prime Minister Winston Churchill who was chalking the message 'Hitler-personal' on a shell which he then fired from one of 3rd Super Heavy Regiment's 240mm guns on 5 March 1945. (IWM B 15220)

Victory in Europe. These smartly turned out Gunners of 3rd Regiment RHA fire a salute at the Victory Parade in Berlin to mark the end of the war in Europe. (IWM BU 9089)

The turning point in the war against the Japanese in Burma came in the battles for Kohima and Imphal. Two Gunners of 82nd LAA/Anti-Tank Regiment look down on the Imphal plain from the Bishenpur road, not far from where 88 LAA Battery of their regiment had fought Japanese infantry at close quarters. Note the stencilled warning on the jeep's tailboard. (S Slade via Ray Goodacre)

On the Tiddim road as Fourteenth Army advance through Burma. Gunners of an unidentified field regiment, possibly of 5th Indian Division, carry out maintenance on their gun which has been roped and chained into position. (Private photo

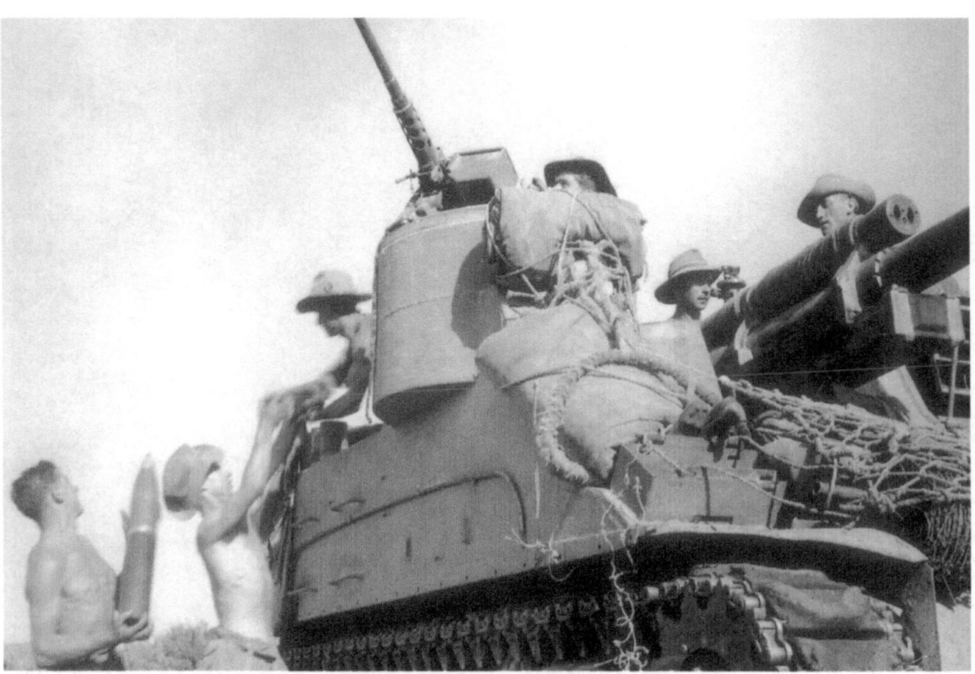

Some self-propelled equipments made their way to Fourteenth Army, including this M7 Priest of 59 Battery 18th Field Regiment in 17th Division. The Battery was in the forefront of 255 Indian Tank Brigade's advance to Meiktila and had a key part in the fighting there, so much so that it was awarded the honour title 'Meiktila'. This detachment is replenishing their Priest at the beginning of the advance to Meiktila. (IWM SE 3279)

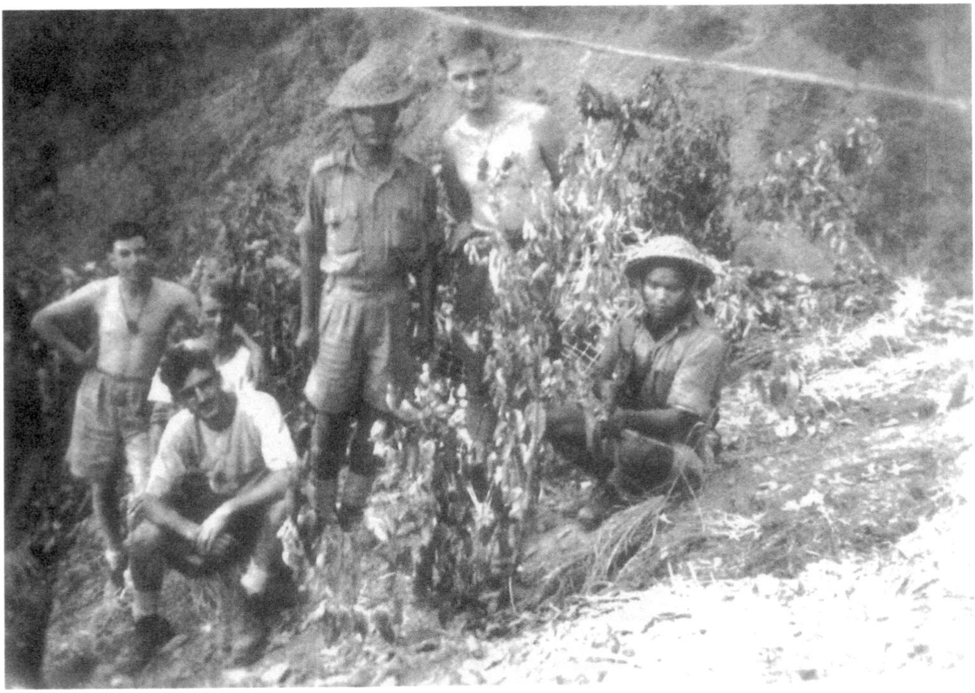

A well-camouflaged 2-pounder anti-tank gun of J Troop 203 Battery 82nd LAA/A-Tk Regiment on the Tiddim road during Fourteenth Army's advance. The Imperial Japanese Army had few tanks and most of those were so lightly armoured that the 2-pounder could deal with them effectively; it could also be used against bunkers. (C C Fuller via Ray Goodacre)

'Come you back, you British soldier; come you back to Mandalay'. And they did in March 1945. So strong were the walls of Fort Dufferin that siege techniques were used to attack them. A 5.5 of 1st Medium Regiment, attached to 134th Medium Regiment in 19th Indian Division, bombards the fort's walls on 9/10 March. (IWM SE 3261)

The sole Victoria Cross to a Gunner other rank was awarded to Havildar Umrao Singh of 30 Battery 30th Indian Mountain Regiment near Tinma in the Kaladan Valley in December 1944. Havildar Singh, a 24-year-old Punjabi, fought off several attacks on his gun by Japanese infantry before being overwhelmed. When the gun was recaptured he was found to be still alive but badly injured. David Rowlands' painting shows Singh wielding a gun bearer to fight off the fifth Japanese attack on his gun. (Courtesy of the artist, David Rowlands; the original painting is held by the School of Artillery, Deolali, India.)

(Left) A 7.2-inch howitzer in its final form on display in Firepower, the Museum of the Royal Artillery at Woolwich. A far cry from the Great War 8-inch howitzer from which the weapon was modified in the early days of the war. (Courtesy Royal Artillery Historical Trust)
(Right) Also in retirement at Firepower is this mobile 3.7-inch HAA gun. One of the most important weapons of the Second World War, the 3.7 served as a field gun and, in some cases, an anti-tank weapon, as well as in its intended role. (Courtesy Royal Artillery Historical Trust)

Chapter Seven

Victory in the Med

We left Eighth Army grappling with Panzer Armee Afrika along the El Alamein line in July. With both armies exhausted by the end of the month, an uneasy stalemate began. In August, General Auchinleck was relieved as C-in-C, Middle East, by Winston Churchill, his place being taken by General Sir Harold Alexander. A new commander, Lieutenant General 'Strafer' Gott, was also appointed to Eighth Army but was killed before he could assume his post. Lieutenant General Bernard Montgomery was flown out from Britain to succeed him.[1] In his *Memoirs*, Montgomery claimed that he turned Eighth Army into a successful fighting machine; in truth, he inherited an army that had already beaten Rommel once and was preparing to beat him again.

Auchinleck had appreciated the importance of using artillery in concentration to produce what Stalin termed 'the God of war', in spite of the limits placed on his field and medium artillery.[2] However, Montgomery brought out from Britain a new artillery commander for Eighth Army, Brigadier Sydney Kirkman, who had so impressed him during Exercise BUMPER in 1941.[3] With Alexander providing a firm buffer between Eighth Army's commander and Churchill's demands for early action, Montgomery was able to concentrate on preparing for the offensive, which he scheduled for the October full moon.

In the meantime, however, he had one major clash with Rommel when the latter attacked at the end of August. Rommel's plan was to strike south of Alam el Halfa ridge with 15th and 21st Panzer Divisions of Afrika Korps, flanked by a group created from the Axis reconnaissance units to the right and an Italian armoured group from Ariete and Littorio Divisions to the left, to hit at the rear of Eighth Army's positions. However, the attack was expected. Instead of rolling up Eighth Army and advancing to Alexandria and Cairo, Rommel took another drubbing from British forces that were well positioned on and about Alam el Halfa ridge. This position, identified by Auchinleck, was garrisoned strongly and Montgomery had added to the defensive strength. Anti-tank guns, including the new 6-pounders, screened the British armour and dealt heavy punishment to the Axis tanks; Allied aircraft added to that punishment.[4] Near Deir el Munassib, south of Bare Ridge, F Battery RHA, with anti-tank guns of 2nd Rifle Brigade, imposed the first check on Rommel's advance. Rommel was forced to change his plan after this first of a series of setbacks.

As the battle continued, there were some localised Axis successes but the overall picture was bleak. A sandstorm added to the confusion while 22 Armoured Brigade positioned itself at Point 102 towards which Axis tanks advanced in the afternoon of 31 August, only to run into the fury of the brigade's units. B Battery RHA took on thirty tanks that detached from the main attack to threaten 133 Brigade's positions and fought the enemy armour over open sights with armour-piercing shot. Supported by tanks of 22 Armoured, sent to help the infantry, they forced an enemy withdrawal as darkness fell. The action at Point 102 was the critical point of the battle. That night, as German and Italian tanks laagered, British aircraft and artillery pounded their positions. Although Rommel tried to move 21st Panzer around 22 Armoured Brigade's left flank this came to naught and, on 2 September, he called off the attack.[5]

Montgomery could now concentrate on planning and training for the offensive. With both sides holding lines that were secure on their northern and southern flanks, Eighth Army's only solution was a deliberate attack. Of course, Rommel expected such an attack and created defences on a par with those of the Western Front in the Great War with minefields, dubbed 'Devil's gardens', along the front. Breaking into the Axis line would require determined and well-trained troops, both infantry and armour, with massive artillery support.[6] The Gunners were not to be found wanting: this was to be 'the first great artilleryman's battle in the Second World War'.[7]

> For the first time, therefore, using on a grand scale all the technical aids which had been developed, it was possible by careful planning and with centralised control to put into practice those principles governing the employment of artillery which played such a decisive part in the later stages of the war.[8]

The detailed planning included the use of aerial photographs and the work of survey batteries, which combined to produce information critical to the successful use of artillery in the battle's opening phase. Hurricanes of No. 208 Squadron RAF flew many dangerous tactical reconnaissance missions, at significant loss, to bring back photographs for the intelligence officers.

> The value of vertical air photos prior to and throughout the battle was immense. Practically all CB locations and the exact whereabouts of enemy defended localities were based on air photos, though in the latter case the information was taken from overprinted maps prepared from photos prior to the battle by an RE Photo Survey Section. In a desert of the type in which the battle was fought, oblique photos are of no use to the Gunner as it is impossible to correlate the photo with the ground.[9]

Survey batteries worked out the locations from which enemy artillery was firing and the two sources of information were collated. This allowed the organisation of counter-battery fire to an extent not before known in North Africa. In fact, it became possible for corps and divisional artilleries to fire concentrations at a few minutes' notice for the first time ever.[10]

Detailed artillery planning for Operation LIGHTFOOT began in the opening days of October. XXX Corps' artillery was reinforced by transferring three field regiments – 78th, 98th and 146th – from X Corps; these were to be deployed in troops reinforcing regiments of the corps' artillery. This manner of deployment was intended to 'reduce the number of reconnaissance parties which would be wandering about the forward area' and thereby arousing enemy suspicions.[11] Although the post of Corps Commander Medium Artillery (CCMA) had been abolished after Dunkirk,[12] and Army Groups Royal Artillery (AGRAs) had yet to appear, a corps' medium artillery staff was established under Lieutenant Colonel 'Stag' Yates. Three medium regiments – 7th, 64th and 69th – were brigaded under Yates' command in XXX Corps; a composite survey battery and corps' counter-battery staff completed his organisation.[13]

Sydney Kirkman arrived in Egypt on 13 September and relieved Brigadier Martin as BRA Eighth Army two days later.[14] His was the overall responsibility for Eighth Army's fireplan in the forthcoming battle. The main burden of the initial artillery bombardment would fall on the guns of XXX Corps, whose CCRA, Brigadier Meade Dennis, transferred from XIII Corps in September.[15] Artillery preparations for LIGHTFOOT included stockpiling ammunition, which had to be dumped in the appropriate locations, a further responsibility for each CCRA. In all, 286,000 rounds of 25-pounder ammunition and 20,000 medium rounds were dumped and concealed in the battle area,[16] with shells being buried at sites chosen as gun positions that would not be occupied until the last moment. The RASC ran the Field Maintenance Centre in the El Imayid area, in which were stocked 3,000 tons of ammunition.[17]

It was impossible to conceal the build-up but it was possible to deceive the Axis about the whereabouts of units and equipment and an elaborate deception plan, Operation BERTRAM, was implemented to this end.[18] For the Gunners this meant concealing from the enemy the positions of Eighth Army's field artillery. Since the plan for LIGHTFOOT required the initial attack to go in to a depth of 6 to 7,000 yards, field guns had to be deployed within 1,500 yards of the forward localities, where they might be observed from the Axis positions. It was decided to conceal these positions by erecting dummy 3-ton lorries in the gun areas with each dummy hiding a 25-pounder and its ammunition limber. On one occasion a strong wind led to concern that the scheme might be detected by the enemy when many 'lorries' began flapping about in the breeze.[19]

An indication of the tempo at which the Gunners would be operating may be gained from XIII Corps' preparations. On 10 October the Corps held 147,000 rounds of 25-pounder ammunition, which would meet the needs of the guns in the opening bombardment, during which each gun would fire 390 rounds, a quarter of which would be supercharge. XIII Corps' holdings would supply the artillery under 7th Armoured Division command, of which 3 RHA, 3rd Field Regiment RA and 1st Fighting French Field Regiment would fire 200 rounds per gun, the same rate as the artillery of 50th (Northumbrian) Division, which included 1st Greek Field Regiment. Once again, additional supplies were held in FMCs, enough for four days' firing at Eighth Army rates and a fifth day at thirty rounds per gun.[20] (In the course of the battle, XIII Corps' artillery fired 578 rounds per gun, a daily average of forty-eight rounds per gun.)[21]

Among the ammunition stockpiled were 105mm rounds for Eighth Army's latest artillery equipments, the American M7 howitzer motor carriage, a 105mm howitzer mounted on a modified M3 medium tank chassis. These were the first M7s delivered and the weapon would first see action at El Alamein. The 105mm equipment with its 33lb round proved a very effective weapon. To 11th (Honourable Artillery Company) Regiment Royal Horse Artillery went the distinction of being the first unit to operate the M7, which became known as 'Priest' in British service from its pulpit-like machine-gun mounting. Such a weapon was appropriate for the 'Galloping Gunners' of 11 (HAC) RHA, but its arrival required retraining in addition to that expected to familiarise personnel with any new weapon. American artillery procedure was based on the French army's, which meant that the HAC personnel had to absorb a new language in which degrees were replaced by 'mils' while other novelties included 'pro-directors' and 'panoramic telescopes'.[22] Another new weapon deployed at El Alamein was the British 5.5-inch medium gun, of which sixteen were with the medium artillery.[23] However, the 5.5 had first seen action in the desert in May.[24]

From about 9.00pm on Friday 23 October there was complete silence save for an occasional burst of fire to 'keep the deception going and the enemy happy' before, at 9.40pm, the 834 field and forty-eight medium guns of Eighth Army opened fire.[25] Along the 12,000 yards of XXX Corps' front, 432 field and all forty-eight medium guns engaged accurately located enemy batteries for twenty minutes at an intense rate. Each target had been 'fixed' by aerial photos from No. 208 Squadron and weeks of work by 4th Survey Regiment (Lieutenant Colonel Whetton) and the Counter Battery staff (Major Temple). Some enemy guns engaged did not return a single round as they had been reduced to scrap metal; many were later found smashed and in pieces. The 'minimum' treatment dealt out to an Axis battery was a concentration of ten guns to one; the maximum was twice that rate.[26] In the first fifteen minutes of the bombardment the medium guns unleashed 1,800 shells. Each Axis battery was struck with ninety-six shells in the space of two minutes.[27]

Such was the intensity of fire that it could be heard and felt sixty miles away in Alexandria. It frightened nuns in the Sacred Heart Convent on Alexandria's rue de Tanis;[28] how much must it have terrified the soldiers of Panzer Armee Afrika?

On one occasion during the night, Rommel was said to be visiting a specific locality in the Axis lines and every gun that could be brought to bear shifted its fire to shell that locality. Although it was believed that Rommel had left the area some minutes before the shells came crashing down, he had never been there at all as he was at home in Germany recovering from ill health.[29] Those guns had been diverted from their assigned task of supporting the infantry as they advanced through no man's land. When not firing to their immediate front, guns were putting down defensive fire for other formations or firing standard concentrations, known as 'stonks'.[30]

The Gunners were in action for twelve days, during which they fired a million rounds from 25-pounders alone. Opportunities for rest were few, although during periods of intense firing, as on the opening night, each gun was rested for ten minutes in every hour to reduce the possibility of shells exploding prematurely in the barrels. Among the outstanding exploits by Gunners during the battle was that which earned the DSO for Lieutenant Colonel William Anthony Sheil, CO of 128th (Highland) Field Regiment, part of the divisional artillery of 51st (Highland) Division. On 27 October the regiment was ordered to engage the German strongpoint codenamed Stirling with concentrated fire from all its guns. Elements of the Highland infantry had closed on Stirling the previous night but were pinned down by enemy fire while some Panzers were also close by. Thus executing these orders would be a difficult task. So difficult, and so important, did Sheil consider the task that he went forward to act as FOO himself. Working his way to within 500 yards of Stirling he identified both his own troops and the German defences and ranged his guns on to the latter. All the while British and Axis tanks were firing at each other over his head. When the British tanks began advancing, Colonel Sheil noticed the enemy anti-tank gunners man their weapons and ordered a 'Mike Target' on them. This soon had the Germans rushing back to their dugouts. When British armour was brought to a standstill by German 88s, firing from a distance on the flank, Sheil ordered 128th Field to pound the Stirling area. They continued this bombardment throughout the daylight hours and, such was their effectiveness, when the Highlanders advanced that night they met very little opposition and found Stirling to be full of German dead. Sheil earned a Bar to his DSO in Sicily.[31]

A day earlier, 1st Armoured Division had been ordered to capture the enemy strongpoints known as Snipe and Woodcock, beyond and about a mile south-west and north-west respectively of the Kidney feature (known usually as Kidney 'ridge', it was actually a depression; the 'ridge' identification arose from a map-reading error). This was to be the first stage of an attempt to reach the Rahman track, 'cut the enemy's main lateral communications [and] force him to attack us on ground of our choosing'.[32] It was unsuccessful but led to one of the most memorable actions of the battle.

Snipe was the objective for Lieutenant Colonel Victor Turner's 2nd Rifle Brigade battlegroup. Although the nominal strength of such a motor battalion was 785 all ranks, the group totalled only 300. In addition to infantry, Turner had G and H Troops 239 Battery 76th Anti-Tank Regiment, although 239 had been with 11th (HAC) Regiment RHA since March.[33] Commanded by Captain A F Baer and Lieutenant F J Wilmore MM respectively, each troop had three 6-pounders while the battalion's own anti-tank company deployed another sixteen. Also included were Sappers of 7 Field Squadron while Captain Noyes, 2 RHA, was the FOO. Turner's force had twenty-two carriers, a Vickers MMG platoon and a 3-inch mortar platoon.[34]

At 11.00pm, the force moved off, the carriers leading; the anti-tank guns, carried portée, remained with the supply lorries until called forward. At fifteen minutes past midnight, Turner transmitted the success signal and the portées and supply vehicles moved up and, by 3.45am, nineteen 6-pounders, thirteen from 2nd Rifle Brigade, and the water, rations and ammunition were in place.[35] Captain Noyes had made his only contribution to the operation when Turner, uncertain about his location, had asked for a smoke shell to be fired on the objective. The round burst within 300 yards of the group and Turner, satisfied that he had reached his objective, occupied an oval depression measuring roughly 900 by 400 yards. Formerly a German engineer depot, this contained a small dugout which became his HQ.[36]

There was one recognisable feature nearby, an oval mound shown on maps as a 35-metre ring contour; this was Hill 37, about three-quarters of a mile long and peaking at thirty-seven metres. However, Turner was about 900 yards south of the true objective, although securing the hollow was to prove fortunate. He established defensive positions with G and H Troops supporting A Company on the perimeter's north-east.[37]

A scout platoon made the first of many contacts with the enemy, in this case *Kampfgruppe* Stiffelmeyer, which was spotted subsequently moving in two columns, one of them making for Snipe. This was led by a Mark IV Special, with a long-barrelled 75mm gun, then the most powerful tank in the desert, but its crew seemed unaware of the British presence. It burst into flames when struck by a Green Jacket 6-pounder at under a hundred yards' range. At the same time 239 Battery destroyed a 76.2mm SPG. Both detachments had waited until a hit was certain before firing as the 6-pounder's sights were poor for night shooting. These kills prompted the remaining enemy tanks to veer off westwards, halt and wait for daylight.[38] Turner's Gunners, both infantry and Royal Artillery, were delighted at their performance and with the quality of their new weapons, so much more effective than the 2-pounders.

> From this moment the garrison was fired to a most astonishing degree with an eager and offensive confidence. As events disclosed themselves, this spirit swelled into something more impressive – the exultant spirit of the happy warrior.[39]

However, a setback followed when Captain Noyes set out on reconnaissance. He was captured by a German patrol, leaving Turner with no channel to his supporting artillery; no replacement could cross the fireswept ground.[40] Just before dawn, the soft-skinned vehicles were sent back and, thirty minutes later, both enemy tank groups moved off, seemingly unaware that a sizeable force had infiltrated their lines. The benefits of the hollow began to be felt, as was the cover afforded by thorn scrub. As the columns presented their flanks, the 6-pounders fired at less than 800 yards. Sixteen vehicles were knocked out before both groups withdrew. Snipe's garrison had now killed eighteen enemy armoured vehicles but the element of surprise had gone: the enemy, aware that the hollow was manned by British troops, subjected it to heavy shellfire. With daylight it became

> ... possible to see what the ground looked like. There were no distinct features, with the exception of the 30 Ring Contour running NW from 867293 to 865295, and the 35 Ring Contour 864293. Even these ... were difficult to distinguish owing to the undulating nature of the ground. There was a lot of sand and scrub which made easy the digging in and camouflaging of the A. Tk gun positions. On the other hand, this ground enabled enemy tanks to take up hull down positions almost anywhere except on the ground to the SW of the position 865292, which was open and ran up to the 35 Ring Contour 864293.[41]

Thus began a long, hard day for the defenders of outpost Snipe. First Armoured Division had intended Snipe and Woodcock to provide points from which the armour could advance to sever the Rahman track. Snipe was to be 24 Armoured Brigade's base but when its first tanks, of 47th Royal Tank Regiment, appeared there was almost catastrophe. Mistaking Snipe for an enemy position the tanks opened fire. The situation was saved only when Turner's intelligence officer drove back in his carrier to explain the situation to the tankmen.[42]

At this point enemy tanks appeared. These were engaged and one detachment claimed to have set alight three tanks. But 47th Royal Tanks also came under heavy fire from those tanks, and from 88s, mostly firing from Kidney, while Axis artillery fire was hitting the outpost into which 47th Royal Tanks had moved by about 8.30am; seven Shermans were hit in just over fifteen minutes. Ordered to withdraw, 24 Armoured Brigade retreated; 47th Royal Tanks was reduced to five Shermans and six Crusaders.[43]

More attacks were made on Snipe but at least eight enemy tanks were set ablaze before the Germans withdrew. By 11 o'clock only thirteen of the nineteen 6-pounders at Snipe remained in action.

> those guns which had been shooting hard in the West and Southwest sectors were running short of ammunition. The transporting of ammunition from one sector ... to another was an extremely hazardous job owing to very heavy enemy shelling ... continually falling into the position.[44]

Two hours later eight Italian M13s, and some SPGs, advanced from the 35-ring contour but only one 6-pounder could engage. The M13s were engaged at close range, the last three less than 200 yards from the gun position. During this action, in which the tanks and one SPG were knocked out, Victor Turner was wounded and earned the Victoria Cross.[45]

Some of 239 Battery's guns had been silent since early morning but that changed when two groups of tanks, about seventy in all, attacked in late afternoon. At 5 o'clock, as one group moved rapidly towards 2 Armoured Brigade, its southernmost element passed within 500 yards of Snipe's north-east corner and several 239 Battery 6-pounders. Since these guns had hitherto been silent, their presence was unknown to the Axis tankmen who were soon shaken from their ignorance as 239 Battery opened up, claiming nine set ablaze and hitting several others.[46] Tragically, Snipe again came under attack from its friends, as Priests of 11th (HAC) Regiment RHA shelled the position in what Turner described as 'the most unpleasant' part of a very unpleasant day.[47]

The Axis attack was stopped just before 5.30pm but Snipe then came under attack again. About fifteen Mark IIIs advanced slowly and only three guns, with an average of ten rounds left, could engage. Three panzers took up hull-down positions in the 35-ring contour area and engaged the Rifle Brigade's positions until well after dark. Those that pressed home their attack suffered heavily and withdrew to hull-down positions nearly a half mile away, but continued machine-gunning Snipe. As the 6-pounders in this sector were down to an average of three rounds per gun, it was fortunate that there were no further attacks, although some twenty enemy tanks were nearby.[48]

At 5.40pm, Turner learned that 2nd Rifle Brigade would be relieved that night. About two hours later the twenty enemy tanks moved off north-westwards. At 10.30pm the British artillery began bombarding the Axis laager some 1,200 yards north-west of Snipe. The enemy took avoiding action, including moving eastwards towards 2nd Rifle Brigade. Forty-five minutes later, the last elements of Turner's command slipped away from Snipe. All but one of the guns were destroyed as it was impossible to bring them back. The surviving weapon, from 239 Battery, was evacuated on a bullet-riddled portée.[49]

There could be no doubt of the gallantry shown by the men of 2nd Rifle Brigade and their Gunner and Sapper comrades at Snipe. Deservedly, the action has become one of the best-known elements of the battle and contributed significantly to weakening Rommel's tank strength, something he could not afford; Rommel described it as 'a tremendously powerful anti-tank defence'. A later examination of the site, from which some vehicles had been recovered by the Axis while others had been towed away by British recovery teams, found twenty-seven hulks. Careful and critical analysis of the performance of each gun established that twenty-one German and eleven Italian tanks had been destroyed, together with five SPGs, while up to twenty additional tanks or SPGs had been immobilised but subsequently recovered. In all, fifty-seven enemy armoured vehicles were destroyed, nineteen of them by 239 Battery. Turner's force had suffered fourteen dead, forty-four wounded and one missing; but Axis losses must have been much higher.[50]

The opposing armies had fought almost to a standstill by the end of October, forcing Montgomery to rethink his plan. A new operation – SUPERCHARGE – was launched on the night of 1/2 November. Once again Gunners played a major part with thirteen field and three medium regiments involved. The medium regiments were from XXX Corps' artillery while the field, or RHA, units were drawn from 1st and 2nd Armoured, 51st (Highland) Divisions, 2nd New Zealand and 9th Australian Divisions. The New Zealand CRA, Brigadier C E 'Steve' Weir had operational control of the artillery since the principal attacking formation was the New Zealand Division, although it deployed brigades from other formations. In preparation for the attack, artillery stockpiles were increased with 110,631 25-pounder rounds drawn from the railheads at El Imayid and Burg el Arab on 31 October and 81,044 the following day. The guns were to open fire at H Hour with a shell being dropped every twelve yards along the opening line and, as the infantry advanced, the bombardment would creep forward by a hundred yards every two-and-a-half minutes. During the first four-and-a-half hours of SUPERCHARGE, Weir's Gunners, manning 192 guns, fired over 50,000 rounds. Meanwhile, another 168 guns deployed to fire concentrations on known enemy locations in and around the flanks of the advancing infantry. Bofors LAA guns fired tracer rounds to mark brigade boundaries as the infantry advanced along a front of 4,000 yards.[51]

Having supported the infantry on to their objectives the Gunners then gave similar support to the advancing armour. At first the tankmen were surprised to be receiving the surrender of many Axis infantry who were so battle-shocked from the artillery pounding they had taken that they lacked the will to continue the fight. But then enemy opposition stiffened and the British armour, advancing against well-sited anti-tank guns and with the sun rising behind them, took fearful punishment. Eventually Eighth Army's armour, backed up by its artillery and the Desert Air Force, prevailed. Axis attempts to give air support to the Panzer Armee were weak and were thwarted by aircraft and anti-aircraft fire: on 2 November the AA defences at the El Alamein railhead were augmented by Right Troop 192 HAA Battery and B and C Troops 6 LAA Battery; the latter's D Troop was protecting Montgomery's tactical HQ.[52]

As the pressure was maintained on Rommel's forces, Gunners supported actions such as that to capture Point 38, or Skinflint, while, on the final night of the battle, barrages were fired to support 5 Indian Brigade as it advanced over unfamiliar country. Over a million rounds had been fired by the Gunners in the twelve days of battle. They had proved themselves to be a battle-winning instrument. Of their performance at El Alamein, General Sir David Fraser has succinctly noted: 'Now they came into their own.'[53] The Gunners' guiding principle had been that 'British artillery should dominate the battlefield and should allow no enemy movement within range to remain unpunished.'[54] They had achieved that at El Alamein, which became the yardstick by which later bombardments would be measured: 'more guns than at Alamein', 'as many rounds as at Alamein', 'a sound like that at Alamein'.[55]

As Eighth Army began its slow pursuit of the retreating Panzer Armee Afrika, First Army was en route to the western end of North Africa and Operation TORCH, the invasion of Vichy French Algeria and Tunisia. The landing of Allied forces in TORCH ensured that Rommel made no attempt to do other than delay Eighth Army as he retreated to Tunisia, abandoning Italy's last colony, Libya, while so doing. There were some actions intended to ensure that the Panzer Armee was able to elude its pursuers but these were not on any significant scale. In his *Memoirs*, Montgomery writes of a battle at El Agheila in December although this was much more of a *son et lumière* demonstration by Rommel than a real battle. It achieved its intention by checking Montgomery's progress at a point where Eighth Army and its predecessors had been stopped twice before. Eighth Army prepared for a major engagement, with the Gunners making their usual contribution, but the attack, when launched, hit thin air. Axis forces had pulled out.[56] There was much more serious fighting as Eighth Army approached Tripoli, with plenty of activity for Gunners. Tripoli fell to Eighth Army on 23 January. Tradition has it that the first British soldiers to enter the city were men of 11th Hussars, the Cherrypickers. However, the Cherrypickers' entry into Tripoli was watched by men already in the city – recce parties of 9th (Londonderry) HAA Regiment. Some cryptic comments were made by those Gunners about both the appearance, and tardiness, of the Hussars.[57]

That redoubtable Irish unit, which had already defended Alexandria and Port Sudan with outstanding success, was to be the key element in the Tripoli defences for the next four months. Lieutenant Colonel L C 'Bob' Aitken, their CO, was appointed AA Defence Commander (AADC) Tripoli with his own regiment, 94th HAA Regiment, 40th and 53rd (KOYLI) LAA Regiments and 306 SL Battery; both 94th HAA and 40th LAA Regiments were Scottish units. Although the composition of the defences changed over the following months, the one constant was the presence of 9th Regiment. In addition to 3.7s and Bofors, the defenders also deployed several captured Italian 90mm HAA guns, and light guns including Breda 20mms.[58]

That Tripoli was vital to Eighth Army's logistical train was recognised by the Germans who soon turned their attention to the port. Between 25 January and 26 April, fifty-four Luftwaffe raids or recce flights were aimed at Tripoli. These were fought off with such loss to the attackers that a captured Luftwaffe airman told his captors that the AA defence of the city was known as a *Wand aus Stahl*, or wall of steel, to his fellow flyers and that the most unpopular order in the region was to fly against Tripoli. Claims were made for a number of aircraft destroyed by guns or fighters and there were few occasions on which bombs fell on or near the harbour. Only once was shipping in the harbour hit. That was during the Luftwaffe's last major raid on 19 March when a bomber struck by AA fire crashed on a cargo ship carrying ammunition, which then exploded; other vessels were also damaged. Nonetheless, the Luftwaffe failed to deny Tripoli as a supply port to Eighth Army and much of that failure was due to the professionalism of Bob Aitken's Gunners.[59]

As Eighth Army entered Tripoli, far to the west First Army was engaged in bitter conflict with Axis forces. Hitler had ordered the reinforcement of Tunisia and a garrison had been flown and shipped in that narrowly prevented leading elements of First Army from capturing Tunis in early December 1942. Those elements had been deployed in a two-pronged advance with the prongs composed of units of 78th Division. On the left was 36 Brigade while 11 Brigade operated some twenty-five miles to the south on the right flank; there were also two small forces, Hartforce, commanded by Major V Hart of 5th Northamptons, operating with 36 Brigade, but drawn from 11 Brigade, and Blade Force, a larger group under Lieutenant Colonel R A Hull, CO of 17th/21st Lancers, which included Hull's regiment, a motorised Rifle Brigade company, armoured cars of the Derbyshire Yeomanry, and 1st Parachute Battalion; Gunner support was provided by C Battery 12th (HAC) Regiment RHA. Blade Force was 'to deny the high ground between these two widely-separated roads, to act as a mobile link between the two brigades and to be ready to help either side over its inner flank or join in any break-through towards Tunis'.[60] Blade Force was the advance guard of 6th Armoured Division.

Thirty-six Brigade had the first major engagement with the enemy. This was at Djebel Abiod on 17 November when 6th Royal West Kents, supported by 360 Battery 138th (City of London) Field Regiment, were attacked by 400 German paratroopers and thirty Mark III and IV tanks. The Germans also enjoyed air superiority with aircraft operating from all-weather airfields whereas the Allies' temporary airstrips were waterlogged following heavy rain. Although the West Kents and 360 Battery put up a strong defence the day belonged to the Germans who, however, had eleven tanks knocked out. British losses included three of 360 Battery's 25-pounders and five of the West Kents' six 2-pounders.[61]

A week later 11 Brigade's 2nd Lancashire Fusiliers and 5th Northamptons advanced on Medjez-el-Bab on the Medjerda river but met such stiff opposition that they were forced to withdraw.

> The withdrawal was made possible by the covering fire of 321 Field [Battery] – the [T]erritorial unit from South Wales which normally supported this brigade. Captain Barker-Benfield, a forward-observation officer, got across the river his wireless set tied to his back, and engaged the machine-gun posts whilst the Fusiliers withdrew in good order. He was awarded an MC for his coolness and courage.[62]

On 27 November a battalion group under Lieutenant Colonel Wilberforce, CO of 1st East Surreys, entered Tebourba, only fifteen miles from Tunis. The Surreys had not had time to dig in when, at mid-morning, seventeen German tanks attacked, engaging both the infantry and their supporting 322 Battery until dusk. With no defensive positions readily at hand, the foot soldiers withdrew through the guns and 322 Battery engaged the tanks. In the course of the day they knocked out fourteen but suffered the loss of all but one of their eight 25-pounders. That last gun had been manned by one Gunner for most of the day: Sergeant Eustace was awarded the DCM. The fourteen dead tanks were ringed around the Battery's positions with one but three yards from the muzzle of the 25-pounder that had claimed it. In addition to Sergeant Eustace's DCM two other awards were made to 322 Battery: Lieutenant Owen Jones received the MC and Gunner Deans the MM. Although under fire, Deans had maintained communications throughout the day from an unarmoured truck. The German tank crews had been especially tenacious and even when their vehicles had been knocked out dismounted to fight as infantry from the cover of cactus clumps.[63]

Tebourba was held and it seemed as if there was still a chance of reaching Tunis, especially when it was learned that the third of 78th Division's brigades – 1 Guards – had landed in Algiers and was en route to the front. The division's third field regiment – 17th Field – was with the Guards. One of the Guards' Brigade battalions – 2nd Hampshires – was soon in the line under 11 Brigade whose 5th Northamptons had suffered heavily on 30 November, their leading company all but wiped out in an attack on Djedeida. The Northamptons had support from 496 Battery 132nd Field Regiment but were forced to pull back with German tanks and infantry in pursuit. This strong reaction from the enemy put an end to Allied plans for an armoured attack on Tunis.[64]

The Hampshires also suffered heavily and, by the evening of 3 December, were down to 210 all ranks, forming square around battalion HQ and launching bayonet attacks on the enemy. Their Gunner comrades of 496 Battery, whose 25-pounders had all been destroyed, joined them as infantrymen as the Hampshires fought their way out from Tebourba.[65] Many who survived this phase of operations in Tunisia were veterans of France in 1940 and saw many parallels in the fighting, with enemy airmen dominating the battlefields. Tunis was to remain in Axis hands for many more months.

As First Army's soldiers fought in the cloying mud of Tunisia, their force was being built up to its intended strength. Initially, the build-up was to corps strength, as V Corps, and then to full army strength. With that came many more Gunner units and the advent of two innovations noted in Chapter Three: aerial observation and AGRAs. But before the tide turned there were many more difficult moments for First Army and its Gunners.

In December, another attempt was made to reach Tunis. Having taken Longstop Hill, 1 Guards and 11 Brigades with an American combat team were to advance to Tebourba while 6th Armoured Division moved up to Massicault. From Massicault and Tebourba, 6th Armoured and 78th Divisions were to race for Tunis. Dry weather was essential if the tanks were to be able to operate in the Medjerda valley and when rain held off for six days the plan was initiated at 10.30pm on 22 December. Only sixteen 25-pounders of 138th Regiment, and some mediums under the Regiment's command, were available to support the initial assault with a fifteen-minute bombardment – a minuscule effort compared to what was available to Eighth Army or would later be on hand in First. Longstop was taken by 2nd Coldstream who were relieved by a battalion of the

US 18th Combat Team. Hardly had the Americans taken over than the Germans counter-attacked and the Coldstream were called back to re-take Longstop. At much the same time the rain came down again and this, plus the realisation that an even greater obstacle – Djebel el Rhar – loomed ahead, led to the main operation being cancelled. Throughout, 138th Field provided excellent support to the infantry and Lieutenant Colonel Clive Usher earned the DSO for his personal action on Longstop.[66] Usher later received a Bar to his DSO in Sicily.[67]

And so the impetus died as the Allies deployed to prevent the Axis breaking through to their rear areas. Gunners were critical in repelling attacks at Two Tree Hill and on the Goubellat Plain in January 1943 where, south of Medjez-el-Bab, the first Uncle Target shoot in Tunisia took place. Under his command the CRA of 6th Armoured Division had eighty-six guns, including mediums, and when the CO of 12th (HAC) Regiment RHA, Lieutenant Colonel J A T Barstow, spotted a group of about thirty tanks and many soft-skinned vehicles engaged in an apparent outflanking move, he called for the fire of the entire divisional artillery. This was granted and the result was devastating for the Axis troops.

> The CRA himself, Brigadier T Lyon-Smith, then appeared, demanded his share of the fun and completed the discomfiture of the dispersed and withdrawing enemy with a further series of 'Uncle targets'.[68]

One of 6th Armoured Division's field regiments – 152nd (Ayrshire Yeomanry) – helped give a drubbing to another German attack on the Goubellat Plain when the improvised Y Division came under determined attack on 26 February. Although firing over open sights at one stage the Ayrshire Gunners, with support from 56th Heavy Regiment, helped break up the attack.[69] It was during this battle that Gunner Spike Milligan earned a Mention in Despatches when he made repeated journeys to an OP under constant fire.[70] In the aftermath of this battle Captain Tulloch of 152nd Field was approached by two senior NCOs of 2nd London Irish Rifles to ask how to set about recommending Captain Atkins for the Victoria Cross. Atkins' 'use of smoke, seated in full view on his carrier, had allowed the remnants of 2 LIR to withdraw'. No VC was awarded but Atkins received the Military Cross. He was killed in action soon after the recommendation had been made.[71]

That attack had been preceded by a German attack on 1st US Armored Division at Kasserine Pass. On 14 February Rommel had struck the raw US armoured troops, who were dispersed between Gafsa and Fondouk, and drove them, in confusion, through the Kasserine Pass. US and British reinforcements stopped the attack, forcing Rommel to return to his main force in the Mareth Line. Among British reinforcements was Gore Force, under Lieutenant Colonel Adrian Gore of 10th Rifle Brigade, which included Gore's own battalion, C Squadron 2nd Lothians and Border Horse, F Battery 12th (HAC) Regiment RHA and a troop of self-propelled anti-tank guns of 93rd (Argyll and Sutherland Highlanders) Anti-Tank Regiment. In the desperate fighting of the next few days, Gore Force slowed Rommel's advance sufficiently for the main body of 6th Armoured Division to establish itself at Thala.[72]

East of Thala, Brigadier Cameron Nicholson, himself a Gunner (and brother of Ronald, whom we met in Chapter Six), deployed his command – Nick Force – to deny to the enemy the road to Le Kef by establishing a blocking position east of Thala.[73] Nick Force included 17th/21st Lancers, 2nd Lothians and Border Horse, a reinforced 10th Rifle Brigade and two troops of 25-pounders, one each from F Battery 12th (HAC) Regiment RHA and 450 Battery 71st (West Riding) Field Regiment. However, Rommel's tanks outgunned the British Valentines and Crusaders which, before long, were retreating from ridge to ridge with the 25-pounders doing their best to impede the enemy's progress. Both armoured regiments lost most of their tanks and the survivors pulled back to Nick Force's final defensive line. Facing the Germans were the remnants of the two armoured regiments, 2nd/5th Leicesters, recently arrived in Tunisia, 90 Battery 23rd Field Regiment and anti-tank guns of 229 Battery 58th (Duke of Wellington's) Anti-Tank Regiment, as well as F Battery 12th (HAC) Regiment RHA. A 4.2-inch mortar company of Royal Engineers and six 37mm anti-tank guns from an American unit were also included. Although 16th/5th Lancers, 26 Armoured Brigade's third regiment, were en route with their new Sherman tanks, the situation looked desperate.[74]

Shortly after dusk, German tanks pushed though the infantry towards the positions of F Battery. Tank and mortar fire had already struck the Battery's lines and as the tanks approached the GPO gave the order to limber up and withdraw. This was countermanded almost immediately by the BC, Major Cecil Middleton, who later wrote of the action.

> The area was shelled at frequent intervals throughout the morning and several tanks which appeared on the crest about 1,500 to 3,000 yards away were engaged furiously over open sights. When AP ran short, HE 119 'cap-on' was used. It is doubtful if any of the tanks were actually knocked out but they were certainly discouraged. OPs were also engaged over open sights. No infantry attack on the position developed during the day, but the shelling was heavy and obviously directed from the ridge in front, and casualties amounted to one killed and thirteen wounded, including Captain Pirie, who had been an inspiration throughout. During the day the Battery was greatly heartened by a visit from the BRA, First Army, Brigadier Parham, who insisted on visiting each gun. While he was there a German motorcyclist with sidecar advanced down the ridge in front and after being greeted with a hail of ill-directed small-arms fire was knocked out by a gun. Too late, and to our great regret, we discovered that he was a medical orderly who had clearly lost his way.
>
> The road from Thala was under shellfire and during the day the quads had to run the gauntlet several times to bring up more ammunition. The evacuation of casualties was undertaken voluntarily by Gunners Kerr and Peters, the driver and wireless operator of one of the troop leader's trucks. They worked untiringly, often

> under shellfire, and succeeded in getting all casualties, both our own and those of other nearby units, back to the ADS at Thala.
>
> Another highlight of the day was Captain Buchanan's OP work. Practically all the time his line was out of action, as it was repeatedly cut by shellfire, but he was able to carry on sending fire orders by 'voice control', which he enlivened with suitable words of encouragement. When his voice failed him he engaged enemy OPs with his rifle and claimed several hits. By the end of the day he could no longer speak. We were later told that his running commentary had been a great encouragement to a company of the Rifle Brigade who, unknown to us, had been in a position on our right.[75]

The arrival of additional artillery, including 9th (US) Division's guns and 152nd Field, with further reinforcements prompted the Germans to withdraw but, on the 24th, they were again advancing, this time towards Hunt's Gap, some five miles north of Beja. At Sidi Nsir, a small village surrounded by hills, twelve miles in front of 128 Brigade's main positions, a forward position had been established by 46th Division. At Sidi Nsir were 5th Hampshires and 155 Battery 172nd Field Regiment with its 25-pounders. This fresh German thrust was made by an armoured battlegroup with over seventy tanks, including some of the new Mark VI, or Tiger, which had first been encountered in January.[76] Sergeants Duncan and Bauer of No 1 Troop 72nd Anti-Tank Regiment had claimed the first Tiger knocked out on 31 January.[77]

In the battle that began with F Troop 155 Battery being mortared from behind a nearby ridge, the Gunners and Hampshires fought desperately as the Germans pressed home their attack, supported by aircraft that strafed with machine-gun and cannon fire. Lieutenant Richard Taylor was the sole officer on F Troop's position, north of the Mateur road. He and Sergeant Henderson 'stood out by reason of their undaunted offensive spirit and the inspiring example they set'.[78] Mortar rounds continued to rain down on the Battery's positions and when the first enemy tanks tried to push down the Mateur road F Troop's No. 1 gun engaged them over open sights, in spite of being under both mortar and machine-gun fire. Three tanks were hit and blocked the road where it passed through a minefield laid by the defenders.

However, 155 Battery lost its best vantage point over the Mateur road when the OP on Point 609 was attacked by German infantry at 9.40am. The wireless sets were smashed by mortar fire, the land lines to the gun positions were cut and Lieutenant McGee was wounded and captured. Later in the morning Messerschmitts strafed the gun positions as well as the Sidi Nsir–Hunt's Gap road, setting alight many vehicles. Undeterred by the risks of explosions, battery personnel salvaged shells from the wreckage throughout the day. However, the Luftwaffe fighters were not given clear runs and were engaged by Gunners with Brens who claimed four shot down in the course of the day.

By midday some thirty tanks, accompanied by infantry, had infiltrated to positions on the flanks of the guns. During this time 155 Battery was 'completely occupied in engaging enemy infantry, machine guns and mortars, which were closing in on the Hampshire company positions'.[79] The guns were cut off from their ammunition supply when, at about 3 o'clock, an infantry column penetrated between Hampshire farm, some two miles west of the Sidi Nsir–Beja road, and the gun positions. Then, at 3.30pm, several tanks attempted to pass down the main road, under cover of machine-gun and main-gun fire from a baker's dozen of tanks in hull-down positions. In the lead was a Tiger which Sergeant Henderson's No. 1 gun hit three times. With the Tiger stopped, a Mark IV tried to pass but Henderson's gun again scored a hit and it, too, was stopped, as was a third tank which was set ablaze by the redoubtable NCO and his detachment.

Another attack was launched at 4 o'clock and, once again, Sergeant Henderson's detachment disabled the leading tank. But then No. 1 gun took a direct hit and, with its valiant detachment, was knocked out. The remaining three guns of F Troop continued firing, with Lieutenant Taylor, the artificer, cooks and other survivors dashing from gun to gun to keep them in action as they engaged the advancing tanks at ranges from fifty down to ten yards. F Troop remained in action for more than an hour before the last gun fell silent. It was probably during this phase that the 22-year-old Taylor was killed.[80]

German attention now turned to E Troop, which was surrounded quickly by tanks and infantry. It was a short-lived battle in which the Gunners fought determinedly against overwhelming odds. No. 4 gun was soon out of action while No. 3 had been peppered with machine-gun fire by a Tiger, but its detachment kept firing. Then No. 3 was knocked out and No. 1 captured. The last gun ceased firing and what was described as 'a seemingly endless queue of Mark IVs, led by a Tiger, rolled slowly nose to tail' across the Battery's front.[81] The last message received from the Battery, at 5.51pm, noted simply that 'Tanks are on us'. A few seconds later this was followed by a Morse message, the letter 'V'.[82]

The suffering of 155 Battery and their infantry comrades may well have bought valuable time for First Army. In the immediate aftermath of the battle, the Germans paused to re-organise but, at the same time, the heavens opened yet again and several days of torrential rain followed. That rain turned the valley to the Hunt's Gap position into a quagmire and the German tanks could not advance. At the same time, reinforcements were reaching 128 Brigade. These included medium artillery and the Gunners began a programme of hammering the German tanks in the valley and the infantry in the hills. Although the Germans were also reinforced, they seem to have lost the will to press on; at the first signs of a British counter-offensive, on 2 March, they pulled out, leaving behind them thirty tanks. Lieutenant Colonel H C C Newnham, CO of 5th Hampshires, had no doubt of the contribution made by 155 Battery when he wrote: 'I voice the feelings of my Battalion when I can only recommend that 155th Battery receive the highest award for valour. Their unshaken devotion to the guns was an epic and as gun by gun was silenced so did survivors make their way to help the guns remaining in action.'[83] In a Special Order of the Day, the CRA of 46th Division paid tribute to 155 Battery:

> For grit and devotion to duty the action of 155 Battery at Sidi Nsir compares with anything in the history of the Royal Regiment. It is no exaggeration to say that the fire of 172nd Regiment Group on the Beja Road decisively influenced the battle in our favour.[84]

It was estimated that each of 155 Battery's guns fired up to 1,800 rounds that day.[85]

> Yes; the twilight came on gently and the shadows grew more deep,
> And the dead seemed faintly smiling; they were smiling in their sleep,
> And though in peace went down at last, that last of all our guns,
> The swan-song of the Battery was the thunder of the guns.
>
> (Vivian Bewick)[86]

Rommel had quit Tunisia, leaving others to oversee the final phase of the North African war. After the fall of Tripoli on 23 January, only the spearhead of Eighth Army had pursued Panzer Armee Afrika into Tunisia. This included 7th Armoured Division with its own 4 and 22 Armoured and 131 (Queen's) Brigades, plus 8 Armoured Brigade; artillery included 69th Medium Regiment in addition to 7th Armoured's own 3 and 5 RHA, 146th Field, 65th A-Tk and 15th LAA. With Tripoli's port open and supplies arriving for Eighth Army, other formations followed into Tunisia where Medenine was taken on 17 February; these included 51st (Highland) and 2nd New Zealand Divisions. All three formations were deployed defensively as Montgomery expected an Axis counter-attack. Ultra intercepts had confirmed Rommel's intention to strike against Eighth Army and Montgomery considered that this might 'upset the preparations for our own attack against the Mareth Line', scheduled for 19 March.[87]

Planning a defence against an armoured attack, Montgomery disposed his anti-tank guns to meet such a threat. Guns were sited in an overall layout rather than to meet local threats and included his three British regiments – 57th (East Surrey), 65th (Norfolk Yeomanry) and 73rd – 7th New Zealand and all the infantry anti-tank guns. This gave a total of 472 guns, of which only forty-eight were 2-pounders. The four Gunner regiments deployed 256 guns, including some of the new 17-pounders which were deployed inconspicuously in 2nd New Zealand Division's rear areas. Eight British and three New Zealand field regiments were also available to Montgomery, as were 7th, 64th and 69th Medium Regiments. The field and medium regiments registered a large number of targets and were also ready to engage as Mike Targets any unregistered target that appeared.[88]

Preceded by dive-bombing attacks, the enemy attack came early on 6 March. The Axis strike force included three panzer divisions, with 160 tanks in all, and some 200 guns, all commanded by the Italian General Messe, a 'competent, conscientious, realistically pessimistic [commander], and not exactly a fighting general'.[89] As the panzers advanced they had, at first, the benefit of fog to conceal them but, as the sun rose and burned through the fog, that cover soon dissipated and the armour met a horrendous barrage from the anti-tank guns, forcing their withdrawal. In spite of this rebuff, they came forward again, not once but three times before finally quitting the battlefield. Most of the fighting of the Battle of Medenine had been done by the anti-tank gun detachments, which held their fire until the enemy were, in some cases, less than a hundred yards away. They had meted out severe punishment to their attackers: over fifty enemy tanks were left on the battlefield, of which all but seven fell victim to anti-tank guns. Eighth Army lost no tanks although only one squadron of Shermans had seen any serious involvement.[90]

Enemy aircraft had also been in action with Ju87 Stukas preceding each of the four ground attacks. These had suffered also as light AA gunners put up a screen of fire with few precedents in North Africa. And the field Gunners had played their part too, at times engaging enemy tanks that made the mistake of bunching, thereby presenting good targets for indirect fire. However, Montgomery chose not to pursue his foe but to continue preparing for Eighth Army's attack on the Mareth Line.

Operation PUGILIST, the assault on the Mareth Line, was a tough battle for Eighth Army in which Montgomery was forced to improvise, when his original plan seemed doomed to stalemate, by sending Brian Horrocks' X Corps, reinforced with 1st Armoured Division, around the left, or southern, flank through the Tebaga Gap while 4th Indian Division was to work its way into the Matmata hills to take a shorter left hook around the line. The plan was complicated by Montgomery's superimposing Horrocks' corps on Freyberg's New Zealand Corps, which had been created specially to deal with the Mareth Line.[91] This Maginot Line in Africa had been built by the French to defend against Italian aggression from Libya and its defences proved too strong for the artillery of 50th (Northumbrian) Division even though the CRA could call on thirteen field and three medium regiments. None, however, fired a shell heavy enough to do more than cause a headache for the occupants of the concrete and steel emplacements.[92]

The revised plan worked with, once again, the Gunner role critical. Eighth Army's artillery was now a finely tuned instrument that could react to critical developments almost as a matter of routine. Such was the case with 76th Anti-Tank Regiment when tanks from both 15th and 21st Panzer Divisions threatened to play havoc with Montgomery's plans at El Hamma. When the German tanks engaged 8 Armoured Brigade and the soft tail of 1st Armoured Division, the anti-tank Gunners, who had been farther forward with the leading armour,

> ... dashed back to form a shield with a combination of 6-pounders on portées and newly issued towed 17-pounders. An extraordinary running fight took place, in which the 17-pounders proved their power, and after much helter-skelter and the eruption of blazes, the attackers withdrew, pounded by gunfire ...[93]

Not only had the 17-pounders proved themselves but the 6-pounders on their portées had tackled the panzers in a running battle and beaten them; their first three rounds knocked out the tractors of two 88s.[94] This action helped Eighth Army overcome the Mareth defences and push deeper into Tunisia.

Included in Eighth Army's artillery at this time was an ad hoc troop named for the commander of 12 AA Brigade, Brigadier H M J McIntyre. Known as Mac Troop, this deployed four captured 88s and had its beginnings in a visit made by General Freyberg and his CRA, Brigadier Weir, to a firing range at Azizia south of Tripoli where they witnessed 3.7-inch HAA guns of 25 Battery 9th (Londonderry) HAA Regiment firing in a field and anti-tank role. So impressed were they by this demonstration that they asked for 3.7s for the New Zealand Division in Tunisia. Although no 3.7s could be spared, several 88s had been captured and these equipped Mac Troop, which was formed from 9th and 51st (London) HAA Regiments and was commanded initially by Captain Downing of 51st HAA Regiment. Mac Troop first saw action at Medenine where it fired in an AA role before being placed under command of 4th New Zealand Field Regiment with whom it remained until the campaign ended.[95] Weir noted that in its first engagement, in the AA role, the troop 'forgot to set the fuzes to "time" with the result that some of the shells completed the trajectory, bursting on percussion in Colonel Crump's replenishment area'. He added that it would 'be unfair to assume that this is why they moved to 4 Field Regiment'.[96]

The troop proved very versatile and fired in AA, field and anti-tank roles. In that last role it knocked out some German tanks, the commanders of which had mistaken the troop for 'friendly' artillery. Captain Hume Stewart-Moore, who had succeeded Downing as troop commander, ordered his Gunners to hold fire until the panzers had passed. They then engaged the tanks from behind, brewing up all of them. The 88s also engaged *Nebelwerfern*, the German multi-barrelled mortars known as 'Moaning Minnies', which were first deployed in Tunisia. Nebelwerfer rounds had hit 4th Field's RHQ and that of 111th Field Regiment RA, whose CO was among several who were killed. The Germans were sited in a gully, presenting a very difficult target for the 25-pounders, but the 88s silenced them by firing airbursts over their position.[97]

The Mareth battle had also seen the arrival of AOPs in Eighth Army's area, although these had been operating with First Army for some time. No. 654 Squadron, with its operational-standard Auster IIIs, arrived in Tunisia on 4 March and was soon available to support Eighth Army's artillery.[98] No. 651 Squadron had been the first to arrive in Tunisia. As we saw in Chapter Three, Brigadier Jack Parham ensured that two flights of the squadron under Major Charles Bazeley were included in the first follow-up convoy to Tunisia. Although equipped with the Auster I, Bazeley's squadron performed sterling duties that proved beyond doubt the value of the AOP. When the third flight arrived in February 1943 it brought with it the Auster III, a much more capable aircraft than its predecessor, which had been intended as a training machine and had neither landing flaps nor self-sealing fuel tanks, while the pilot's rear view was also restricted.[99]

Bazeley's pilots were soon in action, flying thirty-seven operational sorties in their first two weeks. Only two machines had been attacked by enemy aircraft, one of which, with its pilot, Captain A H Newton, was lost when pounced upon by Messerschmitt Bf109s while coming in to land.[100] The men and machines of the squadron provided a valuable service to First Army's Gunners throughout the remaining months of the campaign. One of those pilots was Captain James Magrath who flew sorties for 12th (HAC) Regiment RHA between 23 and 26 April while the regiment was supporting 26 Armoured Brigade. On the 23rd Magrath landed at 26 Armoured's HQ, although no previous ground reconnaissance of the landing strip had been made. Moreover, the HQ was well forward and under occasional enemy shellfire. Over the next few days, as the brigade advanced, Magrath flew many sorties to provide information for the Gunners. In the air several times each day he ran the risks of enemy ground fire and fighter aircraft as well as Axis AA fire and, since he was flying so low, field artillery shells. On one occasion an 88mm AA round passed through his Auster's fuselage without exploding.

Magrath enabled 12th (HAC) to carry out many effective shoots including

> … one most successful shoot against enemy tanks which, from hull-down positions, were holding up our advance, dispersing them and setting one on fire in spite of the fact that he was several times engaged by small-arms fire from the enemy tanks while observing.[101]

The danger from enemy fighters was demonstrated when Magrath was attacked by five Focke-Wulf Fw190s. Evading any one fighter meant that Magrath had to look out for that machine's wingman, but he proved too wily for the Germans.

> The terrain in Tunisia is in sharp relief with deep valleys and abrupt sugar-loaf hills, and Magrath had noted when he began his sortie a circle of hills forming a deep basin which he considered might be a useful refuge in case of trouble, and jinking violently, he tore off at the lowest altitude to seek safety in it. Once inside he flew round and round like a wasp in a jam-jar until the pursuing fighters, who were probably returning from a distant mission, ran out of petrol and went home.[102]

Another AOP pilot proved so elusive that a German fighter pilot, probably frustrated by the little Auster's jinking about at such low levels, flew too low and too fast and hit the ground before he could pull out of his dive. Over time an early warning system was devised for the AOP pilots through the air-raid sentries who were already a standard feature of the batteries, since they were attractive targets for fighter-bombers. With the AOPs on the same radio network as the batteries they worked with, it became the practice for a 'Bandits' warning, with the appropriate bearing, to be called over the radio. Thus warned, the AOP would fly off and drop as low as possible until the raiders departed.[103]

As Eighth Army pushed forward from the Mareth Line it met stiff resistance at Wadi Akarit where it was to fight its last great battle in Africa. The attack by 4th Indian Division through the hills was made without artillery support although guns were available if necessary. Tuker, GOC of 4th Indian, considered that the Battle of Wadi Akarit had been won by his soldiers before the formal attack even began.[104] The latter was launched by 50th (Northumbrian) and 51st (Highland) Divisions with full artillery support.[105] By the end of the day, sixteen infantry battalions from Eighth Army had wrested strong defensive positions from no fewer than nine Axis divisions, including three armoured, and Montgomery's force could move rapidly northwards.[106] It was not, however, to advance to Tunis. Both First and Eighth Armies were under command of 18 Army Group, commanded by General Alexander who decided that Eighth Army would now maintain pressure on the Axis, commanded by General Jürgen von Arnim, while First Army made the final attack on Tunis.[107]

First Army had been reinforced extensively and now included IX Corps, which was to execute that final attack. The plan was for IX Corps, now under Brian Horrocks, to attack through V Corps on 6 May with 4th British and 4th Indian Divisions on a narrow front. Once these formations had broken in, 6th and 7th Armoured, the latter transferred from Eighth Army, and 4th Indian Divisions, also late of Eighth Army, would complete the breakthrough before advancing on Tunis. With ground that favoured good observation and the siting of a mass of artillery, the CCRA of IX Corps, Brigadier Ambrose Platt, could deploy the artillery of seven divisions as well as two strong AGRAs, a concentration of guns that contrasted sharply with the puny packets of artillery which First Army's formations had been forced to employ in the early days of the campaign; with V Corps' guns there were 652 in all.[108] Such was the power of the Allied air forces that it was possible to dump the ammunition for the artillery – 550 rounds per field gun and 350 per medium – in broad daylight without hindrance from Axis aircraft.[109]

At dawn on 6 May the attack began. The guns prepared the way with a barrage that took the attackers to their first objective. Thereafter, concentrations were fired as necessary. Such was the power of the guns that the infantry encountered little opposition and the armour was passed through at 11.30am. This was according to plan and neither Axis artillery nor airmen could provide any succour for the German and Italian infantry who faced First Army's onslaught. Sixth Armoured Division met only token opposition until Hammam Lif, which was reached on the 7th. There the mountains rise abruptly from the plain, leaving a gap of about 300 yards between the rising ground and the sea. An attack by both armour and infantry, supported strongly by 6th Armoured's divisional artillery and a medium regiment, failed to force the defile and a fresh attack was planned involving the firepower of 2nd AGRA. This was scheduled for 7.00pm but, before then, the tanks broke through the defile.[110]

On the 7th, the first British troops entered Tunis and two days later were on the Cape Bon peninsula. By 12 May the Tunisian campaign was over and more than 200,000 Axis prisoners marched into captivity. General Sir Harold Alexander was able to signal to Churchill that 'We are masters of the North African shores'. Almost three years of war in North Africa were at an end and Allied forces could turn their attention to the return to Europe where, once again, Gunners would pave the way to victory.

Notes

1 Pitt, *The Military History of World War II*, p. 122
2 Auchinleck created a higher command course at Sarafand for potential divisional commanders as well as extending the Staff College at Haifa and ensuring that a uniform doctrine for all three arms of artillery, armour and infantry was taught under a single direction. NA Kew, CAB44/97, p. 10
3 Montgomery, *Memoirs*, p. 113; Bidwell, *Gunners at War*, p. 189
4 Doherty, *The Sound of History*, pp. 47–51
5 Ibid, pp. 51–7
6 Ibid, pp. 67–70
7 Duncan, op cit, p. 227
8 Ibid
9 NA Kew, WO201/555, HQ RA Eighth Army, Operations Report, El Alamein
10 Duncan, op cit, p. 227; NA Kew, WO169/4681, war diary 1 Survey Regt 1942
11 Duncan, op cit, p. 228
12 Bidwell, op cit, p. 141
13 Duncan, op cit, p. 228
14 NA Kew, WO169/3940, war diary BRA Eighth Army, 1942
15 NA Kew, WO169/4010, war diary HQ RA XIII Corps, 1942
16 NA Kew, WO201/555, HQ RA Eighth Army, Operations Report, El Alamein
17 Cruickshank, *Deception in World War II*, pp. 26–7
18 Doherty, op cit, p. 81
19 Duncan, op cit, pp. 228–9
20 NA Kew, WO169/4010, HQ RA XIII Corps, 1942, XIII Corps RA Inst No. 26
21 Ibid
22 Lucas Philips, *Alamein*, p. 85
23 Doherty, op cit, p. 115
24 Hogg, *British and American Artillery*, p. 47
25 Duncan, op cit, p. 229
26 Ibid
27 Doherty, op cit, p. 115
28 Sister M Richard Coyle OSF to author, 1997. See Doherty op cit, p. xv
29 Duncan, op cit, p. 229; Doherty, *op cit*, p. 83
30 Duncan, op cit, p. 229

31 Doherty, *Irish Volunteers in the Second World War*, pp. 118–9
32 NA Kew, WO169/3990 war diary, HQ X Corps 1942
33 Frederick, *Lineage Book*, p. 920
34 Doherty, *The Sound of History*, p. 174 & p. 179n
35 NA Kew, WO201/547, 2nd Rifle Brigade Account of Action at 'Snipe'.
36 Doherty, op cit, pp. 176–7
37 Ibid
38 Perrett, *Last Stand*, pp. 119–21
39 Lucas Phillips, op cit, p. 277
40 Doherty, op cit, p. 178
41 NA Kew, WO201/547, op cit
42 Pitt, *The Crucible of War, Vol III*, p. 156
43 Ibid; NA Kew, WO201/547, op cit; Perrett, op cit, p. 122
44 NA Kew, WO201/547, op cit
45 Ibid; Pitt, op cit, p. 160; Doherty, op cit, p. 181
46 Lucas Phillips, op cit, pp. 290–1
47 Ibid, p. 289
48 NA Kew, WO201/547, op cit
49 Ibid
50 Ibid
51 NA Kew, CAB44/104, p. 367
52 Ibid, p. 532; WO169/4913, war diary 6 LAA Bty, 1942
53 Fraser, *And We Shall Shock Them*, p. 246
54 NA Kew, CAB44/103, p. 94
55 Doherty, op cit, p. 75
56 Playfair, *The Mediterranean and the Middle East, Vol IV*, p. 224; Doherty, *A Noble Crusade*, pp. 114–5; Montgomery, op cit, p. 147
57 Mr Thomas McCready, 24 HAA Bty, to author, 1987. Gnr McCready was a member of one of the recce parties.
58 Doherty, *Wall of Steel*, pp. 119–21; Frederick, op cit, pp. 778 (94 HAA Regt), 826 (40 LAA Regt) & 828 (53 LAA Regt)
59 Doherty, op cit, pp. 116–8; NA Kew, WO169/9819, war diary RHQ, 9 HAA Regt, 1943
60 Ray, *Algiers to Austria*, p. 9
61 Ibid, pp. 10–12
62 Ibid, p. 13
63 Ibid, p. 16
64 Blaxland, *The Plain Cook and the Great Showman*, p. 115
65 Ray, op cit, p. 21
66 NA Kew, WO175/338, war diary 138 Fd Regt, Oct '42 – June '43
67 *The London Gazette*, 18 Nov '43
68 Mead, *Gunners at War*, pp. 57–8
69 Brownlie, *The Proud Trooper*, pp. 475–6
70 Doherty, *Clear The Way!*, pp. 40–1
71 Brownlie, op cit, p. 476
72 Doherty, *Ireland's Generals*, pp. 179–80; Wilson, *Unusual Undertakings*, p. 43
73 Mead, op cit, p. 58
74 Ford, *Mailed Fist*, pp. 61–2
75 Duncan, op cit, p. 269
76 Ibid, p. 59
77 Ibid, p. 274
78 Ibid, p. 273
79 Ibid

80 Richard Taylor is commemorated on the Medjez-el-Bab Memorial. He was posthumously Mentioned in Despatches. www.cwgc.org
81 From an account by Lt Col G S Stavert in *British Army Review,* Dec 1977, quoted in Mead, op cit, p. 61
82 Duncan, op cit, p. 274
83 Quoted in Mead, op cit, p. 62
84 Duncan, op cit, p. 276
85 Ibid, pp. 273–4
86 Ibid, p. 277
87 Montgomery, op cit, p. 158
88 Mead, op cit, pp. 62–3
89 Blaxland, op cit, p.189
90 Doherty, *A Noble Crusade*, p. 122; Bidwell, op cit, p. 195
91 Playfair, *The Mediterranean and the Middle East, Vol IV*, p. 344
92 Blaxland, op cit, p. 196
93 Ibid, pp. 207–8
94 Bidwell, op cit, p. 199
95 Doherty, *Wall of Steel*, pp. 213–4; Stevens, *Bardia to Enfidaville*, p. 148
96 Stevens, op cit, p. 148
97 Doherty, op cit, pp. 214–5; S Harwood to author. Sgt Harwood took part in the action described.
98 Mead, op cit, p. 66
99 Bidwell, op cit, p. 1161
100 Mead, op cit, p. 66
101 Doherty, *Irish Volunteers*, pp. 122–3
102 Bidwell, op cit, p. 121
103 Ibid, p. 121
104 Blaxland, op cit, pp. 213–5
105 Ibid, p. 214, who notes that some 300 field and mediums were involved.
106 Ibid, pp. 212–7
107 Ibid, pp. 230–1
108 Playfair, op cit, p. 447
109 Duncan, op cit, p. 278
110 Ibid, p. 280; Playfair, op cit, p. 454

Chapter Eight

Back to Europe

Before the North African campaign had been won, the Allies were planning their next phase of operations: to take the island of Sicily. This was to be achieved by British and American forces, designated 15 Army Group with two armies, one British and one American. Initially, these were Seventh (US) and Twelfth British Armies but General Montgomery succeeded in having the designation Eighth Army retained for the latter.

The invasion of Sicily, Operation HUSKY, was scheduled for 10 July 1943. Gunner contributions to HUSKY included, for the first time, rocket-firing craft. Landing craft were adapted as firing platforms for batteries of rocket projectiles; these LCT (R)s were to be used in greater numbers and to greater effect in Normandy eleven months later. The rocket craft did not gain everyone's confidence immediately, largely due to an unfortunate incident during a demonstration when a rogue projectile landed some sixty yards in front of a motor launch carrying 'a galaxy of prospective buyers'. Eventually, with the assurance that radar control would eliminate such problems, the concept was 'sold' and the GOC and CRA of 51st (Highland) Division accepted rocket support for the Highlanders' part in the invasion.[1]

HUSKY, the largest amphibious operation ever mounted, was to provide many valuable lessons for future such operations, especially OVERLORD, the 1944 invasion of Normandy. There were many problems in the Sicily landings, some occasioned by exceptionally bad weather that at least had the positive effect of putting the defenders off guard as they did not expect an invasion in such conditions. Others were less serious, such as the anti-tank regiment CO who was 'released on the wrong side of his ship and set out for Crete' before finally landing in Sicily 'on a private beach of his own'.[2]

Other problems were less amusing: 1st Canadian Division, sailing from Britain, lost the CRA's vehicles and signals equipment when their ship was torpedoed by a U-boat. However, HQ 5th AGRA, landing in advance of its units, was able to assist; its CAGRA (Commander, AGRA) stood in as CRA 1st Canadian Division.[3]

Although the campaign lasted less than six weeks it was not entirely successful for the Allies, since the Germans, who had reinforced the Italian garrison, were able to evacuate most of their troops, their equipment and heavy weapons to Italy. They had fought a series of delaying actions that were assisted by rivalries between the Allied army commanders, Montgomery and George Patton of Seventh (US) Army.

In the campaign's opening days, the hardest fought battle was at Primosole bridge where Eighth Army tanks and infantry struggled to reach the airborne troops who had landed around the bridge. During this battle XXX Corps' artillery used some Vickers 12-inch howitzers captured from the Italians, firing them against the other half of the Italian artillery unit that owned them.[4]

The Primosole bridge action was a foretaste of what was to follow. Hard as the Sicilian campaign was for the infantry, it was in many respects even harder for the Gunners who supported them. Conditions were difficult and the mountainous nature of the country often made it hard to find suitable gun positions. Roads were primitive and frequently no more than tracks. Worse, they were so narrow, with lava walls skirting them, that guns and tractors could only just make their slow way along them.[5] And, of course, it was high summer with intense heat that made a man sweat from the slightest exertion. The dry dust expected of a landscape toasted by the Mediterranean sun was made worse by volcanic dust from Mount Etna, still active as the glow from its cone proved during the short hours of darkness. Even the makeshift facemasks that many soldiers wore over their mouths and noses proved no protection against Sicily's dust.[6] Combined with sweat, it left men coated in a black paste. All this 'made existence vile and exertion all but intolerable'.[7] Small wonder that one veteran described Sicily to the author as 'a land of heat and smelly socks'.[8]

Added to the misery was the prevalence of malaria in the Catania plain with many men incapacitated by the disease. In spite of all these factors, 'the artillery did not fail to enhance their reputation, and the discipline and morale of the Regiment remained, as ever, very high'.[9]

For the first time, XXX Corps had the use of Air OPs which were always in great demand from the divisional artilleries and the medium regiments. Some senior staff officers seemed to believe that the Austers could be used as air taxis but this abuse was suppressed vigorously and the aircraft performed the role for which they were intended.[10] A considerable number of Gunner units were represented in the Sicilian campaign, including no fewer than twenty-three field regiments, of which three were Royal Canadian Artillery and one was Royal Horse Artillery (11th (HAC) Regiment). Of medium regiments there were six while seven anti-tank regiments, including one Canadian, were also deployed. Since there was still significant Axis airpower in the region, nine heavy and fourteen light AA regiments, including a Canadian LAA regiment, deployed. Two survey regiments and No. 654 OP Squadron completed the Gunner line-up.[11] Eighth Army's formation commanders had 5th AGRA on call to supplement their field artillery under its commander 'Toc' Elton who, tragically, was killed in a plane crash while on his way back to Britain to join 21 Army Group for the invasion of France.[12]

The narrow roads with their lava walls presented many problems to the Gunners. It was often impossible to deploy the guns off the roads and more than one battery had the uncomfortable experience of going into action from the road. Nonetheless, artillery support was provided whenever and wherever it was needed, as when the Canadians were advancing on Catenanuova, an occasion on which E Battery, 11th (HAC) 'registered the first air-burst barrage in the war – 65 rounds per gun'.[13]

Even when it was possible to leave the road, there were many places where it was difficult to site the guns. This was especially true when 78th Division relieved the Canadians to attack the mountaintop town of Centuripe, but the assaulting infantry of the Irish Brigade had the full support of all seventy-two guns of the divisional artillery. The Brigade's attack on Centuripe was planned with the first phase on the left flank having all the guns supporting them while the second phase, by two battalions in the centre and right flank, would see the divisional artillery switch its attention to their objectives. Although the battle did not go entirely to plan, Centuripe was taken and the Gunners had been an essential part of that success.[14]

As 78th Division continued its advance, the Irish Brigade, strengthened by 8th Argyll and Sutherland Highlanders, was assigned the task of capturing Maletto as well as Monte Macherone, Monte Capella and Monte Sperina. The attack was launched at 2.30am on 12 August and had support not only from the divisional artillery but also four medium batteries. Resistance was fierce and with the lava-strewn country making movement difficult for the infantry, further artillery concentrations were called for. Thus it was that a series of Uncle Targets assisted 2nd London Irish Rifles to seize their objectives.[15]

The Gunners faced considerable difficulties in this period as German artillery, mortars and machine guns made such good use of the 'rugged defensive country [that] it was virtually impossible to spot [them] in spite of ground and air observation posts and flash spotters'. Seventy-eighth Division's historian noted that the artillery 'had four particularly difficult days in trying to dominate this fire directed against our leading troops'. Significantly, two members of 17th Field Regiment were decorated at this time: Bombardier G H Evans won an immediate MM when firing in support of the Buffs and Royal West Kents on the road to Randazzo while German artillery was shelling 17th Field's positions and Captain D J Anderson earned the MC for his work with 1st Royal Irish Fusiliers when observing under fire and manhandling ammunition across a minefield.[16]

Among other awards to Gunners in the campaign were DSOs to two commanding officers. That to Lieutenant Colonel Richard Goodbody, of 11th (HAC) Regiment RHA which landed with 23 Armoured Brigade on 10 July, was an immediate award for this service throughout the campaign, in which his regiment 'was constantly in action'. Near Catenanuova, E Battery's air-burst barrage, 'Superimposed on the high explosive barrage furnished by the field and medium batteries ... helped the Canadians to achieve a comprehensive success; and still supported by the Regiment they were able to press on towards the stronghold of Centuripe'.[17] The DSO citation emphasised the regiment's role in actions at Vizzini and on the Dittaino river where Lightbody 'showed great gallantry and leadership in reconnoitring suitable gun areas and observation posts'.[18] The action at Vizzini took place on 13 July, a day before Lieutenant Colonel William Anthony Sheil earned a Bar to the DSO he had been awarded at El Alamein. Sheil was still commanding 128th (Highland) Field Regiment which was supporting 152 (Seaforth & Camerons) Brigade of 51st (Highland) Division in an attack on the hilltop village of Francofonte, which was held by well-dug-in German paratroopers. The enemy were putting up a stubborn resistance but this did not deter Sheil from going forward in person to 'identify the actual centre of resistance which no one else could locate'. With his recce completed he then observed 128th's fire on to several German strongpoints and, where the 25-pounders could not engage, 'himself manhandled 6-pounders and a 17-pounder into action at short range, and then directed their fire'. His work was critical to overcoming the German defenders of Francofonte.[19]

As the campaign progressed it was clear that, although German ground resistance was stout, it was much less so in the air. In fact, the Luftwaffe became a diminishing threat as the Allies pushed towards the north-east of the island. Thus Eighth Army's AA regiments found themselves with little action; although their guard could never be dropped, 78th Division's historian noted that 49th LAA Regiment saw little action after their first three days on the island.[20] (This Division was not included in the invasion force, arriving at the end of July.)[21] However, the Bofors guns of the divisional LAA units could assist in other ways, as at the Dittaino river where a Bofors fired tracer rounds up the Fontana Muralato valley to guide an attack by 5th Cameron Highlanders, supported by a squadron of Sherman tanks and a platoon of 1/7th Middlesex. Of course, the divisional artillery was also in support as the infantry attacked behind a curtain of fire that lifted a hundred yards in three minutes.[22]

Also underemployed in the latter phase of the campaign were the anti-tank guns of the divisional regiments. As the Germans had never intended to hold Sicily, their actions had been intended to slow the Allied advance while their own forces were evacuated to mainland Italy. A shuttle service across the Straits of Messina was organised to transport men and equipment to Italy and, as the defenders withdrew to ever shorter lines, units no longer needed in the line pulled back to Messina to board the vessels that would take them to Italy. Much of the heavier equipment was taken back for evacuation, reducing the number of tanks that faced the advancing Allies. As a result, only one of the four batteries of 64th Anti-Tank (Queen's Own Glasgow Yeomanry) Regiment saw any action at all after its parent 78th Division advanced beyond Adrano.[23]

When Operation HUSKY was in the planning stages, the Americans had intended that this would be a one-off operation rather then a prelude to invading Italy. However, as the Allies advanced through Sicily and the prospect of an armistice with Italy grew stronger, American views changed and agreement was reached that the next phase of operations in the Mediterranean should be in Italy. Thus the largest fire-plan for the Royal Artillery in Sicily came weeks after the campaign on the island had ended.

Two separate landings were to be made in Italy with Fifth (US) Army, including X British Corps, landing at Salerno in Operation AVALANCHE. Before this could happen, it was considered vital to secure the Straits of Messina; this was to be achieved by Eighth Army landing at Reggio di Calabria in Operation BAYTOWN. D-Day for BAYTOWN was fixed for 3 September when elements of XIII Corps crossed the Straits of Messina to land in Reggio. The crossing was covered by an umbrella of fire from 630 guns – 410 field and 120 medium[24] – from XXX Corps and 6th AGRA, all under the command of Brigadier Meade Dennis, CCRA of XXX Corps.[25] However, it was no simple task to assemble all the necessary guns in the Messina area as '[h]ardly any bridges were standing, diversions were as numerous as flies on the wall and the gradients and curves in the immediate vicinity of Messina made a problem for medium and heavy loads.'[26] Nonetheless, these problems were overcome and the guns deployed ready to fire.

At 3.45am on 3 September the order to fire was given and the artillery began bombarding the mainland. Under this umbrella, which unleashed 29,000 rounds, or almost 400 tons of explosives,[27] 5th British and 1st Canadian Divisions began crossing with the first soldiers landing at Reggio at 4.30am. Over eighty-five minutes, 70th Medium Regiment fired 167 rounds per gun.[28] Five field regiments and one medium fired in support of 5th Division but 1st Canadian was supported by four medium regiments, due to the ranges involved; 6th AGRA included four US artillery battalions with 155mm guns.[29] It was noted that observation across the straits 'was magnificent'.[30] Air support was also provided while naval gunfire from 120 guns added to the weight of explosives that fell on Calabria. Rockets, first used in HUSKY, were also deployed.[31] However, most Germans had already departed and opposition was non-existent. In fact, the soldiers of Eighth Army were welcomed as liberators by the people of Calabria, in spite of the fact that Italy and Britain were still officially at war.[32]

From Reggio, Eighth Army's divisions began their slow march through Calabria. It was slow because the Germans had demolished every bridge and corniche, cratered every junction and chopped down many trees to impede their pursuers. The advancing troops continued to have the support of naval vessels off the coast to add to their own artillery, which included 91st, 92nd and 156th Field Regiments with 5th Division, 165th Field with 231 Brigade, and three Canadian field regiments: 1st Regiment Royal Canadian Horse Artillery and 2nd and 3rd Field Regiments Royal Canadian Artillery. There were, of course, also the divisional LAA and anti-tank regiments while, in addition to 6th AGRA, 2 AA Brigade was also under XIII Corps command.[33]

As Eighth Army advanced through Calabria, Fifth Army was making final preparations for Operation AVALANCHE. Much of August had been taken up with amphibious training, waterproofing vehicles and equipment[34] and, with the Straits of Messina secure, it was time to begin embarkation. D-Day was set for 9 September, the moon being 'right' on the night of the 8th/9th – it would not be again until the 21st.[35] On 8 September, General Eisenhower announced that Marshal Pietro Badoglio's new Italian government had reached an armistice agreement with the Allies and an announcement was made that 'Hostilities between the United Nations and Italy have terminated'.[36] However, the Germans were about to take over Italy with the powerful forces that they had already deployed in the peninsula.

At 3.45am on the 9th, landing craft began touching down at Salerno and Gunner recce parties disembarked with the leading infantry with the first 25-pounders and anti-tank guns following closely. By nightfall, elements of thirteen regiments were ashore. This is not to infer that the landings had been straightforward. The LCTs carrying 65th Field Regiment had been attacked by Luftwaffe fighter-bombers although these had been driven off by Allied fighters – twin-engined Lockheed P-38 Lightnings – while the LCT carrying 46th Division's RA stores had been bombed. Vessels waiting in Salerno Bay to run in to the shore suffered 'some very unpleasant bombing' while German demolitions of the ports of Naples and Salerno lit up the horizon with flames and explosions that silhouetted, in pink, the Allied convoys. Those onboard those vessels felt very exposed to air attack as a result.[37]

This was the first occasion on which guided bombs were used in action, when Luftwaffe aircraft launched radio-controlled bombs at the battleship HMS *Warspite*, causing considerable damage and killing nine men.[38] Since German air attacks had been expected, especially as the landings were at the extreme limits of Allied fighters based on Sicily, an AA plan had been drawn up and 'with the well-tried 12 AA Brigade from the Desert we had every reason to be confident that the 'Jerry' bombers would be forcefully dealt with.'[39]

Other casualties included the LST carrying 71st (West Riding) Field Regiment, which was holed by shellfire just off the beaches. Disembarking vehicles were set on fire by 88s and the leading troop had to fight its way into action against both heavy machine-gun and mortar fire. In spite of this opposition, 71st Field had guns in action two miles inland by the evening of D-Day. Meanwhile, 113th Field had a hard battle to cross the beaches and take up positions in the close vineyards and tomato groves. The regiment's Gunners had endured constant harassing fire from enemy snipers who proved very difficult to locate. Another unit to share such adventures was 65th (8th London) Field Regiment, some of whose guns and vehicles landed in soft sand while one landing craft was hit offshore. Considerable exertion on the part of the Gunners reclaimed the guns and vehicles from the sand. They were spurred on by 'the bark of the hostile Bredas and the thump of mortars'. One major loss occurred when the LCT carrying E Troop 506 Battery 142nd (Royal Devon Yeomanry) Field Regiment struck a mine, broke in half and sank 'gracefully without a murmur'; fourteen men, including Sergeant Albert Allen's entire detachment, were killed and their SPGs lost. E Troop had been preparing to land with 64th (7th London) Field Regiment and their SPGs would have been especially valuable in the beachhead. Also coming ashore at the end of the first day were the recce parties and leading troops of two medium regiments – 5th and 69th (Carnavon & Denbigh) (Yeomanry).[40]

Although the opposition on D-Day was determined it was not as strong as it might have been. The Germans had not been certain whether this was a major landing or a feint and did not make their minds up until many more Allied soldiers were ashore. One Gunner officer later commented that it was fortunate that the enemy 'with his excellent observation, had so few field guns available to deal with those beaches during the early hours when our guns could do so little'.[41] However, it was not long before the full ferocity of a counter-offensive was launched against Fifth Army's beachhead. For several days the men in the beachhead fought tenaciously but it looked at one stage as if the Germans might push the Allies back into the sea. Fifth Army's commander, General Mark Clark, even suggested evacuating VI (US) Corps from the southern beaches, below the Sele river, but this was overruled by 15 Army Group's commander, General Sir Harold Alexander and the Allied naval commander, Admiral Sir Andrew Cunningham. Alexander also suggested to Clark that he relieve VI Corps' commander, Lieutenant General Ernest J Dawley, whom he (Alexander) considered a broken reed. However, Alexander also released 82nd (US) Airborne Division from Army Group command to Clark's command and this was one of the key elements in stabilising the beachhead.

Another factor in holding the beachhead was the rapid conversion of British Gunners into infantry. A shortage of shipping meant 7th Armoured Division was still awaiting the infantry of 131 (Queen's) Brigade when the Germans struck. Although Brigade HQ and the battalion and company HQs of its three battalions – 1/5th, 1/6th and 1/7th Queen's – were ashore, the fighting personnel of those battalions were still in North Africa. However, on the night of 15 September, there were men coming ashore who could fill the gaps in the infantry ranks. These were the Gunners of 24, 25 and 26 HAA Batteries 9th (Londonderry) HAA Regiment who began disembarking from their LSTs at 9.00pm completely unaware of the threat faced by X Corps which had no reserve of infantry. Very quickly, the 'Derry Boys' had been designated a Corps Reserve of Infantry with 468 officers and men formed into rifle companies under command of Lieutenant Colonel Browning of 52nd (East Lancashire) LAA Regiment.[42]

Initially deployed near Montecorvino airfield, whence they mounted fighting patrols at dawn, the Gunners then moved closer to the front and were attached to 1/6th Queen's with 24 Battery becoming A Company, 25 Battery B Company, and 26 Battery C Company of the battalion. As this was a lorried infantry unit, the Gunners were then driven to the Incarto area to take up defensive positions until relieved by the arrival of the battalion's own personnel, following which the Gunners were attached to 5th Royal Tanks. During the afternoon of the 17th, 25 Battery's Gunners were withdrawn and returned to their guns for the AA defence of the beaches. The other two batteries remained in a reserve infantry role with 5th Royal Tanks and the Royal Scots Greys before they, too, returned to their guns on the morning of 19 September.[43]

It had been a difficult time for the Gunners who faced an unfamiliar role.

> They always talk about the pen being mightier than the sword. We were made infantrymen just at the stroke of a pen, and up we went into the front line at three or four [o'clock] in the morning. … When we got up in the morning there they were – the Germans in one field and we were in the next.[44]

From the infantry role, 9th HAA Regiment moved to more familiar duties, serving as both AA and medium artillery in the beachhead until the breakout. Working with field and medium units, the AA Gunners – thirty-six 3.7s were deployed – helped to break up the German attacks. One Gunner officer later wrote that the AA detachments 'shot with remarkable effectiveness despite lack of experience in this role'.[45] That was not true of 9th HAA Regiment since their CO had ensured that his men were trained in the field role. When Naples fell at the beginning of October the Regiment deployed around the city to provide air defence with Lieutenant Colonel Bob Aitken once again in the role of AADC.[46]

There had been seven days of desperate fighting in the beachhead before Fifth Army broke out to advance along the road to Naples. In that fighting the Gunners had acquitted themselves superbly, as Gunners and infantry, and 'at the most critical stage the guns stemmed the tide of the German assault and broke his morale.'[47] Fifth Army morale, however, was high and there 'was a perceptible change of atmosphere when good local Marsala was discovered at 10 lire (5d) per four-gallon jerry-can'.[48]

Advancing on either side of the Apennines, Fifth and Eighth Armies met the stubborn opposition that was to be the hallmark of the German defences in Italy. Pushing towards the Volturno river, X Corps' artillery was called upon to support many attacks and provide many defensive tasks for attacking infantry and armour. Across the peninsula, Eighth Army was advancing from the Biferno river towards the Sangro. At the Trigno river, 78th Division was supported by 70th Medium Regiment which, as the sole medium regiment available, fired day and night with an average daily expenditure of 3,000 rounds, about seventy-five tons of ammunition daily.[49] But the weather was changing and winter came early, adding yet another problem for the Allies but aiding the Germans, rivers swelling as the rains ran off the mountains and making crossings even more difficult. Although Fifth Army was across the Volturno by mid-October, it was late November before Eighth Army crossed the Sangro. Gunner support proved critical: at one point

German defences beyond the Sangro were pounded by some 400 guns as Eighth Army prepared to attack.[50] That attention was to become even more impressive as V Corps artillery hammered the enemy. In the first three days of the Sangro battle, each field gun fired over 600 rounds while the 5.5s loosed off over 350 rounds each and the 4.5s some 330 rounds per gun.

> The ridge appeared to be a pleasant countryside with small white houses with red roofs. The supporting fire passed along it and when the dust and smoke cleared, all the ground crossed was a shambles of smashed houses, burning ricks and desolation.[51]

In total, 145,770 rounds were fired, almost 1,623 tons of explosive. The corps artillery included 51st (Midland) Medium Regiment of 1st AGRA, 66th (Lowland), 70th and 80th (Scottish Horse) Medium Regiments of 6th AGRA, the divisional artilleries of 78th Division and 8th Indian Division, plus four army field regiments.[52]

Both armies now found themselves up against the Gustav Line, a series of heavily fortified positions stretching from coast to coast over the rugged Apennines and using the topography of the country to best advantage. Montgomery's plan to take Rome before Christmas was proven to be illusory and Eighth Army came to a standstill as Montgomery departed for Britain and command of 21 Army Group, while major formations were transferred across the country to join Fifth Army. The latter, still including X British Corps, was trying to maintain the impetus but this, too, proved impossible. Although there were some gains along the Gustav Line, it was clear that there would be no breakthrough. A new plan was devised that called for Fifth Army to envelop the critical Monte Cassino position from the north and make a crossing of the Rapido river while II (US) Corps landed behind the Gustav Line at the ports of Anzio and Nettuno, south of Rome, in Operation SHINGLE.

D-Day for SHINGLE and the Rapido crossing was 22 January 1944. Both operations included British divisions, with 1st Division in VI Corps at Anzio, and X Corps assaulting across the Garigliano river with 5th, 46th and 56th Divisions. The initial crossing was made by brigades of 5th and 56th Divisions on the night of 17/18 January. So that the Germans might be taken by surprise, 5th Division's attack was to be 'silent' although strong artillery support was on hand if needed: in addition to the divisional artillery – 91st (4th London), 92nd (5th London) and 156th (Lanarkshire Yeomanry) Field Regiments – they also had 98th Army Field and 102nd (Pembroke Yeomanry) Medium Regiments. On the other hand, 56th Division was to have full artillery support from its own 64th, 65th and 113th Field Regiments, supplemented by 142nd Army Field and 51st Medium Regiments plus 2nd AGRA which deployed 78th Army Field, 69th (Carnavon & Denbigh) (Yeomanry), 74th and 140th (5th London) Medium and 56th Heavy Regiments; 146th Medium Regiment and No. 654 AOP Squadron were deployed as corps troops.[53] Naval fire support was also available from two cruisers and five destroyers. In readiness for the fire plan, ammunition had been dumped at each gunsite: 400 rounds per 25-pounder, 250 rounds per medium and 150 rounds per heavy.[54]

The initial crossing was more successful than anticipated and further advances were made but the inevitable counter-attacks caused many casualties and some ground was lost. On the night of 19/20 January, 46th Division was also to cross the river to protect the flank of II (US) Corps when that formation crossed at Sant'Angelo on 20 January. The crossing, by 128 (Hampshire) Brigade, was supported by 70th (West Riding), 71st (West Riding), 72nd (Northumbrian) Field, 23rd Army Field and 5th Medium Regiments as well as two batteries of the US 59th Armoured Field Artillery Battalion. In spite of all this support, 128 Brigade's attack was repulsed, partly due to the difficulties of crossing the river which was in flood and the loss of many assault boats.[55]

Then followed the repulse of 36th (Texas) Division close to Sant'Angelo, leading Clark to call off his offensive, except for the operations of the French Expeditionary Corps. X Corps continued holding its bridgehead but did not advance. In turn the Germans called off their counter-offensive against X Corps on 22 January. However, Clark began a new operation with 34th (Red Bull) Division on the 24th. Although Fifth Army had suffered heavy losses in these operations it had made some important gains, including Monte Trocchio, overlooking Cassino town, Cáira village and several of the hilltops, some of which overlooked Monte Cassino itself.

The northward attack by X Corps and 36th (Texas) Division had been intended to link up with the troops at Anzio who were now isolated. Operation SHINGLE had gone ahead as planned on 22 January with 1st Division landing on 'Peter' beach. Two Brigade's infantry landed first, all of them being ashore by 2.45am, accompanied by the first Gunners: 67th (South Midland) Field Regiment came ashore with its guns in DUKWs, amphibious 2.5 ton trucks, the first occasion on which 25-pounders had been landed in this fashion. In addition to the field guns, 294 Anti-Tank Battery and 312 (SP) LAA Battery also landed with 2 Brigade.[56] A Flight No. 655 AOP Squadron was soon in the beachhead as well.[57] Once again, all went well initially, with virtually no opposition, which allowed VI Corps to advance but its commander, Major General Lucas, was reluctant to make a dash for Rome (he had been advised by Clark to be cautious) and so the advance was limited. Before long the beachhead was under siege, a situation that would prevail until the end of May.

Artillery with 1st Division at the end of January included the divisional regiments – 2nd, 19th and 67th Field – as well as 24th Army Field, 78th (Lowland) Field, 80th (Scottish Horse) Medium, 81st (Anti-Tank) and 90th (South Wales Borderers) LAA Regiments with 50 Survey Battery, C Troop No. 2 Bombardment Unit and A Flight No. 655 AOP Squadron.[58]

The experience of the Gunners at Anzio may be expressed through that of 1st Division's augmented artillery in the most critical three weeks of the siege, in late

February and early March, when the Gunner units suffered over 600 casualties, including fifty officers, while nineteen gunpits sustained direct hits from bombs or shells. Fifty OP wireless sets were destroyed by enemy action, or to prevent their falling into enemy hands, and two dozen anti-tank guns were overrun and lost. In 19th Field the CO, the second-in-command and two BCs were lost in three days. The Division's guns fired almost half-a-million rounds, one weapon of 78th Field discharging no fewer than 706 rounds in one twenty-four-hour period. Among other noteworthy achievements was that of 111 Battery 80th Medium Regiment, which moved five miles by night, fired 2,174 rounds from its new position and brought 3,742 rounds either from its old position or from a dump at much the same distance away; each man handled three tons of shells.[59]

While the siege of the Anzio beachhead continued, Mark Clark had not given up hope of breaking the Gustav Line in the Cassino area. On 1 February he launched II (US) Corps, supported by the French Expeditionary Corps on a fresh assault on the critical Cassino position but this, too, was rebuffed and led to another attack, this time by the ad-hoc New Zealand Corps – 2nd New Zealand, 4th Indian and 78th Divisions. Launched on 15 February, this assault was called off on the 18th with the two attacking formations, the New Zealand and Indian Divisions, suffering significant casualties for little gain. Clark remained determined and planned yet another assault, before which the Benedictine abbey atop Monte Cassino was pounded to rubble by USAAF heavy bombers, it being believed, wrongly, that the Germans were using it as an observation point. Thereafter, the Germans moved into the ruins, which provided an excellent strongpoint overlooking the valley. This new assault, also by the New Zealand Corps, began on 15 March and was preceded not only by the bombing of Cassino but also by an artillery bombardment of almost 200,000 rounds. When the operation was called off, the attackers had taken much of the town, and the features of Castle Hill and Hangman's Hill, both overlooking Cassino. General Alexander was already planning the final assault on the Gustav Line for which he sidestepped Eighth Army from the east coast to join Fifth Army west of the Apennine spine. Both armies were re-organised to place all British, Commonwealth and Empire formations – save for 1st and 5th Divisions at Anzio, where they would be joined by 56th Division – in Eighth Army, which also included II Polish Corps and an Italian Brigade Group, *1° Raggruppamento Motorizzato*.

The Gunners were to play an even greater part in Alexander's new attack. This was the army group's Operation DIADEM, Eighth Army's part in which was Operation HONKER. D-Day was set for the night of 11/12 May and an ambitious deception plan, Operation DUNTON, led the Germans to believe that the inevitable attack would come at the end of May while also causing them to expect amphibious and airborne landings closer to Rome; they were also deceived about the locations of the French and Canadian corps.

As preparations were made for the offensive, Allied troops held positions around Cassino that were very treacherous and, almost always, under enemy observation. Those in the mountains had to be re-supplied by night by mule and, of course, the Germans knew every inch of the ground. Roads and tracks were registered and under regular attention from artillery and mortars, to combat which the Allies used a smokescreen, codenamed Cigarette, to conceal movement and preparations for the new attack.

> The period during which Cigarette was laid by the 25-pounders – from ten at night until the supply parties were back under cover – was an anxious one for all concerned, and particularly for the Gunner FOO in the town, who had to adjust the points on which the smoke canisters fell according to the wind blowing at the time.[60]

Cigarette was an unpopular task as the majority of field batteries were required to remain silent so that the Germans would be unaware of the great number of guns gathering round the entrance to the Liri valley. As a result the shooting was carried out by a small number of batteries which each had to fire a large number of smoke-shells. This caused wear and tear on the guns, all of which had been calibrated recently, as well as being tiring for the detachments who had to carry large quantities of ammunition and replenish it nightly.[61]

Guns also fired defensive tasks, but there was a real problem facing the Gunners. This was a severe shortage of ammunition, caused by the inability of British industry to keep pace with demands for 25-pounder and medium shells. The problem was aggravated in Italy because of the high expenditure of such rounds to support infantry attacks and break up enemy counter-attacks. On 21 March, just as he was starting to plan Operation DIADEM, Alexander was forced to issue orders rationing the daily expenditure of shells; 25-pounder ammunition was restricted to fifteen rounds per gun daily while the daily ration for a medium gun was ten rounds.[62] Fortunately for the morale of both infantry and Gunners, only Alexander and his staff knew the full extent of the ammunition famine. Thus was the plan for the offensive complicated by the need to stockpile ammunition so that an effective fireplan might be drawn up.

Gunners were kept busy preparing and camouflaging gun positions while a detailed picture of German artillery positions was built up. This was achieved through observation, sound ranging and aerial reconnaissance so that, by D-Day for Operation DIADEM, the location of almost every enemy gun and mortar was known. Throughout the army group, now known as Allied Armies in Italy (AAI), some 1,600 guns were making ready for a bombardment that would surpass that at El Alamein. Eighth Army alone disposed about 1,000 guns; anti-tank and AA guns doubled that figure. Careful husbanding of ammunition meant that each of XIII Corps' heavy guns had 200 rounds available, the mediums each had 350 rounds and there were 600 for every 25-pounder. In II Polish Corps there were 700 rounds per medium gun and 1,090 per 25-pounder. XIII Corps had 700 guns and the Poles had 300 in their sector.[63]

In addition to the divisional artilleries, Eighth Army deployed, as Army artillery, 2nd Regiment RHA, 23rd, 98th (Surrey & Sussex Yeomanry, Queen Mary's), 142nd (Royal Devon Yeomanry) and 165th Field Regiments and 11th Field Regiment, Royal Canadian Artillery. Corps artillery groupings are shown below:[64]

Nor was this the total of Eighth Army's firepower: four AGRAs and two AA brigades were also in the orbat deploying as indicated in the second table:[65]

Corps	Artillery Units
X Corps (protecting Eighth Army's northern flank)	8th Survey, 57th (East Surrey) A-Tk and 56th (East Lancashire) LAA Regiments; No. 654 AOP Squadron
XIII Corps	3rd Survey, 105th A-Tk and 99th (Queen's Royal Regiment) LAA Regiments; No. 655 AOP Squadron
I Canadian Corps	1st Survey, 7th A-Tk and 1st LAA Regiments, RCA; No. 651 AOP Squadron
II Polish Corps	1st Survey, 7th A-Tk, 7th LAA and 8th HAA Regiments, Polish Artillery

AGRA/AA Brigade	Units included
2nd AGRA	5th, 74th, 102nd (Pembroke Yeomanry), 140th (5th London) Medium & 56th Heavy Regiments
6th AGRA	2nd, 66th (Lowland), 75th (Shropshire Yeomanry), 76th (Shropshire Yeomanry), 78th (Duke of Lancaster's Own Yeomanry) Medium & 75th (Highland) Heavy Regiments
1st Canadian AGRA	51st (Midland) Medium RA, 1st, 2nd, 5th Medium RCA, 32nd Heavy RA
2nd Polish AGRA	7th Horse Artillery, 9th Field, 10th & 11th Medium, Polish Artillery
2 AA Brigade	53rd (KOYLI), 74th, 117th (Royal Ulster Rifles) LAA, 51st (London), 84th (Middlesex, London Transport) & 88th HAA Regiments
12 AA Brigade	14th (West Lothian Royal Scots), 52nd (East Lancashire) LAA, 1st, 57th (Wessex) & 97th (London Scottish) HAA Regiments

In addition to the re-organisation of the two armies, Eighth Army had also been reinforced with the arrival in Italy of 6th South African Armoured Division, although it remained initially under AAI command. But there was another 6th Armoured Division in Eighth Army's orbat, the British veterans of Tunisia. The latter had arrived in Italy in dribs and drabs and, for Operation HONKER, was to support the assaulting infantry divisions of XIII Corps. The division brought with it to Italy 12th (HAC) Regiment RHA, 152nd (Ayrshire Yeomanry) Field, 72nd Anti-Tank and 51st (Devon) LAA Regiments. Almost a year earlier, in August 1943, 12th (HAC) RHA had handed in its tired 25-pounders in exchange for M7 Priests with their 105mm gun/howitzers, allowing the Gunners to maintain pace with 26 Armoured Brigade's tanks. The Regiment had also received Sherman tanks for its OPs, as had 152nd Field, which, however, retained towed 25-pounders since it usually supported 1 Guards Brigade.[66]

In Tunisia, 6th Armoured's Gunners had exercised 'artillery in support of tanks both for quick support and as a result of a deliberate fire plan' at the RA ranges south-west of Sidi Mezrich. The CRA had flown to Italy on 17 March and just over three weeks later, on 8 April, HQRA 6th Armoured Division relieved HQ New Zealand Artillery in the Cassino sector and was in turn relieved by HQRA 8th Indian Division on the 22nd.[67] However, 12th (HAC) were still at Piedimonte d'Alife where, on 13 April, they were visited by Lieutenant General Sir Oliver Leese, Eighth Army's commander, who 'walked round, distributing cigarettes and newspapers'.[68]

While in the Cassino sector, HQRA had learned a good deal about conditions there and the need for artillery support, including SOS tasks codenamed 'Murphy' and 'Parker' designed to break up any German attack. Such tasks called for the fire of two field regiments. None was called for during the HQ's time at Cassino although one was almost ordered one night when a telephone caller asked for 'Murphy'. Just before there was 'an unwarranted expenditure of ammunition' the caller clarified that he wished to speak to the Counter-Mortar Officer, Captain Murphy.[69]

On the evening of 11 May the batteries responsible for laying the Cigarette smokescreen carried out their task as usual. To have done otherwise would have aroused German suspicions. That evening was one of the quietest in the sector for some time but that quiet, and any sense of normality, ended at 11.00pm as 1,600 Allied guns crashed out their symphony of death and destruction along the front. Among the regiments involved was 142nd (Royal Devon Yeomanry) Field, whose historian noted:

> Four quick stabs of light followed by the loud bark of the 25-Pdrs shewed where a troop of Field Artillery had fired to their programme; and before their flashes had fully died away half a mile from them two far greater flashes and a longer deeper roar marked where two mediums had taken up the tale; a second's silence and some other Troop or Battery of 25-Pdrs would spring into life a mile or more away from

> any of the previous flashes. Then suddenly, almost without anyone noticing the change, every gun of the thousand gathered below was firing. Two or three groups seemed to break the tape ahead of the others by seconds; there was, as it were, a moment's irresolution, then they came again, and this time were joined by the rest; and now there was no stopping them; they were all firing and re-loading and firing again.[70]

The thunder lasted for forty minutes as the counter-battery programme rained shells down on the known positions of German artillery units along the front. Then the guns switched to the first objectives of the attacking Allied infantry. Operation DIADEM, the final battle of Cassino, was underway.

Infantry from two divisions of XIII Corps – 4th British and 8th Indian – were the first to advance, with the Poles beginning their attack at 1.00am on the 12th. Von Moltke once said that no plan survives the first contact and this was certainly the case with Operation HONKER. German machine guns and mortars harassed British and Indian infantrymen as they made their river crossings while the Poles, although initially successful in scaling heights in their sector, were forced to withdraw, re-organise and await XIII Corps' cutting of Highway 6, the main Rome–Naples road, before resuming their attack. That did not happen until the 16th when, with 78th Division threatening Highway 6, the Poles went forward again.[71] On this occasion their efforts met with complete success. During all this time the Gunners had been hammering away at targets requested by the attacking infantry. Fireplans were devised and implemented quickly and provided a devastating proof of the professionalism of the Gunners. As one Gunner officer commented:

> The concentration of guns of all sizes was awesome. The refinement of survey, communications and fire planning enabled any number to be directed quickly onto a single target with devastating effect on the enemy. The added refinements of the Air OP ... and a Counter-Mortar Organisation, placed the enemy under continuous artillery attack. But always on the high ground, overlooking the valleys, he had to be ejected by the infantry, supported by the artillery FOOs and OPs before the rivers below could be crossed and the way opened for the armoured follow-up.[72]

With the Germans retreating from the main Gustav Line, the next obstacle facing the Allies was the Hitler Line, some eight miles back. The defences of this line were impressive with eighteen Panther tank turrets, with 360-degree traverse, set in concrete emplacements as well as 20-foot-deep steel shelters and mobile steel cylindrical cells, or 'crabs', emplaced in pits to show no more than thirty inches above ground level. It would be a hard line to break as 78th Division found on 19 May. Tanks of 1st Derbyshire Yeomanry, 6th Armoured Division's reconnaissance unit, had made the initial approach the previous day but were withdrawn for lack of infantry support and it was two battalions of 36 Brigade with Canadian tanks that made the first attack. Every tank was hit with thirteen lost.[73] With German reinforcements arriving in the Liri Valley, a new plan was cast with the Canadians making the major effort. This was Operation CHESTERFIELD, launched at 6.00am on the 23rd.[74]

The attack was preceded by an intense bombardment surpassing that at El Alamein. Over 800 British, Canadian, French and Polish guns of all sizes were involved eventually, although the fireplan began with half that number.

> Artillery staffs worked without sleep co-ordinating fire plans and drawing up the necessary task tables. 'For an attack on such a scale as this operation, 72 hours' preparation is only just sufficient,' the CCRA Brigadier E C Plow, was to observe later. Beginning late on 19 May a continuous 'counter-preparation' bombardment of 1,000 rounds per hour from 400 guns (which included artillery of the Corps Expéditionnaire Français and XIII Corps) crashed down on all known enemy strongpoints.[75]

This rate of fire increased to 810 rounds per minute as the attack was launched, just thirty minutes before VI (US) Corps began its breakout from Anzio in Operation BUFFALO. By now 810 guns were involved, ranging from 25-pounders, and 105s in Priests, through mediums up to heavies. No fewer than fifty-eight fire units were deployed with eighteen heavy batteries – 7.2-inch and 240mm – and eleven medium regiments in their ranks.[76] The Ayrshire Yeomanry's historian noted that in one four-hour concentration 360 rounds per gun were fired on the enemy positions.[77]

> A ten-minute bombardment of the positions in front [of XIII Corps], carried out at General Leese's instigation to confuse the enemy as to the direction of the main attack, was followed by a crushing counter-battery programme against German gun positions across the valley. At 5:57 more than 300 guns of all calibres began laying down a barrage 3,200 yards wide across the attacking zone, and three minutes later the three assaulting battalions crossed the start line.[78]

A day of desperate fighting followed in which 2 Canadian Brigade sustained the highest single day's casualties for any Canadian brigade in the entire campaign. It was also during that day that Eighth Army's Gunners set another record when 1st Canadian Division's CRA, Brigadier Ziegler, called for a 'William Target', bringing all Eighth Army's available guns into operation. Little more than twenty minutes later, 668 guns of nineteen field, nine medium and two heavy regiments opened fire to plaster the target, German positions in Aquino town, with 3,509 rounds, or ninety-two tons of ammunition, in two minutes. This was the first time an Allied army had fired a 'William Target'.[79] The Ayrshire Yeomanry were hardly alone in noting that this was 'the only Army target to be fired by the Regiment during the war'.[80] This all but destroyed the last line of resistance and, opening the way for the final advance, 'was a notable Gunner gesture at the conclusion of a battle in which the guns had played so vital a part'.[81] The war diary of A Battery 152nd (Ayrshire Yeomanry) Field Regiment noted that B Troop's shells beat the rest of Eighth Army's artillery by five seconds.[82]

With the Hitler Line broken the Allies advanced towards Rome, although German rearguards snapped at their progress. Meanwhile VI Corps was also advancing with their supporting Gunners, as ever, kept busy. Captain A M Cheetham, 2nd Field Regiment, recalled how, during the night of 23/24 May:

> Our Gunners had a very busy night. Following the attack on Pantoni we fired eighteen Mike Targets before midnight. During the next seven hours a further twenty concentrations were fired, in addition to a small fireplan in support of another diversionary attack by 5th Division on our left. In the evening we participated in a fireplan for 45th US Division.[83]

Rome was liberated on 4 June and Alexander's armies began a pursuit of the retreating Germans who were falling back on their next main defensive line, the Gothic Line, from Pisa to Rimini, although there were intermediate lines intended to delay the Allies. For a time there was a war of movement which led many to believe that the campaign would end soon. The armoured divisions came into their own as 6th British and 6th South African raced along the Tiber valley. This is illustrated by 12th (HAC) Regiment RHA's war diary which noted that the Regiment moved forward with no opposition on 5 June although RHQ and the tail of C Battery were delayed by demolitions at Cave. For the 6th the war diary notes:

> In action. 2 L & B H pushed on slowly up ROUTE 4. Regt shelled FONTE DI PAPA most of day, assisted by 23 Fd Regt and 2 MED REGT.

On the 7th the advance resumed at 7.30am with the Regiment coming into action after 3,000 yards. C Battery and 16th/5th Lancers assumed the lead against stiffening opposition but this was a delaying action as the diary for the next day shows:

> In action same area. Major D E Hughes (D Bty) had field day with 'U' Tgts, resulting in ammunition crisis. Enemy held on during day at [map squares] 8895 and 8995. [At 9.00pm] Elaborate fire plan for night attack by 1 GDS BDE came to nothing as enemy withdrew.[84]

This type of action by the Germans – tenacious defence followed by rapid withdrawal to fresh positions – was a standard tactic with which the Regiment would become familiar in the months to come, resulting in many fire plans that came to nothing.

Alexander had set twin objectives for his armies: Fifth was to advance to Pisa and Eighth to Florence; both cities stand on the Arno river. X Corps, with 6th Armoured and 8th Indian Divisions, led Eighth Army's advance to Florence and the Priests of 12th (HAC) were kept busy dealing with German rearguards. However, those were not the only impediments to progress: there were demolitions to deal with, as at Narni on 14 June,[85] and, on the 16th, near Todi, a landslide 'made further crossing of the Tiber impossible'. However, the Lothians and Border Horse reached Todi to be shelled by enemy guns sited some two miles north of the town to which 12th (HAC) replied in kind.[86] Between these two dates the war diary of HQRA 6th Armoured Division notes the arrival of a new Brigade Major, Major R G S Bidwell.[87] This was Shelford Bidwell, later Brigadier Bidwell, who was not only a distinguished Gunner but also, in later life, a military historian of considerable repute.

As Eighth Army continued its fighting progress to Florence, some Gunners found themselves acting in a new role, as the 'Sheldrake Pioneers' who assisted the Royal Engineers in bridge-building and other tasks. Undertaking labouring duties were the men of the divisional LAA regiments whose role had all but disappeared and anti-tank Gunners who were also underemployed.[88] On 19 June the units of 6th Armoured were approaching Perugia and 12th (HAC) fired several 'Uncle Targets' although the war diary comments that the Regiment was 'bogged down', a situation that continued the following day, before the Germans abandoned the city that night allowing the Regiment to move forward to fire several 'Uncle Targets' to support D Battery and the Lothians.[89]

Eighth Army was approaching Lake Trasimene where Hannibal had trounced Flaminius' Roman army in 217 BC, during the Second Punic War, and where Leese's army would now engage a German army. Once again, the Germans withdrew after some bitter fighting during which the trust built up between Eighth Army's Gunners and other arms was amply demonstrated. Rarely was this clearer than at the battles for Sanfatúcchio and the nearby Pucciarelli ridge where co-operation between infantry of 78th Division, Canadian tankmen of the Ontario Regiment and 17th Field Regiment was of the highest order.

With 2nd Lancashire Fusiliers of 11 Brigade pinned down on the edge of Sanfatúcchio, the task of taking the village was assigned to the Irish Brigade's 2nd London Irish and Ontario tanks. The London Irish CO, John Horsfall, decided on a flanking attack with Ontario tanks supporting his riflemen. With the Lancashires pinned down so close to the village, it was impossible for 17th Field to bombard the German positions but the regiment wreathed the area in smoke, although one gun troop did 'some delicate shooting' at the defending Germans. Eventually the Gunners ran out of smoke shells and a German OP in Sanfatúcchio's church tower was able to call down fire on the advancing tanks and riflemen until a shot from one Canadian tank brought down part of the tower and wiped out the OP team. (The visitor to Sanfatúcchio today can see that the tower has been rebuilt since the war, as have many other towers in the region and throughout Italy.)

After several hours, resistance collapsed and 2nd London Irish advanced to their next objectives. As the Irish Brigade advance continued the Gunners of 17th Field responded rapidly and effectively to every call for support. When the London Irish took the farm at Casa Montemara from its German defenders there was a furious counter-attack which was smashed by 17th Field's FOO, Captain Alan Parsons (later awarded the MC), calling down fire from single guns all around the farm in what John Horsfall described as 'masterly' shooting, 'pitching shells down scarcely fifty yards from the buildings'.[90] Such was the bond between the Irish Brigade and 17th Field Regiment that the latter were by now describing themselves as 17th Field Regiment RHA (Royal Hibernian Artillery) and the Brigade was accepting that title. There can have been few finer tributes to trust and co-operation between the infantry and artillery. And, as in Hannibal's day, the strength of the defence lay at Sanfatúcchio: once that had fallen the Trasimene position was doomed. The Gunner role in that cannot be overstated.

On Fifth Army's front, the Gunners were also playing their part. Not only was 5th AGRA supporting Fifth Army but so, also, were ack-ack Gunners, once again acting out of role, this time as medium artillery along the Arno. The 3.7-inch HAA gun was a splendid weapon in this role and amongst the units displaying their abilities as field artillery was 9th HAA Regiment. Having performed the task so well at Salerno, the Regiment was a natural choice to reprise the role in this phase of the campaign and its Gunners adapted quickly.

On 12 July two batteries of the Regiment – 24 and 25 – were ordered to send troops to Rosignano. B Troop 24 Battery and C Troop 25 Battery were joined at Rosignano by a further eight 3.7s of 55th (Kent) HAA Regiment and, by the 14th, had registered targets in the Montenero area. The 3.7s were deployed to support 34th Red Bull) Division and, in particular, 804th Tank Destroyer (TD) Battalion, which was advancing on Livorno. In this role the 3.7s proved extremely effective and very accurate while their Fuze 208 rounds enabled airbursts to be directed on enemy positions. Such was their effectiveness that the remainder of 24 and 25 Batteries were also deployed as field artillery as were all of 55th HAA Regiment's guns.[91]

With the aid of AOPs as well as their own ground-based OPs, the HAA Gunners carried out some very destructive shooting, knocking out enemy OPs in a tower at Montenero and supporting 804th TD Battalion as it entered Quercianella, almost seven miles from their gun positions at Castiglioncello. When German shelling hit one of 25 Battery's OPs, the reaction was to fire 330 airburst rounds over the offending 88mm and 105mm guns which then fell silent.[92] As the advance continued, 9th Regiment's 3.7s deployed along the Arno close to Pisa with orders not to fire within an arc five degrees on either side of the city's famous Leaning Tower.

> We took a position in facing the Leaning Tower of Pisa. … there was a smaller battery in front of us, 25-pounders. … we had to fire five degrees each side of [the

> Tower] and we could see the Germans coming down inside that five degrees and into the wee river in front of them, and having a swim and going back up again … you had to be dead-on if you were going to fire on either side, because the big scare was to save this Leaning Tower of Pisa. I could never get over that. To hell with the Leaning Tower of Pisa … I wouldn't care about it if it had [fallen] down on top of the Germans.[93]

The order to protect Pisa's most famous landmark had been inspired by reaction to the Allied destruction of the monastery at Monte Cassino, an act that allowed Germany to portray its adversaries as destroyers of culture. Upriver at Florence the German high command had ordered the evacuation of the city to ensure its protection, an order for which the commander of I Parachute Corps, General Schlemm, showed little regard. Fortunately, Florence suffered little damage.

Church towers often provided excellent locations for OPs although it was clear to both sides that this was so and thus towers often received attention that led to damage or destruction. One OP party of 25 HAA Battery had such an experience in the last OP they occupied in Italy. Sergeant Billy Smyth recalled that this was in a church tower in Marina di Pisa. The party approached the church along a street that appeared to be deserted completely with every window shutter closed firmly. They walked along the roadway itself, on paving laid centuries earlier by Roman engineers, to avoid the possibility of anti-personnel mines or booby-traps close to the buildings. Although the church door was open there was no sign of anyone about. A curtain was blowing and the sacristy was empty, as was the body of the church. Access to the tower was by a steel ladder fixed to the wall and from the tower information was passed back to the gunsites. Before long the Germans became aware of the party's presence and the tower was mortared but, although it was damaged, the OP party continued operating. Since no shelling occurred the tower survived, as did the Gunners inside, leading them to believe that the tower was out of range of any available enemy artillery.[94]

The Allied offensive against the Gothic Line was a hard, bitter struggle that eventually saw the enemy defences pushed back in many areas but with considerable loss to the attackers. Although Sir Oliver Leese, commanding Eighth Army, had hoped for a great leap forward to Venice and even to Vienna, both armies were doomed to another cold, wet winter facing an implacable foe. With great losses in infantry and armour – the British 1st Armoured Division was disbanded following the Battle of Coriano Ridge – artillery firepower became an even more valuable asset while many Gunners found themselves re-roled as infantry. This was the fate of many AA units, both heavy and light, as the Luftwaffe had all but disappeared from Italian skies. In some cases, a unit might return to an earlier role as happened with 117th LAA Regiment. Once 8th Battalion The Royal Ulster Rifles, the Regiment was disbanded on 15 June 1944 and its personnel once again became riflemen, this time with battalions of 61 Infantry Brigade, a new Green Jacket formation.[95] For these men the winter that followed became one of infantry warfare. Other Gunner units, although not re-roled, found other tasks assigned to them during the winter: some became road builders, others lumberjacks and still others stretcher-bearers. Gunners of 53rd LAA Regiment manned a mortar battery that provided a small party to screen the San Clemente ford.[96]

The ammunition shortage worsened as the year drew closer to its end. By November, 25-pounders were reduced to fifteen rounds per day, a ration that was cut even more drastically to five rounds per day in January 1945.[97] With these restrictions the guns continued supporting the infantry, as at Monte la Pieve (Point 508) on 18/19 October. This was a difficult task for the Gunners as the direction of attack was almost at right angles to the general line of fire of the supporting artillery. Matters were aggravated by road congestion, the presence of 88th (US) Division to the left and the urgent need to get the guns better placed. Landline communications were long, with a distance of seven miles between OPs and guns while, in the early stages of the operation, HQRA was another eight miles back. It took four attempts before the dominating height of Monte la Pieve was in British hands.[98]

Five nights later the attack on Monte Spaduro proved much more satisfactory for the Gunners who were able to redeploy along the Sillaro valley road in a more orthodox layout. Some initial complications had arisen because of the boundary between 88th US and 78th British Divisions, which followed the road from Pezzolo to Sassoleone before running due north. On the British side there was a precipitous drop with no hope of deploying guns. However, there was a much gentler slope on the American side where guns might be deployed but there was 'no entry for the British into this comparative Eldorado until the proposal had been cleared with the American Command'. Once the US command realised the importance of using this ground the way was clear for 78th Division's artillery to deploy and 17th Field went into action near Pezzolo, 132nd in the hairpin bends below Sassoleone and 138th straddling the valley between Cuviola and San Apollinare. A battery of 7.2-inch howitzers from 6th AGRA supported the 25-pounders. It took two attacks by the Irish Brigade to wrest Monte Spaduro from the Germans, the first effort having been repulsed by a German counter-attack.[99]

In several weeks of hard fighting, 78th Division had seized some key objectives but were prevented from going further by the onset of even worse weather, which brought Fifth Army's offensive to a halt on 27 October. However 'Many tributes to the way our infantry had leant on the barrages were paid by German prisoners'. Capturing Spaduro secured the American flank as, two days earlier, US troops had seized the summit and greater part of Monte Grande but could not have held on had Spaduro remained in enemy hands.[100]

Through the winter of 1944–5, the soldiers of both Allied armies suffered from the cold, from rain that became snow and from frozen conditions while facing the Germans along what would prove to be the latters' final defensive line in Italy. Many Gunners found themselves serving as infantry or as mortar units. The second role was that assigned to 11th (County of London Yeomanry)

LAA Regiment, the Roughriders, which became a mortar unit, operating 3-inch and 4.2-inch mortars, with which they supported infantry units in the mountains around the Sillaro valley and on Monte Grande in February, March and April of 1945.[101]

Changes in the Allied high command during the winter saw General Wilson, the Mediterranean commander-in-chief, move to Washington to succeed Field Marshal Dill who had died of aplastic anaemia on 4 November 1944. General Alexander, promoted to Field Marshal, took over responsibility for the Mediterranean theatre, handing the army group over to General Mark Clark. Fifth Army's new commander was Lucian K Truscott while Eighth Army also had a change of command: Lieutenant General Sir Richard McCreery succeeded Leese, who went off to command 11 Army Group in South-East Asia. With this new command team the Allies planned the final offensive in Italy.[102]

Clark considered that Eighth Army was no longer capable of mounting a major offensive but both army commanders disagreed and the final plan was one that came from their combined brains and which received the blessing of the army group commander. It was to be launched as a two-pronged effort with Eighth Army attacking first, on 9 April, in Operation BUCKLAND, followed by Fifth Army's Operation CRAFTSMAN on the 12th; both were elements of 15th Army Group's Operation GRAPESHOT.[103]

The preparations for BUCKLAND included massing 2,000,000 rounds of ammunition for the 1,020 guns that would support Eighth Army's attack.[104] But Eighth Army's guns were not to be confined to supporting conventional attacks. In the BUCKLAND plans were two novel concepts: the use of amphibious vehicles to assault across Lake Comácchio and the neighbouring area that had been flooded by the Germans, and the creation of a fast-moving mobile force to push through the gap at Argenta, the only strip of dry ground available. This force would carry infantry in improvised APCs, known as Kangaroos, and was dubbed the Kangaroo Army. Gunners were a vital component of the Kangaroo Army, which was composed as follows:[105]

Break-out Force	
1st Royal Irish Fusiliers	2nd Royal Inniskilling Fusiliers
A Squadron Bays	B Squadron Bays
MMG Pl D Spt Gp 1st Kensingtons	MMG Pl D Spt Gp 1st Kensingtons
Recce Party RE	Recce Party RE
Scissors Bridge	C Squadron 51st Royal Tanks (Crocodiles)

Mobile Force (Kangaroo Army)
HQ 2 Armoured Brigade
9th Lancers
4th Hussars (Kangaroos)
Z Tp 209 SP Battery
Assault Detachment RE
2nd London Irish Rifles

Reserve Force for Special Roles
C Squadron Bays
254 Anti-Tank Battery
SP Troop 254 Anti-Tank Battery
Armoured Troop RE
Mortar Pl D Spt Gp 1st Kensingtons
214 Field Company RE
152 Field Ambulance RAMC

In immediate support were 11th (HAC) Regiment RHA and 17th Field Regiment.

The Gunners with both the break-out force and the Kangaroo Army played their parts well, as did all those who provided Eighth Army's initial bombardment of the German positions. The former units also took part in that bombardment: 11th (HAC) fired 13,000 rounds in nine hours of continuous shelling.[106] Advancing infantry and armour met many enemy soldiers who were still shell-shocked, literally, by their experience, which had been made worse by the decision of General Traugott Herr, commanding Tenth German Army, to pull his army's main body back from the Senio Line to the Santerno river, out of range of the British artillery. In doing so, Herr signed the death warrants of many of his men, as the Santerno line was to be bombed by 825 heavy bombers of the US Fifteenth Air Force. Thus Tenth Army would suffer both from the artillery bombardment along the Senio and the aerial bombardment along the Santerno.[107]

At 1.50pm on 9 April, the American bombers arrived over the front to drop 125,000 fragmentation bombs on the German artillery and reserve lines.

Their mission was assisted by Eighth Army's 3.7-inch HAA guns performing one of their last tasks in Italy: the guns fired smoke shells that formed a bomb, or marker, line for the planes.[108] At the same time, medium bombers were also striking at German positions. When the last aircraft flew off, the artillery took their turn with 1,500 guns and mortars opening fire along Eighth Army's front. This lasted for forty-two minutes after which fighter-bombers returned to strafe German positions along the Senio riverbank. As the planes departed the guns and mortars opened up again in a pattern that continued for five-and-a-half hours before 8th Indian and 2nd New Zealand Divisions launched their attacks.[109]

With good progress being made by the attacking formations, the Kangaroo Army was launched on its advance on the 13th. As it and 56th (London) Division, which made the amphibious crossing of Lake Comácchio, pushed forward, Fifth Army launched Operation CRAFTSMAN on the 14th. Next day, 11th (HAC) fired a five-hour barrage to help 56th (London) Division as it converged with 78th Division at Bastia; the Regiment had been firing a constant succession of smokescreens and fireplans to support the Kangaroo Army.[110] As 11th (HAC) moved forward with the Kangaroo Army, leap-frogging battery by battery, the Regiment became, by last light on the 21st, the only guns within range of the advancing battle line. At times those guns were called on to cover a frontage of almost 270 degrees. When A and E Batteries took part in 9th Lancers' race towards Porto Maggiore, their enterprise was rewarded by the capture of four tanks, five 88s and a 150mm gun, which 11th (HAC) laid claim to and with which, directed by an AOP, they carried out some accurate shooting. AOP direction had also allowed A Battery to brew up an enemy tank with a direct hit while B Battery inflicted the same fate on a German anti-tank gun.[111]

Almost immediately, Fifth Army's advance in Operation CRAFTSMAN made good progress, with 1st Armored Division, 10th Mountain and the division-strength Brazilian Expeditionary Force to the fore. Clark's 15th Army Group had now swung both fists to such effect that, in five days, the Germans had lost three important river lines.[112] With 10th Mountain Division were the Gunners of 178th (Lowland) Medium Regiment, whose CO was Lieutenant Colonel H S Freeth. So close to the leading infantry were Freeth's guns that US soldiers asked 'When you are going to put bayonets on the ends of your guns?' On 22 April the commander of 7th AGRA detached Q Battery 17th Medium to Freeth's command so that it would be easier for 178th Medium to support each of the three regiments of 10th Mountain Division (an American regiment equated to a British brigade.)[113]

By St George's Day both armies had reached the Po, the last great water obstacle in Italy where the Germans had believed they could make another stand. But such was the pummelling they had taken in the previous two weeks that, although groups of soldiers might still fight tenaciously, all cohesion had gone from their defence. Thus it was that, early on St George's Day, 178th Medium's batteries were close to the Po as the leading infantry of 10th Mountain Division crossed, in spite of having made a rapid advance of thirty-three miles during the previous night.

> The chief opposition came from the devastating 88mm low airburst fire over the forming-up area, and later over the crossing itself – delivered, as we afterwards learned, by no less than 20 enemy guns. Men were falling fast, but in that flat country there was no hope of locating the guns, which were firing flashless ammunition so that even the Air OPs could not see them.[114]

Such was the situation that, in spite of the enemy fire, Freeth drove forward to the riverbank where he encountered three Austrian prisoners and a young Italian who had just been brought back by the boats that had carried the first wave of infantry across the Po. The Austrians had no idea where the 88s were located but the Italian youth knew their exact location – he had been forced to help dig the gunpits. From a 1/50,000-scale map he pinpointed their positions, allowing Freeth to bring down a 'Yoke Target' with 178th Regiment's guns, those of Q Battery and 2nd Medium Regiment, a total of forty mediums. Firing airbursts, the mediums silenced the enemy guns, allowing 10th Mountain's infantry to establish and consolidate their bridgehead. The 88s were later found to have been destroyed by their own gunners.[115]

The pursuit continued for ninety miles north of the Po until the advancing infantry were moving along Lake Garda's east shore. As they did so, the batteries of 178th Medium leapfrogged each other as they supported the foremost regiment. Then, as the pursuers reached the northern part of the lake, where it points north-eastwards, it was found that the road tunnels through the mountains by the shore had been wrecked by the retreating Germans and, on 28 April, the infantry took to DUKWs to continue their advance. Even while waterborne, they received support from 178th's guns. However, as their targets began to move out of range, Colonel Freeth decided to get one battery forward by water and sought suitable craft to transport his 5.5s.[116]

Three sailing barges were found at Brenzone, Canteletto and Cassone on the 30th. Each looked as if it could carry a 5.5 between the main and mizzen masts. The ships were collected at Malcésine where three guns were loaded, using bridging girders as decking, and landed at Tórbole to be winched ashore using DUKWs. By the end of the day the first gun was in action in spite of having run the gauntlet of enemy 105 shells while moving through Tórbole. Three more 5.5s were ferried over early on 1 May, followed by the final four guns, the last of which arrived on the morning of the 2nd with Advanced RHQ. This allowed the Regiment, with three OPs in the bridgehead, to support the leading infantry as they forged forward on three lines of advance north of Lake Garda. Freeth's 5.5s continued to support 10th Mountain Division until the very last moment of action on the evening of 2 May when the German armies in Italy and Austria decided to surrender.[117]

In those final sixteen days of war in Italy, 178th Medium Regiment had advanced 175 miles by road, river and lake, the last twenty miles through difficult mountainous country. At all times, the Regiment provided close support to the leading infantry who were never out of range of the 5.5s.[118] The commander of 10th Mountain Division wrote:

> After the break-through, the Regiment moved always in close support of our leading elements, sometimes ahead of the infantry and behind the tanks in the marching column. This support continued when no other artillery was available … All members of this command hold the highest regard for this splendid artillery organisation.[119]

In that final advance 178th Medium Regiment earned a DSO for its CO, three MCs and one MBE as well as four US awards – one Silver and three Bronze Stars.[120]

Nothing summarises better the role of the Royal Regiment in the gruelling Italian campaign than the professionalism of 178th (Lowland) Medium Regiment in those closing weeks of war as they, literally, went everywhere with their American infantry.

Notes

1 Duncan, *RA Commemoration Book*, p. 283
2 Ibid, p. 284
3 Ibid; Nicholson, *The Canadians in Italy*, p. 46
4 Duncan, op cit, p. 284
5 Ibid, p. 286
6 Doherty, *Clear The Way!*, p. 67
7 Duncan, op cit, p. 284
8 Ibid, p. 284; Doherty, op cit, p. 67
9 Duncan, op cit, p. 284
10 Ibid, p. 286
11 Ibid, p. 287
12 Ibid, p. 286
13 Johnston, *Regimental Fire*, p. 137
14 Doherty, op cit, pp. 68–73; Russell, *Account of the Service of the Irish Brigade*
15 Doherty, op cit, pp. 77–8; Russell, op cit; Ray, *Algiers to Austria*, pp. 75–6
16 Ray, op cit, pp. 74–5
17 Johnston, op cit, p. 137; NA Kew, WO373/3 citation for DSO
18 NA Kew, WO373/3, citation for DSO
19 Doherty, *Irish Volunteers in the Second World War*, pp. 124–5; NA Kew, WO373/3 citation for Bar to DSO
20 Ray, op cit, p. 77
21 Ibid, p. 61
22 Salmond, *The History of the 51st Highland Division*, pp. 122–3
23 Ray, op cit, p. 77
24 Nicholson, op cit, p. 203

25 Molony, *The Mediterranean and Middle East, vol V*, p. 235
26 Duncan, op cit, p. 289
27 Molony, op cit, p. 235
28 *70th Medium Regt, RA*, p. 5
29 Molony, op cit, p. 235
30 Duncan, op cit, p. 289
31 Nicholson, op cit, p. 203
32 Doherty, *Eighth Army in Italy*, p. 2
33 Nicholson, op cit, p. 203; Duncan, op cit, p. 295
34 Duncan, op cit, p. 295
35 Molony, op cit, pp. 231–2
36 Doherty, op cit, p. 6; Duncan, op cit, p. 295
37 Duncan, op cit, p. 295–6
38 Molony, op cit, p. 322
39 Duncan, op cit, p. 295
40 Ibid, p. 296; *Royal Devon Yeomanry*, p. 56; www.cwgc.org. Sgt Allen is commemorated on the Cassino Memorial.
41 Duncan, op cit, p. 296
42 Doherty, *Wall of Steel*, pp. 130–1
43 Ibid, pp. 131–2
44 Robert Hamilton, 24 HAA Bty, interview with author
45 Duncan, op cit, p. 297
46 Doherty, op cit, pp. 132–4
47 Duncan, op cit, p. 297
48 Ibid, p. 298
49 *70th Medium Regt, RA*, p. 5
50 Ray, op cit, p. 101
51 *70th Medium Regt, RA*, p. 8
52 Molony, op cit, p. 490
53 Ibid, pp. 606–8
54 Ibid, p. 608
55 Ibid, pp. 616–7
56 Ibid, pp. 666–7; Duncan, op cit, p. 301
57 Duncan, op cit, p. 301
58 Ibid, p. 304
59 Ibid, p. 303
60 Williamson, *The Fourth Division*, p. 116
61 Ibid, pp. 116–7
62 Molony, *The Mediterranean and Middle East, Vol VI*, pp. 29–31
63 Ibid, p. 32n
64 Duncan, op cit, p. 319
65 Ibid, p. 321
66 Ford, *Mailed Fist*, p. 115
67 NA Kew, WO170/442, war diary HQRA 6 Armd Div, 1944
68 NA Kew, WO172/918, war diary 12 (HAC) RHA, 1944
69 NA Kew, WO170/442, op cit
70 *Royal Devon Yeomanry*, p. 88
71 Doherty, *Eighth Army in Italy*, p. 99
72 Roberts, *31st Field Regiment RA*, p. 52
73 Doherty, op cit, p. 101; Nicholson, op cit, pp. 410–11
74 Nicholson, op cit, pp. 412–3

75 Ibid, p. 413
76 Ibid, pp. 417–8
77 Brownlie, *The Proud Trooper*, p. 524
78 Nicholson, op cit, p. 418
79 Ibid, p. 423; Doherty, op cit, p. 105
80 Brownlie, op cit, p. 524
81 Duncan, op cit, p. 319
82 Brownlie, op cit, p. 524
83 Cheetham, *Ubique*, p. 131
84 NA Kew, WO170/918, op cit
85 NA Kew, WO170/442, op cit
86 NA Kew, WO170/918, op cit
87 NA Kew, WO170/442, op cit
88 Doherty, op cit, p. 118
89 NA Kew, WO170/918, op cit
90 Horsfall, *Fling Our Banner to the Wind*, p. 168
91 Doherty, *Wall of Steel*, pp. 160–1
92 Ibid, pp. 161–2; NA Kew, WO170/1128 war diary 9 HAA Regt, 1944; WO170/1160, war diary 24 HAA Bty, 1944; WO170/1161, war diary 25 HAA Bty, 1944; WO170/1130, war diary, 55 HAA Regt, 1944
93 Robert Hamilton, interview with author.
94 Billy Smyth, interview with author.
95 *The History of 61 Infantry Brigade*, p. 15
96 NA Kew, WO170/1233, war diary 53 LAA Regt, 1944
97 Jackson, *The Mediterranean and Middle East, Vol VI, Pt III*, pp. 30–1 .
98 Duncan, op cit, p. 325
99 Ibid; Ray, op cit, pp. 169–75; Doherty, *Clear The Way!*, pp. 194–205
100 Ray, op cit, p. 175; Duncan, op cit, p. 325
101 Duncan, op cit, p. 332; WO170/4875, war diary 11 LAA Regt, 1945
102 Doherty, *Eighth Army in Italy*, pp. 184–6
103 Ibid
104 Ibid, p. 188
105 Doherty, *Clear The Way!*, p. 234; Scott, Account of the Service of the Irish Brigade
106 Johnston, op cit, p. 163
107 Doherty, *Eighth Army in Italy*, p. 189
108 Routledge, *Anti-Aircraft Artillery*, p. 284, in which this task is described as 'rather tedious'.
109 Doherty, op cit, pp. 197–8
110 Johnston, op cit, p. 163
111 Ibid, p. 164
112 Doherty, op cit, p. 207
113 Duncan, op cit, p. 327; NA Kew, WO170/4816, war diary 178 Med Regt, 1945
114 Duncan, op cit, p. 327
115 Ibid
116 Ibid; NA Kew, WO170/4816, op cit
117 Duncan, op cit, p. 329; NA Kew, WO170/4816
118 Duncan, op cit, p. 329
119 Quoted in ibid, p. 329; NA Kew, WO170/4816
120 Duncan, op cit, p. 329

Chapter Nine

From Normandy to Victory

When Allied troops landed on the Normandy beaches on the morning of 6 June 1944 it was the culmination of years of development and planning that had begun soon after the BEF had been evicted from France in 1940. Although lessons in landing on a hostile shore had been learned in Sicily and at Salerno, one of the earliest had been in France where a Gunner VC had been earned in 1942 during Operation JUBILEE, the Dieppe raid of 19 August.

In JUBILEE, 2nd Canadian Division landed at Dieppe port in a 'reconnaissance in force'. Failing to make a strong lodgement, the division withdrew after serious losses but one element of the operation was successful – the raid to the west of Dieppe in which No. 4 Commando neutralised a German coast battery and Major Patrick Anthony Porteous became the third Gunner to earn the Victoria Cross in the Second World War.

Major Porteous was the liaison officer between two detachments which were to attack separate points of the heavy coast battery site. During the initial assault Porteous, who was with the smaller detachment,

> ... was shot at close range through the hand, the bullet passing through the palm and entering his upper arm. Undaunted, Major Porteous closed with his assailant, succeeded in disarming him and killed him with his own bayonet, thereby saving the life of a British sergeant on whom the German had turned his aim.
>
> In the meantime the larger detachment was held up, and the officer leading this detachment was killed and the troop sergeant major fell seriously wounded. Almost immediately afterwards the only other officer of the detachment was also killed.
>
> Major Porteous, without hesitation and in the face of withering fire, dashed across the open ground to take over command of this detachment. Rallying them he led them in a charge which carried the German position at the point of the bayonet, and was severely wounded for the second time. Though shot through the thigh, he continued to the final objective, where he eventually collapsed from loss of blood after the last of the guns had been destroyed.[1]

Perhaps the greatest lesson of the Dieppe tragedy was the folly of trying to capture a port and so the final plans for Operation OVERLORD were for an assault over open beaches, with both flanks protected by airborne forces dropped before the main landings.

The supporting fireplan for the Normandy landings included Allied naval vessels, ranging from battleships with 16-inch guns to destroyers with 4-inch guns, which would continue to support the armies as they moved inland. There were also rocket-firing landing craft, first used in the Mediterranean, and an innovative use of Gunners firing their first rounds while still afloat. Assigned to this task were ten field regiments: 3rd British Division's artillery were 7th, 33rd and 76th Field, with M7 Priests; 3rd Canadian Division's artillery included 12th, 13th and 14th Field Regiments RCA, with 19th Field RCA, attached from Army Troops, all with Priests; 50th (Northumbrian) Division deployed 90th Field, attached from Army Troops, 86th and 147th Field, each with Sexton SPGs; these were the assaulting divisions on Sword, Juno and Gold Beaches respectively.[2] RAF and USAAF bombers would also make a contribution and it was intended that

> … every available weapon would join in a crescendo of fire to plaster the beaches with bombs, shells and rockets so that the defenders could no longer serve their weapons and must seek shelter or be killed.[3]

Much ingenuity and planning went into the 'run-in' shoot on D-Day. The Gunners were to fire from LCTs (landing craft, tanks), from which they would then disembark to support the first infantry ashore. The LCT (4) had already

> … proved itself to be an excellent craft for the task of carrying 25-pr SP artillery, but in order to ensure the best possible effects certain modifications [were] desirable.[4]

Modifications included fitting a duplicate means of communication, in this case Tannoy sets, as the close proximity of the gun troops would cause their radios to interfere with each other. Voice pipes were proposed as an additional communications method while permanent waterproof housings for No. 19 radio and Tannoy sets were considered essential. Each control craft would have loud hailers while LCTs were fitted with steel blast screens to protect those outside the guns. LCT compasses were to be adjusted with a full load onboard 'and the position of the lead should be carefully recorded and adhered to on all future occasions'.[5]

LCTs of the gun flotillas were tested over a measured distance while fully laden, thereby ensuring that each could make six knots in calm conditions. A standard procedure for 'run-in' shooting was also evolved: firing would take place while 'steaming toward the beach'; at six knots the LCT would be approaching the shore at 200 yards per minute. To avoid confusion among the smaller landing craft closer inshore, the LCTs were not, normally, to come in closer than 3,000 yards of the beach while, for optimum benefit from the 'run-in' shoot, ranging was to begin 'at the earliest possible moment'. Thus 25-pounders on Ram chassis – Sextons – could open fire from 13,200 yards offshore while 105mm M7s – Priests – could fire from 11,400 yards. These gave, respectively, just over fifty and forty minutes of firing.[6]

On the morning of D-Day, 3rd British Division's regiments set off for the shore in a V formation with 7th Field at the apex, leading the other regiments by 400 yards. Thus it was that 7th Field fired the first rounds in the 'run-in' shoot. These were actually discharged by 9 (Irish) Battery, giving that unit the distinction of being Second Army's first Gunner unit to engage the enemy in Operation OVERLORD.[7] However, they were not the first Gunners in Normandy. That distinction went to FOOs of 3rd Division who had earlier landed by parachute to direct supporting fire for the airborne troops who had dropped on the British left flank in the early hours of 6 June. With them were Forward Observation Bombardment (FOB) parties to direct naval gunfire for the same purpose.[8]

It had been those airborne soldiers who had begun the invasion with 6th British Airborne Division assigned to capturing bridges over the Orne river, and high ground beyond, to protect the left flank of the invading armies. Light artillery and anti-tank units arrived by glider with the Gunners of 4 Airlanding Anti-Tank Battery in action by 10.00am, with nine 6-pounders and two 17-pounders,[9] as was a battery of 53rd (Worcestershire Yeomanry) Airlanding Light Regiment, equipped with air-portable 75mm light guns. F Troop 92nd (Loyals) and some triple 20mm SP guns of 93rd (Loyals) LAA Regiments landed from the sea to protect the Orne bridges.[10] So successful was F Troop that, in six days engaging numerous low-level attacks, the Gunners claimed seventeen enemy aircraft destroyed and the bridges were still intact.[11]

Among the first Gunners ashore was Captain J P Cook's FOO party from 90th (City of London) Field Regiment, in 50th (Northumbrian) Division. Cook, with two signallers and an OP's Assistant, was to land on Gold beach at H+20 minutes, there to collect his OP tank and call for fire from several sources, including a Royal Marine battery of Centaur support tanks, (fitted with 95mm howitzers, these were converted Cromwells), Sextons firing from LCTs, and two destroyers. His own Regiment's guns were to land at H+60 minutes.[12]

At 5.45am, Cook's party set off through the choppy waves for the shore. Before long they could see the coastline through the smoke and then rocket ships fired off two salvos that boosted the morale of those in the assault craft; Cook thought that those on the receiving end had little chance of survival if the projectiles found their targets. Arromanches was spotted, as was the landmark known as 'The Wreck', where there was a slight course alteration, by which time some coast guns had opened fire. Although shells were bursting in the water, the little assault craft were moving fast and, well separated, seemed not to be in great danger.

> We beached perfectly clearing all underwater obstacles, and paddled around in 18 inches of water. A fortunate start. The beach was being liberally swished with automatic fire from the right flank and we doubled smartly into a bomb hole, tore the waterproofing from our wireless sets and got rid of our life-belts. We called our armoured OP and the Centaurs repeatedly but got no answer from either. This was a blow, for we might want the latter at any moment now.[13]

A search of the beach revealed neither Centaurs nor the OP tank, and calls were not answered. Cook later discovered that the Centaurs' LCT had suffered a flooded engine compartment and drifted off the Isle of Wight for two days before being towed back to England. However, he found an infantry company HQ where the battalion CO and 90th Field's CO also appeared, the latter accompanied by another regimental OP party. The first target Cook spotted was a troop of four 88s on the Meuvaines ridge but although he called for fire from the destroyers they were engaging other targets and could not respond immediately. When they later called Cook to ask the result of their shoot on the 88s he was compelled to reply 'Unable to observe – now'; he was then under fire from those very 88s.

A wood on high ground west of Buhot had been chosen as a rendezvous for commanders and FOOs from where a fireplan for further attacks was to be laid on but the wood was held in strength by the Germans and Cook's group was forced into cover by machine-gun fire. With two troops of 90th Field now in action on the beaches, Cook called down fire on the German position which then fell to an attack by tanks and infantry, thus allowing further advances to which 90th Field's guns gave effective support. When, eventually, the enemy position on Meuvaines ridge was taken, the 88s had been abandoned.

By evening Cook's party had joined up with 2nd Devons who were pulling enemy prisoners from dugouts on a railway embankment. DF tasks for the night were arranged and radioed back to the guns before the exhausted party – the signallers had carried a heavy No. 68 set all day – found a German command post in which to spend the night. It was a post

> … of incredible depth and solidity. There we brewed the best cup of tea of all time and took a last look at the colossal armada anchored off the beaches, an unforgettable sight in the light of the setting sun.[14]

On Sword beach, on Second Army's left flank, 20th Anti-Tank Regiment landed with its SP weapons.[15] Commanding B Troop 41 Battery was Captain Perring Thomas, whose M10 Wolverines were to support 2nd King's Shropshire LI of 185 Brigade. Although B Troop landed at 11.00am, it was over three hours before they escaped the congestion on the beach and set off on 185 Brigade's axis of advance.

Meeting up with Staffordshire Yeomanry tanks, Captain Thomas's guns followed as the Staffords swept to the east prior to their planned advance. Before long the guns were in open country on terrain that Thomas likened to Salisbury

Plain; the only cover was from buildings in villages while much of the countryside was covered with growing corn. By late afternoon, near the village of Biéville, the M10s made their first contact with enemy tanks when two Mark IVs appeared from the direction of Périers-sur-le-Dan. The tanks were about 2,000 yards away, too far for effective shooting by the Wolverines. Although the guns could engage at that range there was no guarantee of knocking out the target and the practice was to wait until targets had closed to 800 yards.

> Accordingly the guns laid on the tanks and waited for [them] to approach. Simultaneously with this incident other tanks must have been working their way forward in dead ground and two more tanks suddenly appeared in hull down position about half a mile away. They immediately opened fire on No. 1 Gun and got two or three rounds away before the slow traverse of the SP M10s allowed the troop to reply. A slogging match now followed with the tanks rushing up to join in. The No. 1 Gun was hit very early on by a round which struck at the join of the turret ring just above the driver's head. The sergeant was killed and two gunners wounded, one dying ten days later in England. The driver and wireless operator were unhurt and the SP was immediately backed off the position with the gun hanging helplessly over the front with both trunnions shattered.[16]

As the battle continued it was apparent that the first two tanks had not come any closer to the SPs and the order to engage was given before they could make off towards the beaches. Some ranging shots were fired before the tanks were hit, both grinding to a stop and then going on fire. In spite of the longer range the Wolverines had proved very effective; both panzers had been killed at a distance of over a mile. It was established later that they had been part of a force of twenty-four enemy tanks preparing the way for 21st Panzer Division's counter-attack which, although unsuccessful, put paid to any chance of 3rd Division taking Caen on D-Day. German losses were thirteen tanks knocked out while B Troop's No. 1 gun was the sole British loss. [17]

B Troop's three surviving guns redeployed to cover the flank until moving into a defensive laager with the Staffordshire tanks at last light. There was no enemy aggression during the night, although a feldwebel surrendered to the Yeomanry, and before first light B Troop deployed in orchards west of Biéville to support the KSLI.[18]

In the opening days of OVERLORD much reliance was placed on naval gunfire support since the number of guns ashore was limited. The first equipments ashore were SPs, both field and anti-tank, able to lend immediate support to infantry and armour. However, it was planned that, in the first four days, 450 field guns, ninety-six mediums, twenty heavies and 440 AA guns would be landed.[19]

On 7 June the first AOP parties arrived and, next day, Austers from two squadrons landed in the beachhead and began work almost immediately. The problem of bringing them across the Channel had been resolved by flying them over in long 'crocodiles' 'led by an elderly and responsible Walrus amphibian'.[20] They suffered their first fatal casualty in Normandy on the 10th when Captain Eric Pugh, of A Flight No. 653 Squadron, was killed when his Auster was shot down by five FW190s.[21]

As yet no heavy guns were ashore but these would follow soon. Prior to the invasion four AGRAs – 3rd, 4th, 8th and 9th – had been formed for service in north-west Europe, of which the first three would see service in Normandy together with the North African veterans of 5th AGRA; 9th AGRA would join 21 Army Group later. Although the composition of an AGRA could vary, those of 5th and 9th indicate typical orbats: the former deployed three field regiments – 57th, 58th and 121st – and four mediums – 7th, 51st, 64th and 69th, while the latter had medium regiments only, including 9th, 10th, 11th, 16th, 107th (South Notts Hussars), reformed from the field regiment destroyed at Gazala in 1942, and 146th Medium; it had also included 1st Heavy Regiment which was transferred to 1st Canadian AGRA.[22]

As Allied strength increased in the beachhead, so that beachhead expanded. German troops learned to respect and fear the guns of the Royal Artillery as they put down ever heavier concentrations of fire to support attacks aimed at enlarging the beachhead. One such was Operation EPSOM launched on 25 June by XXX Corps, which had been in Normandy since D-Day, and VIII Corps, elements of which were still arriving. The main burden fell on VIII Corps which was strengthened to 60,000 personnel with over 600 tanks at its disposal. To the almost 300 guns of the corps artillery could be added those of XXX Corps, on the right, and I Corps, on the left, bringing the firepower to over 700 weapons. Naval gunfire, from three cruisers and a monitor, plus bombers and fighter-bombers added to VIII Corps' striking power.[23]

Brigadier Jack Parham, now BRA, Second Army, later wrote that 'The enemy within gun range lived under a constant threat of encountering a sudden squall of several hundred shell, all timed to arrive at the target end within a few seconds of each other.' Mead recounts an example of one such 'squall' when Major Andrew Lyell, commanding No. 658 AOP Squadron, spotted some enemy tanks in harbour and brought down fire from the artillery of three corps that included between 500 and 600 weapons from field guns up to heavies. Perhaps those under that fire would have described it as a storm rather than a squall.[24] The effectiveness of the AOPs is reflected in a 10th SS Panzer Division document on lessons of the Normandy campaign:

> The biggest nuisance, though, are the slow-flying spotter-planes which in utter calmness fly over our positions and direct fire, while our infantry weapons cannot reach them.[25]

The EPSOM battles were fought over several days with the weather seeming to intervene on behalf of the Germans as heavy rain reduced the available air support.

Nonetheless, Second Army created and expanded a bridgehead to the west over the Odon and the Gunners were instrumental in defeating counter-attacks. One planned counter-attack by II SS Panzer Corps was smashed by guns of the Royal Artillery, naval guns and aircraft. Commenting that attacks by fighter-bombers had delayed the move of his attacking force from 7.00am until 2.30pm, SS General Paul Hausser noted:

> Even then it could not get going. The murderous fire from naval guns in the Channel and *the terrible British artillery* [author's italics] destroyed the bulk of our attacking force in its assembly area. The few tanks that did manage to go forward were easily stopped by the British anti-tank guns.[26]

On 1 July another counter-attack was smashed by the co-ordinated artillery of VIII and XXX Corps. On this occasion the counter-attack targeted the Gavrus area but twelve artillery regiments, firing in support of the infantry, stopped any enemy troops reaching the British lines. Attempts to renew the attack brought further heavy artillery retaliation. The same fate met another attack – on the junction of VIII and XXX Corps – which, although some infantry and tanks penetrated British lines under cover of smoke, was smashed under the combined fire of Gunners, tanks and infantry anti-tank gunners.[27]

Second Army's next objective was the city of Caen, which fell, finally, on 8 July. The previous night Caen was pounded by 467 RAF heavy bombers, supported by Gunners firing 'a massive and successful artillery fire programme against located enemy AA guns'.[28] So successful was that programme that only one bomber was lost to AA fire during the raid.[29] The final assault on Caen fell to three divisions under command of I Corps: 59th (Staffordshire) was flanked by 3rd British, to the left, and 3rd Canadian, to the right. Adding yet more muscle to the artillery of those three divisions were the guns of Guards Armoured and 51st (Highland) Divisions, 3rd and 4th AGRAs, the battleship HMS *Rodney*, the monitor HMS *Roberts* and the cruisers *Belfast* and *Emerald*. Prior to the heavy bombers' attack, *Rodney*'s 16-inch guns fired on Point 64 north of the city, a range of 25,000 yards, or over fourteen miles.[30]

In spite of stout resistance the Germans were forced to yield the ruins of Caen. At Buron the Canadians took heavy losses from 12th SS Panzer Division but the SS lost many tanks, including thirteen credited to one 17-pounder anti-tank battery. On the night of 8 July Rommel permitted the withdrawal of the heavy weapons of three German corps from Caen. Although the city continued to be defended by strong infantry forces, by the evening of the 9th it was in British hands.[31]

With the Americans making for St Lô, it was time for 21 Army Group to force the enemy to deploy his strongest armoured forces to fight on the eastern flank while the Americans broke out south of the *bocage* to wheel eastwards for the Seine. To this end, Montgomery launched Operation JUPITER on the 10th, supported by 3rd and 8th AGRAs, the divisional artillery of the attacking 43rd (Wessex) Division and the guns of 11th Armoured and 15th (Scottish) Divisions. In this two-day battle, the Wessex men suffered heavily for little gain, but their guns had done everything possible to support them.[32]

On 18 July, Second Army launched Operation GOODWOOD, an attack by VIII Corps, under which Montgomery had placed Guards, 7th and 11th Armoured Divisions. This seemed to be an attempt by Montgomery and Second Army's commander, Dempsey, to break through with massed armour, over 750 tanks, compensating for the infantry losses in recent operations. VIII Corps were to attack where the enemy had disposed his strongest defences and Montgomery's declared intention was to write down the German armour. This was the last clash between Montgomery and Rommel who had designed the German defences. GOODWOOD also enjoyed the largest force of tactical aircraft and strategic bombers 'ever employed in direct support of ground forces in a single action'.[33]

However, the artillery would operate at a disadvantage since the bulk of that supporting the attack had to remain west of the Orne river and canal until all the armour had crossed into the bridgehead. Moreover, as the battle moved southwards, the guns' effectiveness would reduce until they, too, could cross the river and follow up. With heavy bombers again involved, the artillery was to suppress enemy AA defences as at Caen. Over 1,000 bombers took part and the Gunners' attention to the German AA sites meant that only six bombers were brought down by flak. As the sounds of the bombers receded, the guns of three corps, supplemented again by naval gunfire, opened fire on all known enemy batteries.[34]

Leading the advance were 11th Armoured Division's tanks with over 200 guns in direct support; a similar number engaged selected sites with concentrations. However, the flaws in Montgomery's plan began showing as the armour advanced. Although the bombardments had demoralised many enemy soldiers so much that they surrendered to the advancing tanks, the field guns had to stop firing just after 9.00am when the advance outran their range. They would have to wait until they could cross the river and move up before resuming fire. Furthermore, the passage of traffic over the bridges towards the fighting was falling behind schedule while the enemy was beginning to recover from the bombardment; tougher resistance was met as the Germans recovered their equilibrium.[35]

Although Montgomery signalled Brooke, the CIGS, claiming that the situation was 'very promising' and issued a statement for the BBC, the advance had bogged down due to traffic congestion in the initial bridgehead arising from the shortage of crossing points. The battle became a slogging match in which German defences took a heavy toll of British tanks. When the battle was called off, over 400 tanks had been lost.[36] Worse was the loss of manpower: in all arms 5,537 men were dead, wounded or missing, 1,818 of them in VIII Corps.[37] The Gunners had done their best for the attacking formations as exemplified by 13th (HAC) Regiment RHA, whose G Battery Sextons did much good shooting in support of 23rd Hussars. G Battery's BC, Major Peter Gaunt, 'spent much of the rest of the [first] day trying to locate targets and bring down artillery fire on them'.[38] His SPGs were with the armour, but since their 25-pounders were of limited value against tanks, he called down fire from 5.5s on the far side of the Orne. This fire he concentrated on Bourguébus and was pleased to see that it reduced the shellfire coming towards G Battery and 23rd Hussars. In one case, 'a self-satisfied Panther' in front of Bourguébus disappeared when a 5.5 shell fell directly on it, providing a considerable morale boost for the attackers.[39] Elsewhere, SP anti-tank guns proved equally effective; Brigadier Harvey of 29 Armoured Brigade showed his faith in them by deploying 119 Battery 75th Anti-Tank Regiment with F Company 8th Rifle Brigade to guard against possible German tank counter-attack after Grentheville village was taken.[40]

The Germans had fought a determined defensive battle on Bourguébus ridge but, in spite of the losses, Montgomery considered that GOODWOOD had drawn German armour away from the Americans, paving the way for them to break out. On 25 July General Omar Bradley began that break-out at much the same time as von Kluge, the new German commander, launched his armour against the American flank, giving Montgomery the opportunity to surround a large element of the German army. The brutal Normandy campaign was entering its final phase as First Canadian Army attacked towards Falaise and Bradley swung part of his force northwards to engage the Germans already in battle with British forces. In all these operations Gunners gave untiring support and their role as ever was critical, with the Germans continuing to fear that 'terrible British artillery' as it pounded the units and formations trying to escape the Falaise pocket.

Operation JUPITER, to secure the high ground between the Odon and Orne rivers, was launched on 10 July.[41] The operation was focused on Hill 112, a wide, flat-topped crest dominating the surrounding countryside and for which there had already been bitter fighting, with elements of 11th Armoured Division taking the height before being forced to withdraw. Although Hill 112 is an unremarkable feature, which 'rises gently from the valley of the Odon river, which is itself little more than a stream',[42] General Eberbach of Panzer Group West had told II SS Panzer Corps' commander that it was 'the pivotal point of the whole position … in no circumstances may it be surrendered'.[43] At 4.50am on 10 July, two AGRAs plus the guns of 11th Armoured, 15th (Scottish) and 43rd (Wessex) Divisions opened fire ten minutes before H-hour. The experience of 112th (Wessex) Field Regiment typifies that of the Gunners involved in JUPITER.

> The delivery of this massive fire power will be remembered by all. The entire Corps Arty engaged at rates of up to 5 RPM with the guns having to be cooled with water. The Regtl [War] Diary records Uncle Tgts of 1,260 RPM for 19 minutes. Between

> the 8th and the 11th July C Tp fired 2,753 rounds of HE and D Tp 2,906 rounds. Bty ammunition expenditure on 10th was 3,400 rounds.[44]

The attacking infantry made good progress, such was the bombardment's effect on the defenders. By 9.40am, 7th Hampshires had reached the Maltot road and 'were in a corner of Maltot village by 10.12'. However, the battalion was 'superimposed upon strong German defences' which led to very heavy losses. For almost five hours, Gunners engaged targets in support of the Hampshires and Maltot 'was completely ringed by arty fire controlled by Maj Hubert Penrose and Capt Paul Cash'. Both were awarded the Military Cross for this action.[45] Late afternoon saw the Hampshires being supported by 4th Dorsets who had also entered Maltot. The overall action is summarised in a 112th Field situation report for that day.

> Meanwhile 4 Dorset with 9 RTR were attacking Maltot to relieve 7 Hampshire. They arrived approx 17.30 hrs and reoccupied the village finding elements of the Hampshires and the vehicles of Maj Penrose and Capt Cash burnt out. No sign of personnel. At about 18.30 hrs enemy counter-attacked 4 Dorset very heavily with infantry and tanks. DF fire arranged by BC 477 Bty was brought down. The whole Corps Arty fired Rapid for 15 minutes on this and some 1,560 RPM were being fired. The fire had to be reduced after a time to conserve ammunition and eventually 4 Dorset withdrew with 9 RTR. By 22.00 hrs 4 Dorset had withdrawn to line of main Avenay-Caen road. Majors Steele-Perkins (477 Bty) and Tomlinson (220 Bty) had joined up. The situation was confused but the Germans did not follow up their attack and 130 Bde was able to reorganise on the road. 4 Dorset suffered heavy casualties in their withdrawal from Maltot.
>
> Maj Penrose and Capt Cash returned to the Regt on the evening the 10th. Maj Penrose is wounded in the arms and Capt Cash has slight facial injuries. Both … did a magnificent job under very trying circumstances and without their calm and accurate direction of fire our infantry could not have held out as long as they did.
>
> It is as well to realise that while 130 Bde suffered a bloody nose at the hands of the Bosche, the whole Bde has advanced and the enemy suffered heavy casualties. The Battle of Normandy goes well and the advance of Gen Montgomery's forces continues.[46]

The battle for Hill 112 and the neighbouring Hill 113 raged on. Neither eminence offered much cover for the attackers but the Germans made good use of a wood on the reverse slope of the former. This concealed a pioneer company, part of strong defences that also included a platoon of Mark IV tanks; twenty-five Tigers were not far off. Dubbed 'das Wäldchen der halben Bäume' (the wood of the half trees) by the defenders and the 'Crown of Thorns' by the British – it was also called 'Cornwall Wood' by the Duke of Cornwall's LI, 'Diamond Wood' by 53rd (Welsh) Division and 'das Kästenwäldchen', the little box-shaped wood, by 102nd SS Tank Battalion – it was a critical part of the German defences, which inflicted a heavy toll on the British attackers. Although, by 9.00am, the assaulting infantry and tanks had reached the Eterville road, which runs along the crest of the ridge on which both hills sit, they had already suffered greatly as the ridgetop seemed to disappear in 'the fumes, smoke and dust of battle'.[47]

Atop the ridge, the mile-square plateau that is Hill 112 was still in enemy hands and 'the slopes seemed to be littered with brewed-up Churchills'.[48] All efforts to winkle the Germans out came to naught and, at the end of two days' fighting, 43rd (Wessex) Division and its supporting armour had lost about 2,000 men with little to show for their efforts. Although the Official History comments that the Germans had lost half the hill, the attack had failed in its aim to take the entire hill. However, it had kept 9th and 10th SS Panzer Divisions away from the American front and had tied up elements of 1st and 12th SS Panzer Divisions.[49]

The infantry casualty rate was so bad that Montgomery was forced to break up a division to keep others in existence. Hill 112 illustrates the vicious nature of the Normandy fighting and one can only imagine how bad casualties might have been without the stalwart support of the Gunners. Their efforts are praised in several infantry regimental histories. The historians of 112th (Wessex) Field note the casualties suffered in their own regiment. Captain Paul Atkins, wounded and captured at Maltot, was later reported killed while Captain Kenneth Robinson, who had joined 220 Battery only two days earlier, was killed while controlling fire from a Churchill tank; he had relieved Lieutenant Douglas Goddard as OP officer at the last moment. Lieutenant Joseph Blincow, aged 20, disappeared 'while controlling fire and leading a local attack'. It was later learned that he had been killed. His brother Albert, an infantry officer, was killed in Italy two months later. Gunner Alan Wilson was killed while assisting Captain Robinson while two men of 477 Battery's OP party, Bombardier Fisher and Gunner Carpendale were seriously wounded; Clifford Carpendale succumbed to his wounds.[50]

Captain Paul Cash, whose work at Maltot we have already noted, was killed on 12 July when a mortar exploded over his slit trench. His death brought the number of OP officers killed to four.[51] The history of 7th Hampshires comments:

> Captain Paul Cash, a young arty FOO, was instrumental in saving the reverse at Maltot from being catastrophic. He was awarded an MC, but killed by a stray shell bursting above his slit trench some days later.[52]

And so the fighting in Normandy carried on in its bloody way, with death in all the horrible forms that war can devise claiming its steady toll. Both Hills 112 and 113 continued to be important, as 21 Army Group heaved against the German defenders of the ancient duchy. By 21 August, however, the battle of the Falaise 'gap' was over and, although many German troops had escaped, there was no cohesive force to defend along the Seine. The Germans flooded back towards the Low Countries and Germany and, on 3 September, British troops entered Brussels, five years to the day since war had been declared. Elsewhere, ports such as le Havre and Calais had been liberated by 21 Army Group while others, including Dunkirk, had been masked. Although many believed that Germany would be defeated by Christmas the resilience of the German armies would prove that a fanciful thought. For the Gunners the battle for the Falaise 'gap' was memorable 'for its series of artillery targets beyond their wildest dreams'.[53]

Before considering the remainder of the north-west European campaign, it is worthwhile reflecting on one critical aspect of the Gunners' work in Normandy, the role of the anti-tank regiments. They had suffered a high casualty rate in their encounters with German armour, so much so that Mead described it as 'the most anxious artillery factor'.[54] So high were casualties in these regiments that over 2,000 reinforcements were flown over from England.[55] This is not to suggest that they were equipped with inferior weapons, as had been the case earlier in the war. By the time the Allies landed in Normandy the standard anti-tank weapons were the 6-pounder, which still equipped infantry anti-tank platoons and some Gunner units, and the 17-pounder, while a few regiments had 75mm equipments. However, the closeness of the bocage, with its narrow high-banked lanes, placed an especially heavy strain on anti-tank units.

The 6-pounder had entered service in North Africa in 1942, and had the distinction of being the weapon that knocked out the first Tiger tank in that theatre. However, as it went into service, the Germans began improving their tank armour with face-hardened steel. Thus new capped-steel shot (APC) was issued for the 6-pounder from October 1942, followed three months later by ballistically capped shot (CAPC). Whereas, with the original steel shot, the 6-pounder could defeat 74mm of armour at 1,000 yards and an angle of attack of 30 degrees (74/1000/30), with CAPC this now improved to 88mm of armour at the same range and angle of attack (88/1000/30). Then, in perfect time for OVERLORD, came armour-piercing discarging sabot (APDS) shot; the first deliveries of sabot ammunition were to airborne anti-tank Gunners for D-Day.[56] Quitting the muzzle at 4,050 feet per second (1,235 metres per second), this increased greatly the lethality of the 6-pounder which could now defeat 146mm of armour at 1,000 yards at 30 degrees. Not only could it bore through five inches of face-hardened armour but it could also pass through 6.6 inches (168mm) of steel. The 17-pounder entered service with both armour-piercing (AP) and high-explosive (HE) rounds, giving it a secondary field-gun role with a range of 10,000 yards, a capability that was used but rarely. Initially the weapon's armour-defeating ability was 109/1000/30 degrees which improved to 118/1000/30 degrees with APC shot. APDS for the 17-pounder was approved in April 1944 but did not go into service until August, at the end of the battles for Normandy. With APDS the 17-pounder could defeat 231/1000/30 degrees, fatal to any German tank. The performance of B Troop 41 Anti-Tank Battery at Biéville on D-Day, when its guns knocked out two tanks at 2,000 yards with

APC, shows just how much British anti-tank guns had improved since 1940; after August 1944, they could do even better.[57]

The anti-tank regiments had also received self-propelled equipments, including the American M10 gun motor carriage, which mounted a 3-inch gun in an open-topped turret on a Sherman tank chassis. Known as Wolverine in British service – 1,648 were supplied to Britain – these were upgunned subsequently with 17-pounders to produce a much more effective vehicle; the 17-pounder-equipped M10 was known as Achilles.[58] Work had begun on developing an indigenous self-propelled anti-tank gun, or tank destroyer in US Army parlance, almost as soon as the 17-pounder entered service. The initial problem was that no contemporary British tank turret could accommodate the new gun and thus recourse was had to adapting the Valentine, of which many were available, to create an SPG. The turret was removed and a fixed compartment built atop the hull, as with the earlier Bishop SPG. Unlike Bishop, however, this had a low profile with the gun mounted facing backwards over the engine decking. The end result, Archer, was versatile, low and compact and gave good service in north-west Europe; it served with the Royal Regiment until the early 1950s. Its drawbacks included lack of overhead protection – a problem shared with the M10 – and, since the gun recoiled over the driving position, the driver having to vacate his seat when in action to avoid decapitation. Unlike Achilles, with its rotating turret, the entire vehicle had to be aimed at the target.[59]

The availability of tank destroyers such as Achilles and Archer meant that anti-tank units were highly mobile as their deployment in Normandy and later illustrates with, for example, the presence of anti-tank batteries alongside 11th Armoured Division's leading elements in Operation GOODWOOD. Thus, though the threat of German armour remained, the level of that threat was reduced considerably by the presence of such SPGs. Their detachments were confident that they could defeat any enemy tank and their presence was a tremendous morale booster for both armour and infantry, especially as the Panther tank (Panzer V) was appearing in increasing numbers.[60] However, German tactics remained superior in some respects and during the Normandy battles British tank destroyers were not always aware of 'the inherent tactical dangers for slow-moving guns from well-concealed enemy guns and tanks'.[61]

German tank strength was diminishing and, although large numbers of tanks would be seen during the Ardennes offensive in December, the Panzer divisions no longer had the muscle that they once possessed. That is not to say that they ever ceased to be a threat: even in small packets or as individual tanks, they presented danger until the very end of the war, as would soon be demonstrated near Asten in The Netherlands. At the same time, the power of the Royal Regiment on the mainland of Europe was increasing as shown by the following table illustrating that power from 1 September 1944 until May 1945. (There were seven AGRAs – 3rd, 4th, 5th, 8th, 9th, 17th and 59th – and 1st and 2nd Canadian AGRAs – under command of which were the units shown in the table.)[62]

Nature of Unit	Units
Super Heavy	3rd & 61st (North Midland) Regiments
Heavy	1st, 32nd, 51st (Lowland), 52nd Bedfordshire Yeo), 53rd, 56th, & 59th (Newfoundland) Regiments
Medium	3rd, 7th, 9th, 10th, 11th, 13th, 15th, 51st (Cornwall & Warwickshire), 53rd (London), 59th (4th West Lancs), 61st Carnarvon & Denbigh (Yeomanry), 63rd, 64th (London), 65th (Highland), 67th (Suffolk), 68th (4th West Lancs), 69th (Carnarvon & Denbigh) (Yeomanry), 72nd, 77th (Duke of Lancaster's Own Yeomanry), 79th (Scottish Horse), 84th, 107th (South Notts Hussars), 121st & 146th (Pembroke & Cardiganshire); 1st, 2nd, 3rd, 5th, 5th & 7th RCA
Field	4th RHA, 6th, 25th, 32nd, 86th (East Anglian) (Herts Yeo), 90th (City of London), 98th (Surrey & Sussex Yeo, Queen Mary's), 110th (Manchester), 116th North Midland), 147th (Essex Yeo), 150th South Notts Hussars), 166th (Newfoundland) & 191st; 11th & 19th RCA
Survey	11th

Nature of unit	Units
Heavy AA	60th (City of London), 64th (Northumbrian), 86th (HAC), 90th, 98th, 99th, 103rd, 105th, 108th, 109th, 110th, 111th, 112th, 113th, 115th, 116th, 118th, 121st, 132nd (Mixed), 137th (Mixed), 139th (Mixed), 146th, 155th (Mixed), 165th, 174th (Mixed), 176th & 183rd (Mixed); 3rd (RM); 2nd RCA
Light AA	4th (Ulster), 20th, 26th, 32nd, 54th (A & S Hldrs), 71st, 73rd, 93rd (Loyals), 109th (Royal Sussex), 113th (Durham LI), 114th, 120th, 123rd (City of London Rifles), 124th (Highland), 125th (Cameronians), 126th (Middlesex Regiment), 127th (Queen's), 133rd, 139th, 149th (Sherwood Foresters) & 150th (Loyals); 4th (RM)
Searchlight	1st, 2nd, 41st (5th North Staffs Regt), 42nd (Robin Hoods, Sherwood Foresters) & 54th (Durham LI)

At corps levels the following were deployed as corps troops.[63]

Corps	Artillery units
I Corps	62nd (6th London) A-Tk, 102nd (Lincolns) LAA & 9th Survey Regiments
VIII Corps	63rd (Worcestershire & Oxfordshire Yeo) & 91st (A & S Hldrs) A-Tk, 121st (Leicestershire Regiment) LAA & 10th Survey Regiments
XII Corps	86th A-Tk, 112th (Durham LI) LAA & 7th Survey Regiments
XXX Corps	73rd A-Tk, 27th LAA & 4th Survey

In addition to the AGRAs, 21 Army Group also deployed AA brigades which were underemployed in their original role and available to reinforce the field artillery. There were twelve Royal Artillery AA brigades and a Royal Marine brigade which disposed the following regiments.[64] (See table, bottom left)

Infantry divisions maintained divisional artillery of three field regiments, an anti-tank and a light AA regiment, although with some variations. Reflecting its former mountain role, 52nd (Lowland) Division included 1st Mountain Regiment[65] as well as the usual complement of field, anti-tank and light AA units while the disbandments of 59th (Staffordshire) and 50th (Northumbrian) Divisions allowed some of their artillery units to bolster the divisional artilleries of other formations. The three armoured divisions each had two field regiments and the usual anti-tank and light AA regiments; three RHA regiments – 3rd, 5th and 13th (HAC) – were included in the armoured divisional artilleries.

The 'great swan', the advance through France, ended with Allied troops in Belgium and The Netherlands. Field Marshal Montgomery – he had been promoted on 1 September – believed that the war could be brought to a rapid conclusion by a deep narrow thrust into Germany. General Eisenhower, the Allied Supreme Commander, favoured a continuation of the 'broad front' strategy but permitted another Montgomery concept to go ahead. This was the use of First Allied Airborne Army to lay 'carpets' along the road to the Lower Rhine at Arnhem along which XXX Corps would advance to strike into Germany, outflanking the Siegfried Line. The 'carpets' were the main bridges along the route, the last of them, at Arnhem, to be taken by 1st British Airborne Division. This was Operation MARKET GARDEN, with MARKET the airborne phase and GARDEN being XXX Corps' overland advance.

The story of MARKET GARDEN is too well known to bear rehearsal here. It has passed into history as the story of gallant airborne soldiers holding out against great odds until withdrawal became inevitable. What is not so well known is the role of Gunners at Arnhem and in XXX Corps' operations. By its nature, 1st Airborne Division formation had only two Gunner regiments and 1st Forward Observation Unit. (The latter's role was to provide OP parties trained in directing the fire of XXX Corps' long-range artillery units, which would provide support as they came within range.) The two regiments were 1st Airlanding Light Regiment and 1st Airlanding Anti-Tank Regiment, each of three batteries, although only two anti-tank batteries served at Arnhem. Both regiments fought hard but the increasing strength of the German forces besieging the small British and Polish bridgehead meant that there could be but one outcome, especially as XXX Corps met great problems in their advance, which was on a narrow front and subject to interdiction from enemy forces.

When it became clear that XXX Corps could not fight through to Arnhem in time, it was decided to evacuate as much of 1st Airborne Division as possible in Operation BERLIN. By then 1st Airborne's CRA, Lieutenant Colonel Robert Loder-Symonds, was in contact with 64th Medium Regiment, which reached Nijmegen on 21 September and was within range to provide supporting fire with its guns.[66] 'A tremendous fireplan' was arranged with XXX Corps' Gunners, using the radio link from HQRA 1st Airborne Division, the Division's main contact with the outside world.[67]

That fireplan began at 10.00pm on 25 September and covered the withdrawal of the remaining defenders to the riverbank where Canadian boats awaited. The Germans seemed to have taken this bombardment as the prelude to a major attack and, while they waited, boatload after boatload of airborne soldiers slipped away. Last to leave were the Gunners of 1st Light Regiment who had dropped all their breach-blocks and sights in the river, including those from guns already overrun. When day broke, the Germans, realising what was happening, began machine gunning the riverbanks. Major de Gex, now commanding the Regiment, took the last boatload across but the flimsy vessel was hit and slipped below the water; de Gex, Major Linton and the RSM swam to safety.[68]

Such was the 'survival support' that 64th Medium Regiment provided that 1st Airborne's GOC, Major General Urquhart, with the permission of XXX Corps' Commander, granted the regiment the right to wear the Airborne Pegasus badge on the lower right sleeve of battledress blouses.[69] Subsequently, 7th Medium Regiment provided a battery to support the Arnhem garrison while two field regiments of 43rd (Wessex) Division also came into the picture.[70]

Peter Harclerode writes that the Gunners of 1st Airborne Division 'provided magnificent support' throughout the battle. Although under constant mortaring and counter-battery fire from an enemy artillery force that grew to more than a hundred guns, Lieutenant Colonel W F K 'Sheriff' Thompson's Gunners answered every call for support they received. Their FOOs were in the forefront of the action at Arnhem bridge and Oosterbeek and, at times, called down fire from their 75mm guns almost on their own positions.[71] No finer summary of the

Regiment's service can be made than that of the divisional Brigade Major RA, Major Philip Tower, who wrote:

> It must never be forgotten that on the 1st Airlanding Light Regiment during those last few days fell much of the glory of Arnhem. They were mortared almost continuously, the whole gun area was under observation and swept by machine-gun fire. They were subject to attacks, usually backed with tanks, at least twice a day. Finally, their troop positions were overrun and the whole regiment concentrated in 3 Light Battery's area on the north bank of the river around Oosterbeek Church.
>
> They fought as gunners, normal field gunners firing indirectly in support of the whole division, though like everyone's their ammunition was very short. They fought as anti-tank gunners, over open sights at ranges down to fifty yards, manhandling their 75mm guns round the positions until they could get a shot. They fought as infantry – in defence from the gunpits and command posts – and in attack and counter-attack led by battery commanders and troop commanders alike.[72]

(One of the guns of 1st Airlanding Light Regiment at Arnhem may be seen today in the Royal Artillery Museum, Firepower, at Woolwich, still bearing damage sustained in the battle.)

In mid-October elements of 21 Army Group were engaged in clearing the Germans from the Scheldt estuary to open Antwerp to shipping. Allied troops were on the west bank of the Maas and part of Second Army's front was held by 7th US Armored Division, then under command of VIII Corps. Unfortunately, the American division was deployed on a very wide front which, therefore, was held only lightly. During the night of 26/27 October a German attack penetrated 7th Armored's thin screen and reached Meijel, a small town in the centre of the divisional area. Although, initially, this was not identified as a major threat, 25th Field Regiment was deployed by VIII Corps to reinforce the American division; the regiment included 25 Battery, which was to earn an Honour Title in the days ahead. Ellis, the British official historian, notes that 7th Armored Division counter-attacked but met a fresh German attack whilst so doing.[73]

Until recently, 25 Battery had been 12/25 Battery and had seen much service in North Africa and Eritrea but, with its regiment, had been reduced to cadre following heavy losses and returned to Britain to reform. The re-formed 25th Field Regiment had arrived in France in June and had already experienced considerable action in Europe. As 25 Battery deployed to join 7th Armored Division, it seemed as if this was another routine task. Nothing could have been further from the truth.

> What followed was a classic example of the kind of situation that has led to the award of many of the Honour Titles held by batteries of the Royal Artillery. The battery, apparently undertaking a routine task, is suddenly and unexpectedly faced

with a situation of desperate urgency in which all its skill, courage and endurance are tested to the utmost.[74]

When 25th Field's CO arrived early on 28 October, he discovered a much worse tactical situation than he had anticipated. This had been no minor German action but involved two divisions, 9th Panzer and 15th Panzer Grenadier, in a determined and carefully planned attack; according to the Official History, both divisions were nearly at full strength.[75] At dawn that day the enemy had renewed their offensive and had overrun an American company. On the west-bound road from Meijel, Tiger tanks were advancing towards Asten. Into this precarious situation 25th Field Regiment was now plunged.

The CO brought his Regiment into action about 4,000 yards behind the forward Allied positions near Heusden village. Movement was restricted by the terrain, which was flat, and marshy in many places, but this affected both sides. Very quickly OPs were established and the Gunners prepared to meet the German attack, which was held throughout the morning, but at 2.30pm, another attack hit the Allied left flank. In two hours of hard fighting the Germans advanced between 700 and 1,000 yards but, in so doing, suffered considerable losses in tanks and men. Throughout, 25 Battery was in continuous action and its fire was a major factor in bringing the German attack to a halt at 4.30pm. With US troops still thin on the ground, and thinned even more by significant casualties, it was plain that '25th Field Regiment must be prepared to accept an increasing responsibility for defeating attacks which were bound to be renewed next morning'.[76]

As part of that 'increasing responsibility' 25th Field laid on a programme of harassing fire that night with each gun firing 108 rounds. Nor was the programme as straightforward as that statement of rounds per gun might make it appear: no fewer than eighty alterations to line and range were made during the night. All the while the Regiment's positions were under German counter-battery fire. By 29 October the enemy had penetrated about six miles into the Allied lines but further reinforcements were on their way. That morning the hard-pressed Gunners of 25th Field were pleased to be joined by 131st (Lowland, City of Glasgow) Field, of 15th (Scottish) Division, whose guns were quickly in action, their fire directed by 25th's OPs.[77]

The Germans were attacking again and the Americans were suffering heavily; of one infantry battalion that bore the brunt of the assault only two platoons were still in action and most US tanks in the area had been knocked out. As the tenacious GIs fought on they relied even more on the support of the British guns. In turn, the Gunners depended on those manning the OPs, which were often only a few hundred yards from the Germans and in exposed positions. At any one time during the 29th, four shoots were taking place and occasionally that number rose to five. In the course of the day, the guns engaged over a hundred targets with each 25-pounder firing 400 rounds.[78]

The arrival of 131st Field had indicated that 15th (Scottish) Division was on its way to relieve 7th Armored and, during the afternoon, the approach of the Scots was confirmed. The first brigade arrived that evening while the remainder of the division, with 6 Guards Tank Brigade, concentrated behind 7th Armored Division in readiness to attack next morning. That attack met yet another German attack and battle raged for another few days before the front was stabilised. Having held against sustained attacks for over fifty hours, 7th Armored Division was able to withdraw through 15th (Scottish) to re-organise and re-equip. It also returned to 12 US Army Group. For its part in supporting its American allies, 25 Field Battery received the rare award of a US Presidential Unit Citation, to which was later added the Honour Title 'Asten'.[79] Today 59 (Asten) Battery forms part of one of the Army's training regiments.

At the same time, XII Corps was advancing in an operation intended to assist Second Canadian Army, which brought 53rd (Welsh) Division to the old fortress town of s'Hertogenbosch. On 27 October D Troop 381 Battery 116th (Royal Welch Fusiliers) LAA Regiment, with SP guns, was supporting an infantry battalion during an attack on the outskirts of the town. That day, and the next, Gunner Kenneth Williams drove his troop commander's jeep about the battle area, ignoring the danger from enemy machine-gun fire, rescuing wounded and taking them to the RAP. He drove his troop commander on a recce of the forward area and, on the 29th, with an SPG covering, he, the troop commander and two others attacked a machine-gun position and took nine prisoners. His gallant behaviour continued into the 30th when both his troop commander and troop sergeant major were wounded. Having taken the TSM back for treatment, Gunner Williams returned to rescue his officer. Although wounded himself in the head, he assisted in recovering the officer and took him to the RAP. Not surprisingly, Gunner Williams was decorated with the Distinguished Conduct Medal, the second highest gallantry award then available to other ranks, the citation for which concludes:

> His courage and complete devotion to duty throughout these four days ... were of the very highest order, and there is no doubt that ... he contributed in no small measure to the success of the operation of his tp, which enabled the leading t[roo] ps to press on continuously. His gallant behaviour is still the talk of his fellow men.[80]

The action in which D Troop was involved at s'Hertogenbosch illustrates the variety of duties now being carried out by divisional and corps light AA regiments since the threat from the Luftwaffe had been reduced to a shadow of its old self. Many AA regiments had been disbanded, as was also happening in Italy, and their soldiers were being re-roled. In 21 Army Group infantry battalions were formed from redundant Gunners and deployed on lines of communication duties: they included 600th, 601st, 606th, 608th, 609th, 612th, 613th, 614th, 616th, 617th, 619th, 623rd, 625th, 630th, 631st, and 637th Regiments RA.

However, there had been a significant addition to 21 Army Group's firepower in mid-October when 3rd Super Heavy Regiment came into action in Belgium under command of 9th AGRA. Equipped with 8-inch guns and 240mm howitzers, both the latest American equipments, this Regiment had been formed in November 1940 and after re-equipping underwent two months' intensive training on Salisbury Plain before crossing the Channel to join 21 Army Group. Its move had been disrupted by bad weather in the Channel but the Regiment proved a boon to Second Canadian Army and was in continuous action until the end of March 1945. Its CO throughout that period was Lieutenant Colonel J B Hyde-Smith, who had assumed command in 1942.[81]

By now the crust of the German defence had strengthened while fighting on their own frontiers added to the resolve of German soldiers. Efforts were being made in Germany to increase the manpower available and Allied Intelligence suspected that a 'spoiling attack' might be launched, although they considered that the evidence did not justify confirmation. The British Chiefs of Staff still believed that the war in Europe would be over by 15 May 1945,[82] a prediction that proved accurate, in spite of the fact that the conclusion that there would be no 'spoiling attack' would prove wrong.

Throughout the early winter months there was considerable evidence of toughening in the German defences. Allied operations met determined resistance and the average German soldier appeared resolved to continue the struggle as long as possible. On 2 November, Montgomery issued a directive to 21 Army Group in which he stated that, having opened Antwerp and driven the enemy north of the Lower Maas, Second Army would then push him east of the Maas in the Venlo area. Since this would demand a re-grouping, First Canadian Army would take over the front from the coast to the Reichswald, or State Forest. Second Army's operations to clear the Germans from the west bank of the Meuse were scheduled to start on 12 November and, soon thereafter, the army would extend its flank southwards to Geilenkirchen, assuming responsibility for some of 12 Army Group's front.[83]

The threat of the German V-weapons, the first of which had been launched against Britain a week after D-Day, persisted and, from early September, included targets on the mainland. From then until the end of the year, 5,097 V1 flying bombs and 994 V2 rockets were launched against such targets. The worst single death toll resulted from a V1 hitting an Antwerp cinema and killing 242 service personnel and 250 civilians; there were 500 other serious casualties. In all, 2,219 civilians were killed and 4,493 injured seriously by V-weapons; there were 792 military deaths and 993 injuries.[84] With the opening of Antwerp port, that city became a prime target for attack by both conventional aircraft and V-weapons. To protect against such attacks, strong air defences were provided for the city and the Scheldt estuary, including 336 British 3.7-inch heavy AA guns, 192 American 90mm heavy AA guns and almost 500 light AA guns. In addition, seven searchlight batteries deployed together with six smoke companies, including two American, and a balloon barrage, the latter provided by the RAF.[85]

The threat from V1s and V2s continued until their launch sites had been overrun. By the end of March 1945 the V-weapons offensive had run its course. More V1s and V2s were launched against continental targets than against Britain: 11,988 V1s and 1,766 V2s, which killed about 5,400 people while injuring seriously another 22,000. Over half the deaths occurred in the greater Antwerp area, which was hit by 1,214 V-weapons, although the port itself suffered comparatively lightly. Just over 300 V-weapons struck it – divided almost equally between flying-bombs and rockets – but caused no major problems for the running of the port. Although there was damage to railways, roads and harbour installations, these were repaired quickly: only two large ships were sunk although fifty-eight smaller vessels were lost. Apart from tying up manpower in defences and repair work, the V-weapon assault on Antwerp achieved nothing for the Germans.[86]

Antwerp was not the only location for a major Allied AA layout. We have already noted that Dunkirk was masked by the Allied armies and that port continued to be held by the Germans. The occupying garrison was pinned in place by besieging forces but it was clear that air re-supply was being carried out by night. Night-fighter patrols and radar observation, however, found no Luftwaffe aircraft coming in over the sea. One night, Brigadier Basil Hughes, commanding 51st AA Defence Group, responsible for protecting 21 Army Group's base area and lines of communication, discovered, by chance, how the re-supply flights were operating. Hughes was visiting a night-fighter base of No. 85 Group, which operated alongside his AA Defence Group, and was standing on the airfield with a squadron commander when both men heard an aircraft approaching at low altitude. Looking up they spotted the unmistakable silhouette of a Heinkel 111 – its crews called it the 'spade' from the distinctive shape of its wings – flying in a north-easterly direction. They both realised immediately that this machine was one of those re-supplying Dunkirk and that the Luftwaffe was flying over land rather than over water.[87]

The German use of such a tactic had not been considered since flying so low over land was extremely risky. Later it was discovered that these operations had been entrusted to a squadron of 'very experienced night fighter pilots using radio altimeters'. Even so, the risks were still very high. Hughes decided straightaway to redeploy four LAA/SL batteries from six which had been formed recently and allocated to No. 85 Group for the airfield defence. The Air Officer Commanding (AOC) was agreeable and the batteries were in place around Dunkirk the following night. On five further successive nights, the Luftwaffe made supply-dropping flights to Dunkirk, each time sending a flight of two to four aeroplanes. The LAA/SL batteries proved devastatingly effective: four enemy aircraft were caught in the searchlight beams and shot down while another two were dazzled by searchlights and so disoriented that they flew into the ground. One was claimed as a 'probable' and two as damaged. Their loss ended the night flights to Dunkirk.[88]

The Allied intelligence officers who had concluded that a German counter-offensive was unlikely were proved wrong on 16 December when the Germans launched just such an offensive in the Ardennes with the aim of punching though to Antwerp. Although taken by surprise, Allied commanders rallied quickly to meet the attack, which benefited from weather conditions so bad that Allied tactical air forces were grounded. When the weather changed on the 23rd, the airmen were able to operate with great effect and the German advance had reached its limit. By the turn of the year the Battle of the Bulge was all but over. Although the main weight of the assault had fallen on US troops, British elements had also been involved. These included Gunner regiments which once again reminded the Germans of their effectiveness. On 1 January 1945 the Luftwaffe launched its Operation BODENPLATTE against Allied airfields in the Ardennes and southern Netherlands, an assault that kept the AA Gunners busy. The Battle of the Bulge ended finally with Patton's Third US Army taking Oberhausen on 27 January. By then 21 Army Group was completing preparations for Operation VERITABLE, an attack designed to clear the Reichswald and Hochwald forests and bring Montgomery's command up to the Rhine.

Before that could happen, Montgomery ordered XII Corps to destroy the German salient between Roermond and Geilenkirchen, south-west of the Roer river. It had been intended to do this in November but the operation, now named BLACKCOCK, had been postponed due to bad weather. The salient was triangular and its defences had been strengthened considerably since November while the two divisions holding it were supported by a considerable artillery force including ninety field guns, thirty-six mediums, twenty 88s and eighteen 75mm SPGs.[89] Against this, XIII Corps included 7th Armoured Division, 43rd (Wessex) and 52nd (Lowland) Divisions, with their divisional artilleries, 6 Guards Tank and 8 Armoured Brigades, plus detachments from 79th Armoured Division. Added to this were 3rd and 9th AGRAs with the guns of VIII Corps, to the north, and XIII US Corps, to the south, also available.[90]

The Germans fought skilfully and with determination, their ranks bolstered by reinforcements during the battle, which opened on 16 January and ended on the 26th when the German High Command noted that 'Roer bridgehead no longer exists'.[91] Gunners had been vital in this major action, especially as weather conditions had, again, restricted air support. The historian of 52nd (Lowland) Division pays particular credit to that formation's Gunners who had fired more than 100,000 rounds of 25-pounder ammunition alone.[92] The mass of artillery supporting the infantry had been a cheering sight even before battle was joined:

> As they took up their positions for battle the Lowlanders were astonished and heartened to see what a mass of artillery and weapons new to them had been assembled in their support. Many had their first sight of 'flail' tanks, of the flame-throwing Crocodiles and of the troop-carrying Kangaroos. They would

> have been even more substantially cheered if they could have seen the concentration of guns, up to the mammoth super-heavies, wheel to wheel behind them. (Their old friends of the Scheldt, Brigadier Crosland's 9th AGRA, were again their main support.) They would have wondered to see the queer pieces of the 1st Canadian Rocket Battery, which could fire a ripple salvo of some 350 rockets, each the equivalent of one 5.5-inch shell, at ranges from between 5,000 and 7,000 yards. (... facetiously known as 'the Flying Bedstead'.) This great weight of gun-power undoubtedly speeded the operations and saved many lives, though the Gunners themselves admit that the difficulty of switching so many pieces and units as the battle developed in complexity occasionally tended to slow things up. Finally, one troop of a Moonlight Battery was ready to provide with its searchlights that soft, cloud-reflected glow – 'Monty's Moonlight', they called it – which so greatly assisted movement in darkness.[93]

That same historian reserves one 'special word for the brilliant and devoted work of the divisional Gunners' on 21 January, when they supported six major attacks.[94] As the day progressed new fireplans had to be made for each successive attack, one of them by 43rd Division on Schierwaldenrath. On that day both Gunners and foot soldiers 'were faithfully served' by the artillery Air OPs:

> Up all day in their little Auster planes, they never failed to bring the fire of the medium guns down on any enemy Tiger or Panther that dared to show its nose in the open. Theirs was a great contribution to the victory.[95]

BLACKCOCK cleared the ground for VERITABLE, which was launched on 8 February with XXX Corps leading. Also attacking in VERITABLE was II Canadian Corps – the overall operation was the responsibility of First Canadian Army to which XXX Corps was on loan – while the associated Operation GRENADE was carried out by Ninth US Army, with three corps under command. Over a thousand guns were allocated for VERITABLE and at 5.00am on the 8th, they opened fire in 'a programme which during the course of the day was to provide a concentration of fire exceeding any the British had employed previously in this war.'[96] Of 25-pounders there were 576, while mediums, both 4.5s and 5.5s, numbered 280, with 122 heavy and super-heavy weapons – 155mm, 7.2-inch and 240mm equipments – as well as seventy-two 3.7-inch HAA guns in a ground role, a total of 1,050 weapons.[97] In addition to the divisional artilleries, VERITABLE was supported by 2nd Canadian, 3rd, 4th, 5th and 9th AGRAs.[98] Lieutenant General Sir Brian Horrocks, commanding XXX Corps, described the opening of the artillery programme:

> All across the front shells were exploding. We had arranged for a barrage, a curtain of fire, to move forward at a rate of 300 yards every twelve minutes, or 100 yards every four minutes, in front of the troops. To mark the end of the four-minute

> period when the guns would increase their range by 300 yards they all fired a round of yellow smoke.[99]

Once again, opposition was stiff. Horrocks noted that the Germans rushed up 'more guns and more divisions' so that XXX Corps was eventually facing more than 1,000 guns as well as 700 mortars and ten divisions but 'Slowly and bitterly we advanced through the mud supported by our superb artillery'.[100] As the battle continued, Horrocks, who described it as 'unquestionably the grimmest battle' of his experience in the war, identified 16 February as the turning point. This was the day on which 43rd (Wessex) Division advanced over 8,000 yards to the escarpment above Goch, a fortified town that was later captured by 15th (Scottish) and 51st (Highland) Division. On Horrocks' right flank was 52nd (Lowland) Division while one of the Gunner units supporting the attack on Goch 'was that magnificent medium artillery regiment The Scottish Horse'.[101]

As with BLACKCOCK, the attacking formations were also supported by rocket-firing Gunner units. On this occasion these included 6 LAA Battery[102] whose BC, Major Jack Christie, went forward to act as a FOO. He described the sound of the rocket salvos passing overhead as being 'like ten express trains' and wondered how anyone could survive being on the receiving end. The answer came in the form of large numbers of German troops who came out to surrender; they were 'dazed [and] didn't know what had hit them'.[103]

Christie's battery, of 27th LAA Regiment in XXX Corps artillery, reverted to its normal AA role for its next operation, the Rhine crossing. With the VERITABLE and GRENADE battles over , 21 Army Group was preparing to cross the Rhine and take the war into the German heartland. There were already Allied bridgeheads east of the Rhine and 21 Army Group's crossing, Operation PLUNDER, would put two armies – Second (British) and Ninth (US) – on the eastern side as well. Montgomery's intention was 'to cross the Rhine north of the Ruhr and secure a firm bridgehead, with a view to developing operations to isolate the Ruhr and to penetrate deeper into Germany'.[104]

Operation PLUNDER included an airborne assault – Operation VARSITY – by XVIII US Airborne Corps, which included 6th British Airborne Division, in addition to the formations that would cross by assault boat and, later, by bridge. For this operation, 21 Army Group was supported by 3,500 field, medium and heavy guns.[105] Not all were of the Royal Artillery but the majority were and their covering fire as the assault crossing began must rank as the Gunners' largest of the war. The Germans were also hammered by aerial bombardment from strategic and tactical air forces and resistance to the Allied ground and airborne forces was neither as stiff nor as cohesive as was typical of the German soldier; but there were still cases where the old spirit was evident. Although 51st (Highland) Division had little opposition in their crossing they ran into 8th Parachute Division at Rees and found them unwilling to yield ground. By contrast, 15th (Scottish) Division met so little resistance that they linked up with 6th Airborne early in the afternoon of the first day. The end of that first day of Operation PLUNDER saw 21 Army Group holding a strong position on the east bank of the Rhine. There had been some opposition from the Luftwaffe but Allied air power was overwhelming with over a thousand fighters from the US Eighth Air Force alone.[106] Even so, some German aircraft attacked the bridgehead where at least two were claimed as 'probables' by 113 LAA Battery, which had C Troop of 6 LAA Battery under command.[107]

Among those watching the operation was Winston Churchill, accompanied by the CIGS, Field Marshal Brooke, a Gunner, and Field Marshal Montgomery. The party visited 3rd Super Heavy Regiment which laid on a special shoot by a battery of 240mm howitzers which were deployed close to the Goch–Weeze road. Churchill, who was fascinated by such heavy weaponry, took considerable delight in writing 'Hitler–personal' on one 240mm shell, which weighed 360lbs, before firing the howitzer himself.[108]

Operation VARSITY had also gone well with XII Corps artillery on the west bank of the Rhine supporting 17th US Airborne Division. By the end of the day both 6th British and 17th US Divisions had achieved their objectives with lower casualties than expected.[109] By the 27th the bridgehead was about thirty-five miles wide and twenty deep and VIII Corps was ready to lead Second Army's breakout.[110] Before the airborne soldiers arrived, 1 Commando Brigade had secured their right flank and taken the communications centre of Wesel. In immediate support of the Brigade was 1st Mountain Regiment, commanded by Lieutenant Colonel J R C Christopher. The previous evening, at 9.40pm, the Regiment's 3.7-inch howitzers had shelled the commandos' planned landing points[111] and, eighteen minutes later, six field regiments began a creeping barrage in which, for the first time, British field guns used radar, or proximity, fuses. The results of this innovation were far better than expected. At 10.00pm the first Buffaloes carrying assault troops entered the water and landed close under the barrage.[112] Lancaster bombers then attacked Wesel, with not a bomb dropping short although the target was only a thousand yards from the bridgehead. A German machine-gun position threatening forward troops was silenced by a Mike Target shoot and, just before dawn, a Victor Target ensured that the Germans would not rally to counter-attack 1 Commando Brigade. The guns continued wreaking havoc and when marked tactical maps were found in the German HQ in Wesel the details were soon passed to the guns who dealt with the key positions thus identified.[113]

Second Army's breakout began on 28 March. Throughout April its divisions pushed deeper into Germany against opposition that, although determined, lacked the cohesion of a well-organised defence. It was clear that the end was near but there were still many Germans resolved to fight to the bitter end. However, the Gunners had fired their last great fireplan over the Rhine and although they were called upon for many tasks in the final weeks of war nothing bore comparison with that thunder of the guns. Some regiments were even 'grounded' so that their transport could be used to supply the forward troops during their advance into Germany. Among the units to lose their transport was 3rd Super

Heavy Regiment,[114] which had been operating with 21 Army Group since October 1944 and whose 8-inch guns and 240mm howitzers had been invaluable on many occasions.[115] That is not to say that the Gunners suffered no losses in those last weeks. The Highland Division had lost its outstanding GOC, Major General Tom Rennie, at the Rhine crossing and another fine senior officer a month later. Brigadier W A 'Jerry' Sheil DSO*, CRA of the Division, lost his life on 29 April when his jeep struck a mine. Sheil had been driving the vehicle himself, relieving his driver who, he saw, was exhausted. He had been one of the most respected officers of the Division and 'was popular with the infantry who knew that they could always rely on his guns and with the Gunners who knew and appreciated his professionalism'.[116]

The day after Jerry Sheil's death, Adolf Hitler committed suicide. He was succeeded as Führer by Admiral Karl Dönitz who urged all Germans to fight to the end on 1 May, moved Germany's government to Denmark on the 3rd and then surrendered on the 4th. The surrender took effect from 8.00am on 5 May and, three days later, the Allies marked VE Day.

Gunner units were assigned to a variety of roles. Some guarded displaced persons' camps while others had first-hand experience of the worst horrors of Nazism. At Sand Bostel concentration camp, Major Jack Christie, of 6 LAA Battery, was told of another camp nearby. There he was met by an appalling stench, the source of which was clear when he opened the door of a hut and saw a pile of putrefying corpses. No one was alive and the camp was burned to the ground by flame-thrower tanks, the bodies cremated unceremoniously to prevent the outbreak of disease – which had probably been the cause of death of many of the victims there.[117] Nothing could bring home more forcefully the reasons why the war had been fought.

Notes

1 *The London Gazette*, 2 Oct 1942

2 Lt Col W A H Townend, Secretary RA Historical Society, to author, 21 May 2008

3 Ellis, *Victory in the West, Vol I*, p. 71

4 NA Kew, WO32/10377, 'Artillery support in beach landings'

5 Ibid

6 Ibid

7 NA Kew, WO171/969, war diary 7 Fd Regt. This diary also includes accounts written by the CO and the BCs of the Regiment.

8 Mead, *Gunners at War*, pp. 94–5

9 Ellis, op cit, p. 152

10 Mead, op cit, p. 95; NA Kew, WO171/1123, war diary 92 LAA Regt, 1944; WO171/1124, war diary, 93 LAA Regt, 1944; WO171/1017, war diary LAA Tps (20mm), Jun/Jly 1944

11 Duncan, *RA Commemoration Book*, p. 361; NA Kew, WO171/1123, op cit

12 Mead, op cit, p. 95; WO171/982, war diary 90 Fd Regt, 1944

13 Duncan, op cit, p.
14 Ibid, p.
15 NA Kew, WO171/913, war diary, 20 A-Tk Regt, 1944
16 Duncan, op cit, p.
17 Ibid, p. ; Mead, op cit, p. 98; NA Kew, WO171/913, op cit; Doherty, *Normandy 1944*, pp. 128–9; Ellis, op cit, pp. 203–4
18 Duncan, op cit, p. ; NA Kew, WO171/913, op cit
19 Duncan, op cit, p. 353
20 Ibid, p. 354
21 Farrar Hockley, *The Army in the Air*, p. 155, who gives the date of death as 8 June. www.cwgc.org.uk gives the date as 10 June although it notes Captain Pugh as belonging to 51 Hvy Regt.
22 NA Kew, WO171/908, war diary 5 AGRA, 1944; WO171/911, war diary, 9 AGRA, 1944; Duncan, op cit, p. 610
23 Ellis, op cit, p.275
24 Mead, op cit, p. 102
25 Quoted in Mead, *The Eye in the Air*, p. 210; NA Kew, WO171/132, war diary HQ 21 Army Gp, (G Int), IntSum No. 158
26 Quoted in Ellis, op cit, p. 284
27 Ellis, op cit, p. 285
28 Mead, op cit, p. 103
29 Doherty, op cit, p. 200
30 Ellis, op cit, p. 313
31 Ibid, op cit, pp. 315–6
32 NA Kew, WO171/906, war diary, 3 AGRA, 1944; WO171/909, war diary, 8 AGRA, Jan–Sep 1944
33 Ellis, op cit, pp. 333–5
34 Ibid, op cit, p. 339
35 Ibid, op cit, p. 340
36 Dunphie, *The Pendulum of Battle*, p. 179
37 NA Kew, WO171/139, war diary, HQ 21 Army Gp, A Br
38 Dunphie, op cit, p. 112
39 Ibid; NA Kew, WO171/1015, war diary, 13 (HAC) RHA, 1944
40 Dunphie, op cit, p. 115; NA Kew, WO171/925, war diary, 75 A-Tk Regt, 1944
41 Doherty, op cit, p. 204
42 How, *Hill 112*, p. 146
43 Quoted in Ellis, op cit, p. 318
44 Goddard, *112th (Wessex) Field Regiment*, p. 49; NA Kew, WO171/984, war diary, 112 Fd Regt, 1944
45 Goddard, op cit, p. 50
46 Quoted in Goddard, op cit, p. 51
47 How, op cit, p. 160. The road dates back to Roman times and was known as the Voie Romaine. It is now known as le Chemin du Duc Guillaume, after William, Duke of Normandy, William the Conqueror.
48 Doherty, op cit, p. 205
49 Ibid, p. 206
50 Goddard, op cit, p. 53; www.cwgc.org; NA, Kew, WO304, Army Roll of Honour
51 Goddard, op cit, p. 54
52 Quoted in ibid, op cit, p. 54
53 Duncan, op cit, p. 354
54 Mead, op cit, p. 104

55 Duncan, op cit, p. 354
56 Ibid, p. 572
57 Ibid, p. 354
58 Hogg, *Allied Artillery of World War 2*, pp. 139–143
59 Hogg & Weeks, *Illustrated Encyclopedia of Military Vehicles*, pp. 162–3
60 Eric Woodburn, interview with author.
61 Mead, op cit, p. 104
62 Compiled from Duncan, op cit, p. 610; Ellis, op cit, pp. 521–531; NA Kew, AGRA war diaries
63 Compiled from Ellis, pp. 524–31
64 Ellis, op cit, p. 522
65 Joslen, *Orders of Battle*, p. 86
66 Harclerode, *Arnhem*, p. 145
67 Duncan, op cit, p. 546
68 Ibid, pp. 546–8
69 Litchfield, *The Territorial Artillery*, p. 163
70 Harclerode, op cit, p. 145; Goddard, op cit, pp. 89–92
71 Harclerode, op cit, pp. 145–6
72 Duncan, op cit, p. 546
73 Hughes, *Honour Titles*, p. 195; Ellis, *Victory in the West, Vol. II*, p. 159
74 Hughes, op cit, p. 195
75 Ellis, op cit, p. 159
76 Hughes, op cit, p. 196
77 Ibid; Ellis, op cit, p. 159
78 Hughes, op cit, p. 196; Ellis, op cit, p. 159
79 Ellis, op cit, p. 159; Hughes, op cit, p. 196
80 *The Gunner*, May 2001, p. 5
81 Duncan, op cit, pp. 593–4; NA Kew, WO171/5109, war diary 3 S Hvy Regt, 1945
82 Ellis, op cit, pp. 142–4
83 Ibid, pp. 158
84 Ibid, pp. 149
85 Ibid, pp. 149–50
86 Ibid, pp. 235
87 Mead, op cit, p. 111
88 Ibid, pp. 111–2
89 Ellis, op cit, p. 243
90 Ibid
91 Quoted in Ellis, p. 246
92 Blake, *Mountain and Flood*, p. 145
93 Ibid, pp. 127–8
94 Ibid, p. 140
95 Ibid, pp. 140–1
96 Ellis, op cit, p. 257
97 Ibid, p. 257n
98 Ibid, p. 256n
99 Horrocks, *A Full Life*, p. 249
100 Ibid, p. 251
101 Ibid, pp. 253–4
102 NA Kew, WO171/4941, war diary, 27 LAA Regt, 1945
103 Doherty, *Wall of Steel*, p. 196; NA Kew, WO171/4941, op cit
104 NA Kew, WO171/3850, war diary HQ 21 Army Gp, G (Ops)

105 Ellis, op cit, p. 288
106 Ibid, pp. 288–92
107 NA Kew, WO171/4941, op cit
108 Duncan, op cit, p. 594; NA Kew, WO171/5109, op cit
109 Ellis, op cit, pp. 290–1
110 Ibid, pp. 294
111 NA Kew, WO171/5011, war diary, 1 Mtn Regt, 1945
112 Duncan, op cit, p. 535
113 Ibid, p. 536
114 NA Kew, WO171/5109, op cit
115 Duncan, op cit, p. 594
116 Doherty, *None Bolder*, pp. 254–5
117 Doherty, *Wall of Steel*, p. 196

Chapter Ten

Of Islands and Convoys

One of the epic stories of the war is that of Malta which endured sustained attack from six hours after Italy's declaration of war on 10 June 1940 until the final Axis air raids on 26 February 1943. Three months later, on 26 May, a convoy from Alexandria reached Gibraltar without losing a single ship, the first time in three years that this had happened. Then, on 20 June, HM King George VI visited Malta, on which he had already conferred the distinction of the George Cross on 15 April 1942. (This remains the first of only two communal awards of the George Cross, the second being to the Royal Ulster Constabulary; neither award was 'gazetted'.)

A glance at a map will show the strategic importance of Malta in the Mediterranean region, an importance summarised by Napoleon's comment that he would prefer to see the English on the slopes of Montmartre than on Malta. British forces on Malta dominated the shipping lanes in the Mediterranean, thereby threatening Italian communications with Italy's 'fourth shore', Libya. Less than half an hour's flying time away, however, were Regia Aeronautica bases on Sicily, which allowed the Italians to threaten Malta effectively. In early 1939 the Committee of Imperial Defence agreed to strengthen Malta's defences with additional AA guns, searchlights and fighter aircraft. Thus the island was to be defended by 112 heavy and sixty light guns with twenty-four searchlights.[1]

That first attack on Malta, at dawn on 11 June, lasted only minutes. It was made by ten Savoia-Marchetti SM-79 Sparviero bombers of the Regia Aeronautica, flying in two waves and escorted by nine Macchi C200 Saetta fighters.[2] No fighters intercepted them because there were no modern machines on Malta, in spite of the Committee of Imperial Defence's decision more than a year before; there were but four Gloster Sea Gladiator biplanes flown off from HMS *Eagle*. These were supplemented by four Hawker Hurricane Mk I fighters.[3] Nor were there any warships in Valletta's Grand Harbour: the last elements of the Mediterranean Fleet had departed the previous day. As the day wore on there were further raids by the Regia Aeronautica. The siege of Malta had begun.[4]

These raids were minor compared with what lay ahead. Since September 1939, Malta had been expecting Italian aggression and had prepared for war although deep air raid shelters, recommended some years before, were not constructed. Fortunately, the RAF had had the foresight to build a radar station in 1939 which was working satisfactorily by the time war was declared in September;[5] it would play a vital role in the island's defence. At that time, the Malta garrison included four British infantry battalions and 7th AA Regiment.[6] In total there were only thirty-four heavy and eight light AA guns, although the searchlight complement was complete at twenty-four and there was one GL radar set; a further sixteen guns intended for Malta – eight each of light and heavy equipments – had been sent to Alexandria instead.[7]

Seventh HAA Regiment was later joined by 27th HAA Regiment (it will be remembered that all AA regiments were redesignated HAA in May 1940). Although disposing only two batteries – 10 and 13 – it also commanded 6 AA Battery RMA[8] and had a mixture of 3-inch, 3.7-inch, 4.5-inch heavy and 40mm light guns.[9] In time, these units would be joined by 4th and 10th HAA Regiments RA as well as 2nd and 11th HAA Regiments Royal Malta Artillery (RMA), alongside which were the light units: 32nd, 65th and 74th LAA Regiments RA and 3rd LAA Regiment RMA. Searchlights were manned by 4th Searchlight Regiment RMA. Units were formed into two AA brigades with heavy regiments under HQ 10 AA Brigade and light and searchlight regiments under 7 AA Brigade.[10] Improvised AA defences were also organised in Valletta's dockyard.[11]

AA units were not the sum total of Malta's artillery: 12th Field Regiment, 4th Coast Regiment and 26th Defence Regiment RA stood alongside 1st and 5th Coast Regiments RMA. There was also a School of Artillery, an Officer Cadet Training Unit (OCTU) and both RA and RMA Depots.[12]

British civilians were evacuated and the Mediterranean Fleet left Malta for Alexandria in Egypt. By mid-August more fighters – a squadron of twelve Hawker Hurricanes – had been flown in, taking off from the carrier HMS *Furious*. Joined by No. 431 Flight, with four Martin Baltimore light bombers, these represented a significant increase in the island's defences when Britain was in dangerous straits on the home front. During the autumn of 1940 the AA defences were reinforced with the arrival of an additional battery to come under 7th HAA Regiment's command and two batteries each of 10th HAA and 74th LAA Regiments. The ships transporting the reinforcements had run the gauntlet of enemy attack by sea and air, including the appearance of Luftwaffe bombers. With these additional guns the AA defences totalled seventy heavy and thirty-four light guns, plus the twenty-four searchlights, by January 1941. This timing could not have been better; and the same was true of the arrival of Lieutenant Colonel N V Sadler, posted to Malta by the War Office, which had decided that the island needed 'a senior AA officer, of recent active experience, to supervise AA procedures'. Sadler had been responsible for organising and commanding the Dover defences.[13]

Although there were many attacks on Malta, it was January 1941 before the first major raid occurred. The target was the new carrier HMS *Illustrious* which, damaged badly while escorting a convoy, had put into Grand Harbour for repairs on the 11th. (In November 1940, *Illustrious*'s Swordfish had carried out the raid on the Italian fleet at Taranto.) By now 7 AA Brigade had been established to 'tighten command' and Sadler was appointed its commander. *Illustrious* was the first major test of his skill and experience.

> Clearly such a target would attract enemy attention so special concentrations of AA fire were arranged to cover her berth. Lacking radar capability for 'unseen' engagements any large attack would have to be met by barrages on the approaches. All AA positions prepared their fire tables. Soon after mid-day on 16th, the RAF reported a large raid forming to the east; this proved to consist of about 70 Ju87 and Ju88 aircraft escorted by fighters. HMS *Illustrious* was located and attacked. Intense AA fire was opened and the all too few fighters of the RAF took position immediately behind the fire zone to engage the broken raid stream as it emerged. A second, similar, attack was made on 17th and a third on 19th. Although the surrounding dock area was devastated, *Illustrious* sustained only one minor hit and work on her continued. She sailed for Alexandria on 23 January. The action must be reckoned a success for the combined defences; 16 enemy aircraft were shot down. The heavy air raids were a foretaste of what was to come.[14]

That Axis pressure on Malta was building up was clear to Brigadier C T Beckett, who took command of all Malta's artillery in May 1941. Beckett had to leave the SS *Latona* at Gibraltar as it was no longer considered safe for single ships to sail through the Mediterranean; while *Latona* sailed via South Africa, he had to find another means of reaching Malta.[15]

Until the attacks on *Illustrious*, the Luftwaffe had not been involved heavily in the aerial campaign against Malta. But, with the Afrika Korps despatched to Libya, the German commanders began taking a closer interest in Malta and Luftwaffe units moved on to Sicilian airfields alongside the Regia Aeronautica. At the same time, Axis convoys to North Africa presented important targets for both the Royal Navy and Royal Air Force; Malta provided an excellent platform from which to launch such attacks. In turn, that prompted further Axis attention to the island, and especially to its airfields.

At first, raids on Malta were generally carried out in daylight with attack forces varying from single bombers to large formations. Then came night raids on targets across the island plus minelaying operations. The RAF airfields at Luqa and Hal Far were choice targets and the small force of RAF bombers was withdrawn to Egypt, although the fighters remained. The latter included a squadron of Bristol Beaufighters, which could operate at night in close co-operation with the searchlights; these had been fitted with SLC radar, or Elsie.[16]

That co-operation between the Beaufighters and 4th SL Regiment RMA was an indication of how well co-ordinated the defences had become. The RAF radar station and the Gun Operations Room also worked in harmony: whenever friendly fighters were about, enemy aircraft were engaged by pointer rounds to indicate their location to the fighters while, at night, the GOR used the radar to direct RAF aircraft.[17] Even so, there were still occasions when the zeal of one service led to frustration on the part of another; this occurred when RAF controllers restricted the guns or even banned them from firing.[18]

Enemy operations against Malta were divided into two phases by HQ 7 AA Brigade: the first included those raids between Italy's entry into the war and the initial attack on *Illustrious,* while the second covered the period from that attack, on 16 January, until 31 March 1941. In the first phase the AA guns fired 10,624 rounds, of which 1,078 were from light guns and the remainder from heavies. The increased intensity of operations is shown emphatically by the figures for the second period when 39,836 rounds were fired; of these 21,176 were heavy rounds and the remaining 18,660 were from the light guns.[19] These figures exclude fire from warships in harbour, which was linked to the defences. Farndale comments that Fliegerkorps X suffered heavily and that

> At times attacks were composed of 60 bombers with up to 40 fighter escorts, but by February the Germans were forced to attack at night to cut their losses. They also began aerial minelaying at this time. Then by March even heavier attacks began by both day and night and the shortage of fighters became critical.[20]

In that second phase of attacks, the Luftwaffe admitted to losing sixty aircraft while the Regia Aeronautica lost at least sixteen. The lower Italian losses may be because Italian bombers tended to fly higher, and on steady courses, and it was more difficult for the Hurricanes to reach them, although they presented a better target for the heavy guns. However, there was a complication as far as the latter were concerned. Malta's main defences lay to the east and south-east where the topography prevented heavy AA guns being sited in ideal locations, away from the actual targets. In turn, the GL sets were sited away from their usual location at gun positions but were deployed where they could provide early plots to the GOR. Thus the heavy guns were committed to last-minute engagements, for which a higher gun density was needed with tighter fire control to ensure maximum concentration of fire.[21]

Hitler's decision to invade Russia brought brief relief to Malta. As the Wehrmacht prepared for Operation BARBAROSSA in June, many Luftwaffe units in the Mediterranean were withdrawn to Germany. At the same time, the Royal Navy brought more fighters – 109 in all – to Malta and, in spite of the hazards faced by convoys, also brought 4th HAA Regiment to the island. As well as 4th Regiment's own 3.7s, additional heavy and light guns were shipped in, bringing the totals of those equipments to 112 and 118 respectively.[22] By September, there were also twenty-four field and medium guns for the coast defences, in addition to the coast guns.[23]

In May, Brigadier Beckett re-organised his command to form three brigades, two of which – 7 and 10 – were in the AA role while the third controlled coast defences. He also pressed for the easing of restrictions on AA fire, which led to the creation of a flexible hour-to-hour working system and the division of Malta's airspace into sectors in which priority could be accorded to either guns or fighters according to the tactical situation. Fighters were also to operate above the height limits established for the guns.[24]

The summer of 1941 passed without any Axis attempts to invade the island and the defences were strengthened and re-organised, with many recently-arrived 18-pounders assigned to beach defence. Training was self-contained since no one could leave Malta for courses or exercises and return to the island. One effect of the siege was seen in a doubling of the cost of living between May and October – and yet Malta had not officially been declared a theatre of war.[25] Nonetheless, morale, both civilian and military, remained high and Gunners played their part in this with each regiment finding a ceremonial guard for the Castile for a week. A gun from the regiment was also put on display while the Royal Malta Artillery Band played as the new guard was mounted and gave concerts after the ceremonies had concluded.[26]

Although no invasion fleets appeared off Malta during that summer, there was an attack by Italian Special Forces on Grand Harbour on 26 July. Convoy GM 1 of six ships had reached Malta in Operation SUBSTANCE on the 24th, although the escort had lost the destroyer HMS *Fearless* sunk and the cruiser HMS *Manchester*, a destroyer and the merchant ship, *Sydney Star*, damaged; the last-named limped into Malta behind its sister ships but *Manchester* was forced to return to Gibraltar. There were also seven 'empty' merchant ships in Grand Harbour, awaiting an escort back to Gibraltar. The Italian raid on the 26th was intended to destroy these vessels and was launched by Prince Junio Valerio Borghese's X Mas (*Decima Flottiglia Motoscafi Anti Sommergibili*, 10th Flotilla of Anti-submarine Motorboats), the motto of which was *Memento Audere Semper* – Remember Always to Dare.[27]

Grand Harbour could be entered only through a well-defended harbour mouth. Those defences were formidable, including nets, booms, searchlights and guns. Coast defence artillery was mounted at several commanding points: at Fort St Elmo, where Harbour Fire Command was situated, were six twin-6-pounders of 3 Coast Battery RMA with another three twin 6-pounders of 1 Coast Battery RMA at Fort Ricasoli; 6-inch guns were located at St Rocco and Tigne Forts while 9.2-inch guns were further out at Forts Maddalena and Leonardo. A net hung from the bridge that guarded the harbour mouth at Fort St Elmo where Borghese's men intended to make their entrance.[28]

The MAS attack was to have been synchronised with an air attack on Valletta to drown out the sound of the approaching naval craft. However, the timing of the two forces failed to coincide and the Regia Aeronautica's strike served to alert the defences. The harbour defence lights were switched on and quickly spotted the Italian attack craft. The RAF early-warning radar had also picked up a surface plot moving at about fifteen knots towards Malta, which turned out to be the attackers' support ship, the Regia Marina sloop *Diana*.[29] Furthermore, Ultra intercepts had already alerted the garrison to an impending attack. Instead of achieving surprise, the men of Decima MAS were heading into a killing zone.

The Decima MAS plan was for the attacking craft, nine explosive boats with a one-man crew, known as MTs (*Motoscafo Turismo*, or touring motorboat) to enter the harbour through a gap in the net created by a two-man human torpedo, the type of weapon later adopted by the Royal Navy; two of these SLCs (*Siluro a Lenta Corsa*, or low-speed torpedo) were deployed. Once through the gap, the MTs would then pass in single file via a six-foot-wide gap in the inner boom, intended for fishing vessels, before spreading out and making for their targets.[30] That was the plan; but it was not to work out as the Italian commanders intended.

Lieutenant P S Cassar Torreggiano, a Maltese Gunner officer, described the ensuing battle in Grand Harbour. When the alarm sounded he rushed to Fort St Elmo and one of the twin 6-pounder mountings where he

> … saw what the lookout had reported as the wake of a boat twenty yards from the breakwater heading for a gap in the breakwater viaduct. Almost immediately, a loud explosion shook the harbour and the viaduct fell. The weapon that had caused the damage later proved to have been a baby submarine.
>
> The harbour searchlights illuminated the waters and I could see five fast-moving craft approach the harbour in line ahead making for the gap in the viaduct. The defences immediately engaged the enemy craft and in a few minutes everything was quiet again. The equipment I was on claimed two of the craft, sinking the first with two rounds. At first light fire was re-opened against two abandoned MTs which had been boarded again and were attempting to escape. They were sunk.[31]

This well-planned and courageous attack by Italian Special Forces had failed due to the bad timing of the air attack; the airmen had already been on operations that day which would not have helped. Three Italian bombers were claimed as destroyed by Hurricanes some five miles out to sea and none dropped their bombs on Valletta.[32] As with the British forces, inter-service cooperation between the Regia Marina and Regia Aeronautica could be hit-and-miss. It was fortunate for Malta that this was so on this occasion, as the attack might have inflicted very serious damage on the vessels in the harbour. The raid provided a remarkable baptism of fire for 1st Coast Regiment RMA.

Through the siege the greatest burden fell on the Gunners of the AA regiments, especially from late December 1941 when the intensity of Axis air operations against Malta increased as numbers of Luftwaffe units returned from the Eastern Front. This also marked the arrival of the newly-appointed

Commander-in-Chief, South (*Oberbefehlshaber Süd* or *OB Süd*), Field Marshal Albrecht Kesselring. Under his direction

> A new phase of operations, of increasing violence, began which would last until April 1942. Axis aims were two-fold; to suppress the Royal Navy's attacks on shipping and to eliminate the RAF's presence in Malta by attrition in combat and the destruction of its airfields. There was also the threat of air- or sea-borne invasion.[33]

Initially, the raids were made in daylight with small numbers of aircraft, although attacks were frequent. However, the tempo built up until large air armadas 'with swarms of fighters as escort' were appearing.[34] The Luftwaffe now had some 425 combat aircraft based on Sicily, a formidable threat to an island that measured but fifteen miles by seven. To combat these, and the Regia Aeronautica planes, Brigadier Beckett had thirty AA batteries in five heavy and four light regiments by January 1942; there was also the searchlight regiment.[35]

For several days at a time alerts would be almost continuous. HQ 7 AA Brigade recorded an average of five raids daily and four each night during January, a rate that increased in February. Such was the pace of operations that guns were manned continuously for all but six hours of one three-day period in February, with one alert lasting thirteen and three-quarter hours.[36] It was then that a system of rest and readiness that had been introduced by the CRA paid dividends. AA units were often relieved by field Gunners so that the former might have some rest. However, this could have unexpected tragic consequences as when a leave party on Manoel Island was wiped out, the barracks in which they were staying destroyed by bombing; three guns were also destroyed. Elsewhere, a leave party in the NAAFI on the Barracca during a heavy raid heard a bomb land near a Bofors outside and dashed to the position; the gun detachment were sent to the dressing station while the leave party took over their weapon and manned it until relieved at nightfall.[37]

There were many casualties among the Gunners, including the CO of 74th LAA Regiment, Lieutenant Colonel Guy Wright MC, who was killed in action on 29 December 1941.[38] His and the other light AA regiments were dispersed over three main areas: Valletta and Grand Harbour, Luqa to Hal Far, and Ta Kali. Airfields were the attackers' preferred targets and the light guns were worked hard. The level of attacks was unprecedented and the light guns at the airfields were under attack for days at a time. Even with a light AA regiment to each VP, and a gun density anywhere at about 14,000 feet of some ninety guns, bombers still got through.[39]

RA Headquarters was even forced to go underground for a period of ten days, such was the level of enemy attention.[40] On 8/9 March, German bombers ran a continuous attacking shuttle for more than twenty-one hours.[41] Then, on 20 March, came one of the most determined raids when, from 10.30pm, some 300 ton of bombs fell around Ta Kali during a four-hour period. One effect of the bombing was the destruction of underground water tanks, which not only caused flooding but led to a water shortage over the following four months.[42]

With RAF fighter strength on Malta reduced to thirty-two machines, Lieutenant General Sir William Dobbie, Governor of Malta, appealed for urgent reinforcements and fifteen Spitfires were flown to Ta Kali. Within hours of their arrival they were attacked by Ju88s and several were destroyed; it was little consolation that fourteen attackers were shot down. Air Vice Marshal A P Lloyd, who was at Ta Kali when it came under heavy attack, 'sent a message to the CRA praising the steadfast conduct of gun detachments firing through a hail of bombs and bullets'. There was also praise from an unexpected quarter. A German radio broadcast commented that 'Malta's [AA] artillery must be counted as Tommy's best and plays the greatest part in the defence of the island.' In fact, during March the RAF and the Gunners shared the destruction of sixty-two enemy aircraft, of which thirty-four fell to the fighters and the remainder to the guns.[43] One Gunner officer commented that 'The RAF were the forwards, we the backs of a well-knit team'.[44]

> The physical exhaustion and mental strain of endless hours of manning and action were tremendous yet the future offered little hope of relief. Neither military nor civilian supplies reached the island in any quantity and there was little or no mail, this despite the courage and determination so often demonstrated by the Royal and Merchant Navies.[45]

Yet Malta's defiance continued and the AA guns persisted in their work, although ammunition stocks were depleted and there were restrictions on firing. Even so, such was the level of enemy aggression that ammunition expenditure increased. The arrival of calibration information for GL Mark II had improved the guns' effectiveness which, in turn, seems to have prompted the Luftwaffe to turn their attention to the gun positions in April. This offensive against the guns, especially the 3.7s and 4.5s, lasted for five months during which 115 direct attacks were made on gunsites in which 149 men were killed and 290 wounded. Damage to equipments included three 3.7s, two 4.5s, three Bofors 40mms, three GL sets and three searchlights. Some positions suffered as many as seventeen attacks while 27 HAA Battery, at Luqa, was dive-bombed on seven successive days. Instruments, stores and ammunition were also destroyed and a daily limit of fifteen rounds per gun was imposed. In spite of all this, the defences, both fighter and gun, continued taking a heavy toll of the Axis air forces.[46]

On 7 May Field Marshal Lord Gort of Limerick VC arrived to take up his post as the new governor. With him he brought the George Cross, awarded to Malta the previous month by HM King George VI. At much the same time the intensity of Axis attacks reduced, due to the heavy losses sustained by the Luftwaffe and Regia Aeronautica and a mistaken enemy belief that the RAF airfields had been destroyed. Far from being destroyed they were still in operation and were able to receive sixty-five Spitfires flown in from the aircraft carriers HMS *Eagle* and USS *Wasp*. At much the same time, the fast minelayer HMS *Welshman* reached Malta with food supplies and 84,000 rounds of 40mm ammunition. To protect *Welshman* as she unloaded, 12th Field Regiment laid a smokescreen while lights, guns and fighters also took part in an operation to ensure that unloading went well. *Welshman* sailed again that same day and although attacked was not hit, while six enemy aircraft were shot down.[47]

Welshman repeated the performance in July and was turned around in under five hours, although other convoys were not so successful: only two of the fourteen merchantmen of Operation PEDESTAL reached Malta.[48] The level of raiding reduced in June but the island was in peril of invasion as Axis forces pushed Eighth Army back in North Africa and captured Tobruk on 21 June. In fact, it was probably the fall of Tobruk that ensured no invasion attempt was made. Rommel, elated at the capture of the port that had held out so long the previous year, was confident that he could strike into the Nile Delta and convinced Hitler and Mussolini to allow him to continue his offensive. Kesselring had wanted to attack Malta, the taking of which he believed would have secured the North African theatre but he was over-ruled. Both dictators had baulked at the idea of invading Malta, remembering the losses suffered on Crete the previous year.[49]

The Axis paid heavily for this change of strategy with Malta providing a base for Royal Navy submarines to interdict supplies for Panzer Armee Afrika, a task in which they were aided by RAF bombers and torpedo bombers flying from the island. Over the coming months, Malta was a key asset in Allied strategy in the Mediterranean.

In June Air Vice Marshal Keith Park arrived as the new Air Officer Commanding in Malta. He re-organised the defences to integrate 'more closely the control of both fighters and guns in joint action'. This led to control of all guns being assumed by one GOR with the other becoming an intermediate reserve. With more Spitfires arriving, Park was also able to adopt an offensive stance with longer-range patrols and offensive operations against enemy air bases on Sicily.[50]

Although the Axis resumed their attacks on Malta in October, this offensive did not last as long as earlier efforts. Nonetheless, it was intense, with Luqa again targeted for a series of attacks. The defences had the upper hand and the co-ordinated efforts of guns and fighters led to German losses of forty-four aircraft during the month; Italian losses were probably much the same. Nine 'kills' were definitely attributed to the guns. That the defences were successful was confirmed by two developments:

> the weight of attack rapidly declined and a mixture of warships and merchant vessels regularly used the docks and harbour, without harm, under the AA umbrella. By January 1943, raids were limited to periodic fighter sweeps and high-level reconnaissance flights.[51]

No one could have known it then but the siege of Malta was over. During February, when not a single enemy aircraft crossed the coastline, no bombs fell. By then, Eighth Army was pushing into Tunisia, having taken Tripoli on 23 January and the Luftwaffe's attention was turning to that port. March and April also passed with no hostile air activity, although in May and June there were some fighter sorties and reconnaissance flights. Two large raids were mounted on warships in harbour during July but few bombs found their targets; there was almost no damage and three planes were shot down. And yet reinforcements continued to arrive: 107th and 117th LAA Regiments were among them, which also included three HAA and two LAA batteries of Royal Marines as well as more GL radars.[52] At least one unit, 117th (Royal Ulster Rifles) LAA Regiment, was convinced that it had been sent to Malta by mistake.[53]

Since a threat was still perceived, the air defences of Malta continued to be strengthened and extended but the guns had fired in anger for the last time. The War passed Malta by as the Allies brought the campaign in Tunisia to an end in May and Sicily was invaded in July, to be followed by landings in Italy in September. Now it was time to withdraw units from Malta for service elsewhere and by November 7th HAA and 32nd LAA Regiments had departed for Britain while 74th and 117th LAA Regiments had joined Eighth Army in Italy.[54]

During some of the most intensive aerial bombardment in history, the AA defences of Malta had destroyed 241 enemy aircraft, in some 11,000 sorties against the island, and had fired 297,758 HAA rounds and 226,992 LAA rounds. Gunners had earned a DSO, six MCs, five MMs and twenty-seven Mentions in Despatches; they also shared in Malta's George Cross. It was a remarkable chapter in the history of the Royal Regiment and the Royal Malta Artillery.[55]

Malta had relied on supply by convoy for its survival. The merchant ships in those convoys became prize targets for Axis submarines, surface vessels and aircraft, as was the case with all Allied merchantmen. As a result the ships carried defensive armament which, in many cases, was manned by Gunners. Ships so fitted were termed Defensively Equipped Merchant Ships (DEMS). The Admiralty had foreseen the need for such a practice to protect merchant ships. Initially, most defensively-armed vessels had guns intended to deal with submarines although the aerial danger was also recognised; the first attacks on ships by aircraft occurred in September 1939. However, there was an acute shortage of AA guns and all that could be provided to counter aircraft were Lewis and Bren guns on AA mounts.[56]

These guns were provided by the War Office in response to an Admiralty request for about 500 AA light machine-gun teams, each consisting of two men and a machine gun. Thus began what was to be a huge commitment to the defence of ships. After the first transfer of 1,000 personnel from Home Forces in February 1940 the numbers decreased gradually until August when only sixty-five teams, each of two men, remained but, in that month, the number was brought back to

1,000 personnel and, in October, a further 1,000 with 500 LMGs arrived 'for the AA defence of merchant ships in coastal waters'. By then a further requirement had materialised for men to man 12-pounder guns on merchant ships in UK ports 'as an anti-invasion precaution'; these men were posted in during November.[57] Unlike the AA light machine-gun teams, they were not required to go to sea and were described as 'Port Gunners'; by the end of 1941 their role was redundant and they were transferred to seagoing service.[58]

Numbers aboard ships increased even further in early 1941 with another Admiralty plea for soldiers to man defensive weapons. In February came another 600 men with 300 LMGs 'for merchant ships in West African convoys' followed by '2,500 additional trained LMG personnel ... for Atlantic convoy ships'. The latter were provided with LMGs 'from Naval and Army sources' while a scale of one man per weapon instead of two was introduced.[59] By then the large numbers of Luftwaffe aircraft in western France were carrying out so many attacks on shipping that, in addition to these men with AA light machine guns, another 1,700 with 300 Bofors 40mm guns, on loan from Anti-Aircraft Command, were assigned to the Merchant Navy; 20mm Oerlikon guns were also fitted to merchantmen and manned by soldiers.[60] At the end of 1941 Churchill ordered the transfer of 3-inch AA guns to the Admiralty 'for the defence of ships in the Atlantic'.[61] (Farndale gives a figure of 100 guns whereas Routledge quotes 136.)[62]

These soldiers, who were formed into AA Defence of Merchant Shipping Groups, were drawn from all arms and services but, on 6 May 1941, responsibility for them was assumed by the Royal Artillery.[63] Typical of the early shipboard soldiers was Alfred Tubb, a former infantryman and Lewis gunner, who eventually became a member of 6th Maritime Regiment. Thus was born the latest branch of the Royal Regiment: the Maritime Anti-Aircraft Regiments Royal Artillery. With a strength of 11,200, just 700 of whom were shore-based, the new branch had a small HQ in London within the Directorate of the Royal Artillery and formed three regiments, each with two AALMG batteries and two Bofors batteries.[64] These were based in the UK with 1st Maritime Regiment responsible for all shipping from Scottish ports, 2nd Maritime Regiment that from the north of England and 3rd Maritime Regiment that from the south of England. A training regiment, for the Bofors 40mm, was designated 4th Maritime Regiment. Overseas batteries were based in North America (New York), North Africa (Port Said), South Africa (Simonstown) and India (Bombay).[65] A change in title to Maritime Royal Artillery was made in March 1942. Operational control was 'exercised jointly by the Admiralty and the War Office, in accordance with naval requirements' while, aboard ship, Maritime Royal Artillery personnel 'forming part of the permanent DEMS complement of the ship are under the operational control of the ship's Master, his gunnery officer (Royal Navy or Merchant Navy) or the individual to whom the Master has delegated operational responsibility'.[66]

The Maritime Royal Artillery increased in strength so that, by March 1943, it deployed six regiments with twenty-four port detachments in the UK and four overseas' batteries, based in New York, Port Said, Bombay and South Africa. Its total manpower included 170 officers and more than 14,000 other ranks; some three dozen officers were at sea at any given time while 13,000 of the personnel were regular sea-going Gunners.[67]

The presence of Gunners on merchant ships was an important element in defending those ships and the convoys in which they sailed. On the larger ships there could be as many as thirty Gunners but on coasters the detachment included only two. The average detachment on a liberty ship was seven, of whom four might be naval ratings and three Gunners, or the entire detachment might be naval ratings or Gunners. The Inspector of Merchant Naval Gunnery, Admiral Austin, commented:

> Not only from my own observations, but in all reports received from COs, masters of ships and the many civilians – men and ladies who take an interest in welfare – the conduct, discipline, efficiency and general turnout of the MRA was in all respects a great credit to the RA. In foreign ports they were good ambassadors.
>
> Between the RN and MRA a great friendship and complete trust and co-operation were established, and the job they did was always well done, inspired confidence and helped to raise the morale of the hundreds of thousands of masters, officers and passengers in the ships in which they served.[68]

Since MRA detachments could be so small, often they did not have a Gunner officer in charge and so the senior 'gunlayer' onboard took charge, whether he was a naval petty officer, Royal Marines NCO or Gunner NCO. This system worked well and relations between the services were good, although conditions on many ships were bad; there was no 'hard-lying' money from the Army to compensate, although one officer did claim field allowance. Gunners were trained to use naval 6-inch guns and their training also extended to rockets and balloons, although the Bofors guns fitted to ships remained the responsibility of the MRA personnel.[69] In February 1943 Admiralty permission was given for Maritime RA NCOs who qualified as DEMS gunlayers to wear the naval gunlayer's badge, although it was noted that this would 'not entitle the Maritime Regiment, Royal Artillery personnel to the additional payment of 9d per day paid to Naval ratings' with the same qualification.[70] Another badge, the regimental flash of the Maritime Royal Artillery, 'a foul anchor on a blue ground, with the letters AA (to be altered to RA) in white enables them to have access to all Royal Naval canteens and welfare establishments'.[71] The alliance with the senior service might have been even closer had a 1943 proposal been implemented. This was for the transfer of the Maritime RA to the Royal Marines; but the proposal went no further and the Maritime Gunners remained as members of the Royal Regiment.[72]

Many Gunners lost their lives at sea or were forced to take to lifeboats or rafts when their ships were sunk. General Pile, of AA Command, wrote

> That the job was hazardous is evident by the fact that in the first 18 months one man in every three had had to swim for his life after his ship had been torpedoed. There were never enough of these crews, so they were transferred as soon as their ship got safely into dock to one about to sail.[73]

Gunner Victor George Gurney, of 6th Maritime Regiment, was awarded the British Empire Medal (Military Division) 'for fortitude and gallant conduct in a lifeboat, though he was severely wounded, after a defensively equipped Merchantman was lost'.[74] Two Gunners who had to abandon ship found themselves in an open boat for forty-eight days and must have wondered if survival was possible. Another trio were largely responsible for saving the lives of the master and some of the ship's company when their vessel was stricken and they were shipwrecked in the Svalbard archipelago north of the Arctic Circle. These Gunners helped their companions through frostbite and gangrenous infection. Yet another Gunner, in spite of being wounded three times, tried for 'two interminable hours' to use his body to shield his comrades on a Carley float from the attentions of a Japanese submarine crew who were using the float, and its occupants, for light machine-gun practice.[75]

Also victims of the Japanese were the crew of the cargo-liner SS *Behar,* which left Melbourne on 29 February 1944 bound for Bombay. *Behar* had a cargo of war material but was destined not to deliver it as, on 9 March, southwest of the Cocos Islands, the ship spotted a Japanese cruiser, the *Tone*, which sped to intercept the merchantman. Although *Behar* was armed, its guns were no match for the cruiser's, especially as *Tone* opened fire well beyond range of *Behar*'s guns. The merchant ship took so many hits that it capsized and sank and most of its crew took to the water. Until then the only fatalities on *Behar* had been an Indian seaman, Noor Khan, and Gunner Stanley Pycroft, aged 21, of 4th Maritime Regiment RA, who was killed at his gun.[76] All the survivors were picked up by the *Tone* and taken to Batavia. Captain Haruo Mayazumi, *Tone*'s captain, was then ordered by Admiral Naomasa Sakonju, commanding 16th Cruiser Squadron, to dispose of the prisoners immediately. This meant quite simply that the men were to be killed in accordance with a directive received by the Admiral, which he had already passed to his commanding officers. Mayazumi pleaded for the men's lives and thirty-six of them were put ashore. However, seventy-two were taken to sea where, on the night of 18/19 March, they were murdered. Each prisoner was hit in the stomach, then kicked in the testicles and, while doubled in pain, beheaded. Those who died included five Gunners: Sergeant Charlie Ratcliffe, Bombardier Neil Brodie and Gunner Alex Rodney of 1st Maritime Regiment and Bombardier Arthur Bowers and Gunner Alfred Street of 4th Maritime Regiment.[77] After the War, Admiral Sakonju was tried as a war criminal and executed; Captain Mayazumi was sentenced to seven years in prison.

There were occasions when a ship's entire complement, including its Gunners, was lost. SS *Ceramic* was torpedoed and went down with only one survivor on 7 December 1942. Of the 656 crew and passengers on board the ship, eighteen were Maritime Gunners; three other Gunners were also travelling on *Ceramic*. The ship was sailing independently west of the Azores when, shortly after midnight on the night of 6/7 December, it was struck by three torpedoes from U-515. With the engines disabled the order was given to abandon ship and most passengers and crew took to the lifeboats. The ship was still afloat and remained so until U-515 fired another two torpedoes into it which broke *Ceramic*'s keel in two; the vessel vanished below the waves in a matter of seconds. Tragically, a storm blew up in the morning and sea conditions in the area were such that the lifeboats were swamped, thus leading to the loss of all but one life from *Ceramic*. The sole survivor was a Royal Engineer who was pulled from the water by U-515's crew at about midday on the 7th. By this time the wind was blowing at force 10 and seamen in the area later reported that this was one of the worst storms they had ever encountered. The Maritime Gunners who died were: Gunners Thomas Eric Ernest Bedford, Frank Bullock, John Henry Carlile, William Orlando Donnell, Joseph Dyson, Alfred Yarwood Gibbons, Douglas Haig Nivelle Henrick, Frederick William Hills, Cyril Graham Lines, John James Little, Patrick Joseph McKenna, William Nicks, Gordon Smith, Cyril George Stokes, Charles Sullivan, William Timmins, Lance Bombardier Edward Vokes and Bombardier Leonard Arthur Osborn. Lieutenant James Alan Prentis, Staff Sergeant Frank Edward Ridout and Bombardier Douglas Northcote Kennedy were the other Gunners who died.[78]

Examples of the courage and skill of the Maritime Gunners are legion and would require at least one volume to relate. They were prepared to engage any threat to their ships, which is how one Gunner managed to sink an approaching torpedo. Spotting the weapon surging through the water towards him, he opened fire with his 20mm Oerlikon and hit the torpedo, which then sank. It was afterwards realised that his feat had been possible only because the torpedo had been set to run at the wrong depth. Nonetheless, without his intervention, and good shooting, the torpedo would have struck the ship causing severe damage at least, if not sinking it.[79] Likewise, the following story of an unnamed Gunner illustrates the effectiveness of the AA defences on board even small ships. On 20 August 1940 the *Macville* was sailing off the west coast of Ireland en route to Limerick with a cargo of coal when, at 1.00pm, a Focke Wulf FW 200 Kondor attacked with bombs and machine-gun fire. *Macville*'s Lewis engaged the attacker and after a few bursts the German flew off. Built originally as the Kurier airliner, the Kondor was not strong enough to indulge in the aerobatics needed to avoid effective AA fire.[80]

The most outstanding story of service of a Maritime Gunner is that of Bombardier Henry Herbert Reed of 1st Maritime AA Regiment, who was awarded a posthumous George Cross on 23 September 1941. Bombardier Reed (referred to as Gunner Reed in *The London Gazette*) was manning an AA gun on the SS *Cormount* in a coastal convoy from Blyth to London on 20/21 June 1941 when it came under attack.

> The ship was attacked by enemy aircraft with cannon, machine-guns and bombs. She replied at once with her defensive armament and the men at the guns went on firing despite the hail of bullets and cannon shell.
>
> Gunner Reed behaved with the utmost gallantry. He was badly wounded but when the Master asked how he was, he said that he would carry on. The Chief Officer was also badly wounded. Reed carried him from the bridge down two ladders to the deck below and placed him in shelter near a lifeboat. Gunner Reed then died. It was afterwards found that his stomach had been ripped open by machine-gun bullets.
>
> By his gallant and utterly selfless action Gunner Reed saved the life of the Chief Officer.[81]

There can be no doubt that Henry Reed deserved this posthumous recognition. However, the award of the George Cross, instituted by HM King George VI on 24 September 1940, prompts the question: why not the Victoria Cross? According to *The Register of the George Cross*, the award was

> intended to be an award for outstanding civilian bravery, but as many people in the armed services were unavoidably engaged in work not appropriate for strictly military awards (that is, under direct orders of commanders in the battlefield) they became eligible for recommendation for the George Cross equally with civilians. Consequently, 76 of the first 100 awards were made to members of the armed forces.[82]

Can it be argued that Reed was 'unavoidably engaged in work not appropriate for strictly military awards' and that he was not 'under direct orders of commanders in the battlefield'? Since he was a soldier in uniform carrying out a soldier's role in the direct face of enemy forces, it is hard to argue that he was not eligible for the Victoria Cross. It cannot be argued logically that he was not under the direct orders of commanders in the battlefield since the North Sea was a battlefield, as were the oceans of the world on which sailed British merchant ships. And it should be remembered that those ships had come under Admiralty control in August 1939. Compare Bombardier Reed's case with that of Leading Seaman Jack Mantle who received a posthumous Victoria Cross. Jack Mantle was a naval AA gunner on board HMS *Foylebank*, a merchant vessel taken over by the Admiralty and pressed into Royal Navy service. On 4 July 1940, during a Luftwaffe raid on Portsmouth, Mantle was manning a 20mm pom-pom gun and although wounded many times, including having his left leg shattered by bomb blast, remained at his gun until he collapsed and died.[83] It would appear that the principal difference between Mantle and Reed was that the former was on board a ship of the Royal Navy while the latter was on a Merchant Navy vessel, albeit under Admiralty control; but *Foylebank* had been a Merchant Navy ship until September 1939. There are many who believe that Henry Herbert Reed ought to have been one of the Royal Regiment's VCs of the Second World War.

With the expansion to six regiments there were also additional bases for the Maritime RA. These included the Italian ports of Naples, Taranto, Bari and Brindisi, all liberated by the Allies in late 1943; Naples was home to a Troop HQ with a detachment and detachments at each of the other three ports. Additional bases for detachments were added in North America, including San Francisco, while, in the Indian ocean, Bombay had a battery HQ and a detachment with a further seven regional detachments were at ports including Karachi, Calcutta, Trincomalee and Madras. The South and East African Battery had its HQ ar Capetown with detachments at Simonstown and Durban and sub-detachments at Port Elizabeth and Mombassa. Freetown was the HQ of the West African Independent Troop while there was a sub-detachment at Lagos. In the South Pacific Sydney was home to another independent troop HQ, with a detachment; sub-detachments were based at Melbourne, Freemantle, Townsville, Milne Bay and Wellington, New Zealand.[84]

With peace in Europe the Maritime Royal Artillery was reduced but there remained a job to do in the Pacific and Indian oceans, although this was not as great a burden as had been the case in the Atlantic, the Mediterranean and home waters. When Japan surrendered in August 1945, the work of the Maritime Gunners was all but finished. In September the War Office issued a letter, marked 'secret', noting

> I am commanded by the Army Council to inform you that instructions have been issued by the Admiralty for the withdrawal of all Maritime Royal Artillery personnel from operational duty in the Defence of Merchant Ships.[85]

Arrangements were begun to repatriate Maritime Gunners to the UK as soon as possible so that the Maritime Royal Artillery might be disbanded.[86] So ended a unique chapter in the history of the Royal Regiment.

Farndale noted that, in their five years of service, the Maritime Gunners fought over 3,500 actions 'ranging from long drawn out convoy battles to sudden brief encounters'. They could be at sea for lengthy periods as with the eight Gunners who embarked on the MV *Ajax* in Liverpool on 15 September 1941. Little did they suspect that they would not return to the UK for more than a year, until 30 October 1942. During that time *Ajax* took part in six convoy runs to Malta, surviving almost constant air attack and firing 6,000 rounds against enemy aircraft. From Malta the ship sailed to Egypt and operated between Port Tewfiq, Sofaga, Haifa and Port Said before sailing through the Suez canal to Aden for Capetown and New York. It was from New York that Ajax joined a UK-bound convoy and finally came home.[87]

The men who served in the Maritime Royal Artillery fully lived up to the additional motto adopted by that branch of the Royal Regiment, *Intrepide per Oceanos Mundi* – Fearless through the oceans of the world. In the words of Martin Farndale 'They carried the good name of the Royal Regiment across the oceans to nearly every port in the world, giving protection to their ships from air and surface attack.'[88]

Notes

1 Farndale, *The Years of Defeat*, p. 117
2 Wragg, *Malta: The Last Great Siege*, p. 3
3 Routledge, *Anti-Aircraft Artillery*, p. 167
4 Wragg, op cit, pp. 3–4
5 Ibid, pp. 35–7
6 Ibid, p. 40
7 Farndale, op cit, p. 117
8 Frederick, *Lineage Book*, p. 766
9 Routledge, op cit, p. 166
10 Duncan, *RA Commemoration Book*, p. 166; Routledge, op cit, p. 174 for orbat of 7 and 10 AA Brigades
11 Wragg, op cit, p. 51
12 Duncan, op cit, p. 166
13 Routledge, op cit, p. 167
14 Ibid; Duncan, op cit, p. 161 (which suggests that the raids on *Illustrious* occurred in April)
15 Duncan, op cit, p. 161
16 Routledge, op cit, pp. 167–8
17 Duncan, op cit, p. 162
18 Routledge, op cit, p. 168
19 Ibid; Farndale, op cit, p. 169
20 Ibid
21 Routledge, op cit, p. 168
22 Ibid
23 Farndale, op cit, p. 199
24 Routledge, op cit, p. 168
25 Duncan, op cit, pp. 161–2
26 Routledge, op cit, p. 168
27 Wragg, op cit, p. 95; Greene & Massignani, *The Black Prince and the Sea Devils*, p. 3
28 Farndale, op cit, p. 199
29 Greene & Massignani, op cit, p. 81
30 Ibid, p. 80
31 Duncan, op cit, p. 163
32 Ibid
33 Routledge, op cit, p. 169
34 Duncan, op cit, p. 163

35 Routledge, op cit, p. 169
36 Ibid
37 Duncan, op cit, p. 163
38 www.cwgc.org
39 Duncan, op cit, p. 164
40 Ibid, p. 163
41 Routledge, op cit, p. 170
42 Duncan, op cit, p. 165
43 Routledge, op cit, p. 170
44 Duncan, op cit, p. 166
45 Routledge, op cit, p. 170
46 Ibid
47 Routledge, op cit, pp. 170–1
48 Ibid, p. 171
49 Doherty, *The Sound of History*, p. 9
50 Routledge, op cit, p. 171
51 Ibid, p. 173
52 Ibid, pp. 173–4
53 Graves, *The History of The Royal Ulster Rifles, Vol III*, p. 197
54 Routledge, op cit, p. 174
55 Ibid
56 Farndale, op cit, p. 111
57 NA Kew, WO32/9756, 'Creation of Maritime AA RA'
58 Farndale, op cit, p. 111
59 NA Kew, WO32/9756, op cit
60 Farndale, op cit, p. 111
61 Farndale, op cit p. 111
62 Farndale, op cit, p. 111; Routledge, op cit, p. 392
63 NA Kew, WO32/9756, op cit; Farndale, op cit, p. 111
64 NA Kew, WO32/9756, op cit
65 Farndale, op cit, p. 111
66 NA Kew, WO32/9756, op cit
67 Duncan, op cit, p. 576
68 Ibid, p. 577
69 Duncan, p. 577
70 NA Kew, WO19373, 'Maritime Royal Artillery, 1943–45' Admiralty letter dated 15 Feb.
71 NA Kew, WO32/9756, op cit
72 NA Kew, WO32/10374, 'Note of a Conversation between DRA and Sir Ralph Glyn on the Future of the Maritime Regiment RA'.
73 Pile, *Ack-Ack*, p. 199
74 Supplement to *The London Gazette*, 2 Jul 1943, published 6 Jul 1943
75 Duncan, op cit, p. 578
76 www.cwgc.org Stanley Pycroft, from Nottingham, is commemorated on the Plymouth Naval Memorial.
77 Farndale, *The Far East Theatre*, p. 176; www.cwgc.org The Gunners of 1st Maritime Regiment are commemorated on the Portsmouth Naval Memorial while those of 4th Regiment are on the Plymouth Memorial; www.nes.org.uk The Sinking of the SS *Behar*.
78 www.geocities.com/mulderspants SS *Ceramic* Home Page; www.uboat.net/forums The SS Ceramic incident; www.cwgc.org
79 Duncan, op cit, p. 578

[80] Kennedy, *Guarding Neutral Ireland*, p. 106

[81] Supplement to *The London Gazette* of 19 September 1941, published 23 September 1941.

[82] Carroll, *The Register of the George Cross*, p. 6

[83] *The London Gazette*, 3 Sep 1940

[84] NA Kew, WO32/10373, op cit

[85] NA Kew, WO32/10913, 'History of the Maritime RA, 1944–45'

[86] Ibid

[87] Farndale, op cit, pp. 111–2

[88] Ibid, p. 111

Epilogue

The story of the Royal Artillery in the Second World War is very much the story of the Army in that cataclysmic conflict but it is a little broader than the general perception of the Army's story, as it also encompasses some of the Royal and Merchant Navies' experience with the Maritime Regiments, and the Royal Air Force's story with both AA Command and the AOPs. It is a narrative that proves the truth of the Regiment's single but all-encompassing battle honour: Ubique. For the Gunners were everywhere.

It has not been possible in this volume to relate the histories of every campaign in which Gunners fought and some of the minor campaigns, such as Madagascar and Habbinaya, Iraq, have had to be omitted. Truth to tell, it would require many volumes to cover the Regiment's history in the Second World War, and that task of course has been underway through the Royal Artillery Institution. However, it is possible to demonstrate how the Regiment met the demands of war, through tactical innovation, technical development in equipment, and training of personnel. It is also possible to demonstrate how important the Regiment was to the other arms, especially the infantry, as they refined ways of working together in closer harmony.

The Regiment's story in the war is a remarkable one, from the pre-war Regiment that was, in too many ways, equipped and organised to fight the Great War over again, to the war-winning 'terrible British artillery', as SS General Paul Hausser defined it, that won the grudging respect of the German soldier, instilling fear into him as no other British arm did and cleared the way to so many objectives for British soldiers.

When war broke out the Regiment had many vintage equipments that were long past their prime, especially in the field of medium and heavy artillery, alongside some of the most modern equipment in the world. The latter included the new 25-pounder gun/howitzer that was to give such long and effective service – but how often must Gunners have wished for the extra 1,500 yards' range that the original design would have provided? – the 2-pounder anti-tank gun that was soon overtaken by German tank development, and the 3.7-inch heavy anti-aircraft gun that was the best in its class anywhere. Planned replacements for the heavy guns never materialised and American equipment was used instead, the 155mm and 240mm weapons proving excellent and effective. Other weapons also came along, with anti-tank gunnery benefiting from, first, the 6-pounder and, then, the redoubtable 17-pounder. But the 4.5-inch heavy anti-aircraft gun, an adapted naval equipment, never quite lived up to its promise and towards the end of the war most had their barrels relined to become 3.7s.

Mobility was a critically important factor in every theatre and the Royal Regiment was the only artillery arm in the world to enter the war fully equipped with mechanised gun tractors. But the stagnation of the inter-war years, and the friction between tankmen and artillerymen, had stopped the development of self-propelled guns. War hastened their development with the first 25-pounder not reliant on a Quad being Bishop, the hasty marriage of a Valentine tank with the gun. Although far from ideal – and uncomfortable for detachments – Bishop did provide experience in the use of SPGs and a stepping stone to the fine American M7 Priest, with its 105mm howitzer, and home-grown Sexton, mounting the 25-pounder. These equipments ensured that Gunners could keep pace with armoured divisions, as was shown by the outstanding work of 13th (HAC) Regiment RHA in Normandy; they also allowed the detachments a greater degree of protection with their armoured carapaces. Valentine proved a much better platform for the 17-pounder anti-tank gun, providing an excellent self-propelled equipment to supplement and then supersede the American M10 Wolverine and its upgunned brother Achilles, also fitted with the 17-pounder. Before these SPGs had come along, anti-tank Gunners had opted to carry rather than tow their weapons on trucks and thus the portée 2-pounder and 6-pounder came into service.

For some years before the war a number of Gunner officers had been advocating, and experimenting with, aerial observation for field artillery. Their work bore fruit in the form of Aerial Observation Posts which began front-line operations in the Tunisian campaign and increased considerably the effectiveness of the guns. By the end of the war, the AOPs had been active in every theatre and had carried out excellent work. Those words in 10th SS Panzer Division's report on the lessons of the Normandy campaign – 'the biggest nuisance, though, are the slow-flying spotter-planes' – indicate just how effective were the AOPs.

One of the men behind the birth of AOPs was Jack Parham, who retired from the Royal Regiment as a major general. But not only did Parham help create the AOP squadrons, he was also instrumental in introducing more effective fire control, allowing batteries, regiments and ever larger groupings of guns to engage targets rapidly so that infantry on the ground, through their attached Gunner officers, could call down heavy fire on demand. We have seen how Parham first concentrated the fire of his regiment's guns, with devastating effect, on a German tank battalion in France in May 1940 and how he later went on as a divisional BRA to apply that lesson to a division's artillery, firing its seventy-two guns as if they were a single battery. And as the chief Gunner of First and then Second Armies in Tunisia and North-West Europe respectively he was able to take the principle even further. The creation of AGRAs provided even more flexible firepower to corps and army commanders and brought the reputation of the Royal Regiment to even greater heights.

Gunners have always recognised the importance of concentration of firepower. It was not a lesson that was learned only with Montgomery and Kirkman's arrival in the desert in 1942 although the Montgomery legend would tend to give that impression. The opening bombardment of Operation LIGHTFOOT helped create that belief. It may have been the largest concentration of fire provided by the Gunners since the Great War but that ignores the concentration of some 200 guns by Eighth Army along the El Alamein line in July, the fire of the South African artillery, supplemented by 11th Field Regiment (some ninety-six guns) that broke the Axis attack at El Alamein at the beginning of July, and the bombardment of Bardia as far back as January 1941 in which 120 guns – all but thirty-four of those available to XIII Corps – were deployed to tremendous effect, doing much to bring about the Italian surrender. As the war went on it became possible to concentrate ever greater numbers of guns, providing bombardments that eclipsed that at El Alamein: Cassino is one example while those in Normandy and, especially, at the Rhine crossing, show the developing power of the Royal Regiment. That power was available at short notice at any time of day or night and it was not restricted by adverse weather, unlike the striking power of the tactical air forces which was limited to daylight hours and by weather.

The guns improved during the course of the war although the 25-pounder needed little improvement – it was fitted with the Solothurn muzzle brake in 1942 and a Mark III version was introduced in 1944 but with little obvious change – while the 3.7-inch heavy AA gun saw a series of improvements that maintained its position as the best in its role. As already noted there were great changes in anti-tank guns with the 17-pounder – 'Pheasant' as it was first known – the peak of British wartime development and capable of killing any tank it met. Medium guns saw commensurate changes, the 5.5-inch weapon the standard by War's end while the old 8-inch howitzer became the 'new' 7.2-inch howitzer, which was further refined to become an ever more capable equipment.

Tactics changed during the war to allow greater flexibility in the deployment of artillery and faster responses to calls for artillery support. Alongside these were technical developments that increased the effectiveness of artillery, chief among them being the great improvements in radio communications. Among other developments was the VT fuse, which was developed for and first used by anti-aircraft Gunners but which was also used by field artillery in the closing months of the war. The VT fuse had the effect of placing a small radar detector in the shell and was especially effective against aircraft, including the flying bombs. Radar had also played a major part in the development of AA artillery with Chain Home providing early warning of raids and the primitive GL Mark I sets at gunsites setting the foundation for radar-controlled gunnery, which came closer to realisation with GL Mark II, and Mr Bedford's mats, the Canadian GL Mark III and the American SCR584. But radar had other uses, one of which was discovered during the Italian campaign: the location of incoming shells and mortar rounds. At Salerno and, later, at Anzio, where AA radars maintained vigils against air attack, operators noticed that during German artillery bombardments, shells, especially heavy calibre rounds, showed up as radar signals. This led to experimentation in the Anzio beachhead with a GL Mark II set, the results of which led to more sophisticated experimentation in 12 AA Brigade using No. 4 GL Mark III, GL Mark II and SCR 584 to observe the fire of captured German mortars and artillery. Some fine-tuning of the radar sets allowed 'head-on' detection of the smallest calibre rounds. Such was the promise shown by these experiments that field trials were carried out on Eighth Army's front and, by early 1945, a Field Artillery Radar Regiment was formed, two batteries of which supported Eighth Army and proved very effective, directing the fire of 3.7s on enemy mortar positions. The locating batteries found that they could even detect road traffic which allowed accurate fire to be put down on German convoys travelling under cover of darkness. Thus was born the art of field artillery radar location, for which the AA teams who first made the concept work are owed a debt of gratitude.[1]

Irrespective of developments in technology, tactics or weapons, there was one constant critical factor in the story of the Royal Regiment throughout the war: the skill and courage of individual Gunners. From the dark days of Norway and France in 1940, through the years of sand, sun and sweat in North Africa, in the mountains, jungles and valleys of Burma, the malarial plains and volcanic dust of Sicily, the grinding slog of Italy, the brutal battles from Normandy to Germany, the battles against the Luftwaffe's bombers and V1s over Britain and the defence of merchant ships across the globe, Gunners went wherever right and glory called. The author recalls one Gunner veteran telling him not to portray him and his comrades as heroes: 'We were no heroes, we only went where we were sent and did as we were bid.'[2] But in going where they were sent and doing as they were bid, they were carrying out their duty and the manner in which they did so contributed much to the final Allied victory.

It may be invidious to recall some individuals among so many, but their deeds emphasise the role of the Royal Regiment. Men such as Alan Parsons MC of 17th Field in Italy, calmly calling down fire from single guns to support 2nd Irish Rifles at Casa Montemara, or the anonymous FOO, also in Italy, seen atop a step ladder observing and directing fire; Nora Caveney in the last minutes of her young life working her predictor as bombs fell around her gunsite; Bobby McClay of 25 HAA Battery in the Western Desert doing exactly the same but surviving (he was Mentioned in Despatches); Herbert Reed GC manning his gun and saving the life of a comrade while he himself was wounded mortally as enemy aircraft attacked his ship; Robin Reade MC of 21 HAA Battery with his inspiring leadership in the box at Ngakyedauk Pass; Richard Taylor on the Mateur road in Tunisia; Paul Cash at Maltot; John Johnson at El Alamein, firing even though his arm had been shot off. And there were many, many others, not least of whom were the VC laureates: Ward Gunn and Jock Campbell at Sidi Rezegh; Pat Porteous at Dieppe; Umrao Singh in the Arakan. Nor should it be forgotten that Violette Szabo GC had served with the Gunners. Others did their duty uncomplainingly in extremes of conditions, under intense pressure from enemy action but always with the professionalism instilled into them from training, so that the enemy would learn to dread that 'terrible British artillery' as it pounded the way to victory.

The Royal Regiment also produced many well-known officers, including Field Marshal Sir Alan Brooke, later Lord Alanbrooke, CIGS for much of the war, General Sir Alan Cunningham, first commander of Eighth Army, General Sir Frederick – Tim – Pile, the remarkable supremo of AA Command and one of the most outstanding Gunners of the War, Sydney Kirkman, Montgomery's chief Gunner at El Alamein and later a corps commander, Jack Parham, whose contribution to Gunner history was remarkable, Meade Dennis, commander of XXX Corps' artillery at El Alamein, and many others. Such professionalism arose from a body of officers that many popular writers would have us believe had been amateurs who only been playing at soldiers between the wars.

In all, some 800,000 personnel served in the Royal Artillery between 1939 and 1945. Of that number, 28,924 died. But the contribution they made was beyond price. To paraphrase Montgomery's tribute to 21 Army Group's Gunners, the artillery was terrific and made an immense contribution to victory in every campaign.

Notes

1 Routledge, *Anti-Aircraft Artillery*, p. 292

2 Mr Bertie Cuthbert, Secretary, Londonderry Branch RAA, to author, 1987

Appendix

The Victoria Cross and the George Cross

Four Victoria Crosses and two George Crosses were awarded to Gunners during the war. Of the VCs, two were for actions during the battle of Sidi Rezegh in Libya, the opening phase of Eighth Army's Operation CRUSADER, in November 1941 while the third was awarded for the Dieppe raid, Operation JUBILEE, in August 1942. The final Gunner VC went to a member of the Indian Artillery, Havildar Umrao Singh, for his gallantry in Burma's Kaladan Valley. One of the Sidi Rezegh VCs was awarded posthumously while the second awardee was killed shortly afterwards in a car crash, leaving only two Gunner VCs to survive the war. The first GC awardee, a member of a Maritime Regiment, died as a result of the action in which he earned his Cross while the second, Violette Szabo, was executed in a German concentration camp. The backgrounds to the awards have been described in the relevant chapters and the citations are reproduced below:

Second Lieutenant George Ward Gunn MC, 3rd Anti-Tank Regiment Royal Horse Artillery. Sidi Rezegh, 21 November 1941

On 21 November 1941, at Sidi Rezegh, Second Lieutenant Gunn was in command of a troop of four anti-tank guns which was part of a battery of twelve guns attached to the Rifle Brigade Column. At 10.00 hours a covering force of enemy tanks was engaged and driven off but an hour later the main attack developed by about sixty enemy tanks. Second Lieutenant Gunn drove from gun to gun during this period in an unarmoured vehicle encouraging his men and reorganising his dispositions as first one gun and then another were knocked out. Finally only two guns remained in action and were subjected to very heavy fire. Immediately afterwards one of these guns was destroyed and the portée of another was set on fire and all the crew killed or wounded except the Sergeant, though the gun itself remained undamaged. The Battery Commander then arrived and started to fight the flames. When he saw this, Second Lieutenant Gunn ran to his aid through intense fire and immediately got the one remaining anti-tank gun into action on the burning portée, himself sighting it while the Sergeant acted as loader. He continued to fight the gun, firing between forty and fifty rounds regardless alike of the enemy fire which was by then concentrated on this one vehicle, and of the flames which at any moment would have reached the ammunition with which the portée was loaded. In spite of this, Second Lieutenant Gunn's shooting was so accurate at a range of about 800 yards that at least two enemy tanks were hit and set on fire and others were damaged before he fell dead, having been shot through the forehead.

Second Lieutenant Gunn showed conspicuous courage in attacking this large number of enemy tanks with a single unarmoured gun, and his utter disregard for extreme danger was an example which inspired all who saw it. He remained undismayed by intense fire and overwhelming odds, and his gallant resistance only ceased with his death.

But for this very gallant action the enemy tanks would undoubtedly have over-run our position.

(Second supplement to *The London Gazette* of 17 April 1942)

Brigadier (later Major-General) John Charles Campbell DSO MC RHA, commanding 7th Armoured Division Support Group, Sidi Rezegh, 21st November 1941

In recognition of most conspicuous gallantry and devotion to duty at Sidi Rezegh on 21 and 22 November 1941.

On 21 November 1941 Brigadier Campbell was commanding the troops, including one regiment of tanks, in the area of Sidi Rezegh ridge and the aerodrome. His small force holding this important ground was repeatedly attacked by large numbers of tanks and infantry. Wherever the situation was most difficult and the fighting hardest he was to be seen with his forward troops, either on his feet or in his open car. In this car he carried out several reconnaissances for counter-attacks by his tanks, whose senior officers had all become casualties earlier in the day. Standing in his car with a blue flag this officer personally formed up tanks under close and intense fire from all natures of enemy weapons.

On the following day the enemy attacks were intensified and again Brigadier Campbell was always in the forefront of the heaviest fighting, encouraging his troops, staging counter-attacks with his remaining tanks and personally controlling the fire of his guns. On two occasions he himself manned a gun to replace casualties. During the final enemy attack on 22 November he was wounded, but continued most actively in the foremost positions, controlling the fire of batteries which inflicted heavy losses on enemy tanks at point blank range, and finally acted as loader to one of the guns himself.

Throughout these two days his magnificent example and his utter disregard of personal danger were an inspiration to his men and to all who saw him. His

brilliant leadership was the direct cause of the very heavy casualties inflicted on the enemy. In spite of his wound he refused to be evacuated and remained with his command, where his outstanding bravery and consistent determination had a marked effect in maintaining the splendid fighting spirit of those under him.
(Second supplement to *The London Gazette* of 30 January 1942)

Captain (T/Major) Patrick Anthony Porteous, RA. Dieppe, 19th August 1942

At Dieppe on 19 August 1942 at Dieppe, Major Porteous was detailed to act as Liaison Officer between two detachments whose task was to attack the heavy coast defence guns.

In the initial assault Major Porteous, working with the smaller of the two detachments, was shot at close range through the hand, the bullet passing through his palm and entering his upper arm. Undaunted, Major Porteous closed with his assailant, succeeded in disarming him and killed him with his own bayonet thereby saving the life of a British sergeant on whom the German had turned his aim.

In the meantime the larger detachment was held up, and the officer leading this detachment was killed and the Troop Sergeant Major fell seriously wounded. Almost immediately afterwards the only other officer of the detachment was also killed.

Major Porteous, without hesitation and in the face of withering fire, dashed across open ground to take over the command of this detachment. Rallying them, he led them in a charge which carried the German position at the point of the bayonet, and was severely wounded for the second time. Though shot through the thigh he continued to the final objective where he eventually collapsed from loss of blood after the last of the guns had been destroyed.

Major Porteous's most gallant conduct, his brilliant leadership and tenacious devotion to a duty which was supplementary to the role originally assigned to him, was an inspiration to the whole detachment.
(Supplement to *The London Gazette*, 2 October 1942)

Havildar Umrao Singh, Indian Artillery, Kaladan Valley, Burma, 15/16 December 1944

In the Kaladan Valley, in Burma, on 15/16 December 1944, Havildar Umrao Singh was in charge of one gun in an advanced section of his battery when it was subjected to heavy fire from 75mm guns and mortars for 1½ hours prior to being attacked by two companies of Japanese.

When the attack came he so inspired his gun detachment by his personal example and encouragement to fight and defend their gun, that they were able to beat off the attack with losses to the enemy.

Though twice wounded by grenades in the first attack, he again held off the second enemy attack by skilful control of his detachment's small arms fire, and by manning a Bren gun himself which he fired over the shield of his gun at the Japanese who had got to within five yards range. Again the enemy were beaten off with heavy losses. Third and fourth attacks were also beaten off in the same manner by the resolute action and great courage of Havildar Umrao Singh.

By this time all his gun detachment had been killed or wounded with the exception of himself and two others.

When the final attack came, the other gun having been over-run and all his ammunition expended, he seized a gun bearer and calling once again on all who remained, he closed with the enemy in furious hand-to-hand fighting and was seen to strike down three Japanese in a desperate effort to save his gun, until he was overwhelmed and knocked senseless.

Six hours later, when a counter-attack restored the position, he was found in an exhausted state beside his gun and almost unrecognisable with seven severe wounds, and ten dead Japanese round him.

(Supplement to *The London Gazette*, 29 May 1945)

Bombardier Henry Herbert Reed, 1st Maritime Regiment. At sea, between Blyth, Northumberland and London, 20/21 June 1941

The ship [SS *Cormount*] was attacked by enemy aircraft with cannon, machine guns and bombs. She replied at once with her defensive armament and the men at the guns went on firing despite the hail of bullets and cannon shell.

Gunner Reed behaved with the utmost gallantry. He was badly wounded but when the Master asked how he was, he said that he would carry on. The Chief Officer was also badly wounded. Reed carried him from the bridge down two ladders to the deck below and placed him in a shelter near a lifeboat. Gunner Reed then died. It was afterwards found that his stomach had been ripped open by machine-gun bullets.

By his gallant and utterly selfless action Gunner Reed saved the life of the Chief Officer.

(Supplement to *The London Gazette*, 19 September 1941)

Violette, Madame Szabo (deceased), Women's Transport Service (First Aid Nursing Yeomanry)

Madame Szabo volunteered to undertake a particularly dangerous mission in France. She was parachuted into France in April 1944 and undertook the task with

enthusiasm. In her execution of the delicate researches entailed she showed great presence of mind and astuteness. She was twice arrested by the German security authorities, but each time managed to get away. Eventually, however, with other members of her group, she was surrounded by the Gestapo in a house in the south-west of France. Resistance appeared hopeless, but Mme Szabo, seizing a Sten-gun and as much ammunition as she could carry, barricaded herself in part of the house and, exchanging shot for shot with the enemy, killed or wounded several of them. By constant movement, she avoided being cornered and fought until she dropped exhausted. She was arrested and had to undergo solitary confinement. She was then continuously and atrociously tortured, but never by word or deed gave away any of her acquaintances or told the enemy anything of any value. She was ultimately executed. Madame Szabo gave a magnificent example of courage and steadfastness.
(Fourth supplement to *The London Gazette*, 13 December 1946)

Bibliography

Adams, Jack, *The Doomed Expedition: The Campaign in Norway 1940* (London 1989)

Allen, Louis, *Burma. The Longest War, 1941–45* (London 1984)

Anon, *70th Medium Regt, RA* (np, Italy 1945)

Anon, *Royal Devon Yeomanry: The History of 142 Field Regiment RA, 1939–1945* (Eastbourne 1947)

Anon, *The History of 61 Infantry Brigade, May 1944–June 1945* (np, nd)

Aris, George, *The Fifth British Division 1939 to 1945* (London 1959)

Atkin, Ronald, *Pillar of Fire: Dunkirk 1940* (London 1990)

Baldwin, Michael and Miller, Keith, *The Gunners' Favourite: The 25-Pounder Gun. A Brief History* (London 1991)

Barclay, Brig C N, CBE DSO, *The History of the 53rd (Welsh) Division in the Second World War* (London 1956)

Barr, Niall, *The Pendulum of War: The Three Battles of El Alamein* (London 2004)

Bates, Peter, *Dance of War. The Story of the Battle of Egypt* (London 1992)

Beckett, Frank, *Algiers to Austria with the First and Eighth Armies* (Grimsby 1986)

Bellis, Malcolm A, *Brigades of the British Army 1939–45* (Crewe 1986)

Bidwell, Shelford, *Gunners at War. A Tactical Study of the Royal Artillery in the Twentieth Century* (London 1970)

______, *The Chindit War. The Campaign in Burma 1944* (London 1979)

______, & Graham, Dominic, *Fire-Power. British Army Weapons and Theories of War, 1904–1945* (London 1982)

Blake, George, *Mountain and Flood. History of the 52nd (Lowland) Division 1939–1946* (Glasgow 1950)

Bonnet, Maj Gen P R F, CB MBE, *A Short History of the Royal Regiment of Artillery* (Woolwich, 1995)

Brassey, Lt Col B, MC, & Winslow, Maj P, *153rd Leicestershire Yeomanry Field Regiment RA, TA, 1939–1945* (Pickering, 1947)

Brett-James, Antony, *Ball of Fire: The Fifth Indian Division in the Second World War* (Aldershot 1951)

Brewer Kerr, Dorothy, *The Girls Behind the Guns. With the ATS in World War II* (London 1990)

Brownlie, Maj W Steel, MC TD, *The Proud Trooper: The History of the Ayrshire (Earl of Carrick's Own) Yeomanry* (Glasgow 1964)

Carver, Field Marshal Lord, *Britain's Army in the 20th Century* (London 1998)

Cheetham, A M, MC, *Ubique* (Formby 1987)

Chinnery, Philip D, *March or Die: The Story of Wingate's Chindits* (Shrewsbury 1997)
Churchill, Sir Winston, *The Second World War* (London 1949–54)
Clark, Wallace, *Five Years on Full Alert. WWII AA Gunner Memoirs* (Upperlands 2007)
Clements, Bill, *Defending the North. The Fortifications of Ulster 1796–1956* (Newtownards 2003)
Cooper, Anthony J, *Anti-Aircraft Command 1939–55. The Other Forgotten Army* (Fleet Hargate 2004)
Corrigan, Gordon, *Blood, Sweat and Arrogance and the Myths of Churchill's War* (London 2006)
Davis, Brian L, *British Army Uniform & Insignia of World War Two* (London 1983)
Davis, Lt Col T B, MC RA, *The Story of 98th & 144th Field Regiments (Surrey & Sussex Yeomanry) RA (TA) 1939–1945* (Ditchling 1980)
Delaforce, Patrick, *The Black Bull. From Normandy to the Baltic with the 11th Armoured Division* (Stroud 1993)
_____, *The Fighting Wessex Wyverns. From Normandy to Bremerhaven with the 43rd Wessex Division* (Stroud 1994)
_____, *Monty's Iron Sides. From the Normandy Beaches to Bremen with the 3rd Division* (Stroud 1995)
_____, *The Polar Bears. Monty's Left Flank. From Normandy to the relief of Holland with the 49th Division* (Stroud 1995)
_____, *Red Crown & Dragon: 53rd Welsh Division in North-West Europe, 1944–1945* (Brighton 1996)
_____, *Monty's Highlanders: 51st Highland Division in World War Two* (Brighton 1997)
_____, *Monty's Northern Legions: 50th Northumbrian and 15th Scottish Divisions at War 1939–1945* (Stroud 2004)
Derry, T K, *History of the Second World War: The Campaign in Norway* (London 1952)
Dobinson, Colin, *Fields of Deception: Britain's bombing decoys of World War II* (London 2000)
_____, *AA Command. Britain's Anti-Aircraft Defences of the Second World War* (London 2001)
Doherty, Richard, *Wall of Steel. The History of the 9th (Londonderry) Heavy Anti-Aircraft Regiment Royal Artillery (SR)* (Limavady 1988)
_____, *Clear The Way! A History of the 38th (Irish) Brigade, 1941–1947* (Dublin 1993)
_____, *A Noble Crusade. The History of Eighth Army 1941–45* (Staplehurst 1999)
_____, *The Sound of History. El Alamein 1942* (Staplehurst 2002)
_____, *Normandy 1944. The Road to Victory* (Staplehurst 2004)
_____, *None Bolder: The History of the 51st Highland Division in the Second World War* (Stroud 2006)
_____, *Eighth Army in Italy 1943–45. The Long Hard Slog* (Barnsley, 2007)
Duncan, W E (Ed), *The Royal Artillery Commemoration Book 1939–1945* (London 1950)
Dunphie, Christopher, *The Pendulum of Battle: Operation Goodwood, July 1944* (Barnsley 2004)
Ellis, Chris and Chamberlain, Peter (eds), *Handbook on the British Army 1943* (London 1943 & 1974)
Ellis, Maj L F, *History of the Second World War: The War in France and Flanders* (London 1953)
_____, *History of the Second World War: Victory in the West. Vol I: The Battle of Normandy* (London 1962)
_____, *History of the Second World War: Victory in the West. Vol II The Defeat of Germany* (London 1968)
Erwood, Peter (Ed), *A Fury of Guns: The War Diary of the 75th (Cinque Ports) Heavy Anti-Aircraft Regiment, Royal Artillery (Territorial Army), Dover 1939–40 (Including the Battle of Britain)* (Fleet Hargate 2002)
Farndale, Gen Sir Martin, KCB, *History of the Royal Regiment of Artillery. Western Front 1914–18* (Woolwich 1986)
_____ *History of the Royal Regiment of Artillery. The Years of Defeat, 1939–41* (London 1996)

_____, History *of the Royal Regiment of Artillery. The Far East Theatre, 1941–46* (London 2002)
Farrar-Hockley, Gen Sir Anthony, *The Army in the Air. The History of the Army Air Corps* (Stroud 1994)
Ford, Ken, *Battleaxe Division. From Africa to Italy with the 78th Division 1942–45* (Stroud 1999)
_____, *Mailed Fist: 6th Armoured Division at War 1940–1945* (Stroud 2005)
_____, *Assault on Sicily. Monty and Patton at War* (Stroud 2007)
Forty, George, *The First Victory. O'Connor's Desert Triumph* (Speldhurst 1990)
_____, *British Army Handbook 1939–1945* (Stroud 1998)
Frankland, Dr Noble (ed), *The Encyclopedia of Twentieth Century Warfare* (New York NY 1989)
Fraser, David, *Alanbrooke* (London 1982)
_____, *And We Shall Shock Them. The British Army in the Second World War* (London 1983)
Frederick, J B M, *Lineage Book of British Land Forces 1660–1978* (Wakefield 1984)
Gailey, I B, Gillespie, W F & Hassett, J, *An Account of the Territorials in Northern Ireland 1947–1978* (Belfast 1979)
Gamble, Ronnie, *The Coleraine Battery. The History of 6 Light Anti-Aircraft Battery RA (SR) 1939–1945* (Coleraine 2006)
Gee, Capt P W, (Ed), *A History of the Essex Yeomanry 1919–1949* (Colchester 1950)
Glover, Michael, *An Improvised War. The Abyssinian Campaign of 1940–1941* (London 1987)
Goodacre, Ray, *With the Fighting Cock and the Black Cat in India and Burma: A History of 82nd Anti-Tank Regiment (and 82nd Light Anti-Aircraft/Anti-Tank Regiment) Royal Artillery,1941–1945* (Banstead 2002)
_____, *The Story of the 57th (East Surrey) Anti-Tank Regiment, Royal Artillery (TA). Pt One: Conversion and Confrontation 1938–1940* (Banstead 2007)
Graham, Brig C A L, DSO, *The Story of the Royal Regiment of Artillery* (Woolwich 1983)
Graves, Charles, *The History of The Royal Ulster Rifles, Vol III* (Belfast 1950)
Greene, Jack and Massignani, Alessandro, *The Black Prince and the Sea Devils: The story of Valerio Borghese and the elite units of the Decima Mas* (Cambridge MA 2004)
Hamilton, Nigel, *Monty: The Making of a General 1887–1942* (London 1981)
Harclerode, Peter, *Arnhem: A Tragedy of Errors* (London 1994)
Harrison, Frank, *Tobruk. The Great Siege Reassessed* (London 1996)
Hart, Peter, *To The Last Round. South Notts Hussars 1938–42* (Barnsley 1996)
Henry, Chris, *The 25-pounder Field Gun 1939–72* (Botley 2002)
_____, *British Anti-Tank Artillery 1939–45* (Botley 2004)
Hickey, Michael, *The Unforgettable Army: Slim's XIVth Army in Burma* (Staplehurst 1992)
Hogg, Ian V, *Barrage. The Guns in Action* (New York 1970)
_____, *British & American Artillery of World War 2* (London 1978)
_____, *The Illustrated Encyclopedia of Artillery* (London 1987)
_____, *Allied Artillery of World War Two* (Marlborough 1998)
_____, & Weeks, John, *The Illustrated Encyclopedia of Military Vehicles* (London 1980)
Horrocks, Lt Gen Sir Brian, *A Full Life* (London 1960)
Horsfall, John, *Fling Our Banner to the Wind* (Kineton 1978)
How, Major J J, MC, *Hill 112.Cornerstone of the Normandy Campaign* (London 1984)
Hughes, Maj Gen B P, CB CBE, *Honour Titles of The Royal Artillery* (Dorchester, 1988)
_____, *History of the Royal Regiment of Artillery. Between the Wars, 1919–39* (London, 1992)
Humble, Richard, *CRUSADER. The Eighth Army's Forgotten Victory, November 1941–January 1941* (London, 1987)
Ireland, Bernard, *The War in the Mediterranean 1940–1943* (London 1993)
Jackson, Gen Sir William, *History of the Second World War: The Mediterranean and Middle East. Vol VI: Victory in the Mediterranean. Part II – June to October 1944* (London 1986)

_____, *History of the Second World War: The Mediterranean and Middle East. Vol VI: Victory in the Mediterranean. Part III – November 1944 to May 1945* (London 1986)

Johnson, Brig. R F, *Regimental Fire: The Honourable Artillery Company in World War II 1939–1945* (London 1958)

Joslen, Lt Col H F, *Orders of Battle Second World War 1939–1945* (London 1960 & 1990)

Kennedy, Michael, *Guarding Neutral Ireland: The Coast Watching Service and Military Intelligence, 1939–1945* (Dublin 2008)

Kirby, Gen S Woodburn, *History of the Second World War: The War against Japan Vol I: The Loss of Singapore* (London 1957)

_____, *History of the Second World War: The War against Japan Vol II: India's Most Dangerous Hour* (London 1958)

_____, *History of the Second World War: The War against Japan Vol III: The Decisive Battles* (London 1961)

_____, *History of the Second World War: The War against Japan Vol IV: The Reconquest of Burma* (London 1965)

_____, *History of the Second World War: The War against Japan Vol V: The Surrender of Japan* (London 1969)

Latimer, Jon, *Operation Compass 1940. Wavell's Whirlwind Offensive* (Botley 2000)

_____, *Tobruk 1941* (Botley 2001)

Lindsay, Oliver, with the Memories of John R Harris, *The Battle for Hong Kong 1941–1945* (Staplehurst 2005)

Litchfield, Norman E H, *The Territorial Artillery 1908–1988* (Nottingham 1992)

Lucas Philips, C E, *Alamein* (London 1962)

_____, *Springboard to Victory: Battle for Kohima* (London 1966)

McCusker, Breege, *Castle Archdale and Fermanagh in World War II*, (Irvinestown 1993)

Macksey, Kenneth, *Technology and War. The Impact of Science on Weapon Development and Modern Battle* (London 1986)

Mead, Peter, *Gunners at War, 1939–1945* (London 1982)

_____, *The Eye in the Air. History of Aerial Observation and Reconnaissance for the Army 1785–1945* (London 1983)

Mead, Richard, *Churchill's Lions: A Biographical Guide to the Key British Generals of World War II* (Stroud 2007)

Ministry of Information, *Roof Over Britain. The Official Story of the AA Defences, 1939–1942* (London 1943)

_____, *The Battle of Egypt: The Official Record in Pictures and Map* (London 1943)

Molony, Brig C J C, *History of the Second World War: The Mediterranean and Middle East. Vol V: The Campaign in Sicily 1943 and The Campaign in Italy 3rd September 1943 to 31st March 1944* (London 1973)

_____, *History of the Second World War: The Mediterranean and Middle East. Vol VI: Victory in the Mediterranean. Part I – 1st April to 4th June 1944* (London 1976)

Montgomery, Bernard Law, *The Memoirs of Field Marshal the Viscount Montgomery of Alamein KG* (London 1958)

Moorehead, Alan, *The Desert War* (London 1965)

Neillands, Robin, *The Desert Rats: 7th Armoured Division 1940–1945* (London 1991)

Nicholls, Mark & Washington, Linda (eds), *Against All Odds. The British Army of 1939–40* (London 1989)

Norris, John, *Artillery: A History* (Stroud 2000)

Oates, Edward A Oates, *Gunfire Target: Six Years with The Royal Artillery* (Brighton 1996)

Parham, Maj Gen H J, CB CBE DSO & Belfield, E M G, MA, *Unarmed into Battle. The Story of the Air Observation Post* (Winchester 1956)

Parker, Matthew, *Monte Cassino. The Story of the Hardest-Fought Battle of World War Two* (London 2003)

Pemberton, Brigadier A L, *The Development of Artillery Tactics and Equipment* (London 1951)

Pile, Gen Sir Frederick GCB DSO MC, *Ack-Ack. Britain's Defence Against Air Attack During the Second World War* (London 1949)

Pitt, Barrie (ed), *The Military History of World War II* (London 1986)

Playfair, Maj Gen I S O, *History of the Second World War: The Mediterranean and Middle East. Vol I: The Early Successes against Italy [to May 1941]* (London 1954)

______, *History of the Second World War: The Mediterranean and Middle East. Vol II: The Germans come to the help of their Ally [1941]* (London 1956)

______, *History of the Second World War: The Mediterranean and Middle East. Vol III: British Fortunes reach their Lowest Ebb [September 1941 to September 1942]* (London 1960)

______, *History of the Second World War: The Mediterranean and Middle East. Vol IV: The Destruction of the Axis Forces in Africa* (London 1966)

Price, Alfred, & Pavlovic, Darko, *Britain's Air Defences 1939–45* (Oxford 2004)

Rankin, Kenneth, *Top Hats in Tobruk* (Odiham 1983)

Ray, Cyril, *Algiers to Austria. The History of 78 Division 1942–1946* (London 1952)

Raugh, Harold E, Jr, *Wavell in the Middle East 1939–1941. A Study in Generalship* (London 1993)

Reckitt, B N, *Diary of Anti-Aircraft Defence 1938–1944* (Ilfracombe 1990)

Reynolds, Michael, *Eagles & Bulldogs in Normandy 1944* (Staplehurst 2003)

Roberts, Owen N, *31st Field Regiment RA. A Record* (Bristol 1994)

Robertson, Bruce, *The Army and Aviation* (London 1981)

Robertson, Maj G W, *The Rose and the Arrow. A Life Story of 136th (1st West Lancashire) Field Regiment, Royal Artillery 1939–1946* (136th Field Regiment OCA, 1986)

Roskill, Stephen, *The Navy at War 1939–1945* (London 1960 & Ware 1998)

Routledge, Brig N W OBE TD, *History of the Royal Regiment of Artillery. Anti-Aircraft Artillery, 1914–55* (London 1994)

Sainsbury, J D, *The Hertfordshire Yeomanry Regiments Royal Artillery. Part 1: The Field Regiments 1920–1946* (Welwyn 1999)

______, *The Hertfordshire Yeomanry Regiments Royal Artillery. Part 2: The Heavy Anti-Aircraft Regiment 1939–1945 & the Searchlight Battery 1937–1945. Part 3: The Post-War Units 1947–2002* (Welwyn 2003)

Salmond, J B, *The History of the 51st Highland Division* (Edinburgh 1953)

Seaman, Harry, *The Battle at Sangshak* (London 1989)

Sherrard, William, *The War Diary of William Sherrard, 9th (Londonderry) Heavy Anti-Aircraft Regiment Royal Artillery (SR)* (Londonderry 2005)

Smart, Nick, *Biographical Dictionary of British Generals of the Second World War* (Barnsley 2005)

Stevens, Lt Col G R, OBE, *Fourth Indian Division* (Toronto nd)

Stevens, Maj Gen W G, *New Zealand in the Second World War 1939–45. Bardia to Enfidaville* (Wellington, NZ 1962)

Swaab, Jack, *Field of Fire. Diary of a Gunner Officer* (Stroud 2005)

Ventham, Philip and Fletcher, David, *Moving the Guns. The Mechanisation of the Royal Artillery, 1854–1939* (London 1990)

Verney, Maj Gen G L, DSO MVO, *The Desert Rats: The 7th Armoured Division in World War II* (London 1954)

Wilson, Lt A W, RA, *The Story of the Gun* (Woolwich 1985)

Wilson, Lt Gen Sir James, *Unusual Undertakings* (Barnsley 2002)

Williams, David, *The Black Cats at War. The Story of the 56th (London) Division TA, 1939–1945* (London 1995)

Williamson, Hugh, *The Fourth Division 1939 to 1945* (London 1951)

Wood, Tony, & Gunston, Bill, *Hitler's Luftwaffe* (London 1977)
Woollacott, Robert, *Winged Gunners*, (Harare 1994)
Wragg, David, *Malta. The Last Great Siege 1940–1943* (Barnsley 2003)

Journals/Magazines/Newspapers

Britain at War

Gunner/The Gunner: The Magazine of the Royal Regiment of Artillery

The Irish Sword

Journal of the Royal Artillery

The London Gazette

RUSI Journal

Unpublished

Letters from Captain Alan Parsons MC to his parents

Notes on 26/92 Battery, 17th Field Regiment RA (courtesy of the late Captain Alan Parsons MC)

Notes on 112th (Wessex) Field Regiment RA (TA) (courtesy of Major Douglas Goddard MBE FCIS)

Narratives of the Service of the Irish Brigade 1942–45 by Brigadiers Nelson Russell DSO MC and Pat Scott DSO (in author's possession)

National Archives, Kew

Documents from the series CAB44: Committee of Imperial Defence, Historical Branch and Cabinet Office, Historical Section: War Histories: Draft Chapters and Narratives, Military

Documents from the series CAB106: War Cabinet and Cabinet Office: Historical Section: Archivist and Librarian Files: (AL Series)

WO32/2840: Mechanisation of Divisional Artillery (1935)

WO32/4617: Heavy Artillery – Re-organization and Re-equipment

WO32/4618: Heavy Artillery (Field Army) – Modernization (1937–9)

WO32/4619: Formation of a separate Coast Defence and Anti-Aircraft Branch (1938)

WO32/9659: Middle East – Re-organization of artillery regiments (1941–3)

WO32/9755: Report of the Browning committee on the role of the Royal Artillery in France, 1940

WO32/9756: Creation of Maritime Anti-Aircraft: Royal Artillery

WO32/9757: Employment of Home Guard in Coast Artillery

WO32/9758: Handling of Royal Artillery (1941)

WO32/9805: Experience gained in employment of Royal Artillery units

WO32/10373: Maritime Royal Artillery (1942–5)

WO32/10374: Proposals to transfer Maritime Regiments, Royal Artillery to the Royal Marines (1942)

WO32/10375: Bombardment sub-committee to review existing information (1943–4)

WO32/10376: Reduction in Coast artillery for flood tide (1943–4)

WO32/10377: Artillery support in beach landings (1943)

WO32/10377: Royal Artillery – organization (1943)
WO32/10913: History of Maritime Royal Artillery (Defensively Equipped Merchant Ships) (1944–5)
WO32/14004: Mounting of 25-pounder self propelled guns and tanks with 105mm or 95mm howitzers in landing craft tank
WO32/14213: Royal Artillery in Malta – reports by Major General Beckett
WO32/14238: Titles and designations of units: Honour titles for Royal Artillery units (1946–61)
From the series WO167: war diaries of units in the campaign in France and Flanders, 1940
From the series WO168: war diaries of units in the Norwegian campaign, 1940
From the series WO169: war diaries of units in the North African campaign, 1940–43
From the series WO170: war diaries of units in Central Mediterranean Forces – Tunisia, Sicily and Italy, 1942–3
From the series WO171: war diaries of units in the campaign in North-West Europe, 1944–5
From the series WO172: war diaries of units in the campaigns in South-East Asia, 1941–5
From the series WO176: war diaries of units in various smaller theatres, 1939–45

Websites

www.cwgc.org.uk Commonwealth War Graves Commission: Debt of Honour Register
www.members.tripod.com British Artillery in World War 2
www.ra.39-45.pwp.blueyonder.co.uk Royal Artillery 1939–45 including regimental and battery histories, tactical markings, bibliography etc
www.firepower.org.uk Firepower, Museum of the Royal Artillery
www.army.mod.uk/royalartillery Ministry of Defence Army website; includes historical information
www.36regimentra.org.uk/RARecTroop/id62.htm Royal Artillery Recruiting Troop; includes historical information
www.21bty.org.uk/r_a/orbat.html 21 AD Battery; includes 2004 Order of Battle with historical notes
www.u-boat.net/forums The SS *Ceramic* incident
www.geocities.com/mulderspants SS *Ceramic*
www.nes.org.uk The Sinking of the SS *Behar*

Index

Part 1: Military, Naval and Air Formations, Units etc

Part 2: Persons

Part 3: General